SOUTH AFRICA
AND
THE UNITED STATES

South Africa and the United States:

THE DECLASSIFIED HISTORY

EDITED BY

KENNETH MOKOENA

FOREWORD BY

DONALD ROTHCHILD

PREFACE BY

RANDALL ROBINSON

A NATIONAL SECURITY ARCHIVE DOCUMENTS READER

THE NEW PRESS · NEW YORK 1993

PUBLISHED IN THE UNITED STATES BY THE NEW PRESS, NEW YORK

DISTRIBUTED BY W. W. NORTON & COMPANY, INC.

500 FIFTH AVENUE, NEW YORK, NY 10110

LIBRARY OF CONGRESS CATALOGING-IN-PUBLICATION DATA

South Africa and the United States: a National Security Archive
the declassified history / edited by Kenneth Mokoena.—1st ed.
p.   cm.
Includes bibliographical references.
ISBN 1–56584–081–X
1. United States—Foreign relations—South Africa—Sources.
2. South Africa—Foreign relations—United States—Sources.
3. United States—Foreign relations—Africa, Southern—Sources.
4. Africa, Southern—Foreign Relations—United States—Sources.
I. Mokoena, Kenneth. II. National Security Archive (U.S.)
E183.8.S6S68 1993
327.73068 — dc20   92–59956
                                                            CIP

First Edition

ESTABLISHED IN 1990 AS A MAJOR ALTERNATIVE TO THE LARGE, COMMERCIAL PUB-
LISHING HOUSES, THE NEW PRESS IS INTENDED TO BE THE FIRST FULL-SCALE
NONPROFIT AMERICAN BOOK PUBLISHER OUTSIDE OF THE UNIVERSITY PRESSES.
THE PRESS IS OPERATED EDITORIALLY IN THE PUBLIC INTEREST, RATHER THAN
FOR PRIVATE GAIN; IT IS COMMITTED TO PUBLISHING IN INNOVATIVE WAYS WORKS OF
EDUCATIONAL, CULTURAL, AND COMMUNITY VALUE THAT, DESPITE THEIR INTEL-
LECTUAL MERITS, MIGHT NOT NORMALLY BE "COMMERCIALLY VIABLE." THE NEW
PRESS'S EDITORIAL OFFICES ARE LOCATED AT THE CITY UNIVERSITY OF NEW YORK.

IN LOVING MEMORY OF MY LATE MOTHER, NOMASWAZI IRENE MOKOENA,
FOR HER LOVE, DETERMINATION, COURAGE, AND PATIENCE.

CONTENTS

CONTENTS

CONTENTS

CONTENTS

FOREWORD

As the Cold War recedes into history, we are becoming increasingly aware of the ways and extent to which the lens of anti-Sovietism distorted the United States' formulation of its postwar foreign policy. The U.S. foreign policy establishment, rather than examining Africa's affairs in terms of regional concerns with poverty, human rights, and self-determination, frequently adopted a narrowly ideological view of the issues at stake. The key decisionmakers became so riveted with gaining a competitive advantage over their superpower adversary that short-term expedients in alliance-building often gained precedence over long-term concerns involving the promotion of economic development and effective governance. As a consequence, the demise of Soviet power in the mid 1980s brought little relief to Africa. Many opportunities to encourage civil society and economic development had been squandered, and it became difficult, in the recession-prone years of the early 1990s, to give a new impetus to the continent's developmental process.

In order to understand the African dilemma at the beginning of the 1990s, we must try to go back in time and recapture the mood of international politics in the decades following the transfer of political power to African rulers. Fortunately, in this endeavor time is clearly on our side. Thanks to the painstaking efforts of Kenneth Mokoena and the staff of the National Security Archive, we are now in a position to take a firsthand look at the ideas and values held by some of the most powerful officials in the Washington bureaucracy, as well as those held by the myriad of civil servants underneath them. The primary documents collected and presented to the public in this volume are of great value in giving insight into official thinking on such critical issues as regional conflicts

in southern Africa; possible sanctions against South Africa; peace negotiations in Angola; the evolving relationships between Namibia, Rhodesia/Zimbabwe, South Africa, and Mozambique; and the prevention of nuclear proliferation. Above all, these documents convey a kind of rare excitement that comes from a direct encounter with crucial personalities and events in the historical record. We are all profoundly indebted to Mr. Mokoena for his perseverance and commitment to the task of prying these primary materials from restricted government access and bringing them to the public's attention.

In the large, the documents show the U.S. to be a status quo power, intent upon encouraging moderate forces in southern Africa and profoundly suspicious of, even hostile to, radical change. This is not in and of itself a bad thing, particularly if it leads to the emergence of values and structures that nurture economic growth and stable patterns of social relations; but it became self-defeating to the extent that U.S. suspicion of militant zeal diverted the attention of local leaders away from effective state- and nation-building priorities, and toward externally determined ideological battles of little relevance to Africa's immediate needs.

All too often in the past, Western and Eastern preferences have reflected their own needs and strategic imperatives in Africa. In the case of the United States, cautious and restrained nationalists were praised in Rhodesia/Zimbabwe (Abel Muzorewa), Angola (the National Front for the Liberation of Angola [FNLA] and the National Union for the Total Independence of Angola [UNITA]), and South Africa (Inkatha), mainly because these moderates were understood as denying Soviet interests and promoting the kind of environment that would facilitate political and economic links with Western interests. By contrast, extreme nationalism, particularly when it seemed tinged with an adherence to Marxist-Leninist doctrine, was viewed with deep antipathy. The thread running through many of the papers collected here is a determination to confront and weaken the connections that radical African nationalism was perceived to have with the Soviet Union. As the May 1987 White House memorandum on U.S. policy toward Angola states most explicitly, the United States sought "to reduce and, if possible, eliminate Soviet and Soviet-proxy influence, military presence, and opportunities in Angola and southern Africa" (Document 54). This is the language not of coexistence but of grim, zero-sum politics. Even as Soviet leaders were beginning to speak of a new flexibility in their relations with the United States, ideological thinking was triumphing over pragmatic adjustment in the statements of high U.S. officials regarding the Angolan issue—that is, until the 1988 negotiations, when the Great Powers collaborated in brokering a peace agreement among the international rivals on the scene. By the late 1980s, then, the conflict between the great powers gradually diminished. Nevertheless, the civil war between the internal African adversaries, the Popular Movement for the Liberation of Angola (MPLA) and UNITA, continued. Tragically, even after an externally mediated effort succeeded in hammering out the 1991 Bicesse Accords between these rivals, UNITA leader Jonas Savimbi, dissatisfied with the outcome of the national elections, decided to use the foreign-supplied arms still under his control to resume the military struggle in his country. In a most cruel way, then, the past still held the present ransom.

Besides the U.S. determination to reduce and, if possible, eliminate Soviet and Cuban influence in southern Africa, what do these documents tell us about American foreign policy in this region? They point quite clearly to the risks inherent in a tendency to simplify reality by dichotomizing between friends and enemies. The problem in such a specious under-

standing of the forces actually at work in the southern African region is that, by being too hard on "enemies" and too soft on "friends," they limit and distort the development of an effective, long-term policy. Conceived in the name of a purported Realpolitik, they may prove to be myopic in terms of lasting interests.

The inclination to be too hard on enemies emerges clearly in these documents. For example, the 1984 telegram on the implications of the Nkomati Accord for peace in the region, although noting the range of viewpoints within South Africa's African National Congress (ANC), tendentiously emphasizes the movement's "hardened, Soviet-backed terrorist cadre and teenagers with AK-47s" (Document 50). True, the telegram notes that "it is not inevitable that the ANC [will] remain heavily oriented toward armed terrorism or strongly influenced by Moscow via the South African Communist Party," but the "realist" logic underlying the message seems to encourage a serious skepticism about such a prospect. In fact, despite the pressures of radical elements from within its ranks, the ANC leadership has been cautious and pragmatic, offering political guarantees to minority interests. All along, it would have been a sound policy for the U.S. to distance itself from the misperceptions of white South Africans and make an accurate appraisal of the dominant leadership cadres within the ANC.

Similarly, even though U.S. diplomats and businessmen negotiated constructively with Angola's MPLA government officials during most of the 1980s, the American establishment remained fixed, ideologically at least, in its hostility toward this movement. The MPLA was perceived in adversarial terms as a Marxist organization with close ties to Portuguese communists, the USSR, and Cuba. Dealing effectively with the MPLA's hard-line leadership, then, meant confronting it diplomatically and militarily and bolstering its opponents in the field. As a consequence, the United States refused to recognize the MPLA government, placed a high priority on the withdrawal of all Cuban combat forces, and gave critically important military assistance to UNITA at various stages. "Our public and private position with all the parties to the negotiation," declared Assistant Secretary Chester A. Crocker in the 1982 briefing memorandum, "has been that UNITA is a viable force which must be taken into account in Angola" (Document 45). Thus, the United States built up UNITA and thwarted the MPLA's efforts to consolidate a military victory, but it failed to lay the basis for implementing the peace that followed.

The converse of this, the inclination to be too easy on friends, is evident in the desire to strengthen and give legitimacy to such leaders as Zaire's Mobutu Sese Seko and Angola's Jonas Savimbi. Not only has this proved embarrassing to various U.S. administrations but, despite a consistently stated abhorrence for apartheid, the United States has maintained a functional relationship with South Africa's rulers, leading to exchanges of information, cooperative policies on limiting the Soviet presence in southern Africa, and the easing of restrictions on commerce in military-related equipment and nuclear technology and materials. The United States' 1975 policy statement on Angola, contending that America should not terminate its support to the insurgent movements there, went on to observe, "we believe our withdrawal would also precipitate a South African withdrawal"

(Document 37). South Africa's presence was deemed to be a "balancing intervention" necessary to prevent "a Soviet victory" and to provide an incentive for a "political compromise." However, using a government in this way risked entanglement in its problems—which is precisely what happened, as the documents show, and led to a whittling-down of the sanctions that successive American administrations had laboriously pushed through.

With the end of the Cold War, U.S. policymakers have been handed a new opportunity to rethink their priorities in Africa. It no longer seems necessary to make the same embarrassing trade-offs of past years, supporting dictatorial and racist regimes in the name of the more pressing strategic objective, the defeat of global communism. Even so, a legitimate question remains: How did a powerful and liberally minded United States come to back the Savimbis, Mobutus, and Bothas in the first place? To answer this query, it is most helpful indeed to study the documents in this collection. To my mind, they are required reading for anyone who would learn how the ideology and confrontations of the past carry over and complicate the present.

Donald Rothchild
University of California, Davis
Brookings Institution

American policy toward Africa—and particularly South Africa—over the last thirty years has been driven by two forces: the imperative of Soviet containment and race. We have never cared much about Africa, not nearly as much, by comparison, as we cared about Europe and other parts of the world.

Yet, in recent years, there has been no graver moral-political crisis facing the world than apartheid. Since its conception, apartheid has held terrible if obvious dangers for all the people of South Africa. What may have been less obvious but perhaps more dangerous is the grave risk it has posed to the moral and political fibre and international interests of the United States. It has therefore always been in our direct moral, political, and security interests to do everything we could to help end this crime against humanity.

Apartheid is no case of mild, unfortunate discrimination. It is a horrendous, ongoing political nightmare that has continued far too long. Under apartheid, the fundamental law of the land requires—demands—that the overwhelming majority of the South African people be brutally oppressed solely because they happen to be the wrong color. They have no political representation of any kind. They have been stripped of citizenship. Their land has been shamelessly stolen from them. They have been herded into overcrowded, unproductive *bantustans* and pen-like townships. They are brutally exploited, paid starvation wages, and over-taxed. They are given inferior education and what was called health care only for want of a more appropriate description.

The instruments by which the tiny minority manages all of this are violence, brutality, and pervasive state terrorism. When the victims of apartheid—most of whom have been mere children—protest, they are exiled, imprisoned, kidnapped, tortured, or murdered.

Tragically, American entities continue to support apartheid, as some of the documents in this volume show. American-owned companies supplied as much as 40 percent of the oil that powered Pretoria's oppression of the people. They provided the computers and other supplies that were used not only for keeping tabs on citizens in the fashion of Big Brother, but for nuclear research as well. Our banks advanced the loans and other financial instruments that have kept the wheels of the apartheid political economy well oiled. Our corporations have made America the number one trading partner of apartheid. American-owned factories manufacture trucks and other vehicles for the murderous South African security forces. On countless occasions our government has protected Pretoria even from the verbal criticism of the world by vetoing U.N. Security Council resolutions. We winked when convincing evidence indicated that apartheid South Africa was developing nuclear weaponry. The public need go no further than this reader to find ample evidence of these practices.

Apartheid, it should be remembered, really comes in two forms. There is internal apartheid and there is external apartheid—the kind that has been exported to other parts of southern Africa.

The region has been devastated by South Africa. Ever since the mid 1970s when Mozambique and Angola won their independence from the Portuguese, South Africa has pursued a policy of aggression in an effort to politically and economically cripple the surrounding nations. This policy of aggression has cost the southern African states billions of dollars. The costs that I am referring to do not include loss of life, personal property, or human suffering—it is impossible to place a dollar figure on these losses. It has been documented elsewhere, however, that at least

250,000 people have died at the hands of the South African aggressors and their surrogates—UNITA and RENAMO—and over 100,000 displaced people are known to have fled war-torn districts to seek refuge in neighboring nations. The documents included here have much to say about the role the United States played in these surrogate wars.

For most of the last three decades, economic sanctions have been the mechanism with the greatest potential for bringing an end to South Africa's racist policies. Groups such as TransAfrica advocated sanctions over the years out of the conviction that economic pressure represented the only realistic alternative to increased violence and bloodshed. When Congress passed the Comprehensive Anti-Apartheid Act (CAAA) in 1986, against the determined opposition of President Reagan, it started down the right road. A primary objective of the law was to alert the Botha regime to the grave concerns the American people had about its policies. Hence the law was limited in scope and made some reasonable demands on the regime to obviate the necessity for additional measures. Unhappily, Pretoria made no effort to meet any of the act's criteria for significant progress toward ending apartheid.

Despite its limited scope and South Africa's intransigence, the 1986 law might have had greater impact if it hadn't had to contend with the unbridled hostility of the Reagan administration. This hostility led to lax enforcement, which in turn fed the Pretoria regime's obstinacy.

In other circumstances, the United States has used economic sanctions quite readily. We have applied sanctions against some thirty-four countries whose behavior we sought to change. Nicaragua, Cuba, Afghanistan, and Libya come immediately to mind. In arguing to the world, as we did consistently during the past three decades, that an exception should be made for the only country on the planet whose constitution mandates racially based oppression for the majority, we appeared to be hypocritical racists. In the process

we did great harm to our international standing—and undermined the national security we ostensibly sought to protect.

In 1990, the F. W. de Klerk government, thanks largely to the CAAA, finally began to make changes. Nelson Mandela was released, and the regime scrapped the state of emergency. The following year, Pretoria repealed three fundamental apartheid laws, although it immediately negated this reform by replacing those laws with measures that had the same effect. For some time now, de Klerk's government has also been holding "talks about talks" with the ANC. In July 1993, participants in the multiparty negotiations agreed to hold the country's first nonracial elections in April 1994. Whether this will come to pass is by no means clear at this writing; among other potential roadblocks, sabotage of the process by extreme right-wing groups such as the Committee of Generals is a real possibility.

Whatever the outcome of the ongoing negotiations, the importance of understanding how we got to this point cannot be overstated. The extraordinary collection of materials presented in this volume gives an unusually clear guide to the important role played by the United States. Broken down according to the main subplots of the story—sanctions policy, nuclear collaboration, and regional issues—the documents highlight the dilemmas faced by policy makers in Washington from Kennedy to Bush. They show that in choosing between anticommunism and race, every U.S. administration invariably came down (lamentably, in my view) to a policy that invoked democracy but in fact propped up the Afrikaner regime at the expense of the rights of millions. Whatever conclusions one draws, we owe our thanks to Kenneth Mokoena and the National Security Archive for making this critical history available for public scrutiny.

Randall Robinson
Executive Director
TransAfrica

ACKNOWLEDGMENTS

This book is the second major publication of the National Security Archive's seven-year effort to open up the internal documentation generated by U.S. policymakers during their often-fierce debates over the past thirty years about relations with South Africa. In late 1991, the Archive and the scholarly microform company Chadwyck-Healey published on microfiche, with a printed 2,100-page catalog/index/guide, more than twenty-five hundred previously classified U.S. documents on South Africa policy, obtained primarily through the Archive's use of the Freedom of Information Act (FOIA). This book makes the most interesting and controversial of these documents—together with certain newly released materials—available to the public for the first time in a format more congenial to classroom use and to the general reader.

The fact that we have succeeded to such an extent in piercing the veil of "national security" secrecy, which too often shrouded the U.S. government's deliberations and kept them unnecessarily from public scrutiny, is a tribute to the extraordinary tenacity and intellect of Kenneth Mokoena, the project's director from its inception in 1986 and the editor of both the microfiche collection and this volume. Forcing the U.S. government to release such a comprehensive collection of documents required Kenneth to plan and follow through on 917 Freedom of Information Act requests and forty-nine appeals. Anyone who has experienced the government's typical stonewalling on a single FOIA request will understand what an enormous task Kenneth undertook, and what superlatives he has earned the old-fashioned way.

This arduous work, and especially the demands of this publication, have often separated Kenneth from the most important people related to this project—his wife Susan and his children, Sechaba, Kgomotso, and Thabo. Their contributions to this book, in love, patience, and time, are immeasurable.

Kenneth had the great fortune to attract and supervise a series of top-notch research assistants. For this book in particular, Sipho Shezi performed yeoman work in helping to finalize the manuscript. Sipho is currently a PhD candidate at the Paul Nitze School of Advanced International Studies at Johns Hopkins University; formerly, he served as lecturer in the Department of Political Studies, University of Natal (South Africa), where he was in the forefront of the peace initiatives currently unfolding in Natal. In addition, Sipho coedited the introductory essay with Kenneth and helped to develop the entire conceptual framework of the book. Earlier in the project, Katherine Perkins (BA, Mount Holyoke College; MA, George Washington University) and Nicole Gaymon (BA, Guilford College; MA, George Washington University) earned the respect and gratitude of the entire Archive staff for their herculean efforts in preparing the South Africa collection for microform publication. Katherine's and Nicole's superb work built the foundation for this book.

Malcolm Byrne, the Archive's director of analysis, supervised the South Africa project from the final stages of the microform publication through the first prototype of this reader, to the final manuscript. His finely honed editorial skills and his unfailing capacity to defuse crises with beyond-the-call-of-duty patience and calm were essential to this publication. Malcolm's predecessor, Nicole Ball, deserves significant credit for her indefatigable efforts during the first several years of research and document-gathering for this project. The founder and first executive director of the Archive, Scott Armstrong, provided the initial energy and concept for the project, and made it a pri-

ACKNOWLEDGMENTS

ority as one of the Archive's first sustained documentation efforts.

Everyone on the Archive staff contributed in ways large and small to this book. Two archivists in particular deserve special recognition: Lynda Davis, who not only channeled the flood of Kenneth's FOIA requests and responses in her capacity as FOIA coordinator, but also applied her keen editorial eye and exemplary work ethic to perfect the final manuscript; and Mary Burroughs, transcriber and proofreader extraordinaire, and the eye of the Archive hurricane. We also appreciate the efforts of Lynne Quinto, Will Ferroggiaro, and Bill Carnell, who were always willing to help in a pinch.

Special thanks also to Scott Forrey for applying his professional skills to proofing the entire manuscript.

We owe our thanks to Donald Rothchild, wise adviser and colleague. Professor Rothchild generously contributed this volume's Foreword, which places the documents in the larger context of events in southern Africa and the successes and failures of the policymakers. We also thank Randall Robinson, whose work through TransAfrica pioneered the movement in the United States to seek an end to apartheid, for graciously providing the preface for this book.

Pauline Baker of the Carnegie Endowment for International Peace and Helen Kitchen of the Center for Strategic and International Studies extended special kindnesses to Kenneth by inviting his participation in their respective working groups on the ongoing crisis in southern Africa.

The essential financial underwriting for this lengthy project came primarily from several foundations, which provided major grants of general support funding to the Archive. The Carnegie Corporation of New York has been one of the earliest and most generous of the Archive's financial angels. We have deeply appreciated the encouragement, responsiveness, and professionalism of Fritz Mosher, his successor, Jane Wales, and now our program officer, David Speedie III. Similarly, the consistent, timely, and generous support of the John D. and Catherine T. MacArthur Foundation has been essential to the Archive's survival and success.

We have a special debt of gratitude to MacArthur's superb staff of the Program on Peace and International Cooperation, particularly former director, Ruth Adams, her successor, Kennette Benedict, and research associate Kimberly Stanton.

At the Ford Foundation, we owe special thanks to the far-sighted leadership of Susan Berresford, Gary Sick, and Stanley Heginbotham, who were responsible for the International Affairs Program's early grantmaking support to the Archive. In addition, the Ford Foundation's Program-Related Investment Division made possible the Archive's publishing program with an extensive line of credit, which ultimately converted into grant support. Tom Miller led the PRI effort, and his deputy, Nancy Andrews, was the ideal, tough but fair, hands-on loan officer.

Over the past four years, general support grants from the Compton Foundation have become a crucial contributor to the Archive's success. We particularly appreciate the deep understanding of, and support for, the Archive shown by the foundation's president, James Compton. We also thank Edith T. Eddy, administrative director of the Compton Foundation, for her efforts to make these essential grants possible.

As the third in our series of documents readers with The New Press, this book represents a collective endeavor with the remarkable staff of that unique nonprofit publishing house, a tribute to André Schiffrin's vision. In particular, we are very grateful for the nurturing, pruning, and harvesting skills of our esteemed editors, David Sternbach and Ted Byfield, and for the efforts of Akiko Takano in the book's final stages. If any mistakes survive their eagle eyes, well, it's all their fault.

We owe our thanks to many other individuals and institutions—too numerous to name—who contributed to this project and this book. We can only hope that, in the course of incurring these debts, we have also repaid them at least partially.

Thomas S. Blanton
Executive Director
The National Security Archive

Introduction
U.S. POLICY TOWARD SOUTHERN AFRICA:
AN OVERVIEW

The 1990s have ushered in a new phase in South Africa's history of racial conflict and inequality. Since 1948, the ruling Nationalist party, made up mostly of Afrikaners (whites of Dutch ancestry), has maintained the rigid doctrine of separate development of the races, known as apartheid, and has enforced segregation throughout virtually every facet of professional and personal life. South Africa's apartheid system has left the white minority, totaling some 13 percent of a population of approximately 35 million people, in absolute control of the political and economic levers of power. At the bottom of the racial ladder in this system, blacks, who constitute 75 percent of the population, have been denied some of the most basic human rights, including the right to vote and the free choice of where to live and work. Since February 1990, however, the country has decisively embarked on the road toward political transformation: the repeal of several racially discriminatory laws, such as the Land Acts of 1913 and 1936, the Group Areas Act of 1950, and the Population Registration Act of 1950, are concrete examples of the country's entry into a new political era.

These initial steps in the transformation of the apartheid state took place in the context of rapidly shifting circumstances in the domestic, regional, and international spheres. In the early 1980s, the P. W. Botha administration had suffered a number of setbacks, particularly the failure of both the "total strategy" and its successor, WHAM ("winning hearts and minds"). These approaches involved offering token gestures of appeasement at home, such as injecting money into "betterment" schemes in the black townships, while simultaneously cracking down on internal political opposition and mounting a wave of military aggression against neighboring countries.

The government's strategies resulted in stalemate, as the political process became polarized between the defenders and challengers of apartheid. A struggle over state power and resources ensued, precipitating a condition of dual power in the country: the African National Congress (ANC) and allied liberation forces, which led the antiapartheid movement, came to dominate the townships and international public opinion, whereas the government increasingly relied on its control of the central organs of the state, notably the security forces and the agencies guiding the economy.

Although Pretoria was forced to take account of the new global realities, these changes were not wholly unfavorable from its point of view. Glasnost, perestroika, and "new thinking" in the Soviet Union had undermined the South African government's ability to capitalize on Western fears of Soviet aggression in the region; yet the new conditions also held out opportunities for the regime to end its isolation by seeking acceptance as a negotiating partner, and to play a larger role in the search for a "political solution" to the conflict in southern Africa.

The de Klerk regime came to power in August 1989 with a clear understanding that there could be no solution to the continuing crisis of apartheid without a credible process of constitutional negotiations. On February 2, 1990, de Klerk announced a variety of initiatives intended to encourage talks. Among other steps, he declared his intention to identify and release political prisoners, and to lift the ban on liberation movements; a month later, he freed Nelson Mandela, who, for many people, was the embodiment of sacrifice and freedom. During this period, de Klerk also lifted the national state of emergency and repealed the Separate Amenities Act, a law that required the segregation of public facilities. On

speech to parliament, he announced plans to repeal the three major pillars of apartheid: the Land Acts of 1913 and 1936, which effectively denied black South Africans the right to own land, giving 87 percent of the land to whites; the Group Areas Act of 1950, which segregated residential areas on the basis of race, thus preventing blacks from owning land or property in cities and so-called white residential areas; and the Population Registration Act of 1950, which strictly defined citizenship—and therefore the right to vote and take part in running the country—on the basis of skin color. Although more than sixty pieces of apartheid legislation remained intact, the repeal of these laws indicated that South Africa had begun the irreversible process of dismantling the racially based system.

President de Klerk decided to undertake these drastic measures under intensifying antiapartheid pressure, both domestic and, increasingly, from abroad. Certainly, African states and international organizations all played a part in squeezing Pretoria, but it was not until the United States came on board that the balance began to shift toward the anti-apartheid forces. For decades, many groups had looked to Washington to play a leading role in pressuring Pretoria to change its ways. But as the following overview of U.S. policy suggests—and the documents confirm—successive administrations beginning with that of John F. Kennedy failed to fulfill those expectations in their struggle to balance the powerful economic, scientific, and strategic benefits of smooth bilateral relations, on the one hand, with the moral and political costs, both domestic and regional, of implicitly supporting South Africa's repressive racial policies, on the other.

THE KENNEDY YEARS

The United States' response to the Sharpeville massacre in many ways exemplifies the reactive nature of its policies toward South Africa since then. On March 21, 1960, police in the town of Sharpeville opened fire on a large crowd gathered to demonstrate against the pass laws (which required black people to carry an identity document at all times), killing sixty-nine people and wounding one hundred eighty more. Following a wave of negative reaction around the country, the government declared a state of emergency and outlawed various political organizations. Although South Africa had been practicing racially based policies since 1948, the year the Nationalist party and their allies won a working majority in parliament and introduced apartheid policy, it was only after the Sharpeville massacre that Washington declared its "abhorrence" of apartheid to the U.N. General Assembly. The pronouncement offended the Pretoria government but to no great effect—for the regime subsequently enacted the draconian Anti-Terrorism Act of 1960, an "antisabotage" law that provided for banning and imprisoning political opponents.

African governments responded to the Sharpeville massacre and the new law by introducing a U.N. Security Council resolution calling for economic sanctions, including a total arms embargo, and for South Africa's expulsion from the organization. Despite statements condemning Pretoria for its brutal actions, however, the Sharpeville massacre did not have lasting consequences for U.S.–South African relations. On September 13, 1960, for example, the U.S. National Aeronautics and Space Administration (NASA) announced an agreement to establish tracking stations in South Africa.

South Africa's continued blatant defiance of condemnatory U.N. resolutions, in addition to increased African membership in the U.N., led to the adoption of a harder line by U.N. member states against South Africa. The Security Council resolution of November 1962 signaled the beginning of this shift. The resolution requested member states to break diplomatic relations, close ports to ships flying the South African flag, boycott South African goods, and refuse landing and passage facilities. It also requested the Security Council to call for economic sanctions and an arms embargo. The resolution passed despite the United States' vote against it.

The arms embargo proposal triggered serious disagreements within the U.S. government. The Kennedy administration had agreed, in an aide memoire prepared in June 1962, to sell military equipment to South Africa for purposes of containing international communist aggression; the South Africans, in turn, had allowed the United States to establish a deep-space military tracking facility near Pretoria—on further condition that Washington give "prompt and sympathetic attention" to future requests for military equipment. Thus, while the Pentagon wanted the United States to oppose the U.N. resolution, the State Department wanted it to abstain; in an ambivalent compromise, on August 2, 1963, President Kennedy instructed U.N. Ambassador Adlai Stevenson to vote in favor of a partial, voluntary arms embargo against Pretoria. Resolution 181 of August 1963 passed by nine votes to none, with two abstentions (France and the United Kingdom).

However, the United States nevertheless entered into subsequent contracts with South Africa involving strategic items such as submarines, helicopters, missiles, and torpedoes—a decision it justified as being in the interests of international peace and security. This dichotomy typified the U.S. approach to South Africa in the 1960s. Indeed, prior to the imposition of economic sanctions in the mid 1980s, Washington typically coupled its criticism of Pretoria's racial policies with partial restrictions on arms sales, only to undercut any impact those prohibitions might have had by exploiting loopholes of its own making. For many observers, this contradictory approach cast doubt on America's sincerity in its public opposition to apartheid.

THE JOHNSON PERIOD

In essence, President Lyndon Johnson maintained the Kennedy administration's policies. He continued to restrict exports of military equipment that could be used to enforce apartheid policies, blocked U.S. participation in South Africa's annual Capex naval exercises, and enjoined U.S. Navy ships from visiting South African ports, even as he allowed trade and investments, nuclear collaboration, and intelligence cooperation to carry on relatively unimpeded.

A major policy test for the Johnson administration came early in 1964 with regard to the question of Namibia (then South West Africa). South Africa had invaded the former German colony in 1915, and the League of Nations had subsequently transferred it to South Africa as a Mandate Territory, effectively giving Pretoria the right to determine the direction of Namibia's development until the territory took over governing its own affairs. However, after South Africa was denied the right to annex Namibia in 1946, it refused to place the territory under the new United Nations' trusteeship system. In addition, South Africa further violated the international obligations it had assumed under the 1920 mandate agreement (which the U.N. had inherited) by introducing apartheid and refusing to recognize U.N. supervisory responsibility for the territory. In 1960, Ethiopia and Liberia, with the full support of the Organization of African Unity nations, brought an action in the International Court of Justice (ICJ) charging South Africa with violating the mandate on several counts. They argued that various discriminatory aspects of apartheid, as well as South Africa's refusal to submit to U.N. supervisory jurisdiction, were in violation of the mandate. At the U.N., the United States and other Western countries encountered increasing demands from the Afro-Asian nations, with strong backing from the communist bloc and varying degrees of support from Latin America, that the U.N. take action. But Washington and its allies resisted, pointing out that the ICJ was adjudicating the case.

In South Africa, a government-appointed board, the Odendaal Commission, formally recommended in January 1964 to the administration of Prime Minister Hendrik Verwoerd that Namibia be incorporated into the Republic under the apartheid system. In the United Nations, the commission's report produced a wave of controversy. The United States' response, along with other member states, was an angry protest.

On April 24, 1964, National Security Advisor Mc-George Bundy issued National Security Action Memorandum 295, which directed the State Department to "consider all available diplomatic techniques, including the use of special emissaries, Presidential communications, etc." to ensure that South Africa delayed implementing the recommendations (Document 7). In the end, State opted to threaten sanctions if the Verwoerd administration went ahead, and in less than a week, on April 29, Pretoria issued a white paper announcing that they would defer the Odendaal provisions.

Washington's tough response in this instance, though, is an exception in U.S.–South African relations. Up to that point, the United States had picked fights with Pretoria only when high-profile issues surfaced in the international political arena. Otherwise, Johnson, like Kennedy, chose to minimize conflicts with South Africa in order to protect America's considerable interests there.

A further sign of American reluctance to be firm or even consistent with South Africa was its failure to adopt procedures that would effectively implement the partial arms embargo it had declared. Transactions continued to take place through wholly or partially owned subsidiaries of U.S. firms in third countries, through illegal direct corporate sales, and under the guise of "dual-use" equipment—that is, equipment with civilian "or" military uses, such as transport planes, helicopters, communications systems, and computers. Other sales of prohibited items were made through South African licensees; and occasionally firms in France, West Germany, Belgium, the United Kingdom, Switzerland, and Italy were willing to fill gaps created by the embargo. Washington, by turning a blind eye to these transactions, sent a very mixed message indeed to South Africa about its commitment to end apartheid.

THE NIXON APPROACH

Guided by Henry Kissinger, his national security adviser and later his secretary of state, President Richard Nixon adopted a moderate policy of broadening ties with both the region's white- and black-ruled states and softening political and economic restrictions on the former. This shift in policy was embodied in National Security Study Memorandum (NSSM) 39, which ordered a study to identify the spectrum of policy options available to the administration. The resulting assessment proposed six alternatives ranging from closer association with the white regimes, to a tilt away from the whites and toward the black states, to a complete withdrawal from southern Africa. The Nixon administration picked an alternative known as "the tar-baby option," which was based on the following premise:

> The whites are here to stay and the only way constructive change can come about is through them. There is no hope for blacks to gain the political rights they seek through violence, which will only lead to chaos and increased opportunities for the communists (Document 36).

The administration's policy change included, among other things, resuming gray sales of communications equipment and aircraft; conducting exchanges of high-level officials; renegotiating nuclear collaboration accords to facilitate supplies of enrichment services to South African nuclear power stations; relaxing restrictions on Export-Import Bank financing; and, generally, adopting a nonconfrontational policy toward South Africa. The logic of this approach encouraged South African leaders, during Gerald Ford's presidency, to try to boost their country's importance as an American ally by intervening in the Angolan Civil War of 1975–76 on behalf of the National Front for the Liberation of Angola (FNLA) and the National Union for the Total Independence of Angola (UNITA), to whom both South Africa and the United States gave their support. South African involvement was an attempt to forestall a Soviet- and Cuban-backed military victory for the Marxist-oriented Popular Movement for the Liberation of Angola (MPLA), and thereby provide time and opportunity for the U.S. to assess the situation and, Pretoria hoped, to take meaningful action. For its part,

America's fixation on the Soviet threat in the region led to a policy of covert intervention in the Angolan conflict. The intervention did not succeed in stemming Soviet involvement, however; on the contrary, it triggered increases in Soviet and Cuban military assistance to the MPLA government.

South Africa's involvement on the side of the FNLA and UNITA would later create a dilemma for the United States by diverting African concerns away from Soviet/Cuban intervention and creating pressure among African governments to recognize the MPLA government. Many countries, including Nigeria, Tanzania, and Zambia, which had initially supported UNITA and the FNLA, reversed themselves and recognized the MPLA government, pointing to South African actions as one reason for their decision.

In an attempt to placate African leaders in the wake of the discredited U.S. policy in Angola, Secretary of State Kissinger visited southern Africa and, in a speech in Lusaka, Zambia, promised a thorough reevaluation and revision of U.S. policy toward the region. He stated that Washington was wholly committed to a rapid, just, and African solution in Rhodesia—a declaration that itself marked a shift in U.S. policy. As a result of a meeting in Pretoria between Kissinger and Rhodesian Prime Minister Ian Smith, and the combined pressures of the United States, South Africa, and the frontline states, Smith announced in September 1976 that Rhodesia would negotiate a transition to majority rule. That month, Kissinger submitted proposals for a settlement. Smith, along with the principal African nationalist leaders of the Zimbabwe African People's Union (ZAPU), the Zimbabwe African National Union (ZANU), and the ANC, was invited to a conference in Geneva in October–December 1976, held under British chairmanship; but the conference and subsequent round of consultations failed to achieve an agreement.

THE CARTER PRESIDENCY

Jimmy Carter's approach to the region, and the language in which he framed it, took a more confronta-

tional turn: in contrast to Kissinger's approach, which emphasized Rhodesia to the exclusion of South Africa and Namibia, the Carter administration sought to focus directly on South Africa, Namibia, and Rhodesia. Vice President Mondale's May 1977 meetings with Prime Minister Vorster signaled this shift; after his meetings, he told a press conference that "the policy which the President wished me to convey was that there was need for progress on all three issues: majority rule for Rhodesia and Namibia and progressive transformation of South African society to the same end."[1]

Unfortunately, though, the legacy of earlier, more lenient policies caused relations to deteriorate further in 1977. That summer, Soviet satellites detected what appeared to be a nuclear test facility in the Kalahari Desert, and Moscow relayed the information to the United States. Carter ordered an independent investigation; when the Soviet findings were confirmed, the administration immediately warned South Africa against using the facility, and received assurances that Pretoria had no plans to develop nuclear weapons.

Relations nevertheless worsened in September when Steve Biko, leader of the black consciousness movement, died in police detention after being subjected to brutal interrogation. Biko's murder (the South African government insisted it was a suicide), which followed on the heels of a series of crackdowns, brought international censure upon South Africa. The United States voted in support of U.N. Resolution 418, which condemned the system of apartheid and called for a new—mandatory—arms embargo against South Africa. President Carter called the vote a sign of "our deep and legitimate concern" about South Africa's actions.[2] However, this vote was a typical example of the United States adopting a strong public stance while working behind the scenes to minimize any impact on South Africa. A confidential State Department cable of November 1, 1977, shows that the administration vehemently opposed African resolutions calling for harsher measures, including economic sanctions, which might have placed real pressure on Pretoria. Instead, it preferred an arms embargo, which South Africa had easily outmaneuvered for years.[3]

Ultimately, Carter's approach did not break from prior U.S. policy in southern Africa at all. In keeping with previous administrations, Carter sought to protect vested U.S. economic interests in the region, and his administration adhered to the consistent view of South Africa as the United States' lone ally in a part of the world vulnerable to Soviet influence. As a result, U.S. policy generally supported the status quo in southern Africa, including, for example, the refusal to recognize the government of Angola, which Washington saw as a springboard for Soviet expansionism in the region. Carter's administration also did not weigh in with Congress to strengthen *or* weaken the Clark Amendment, which prohibited aid to all factions in Angola, because doing so might have implied that Washington wanted to intervene in Angolan affairs.

At the same time, though, administration officials tacitly allowed—and in some cases quietly encouraged—others to do those things the White House did not want to be identified with directly. For example, during a high-level Special Coordination Committee meeting on March 2, 1978, National Security Advisor Zbigniew Brzezinski suggested that the United States let the Soviets and Cubans get "pinched" by luring them into increasing their involvement in Angola. Ultimately, his proposal, short of directly supporting UNITA, was to "stop advising friendly countries *against* aid to Savimbi."[4] In general, Carter actively discouraged revolutionary change in South Africa, preferring instead to advocate moderate reforms.

THE REAGAN ERA

When Ronald Reagan entered office in 1981, his administration undertook a review of U.S. policy in southern Africa. Starting from the assumption that Carter had been too soft on communists in the region and too harsh on America's traditional allies in South Africa, the Reagan administration developed a new approach, "constructive engagement." Chester Crocker coined the phrase in an article in the journal *Foreign*

Affairs before he was appointed assistant secretary of state for African affairs. According to the 1987 Report of the Secretary of State's Advisory Committee on South Africa, constructive engagement rested on four interrelated assumptions:

1. South Africa's overwhelming economic and military predominance in southern Africa, and its powerful internal security apparatus, would, at least in the short term, enable Pretoria to "manage" internal and external pressures for change;

2. The Botha government could be induced to agree to an internationally acceptable settlement in Namibia if South African withdrawal from Namibia were linked to both a Cuban pullout from Angola and to prospects for an improvement in U.S.–South African relations;

3. An early Namibian settlement would set in motion a self-reinforcing spiral of positive developments throughout southern Africa, thus validating the constructive engagement approach; and

4. Progress could be made more quickly on apartheid issues if the U.S. government used official, rather than public, channels for its criticism and pressure.[5]

Throughout his tenure, President Reagan did not merely avoid criticizing the South African government; in fact, despite overwhelming evidence of widespread exploitation and oppression of the black majority, he repeatedly praised the Botha administration for making substantial reforms. By openly embracing that regime as "an ally and friend," Reagan demonstrated what many saw as a callous indifference to worldwide demands for human rights and basic freedoms for blacks. The administration's regressive attitude in the face of continued repression and growing internal protests in South Africa revived the sanctions debate in the United States—and this, in turn, led to a 1985 Executive Order imposing limited sanctions and eventually to the Comprehensive Anti-Apartheid Act (CAAA) of 1986.

On regional issues, Reagan adopted an equally controversial stance. In response to a reporter's question in May 1980 about aid to the Angolan rebels, presidential candidate Reagan replied, "Well, frankly, I would provide them with weapons."[6] That, of course, would have been illegal, because the Clark Amendment of 1976 prohibited U.S. assistance of any kind to factions in Angola. Upon assuming office, Reagan made it known that he had no intention of recognizing the MPLA government of Angola as long as Cuban troops were stationed there. In his first year as president, Reagan endorsed UNITA, and urged Congress to repeal the Clark Amendment, a move he justified as necessary to allow the president— himself—a free hand in conducting foreign affairs. Although the administration initially lost this legislative battle, it nevertheless established contact with UNITA and invited Jonas Savimbi to visit Washington, D.C., in November 1981, thereby signaling its determination to make Angola a priority in American foreign policy.

Following his visit to the United States, Savimbi stated that the Clark Amendment was meaningless, that the United States had "other channels" through which it could deliver material assistance, and that Washington was encouraging other countries to support UNITA. Administration officials, anonymously cited in the press, indicated that the White House had requested financial help for the rebel group several times from its allies and pointedly noted that King Fahd of Saudi Arabia had agreed in 1981 to aid anticommunists around the world as part of the arrangement allowing Saudi Arabia to buy American AWACS radar planes.[7] These activities, which clearly violated the Clark Amendment, set the stage for a long-term U.S. policy of destabilizing the legitimate government of Angola.

THE BUSH ERA

Like Reagan, President George Bush embraced constructive engagement as the core of U.S. policy toward southern Africa in general and South Africa in particular. However, the Bush administration also sought to avoid the controversy that had marked Reagan's approach by trying to accommodate the region's realities. For example, Bush did not at first attempt to lift the Comprehensive Anti-Apartheid Act.

Like Reagan before him, though, Bush consistently gave the South African government the benefit of the doubt and generally showed no urgency in pushing Pretoria to embrace democracy. Even as the administration ignored evidence of the regime's extensive involvement in fomenting political violence, its low-profile approach encouraged Pretoria to delay releasing political prisoners, curbing violence, and advancing good-faith negotiations for a democratic South Africa.

During Nelson Mandela's visit to Washington, D.C., in June 1990, President Bush made a point of calling on the ANC to renounce its armed struggle, yet he made no corresponding appeal to Pretoria, for example, to cease covert operations, such as the activities of the death squads established by the South African Defense Force (SADF). Outside observers noted this obvious double standard, to which Bush seemed oblivious: his administration had no qualms about supplying arms to guerrillas in Afghanistan and Central America, and even in Angola, while it deplored the use of violence by opponents of apartheid.

Following President de Klerk's visit to the United States in September 1990 (the first such visit by a South African president in forty-five years), the Bush administration shifted its stance on sanctions, indicating its willingness to seek the earliest possible opportunity to modify or lift restrictions against Pretoria. On July 10, 1991, Bush followed through, removing all sanctions imposed by the CAAA. Although this action was justified as a clear message that the United States fully supported efforts to end apartheid, it conveyed precisely the opposite message.

The South African antiapartheid movement responded by declaring Bush's actions irresponsible in light of South Africa's failure to meet one of the CAAA's requirements, namely the release of all political prisoners. The Bush administration was determined to welcome South Africa as a full partner in the community of nations, despite the glaring fact that democratic change had not been achieved—nor even seriously initiated.

The Bush administration's partiality toward two of the principal sources of violence in the region—South African and UNITA forces in Angola—hindered the resolution of conflict in southern Africa. Occasionally, U.S. activities seemed to promote efforts toward peace; but even as the administration condemned violence on all sides, it refused to penalize those involved in the most brutal violations.

THE FUTURE

The Clinton administration comes to office at a crucial moment in the politics of southern Africa; political instability remains a problem for almost every prominent state in the region. After fifteen years of civil strife in Angola, Jonas Savimbi's rejection of the national election results of September 1992 threatens a return to civil war and demonstrates the fragility of the peace process. In Mozambique, the short-lived peace accords similarly point up how elusive stability continues to be. Yet on a more positive note, the changes in East-West relations have begun to appear in a clear, often radical, way throughout southern Africa. Despite problems in Angola, Mozambique, South Africa, and elsewhere, the political variables point increasingly toward containing and even eliminating the civil wars and strife that have afflicted almost every society in the region. The waning of the U.S.-Soviet rivalry has had much to do with this, as have efforts within each country to resolve specific disputes. Various U.S. administrations also deserve credit for helping to neutralize some of these conflicts—Rhodesia, Namibia—although they did so with their own strategic, geopolitical, and economic interests in mind.

Considering how South Africa's apartheid policy has destabilized the region politically and economically over the years, the final dismantling of that inhumane system will go far toward defusing other hotspots in the area. The United States has an important role to play in this regard, but the Clinton team will have to appreciate that establishing democracy in South Africa means more than simply replacing the white minority government with a predominantly black one. The issues involved are far more complex than that. If the transition is to succeed, Washington must go beyond the traditional political and strategic calculations that have formed the basis of its policy thus far, and address the basic issues—most critically, economic underdevelopment—that face the majority of black South Africans, for they have been the main victims of apartheid.

USING THIS DOCUMENTS READER

This book provides an account of U.S. policy toward southern Africa through the medium of primary U.S. government documents that record the course of thirty years of American engagement in the region. The history of Washington's relationships with the various regimes in that part of the world is indeed wide and diverse. Few people have the time or resources to sift through the vast quantity of primary and secondary material in the public domain, and access to some crucial sources can prove extraordinarily difficult. This reader includes the most important declassified documentation available so that the broader public can explore, understand, and discuss in a critical way the issues involved.

As with other Archive readers, the records in this volume were obtained primarily through the Freedom of Information Act from a variety of U.S. government agencies. Most of these materials are original photoreproductions; a few have been transcribed for reasons of legibility and length. Almost all of these documents were once classified.

It must be emphasized that the documentation in this reader is in no way exhaustive; it is merely intended to serve as a guide. Space limitations, problems in forcing the government to declassify records that are no longer truly sensitive, and the inaccessibility of materials from the other countries under study here are all obstacles that have prevented truly comprehensive coverage of the subject.[8]

The documents are divided into three sections—on sanctions, nuclear issues, and the southern African region—each of which is preceded by a contextual introduction in which the documents are cited by number. Generally, the documents are organized chronologically, although in a few cases materials on a specific topic have been gathered together for continuity. Those readers who prefer to start with a comprehensive overview of events are urged to read the chronology in Part I of the book. This will also help to place the individual documents in the broader context of events.

Until the countries of southern Africa are in a position to bring to bear their own perspectives on their relationship with the U.S., a balanced public understanding of these issues will remain seriously hampered. Nevertheless, it is our sincere belief and hope that the documents presented in this book will serve as an important vehicle to inform and generate critical public and scholarly debate on these issues.

Kenneth Mokoena
Sipho Shezi
April 28, 1993

NOTES

1. "First Meeting Between Vice-President Mondale and Prime Minister Vorster, Morning, May 19," May 26, 1977. This document is available at the National Security Archive.

2. Cyrus R. Vance, Cable for various posts, "Murrey Marder Article in Washington Post," October 28, 1977. This document is included in the National Security Archive's microfiche collection, *South Africa: The Making of U.S. Policy, 1962–1989*, (Alexandria, Va.: Chadwyck-Healey, 1991).

3. Andrew Young, Cable for the Secretary, "West Vetoes African Resolutions on South Africa in Security Council October 31," November 1, 1977. This document is included in the National Security Archive's microfiche collection, *South Africa: The Making of U.S. Policy, 1962–1989*.

4. "Horn of Africa," Summary of Conclusions of Special Coordination Committee meeting, March 2, 1978 (emphasis in original).

This document is available at the National Security Archive.

5. This document is available at the National Security Archive.

6. Raymond W. Copson and Robert B. Shepard, Congressional Research Service, "Angola and the Clark Amendment," 1B81063, Sept. 13, 1985.

7. Ibid.

8. Those who want to pursue these issues further are encouraged to consult other published sources, including the National Security Archive's microfiche collection, *South Africa: The Making of U.S. Policy, 1962–1989*. The Archive also has available a large number of declassified documents received since the publication of this set.

SOUTH AFRICA
AND
THE UNITED STATES

PART I

BACKGROUND MATERIALS

Selected Glossaries

PRINCIPAL ACTORS

Ahtisaari, Martti

Finnish diplomat Martti Ahtisaari served as U.N. Commissioner for Namibia 1977–1981 and held the position of U.N. Special Representative there 1978–1986. He was responsible for implementing Resolution 435 for the independence of Namibia.

Baker, James A. III

As secretary of state under President Bush from 1989 to 1993, James Baker maintained the Reagan administration's strategy toward Angola. The strategy emphasized a combination of diplomatic and military pressures (the latter from UNITA) against the government of Angola.

Baldrige, Malcolm

Malcolm Baldrige served as U.S. secretary of commerce from 1981 until his death in 1987. During his tenure, the Commerce Department implemented the Reagan administration's flexible policy on nuclear-related exports to South Africa.

Biko, Steven B.

Black consciousness leader Steven Biko began his political activities as a student, when he became involved with the National Union of South African Students (NUSAS). At the NUSAS congress held in July 1968, Biko began to canvass support for the idea of an all-black movement that would eliminate "the artificiality of symbolic integration and white liberal leadership." In July 1969, he became president of the South African Students Organization (SASO). He died on September 12, 1977, as a result of injuries received while in police detention.

Botha, Pieter Willem

P. W. Botha served as South Africa's minister of defense (1966–1980), prime minister (1978–1984), and state president (1984–1989). The Botha administration's domestic program focused on reducing certain officially mandated racial discrimination programs without endangering contin-

ued white control of the political and economic system. Botha became instrumental in the formulation of South Africa's "total strategy" policy, the main objective of which was to create a "constellation of states" that would include the ethnic homelands—such as Bophuthatswana, Transkei, and Ciskei, which Pretoria had designated for use by black South Africans—in a cooperative economic, political, and military framework.

Botha, Roelof Frederik ("Pik")

Pik Botha served as South Africa's permanent representative to the United Nations in 1974 and as ambassador to the United States 1975–1977. In 1977, he was appointed minister of foreign affairs.

Bowdler, William G.

William Bowdler was appointed U.S. ambassador to South Africa in March 1975; he left this post in April 1978.

Bundy, McGeorge

As special assistant to the president for national securtiy affairs from 1961 to 1966, McGeorge Bundy announced the president's decision to continue licensing the sale of such equipment as antisubmarine aircraft and C-130 aircraft spare parts to South Africa.

Carter, Jimmy

Although Jimmy Carter gave early indications to the contrary, his presidency (1977–1981) broke none of the traditions of U.S. policy toward South Africa and the region. The Carter administration resisted international calls for economic sanctions and refused to recognize the government of Angola.

Clark, Dick

Dick Clark (D–Iowa) was a member of the U.S. Senate 1973–1979, where he served as chairman of the Foreign Relations Subcommittee on Africa 1975–1979. He sponsored the Clark Amendment, prohibiting U.S. assistance to all parties in the Angolan civil war, which Congress enacted on June 30, 1976.

Cohen, Herman
Herman Cohen served as special assistant to Presidents Bush and Reagan, and as senior director of African affairs on the National Security Council 1987–1989. He was appointed assistant secretary of state for African affairs on May 21, 1989, and served until January 1993.

Crocker, Chester A.
A university professor, Chester Crocker served as assistant secretary of state for African affairs throughout the Reagan administration. He was the architect of the "constructive engagement" policy, which he saw as a framework for U.S. relations with all of southern Africa. The central argument of this policy was that "purposeful, evolutionary change toward a nonracial system was a genuine possibility in South Africa and that U.S. interests lay in fostering such change."

Davis, Nathaniel
Nathaniel Davis was appointed assistant secretary of state for African affairs on March 17, 1975. He resigned in December of that year after his arguments that a political or diplomatic approach to a settlement in Angola was preferable to covert military action went unheeded.

De Klerk, Frederik W.
In February 1989, F. W. de Klerk became head of the National Party after P. W. Botha suffered a stroke. In August of that year he became state president and presided over a period of broad political transformation, including the repeal of a number of racially based laws that had been pillars of the apartheid system.

Dellums, Ronald V.
Throughout his political career, Representative Ronald Dellums (D–Calif.) has been a leader of congressional efforts to terminate U.S. government support for the regime in South Africa.

Diggs, Charles C., Jr.
Representative Charles C. Diggs (D–Mich.), chairman of the House Subcommittee on Africa, was a founder and former member of the congressional Black Caucus. In 1977, he helped to found TransAfrica, a black lobbying organization concerned with African and Caribbean affairs.

Du Plessis, Willem Naude
Willem Naude du Plessis was South African defense attaché in Washington, D.C., but was expelled in April 1979 in retaliation for the South African government's expulsion of U.S. diplomats for allegedly taking aerial photographs of South African military installations. He became deputy chief of staff for intelligence of the South African Defense Force (SADF) on September 1, 1983.

Easum, Donald B.
Donald Easum served as assistant secretary of state for African affairs from March 1974 to March 1975. He opposed Henry Kissinger's proposal to provide covert assistance to the FNLA in the Angolan civil war, and was eventually replaced.

Edmondson, William B.
William Edmondson was appointed U.S. ambassador to South Africa in 1978 and served until July 1981.

Ford, Gerald R.
President Gerald Ford continued the Nixon administration's policy of communicating with white minority regimes in southern Africa. Following Henry Kissinger's guidance, in 1975 Ford authorized CIA covert assistance to the FNLA in the Angolan civil war.

Geldenhuys, Johannes Jacobus
J. J. Geldenhuys became chief of the South African Defense Force (SADF) in 1985 after earlier involvement in both OPERATION SAVANNAH, South Africa's incursion into Angola, and major SADF operations in Namibia. During his tenure, the clandestine Civil Cooperation Bureau (CCB), an SADF unit, played a part in assassination bombings as well as assaults and intimidation of political activists.

Gray, William H.
A seven-term representative, William H. Gray (D–Penn.) rose to the position of House majority whip. He was a leading spokesman on U.S. policy in Africa, authoring the House version of the Anti-Apartheid Acts of 1985 and 1986. In 1991, he left Congress to become head of the United Negro College Fund.

Haig, Alexander M., Jr.
Alexander Haig served as secretary of state from January 1981 to July 1982. Among his principal goals in southern Africa were countering Soviet influence and bolstering U.S. and South African mutual interests.

Helms, Jesse A.
Jesse Helms (R–N.C.) was first elected to the U.S. Senate in 1972. A senior member of the Senate Foreign Relations Committee, he has taken a strong interest in southern Africa as an outspoken opponent of antiapartheid measures in Congress.

Hurd, John G.
John Hurd was appointed U.S. ambassador to South Africa in July 1970 and served until April 1975.

Johnson, Lyndon B.
Lyndon Johnson served as president 1963–1968. He continued the South Africa policies of the Kennedy administration by strengthening the arms embargo and limiting military contacts with Pretoria. However, he continued to foster trade and investments, nuclear collaboration, and intelligence cooperation between the two countries.

Jorge, Paulo Teixeira
As foreign minister of the People's Republic of Angola, Paulo Jorge held numerous discussions in the 1980s with U.S. and South African officials on Angola and regional issues.

Kassebaum, Nancy
As chairwoman of the Senate Subcommittee on African Affairs, Nancy Kassebaum (R–Kan.) was a supporter of constructive engagement from the start. Following a trip to South Africa in February 1983, she became disillusioned with the way the policy had been implemented and its lack of results. She and several other Republicans joined liberal Democrats in August 1986 to support tougher sanctions against South Africa.

Kaunda, Kenneth
Kenneth Kaunda was the first president of Zambia. His political party, the United National Independence Party (UNIP), has been in power since Zambia gained independence in 1964. Kaunda was long regarded as a senior statesman in southern Africa and, as such, participated in discussions relating to virtually all major political issues in the region. He was defeated in presidential elections held in 1990.

Kennedy, Edward M.
Edward Kennedy (D–Mass.) was first elected to the U.S. Senate in 1962. A human rights advocate and outspoken supporter of antiapartheid legislation in the Senate, Kennedy introduced the Anti-Apartheid Act of 1985 (S. 635), which later passed the Senate, but was preempted by Reagan's September 9, 1985, Executive Order imposing only limited sanctions.

Kennedy, John F.
President John Kennedy, who served 1961–1963, gave South Africa a new prominence in U.S. foreign policy following the Sharpeville massacre of March 21, 1960. The incident drew his administration's attention to the problems of apartheid in a dramatic way and led to a gradual hardening of the U.S. approach toward Pretoria. In 1963, President Kennedy declared his intention to end military sales to South Africa; however, U.S. trade investments and intelligence cooperation with South Africa continued.

Kirkpatrick, Jeane J.
President Reagan appointed Jeane Kirkpatrick ambassador to the United Nations in 1981, where she served until 1985. Considered a hard-liner, she opposed economic sanctions against South Africa, and supported U.S. military aid to the UNITA rebels in Angola.

Kissinger, Henry A.
In April 1969, National Security Advisor Henry Kissinger signed National Security Study Memorandum 39 (NSSM 39), ordering a review of U.S. policy toward southern Africa. The subsequent study, proceeding from the premise that "the whites are here to stay and the only way constructive change can come about is through them" (see Document 36), suggested that the United States "can, through the selective relaxation of our stance toward white regimes, encourage some modification of their current racial and colonial policies." The Portuguese coup of 1974 shook this assumption and the policies deriving from it. As secretary of state 1973–1977, Kissinger emphasized the Soviet threat to the region and approved, over the objections of an interagency Angola task force, a program of covert intervention in Angola's 1975–76 civil war.

Lugar, Richard G.
Richard Lugar (R–Ind.) was elected to the U.S. Senate in 1976. In April 1985, as chairman of the Foreign Relations Committee, he introduced a Republican version of an antiapartheid bill to counter efforts to impose economic sanctions against South Africa.

Lyman, Princeton
Princeton Lyman became U.S. ambassador to South Africa in July 1992, and he remains there as of this writing.

Machel, Samora
As president of Mozambique, Samora Machel signed the Nkomati Accord, a nonaggression pact with South Africa, on March 16, 1984. On October 19, 1986, Machel was killed in a plane crash over the South African border. The Pretoria government denied charges it was involved in the incident.

Malan, Magnus A.
General Magnus Malan served as chief of the SADF 1976–

1980 and, concurrently, as chairman of both the Defense Planning Committee and the Defense Council Staff. In 1976, he helped to set up the Mozambique National Resistance (MNR or RENAMO)—a fraudulent black liberation movement in Mozambique. Malan was forced to resign in 1992 following revelations of covert military activities aimed at undermining the ANC and various antiapartheid activities in South Africa.

Mandela, Nelson
Nelson Mandela is currently president of the African National Congress of South Africa. In 1963, he received a life sentence for his leadership role in antiapartheid activities, but the government cut short his term, releasing him in February 1990. In July 1991, he was elected to his present position, where he plays a prominent part in constitutional negotiations with the South African government.

Markey, Edward J.
In January 1985, Chairman of the House Subcommittee on Energy Conservation and Power Edward Markey (D–Mass.) sparked a congressional investigation into South Africa's unauthorized employment of U.S. nuclear workers.

McFarlane, Robert C.
As national security advisor from 1983 to 1985, Robert McFarlane approved the extablishment of a special public diplomacy working group to plan and implement a strategy for gaining broader public support for U.S. policy toward South and southern Africa.

McHenry, Donald
Donald McHenry served as U.S. deputy envoy to the United Nations 1977–1979 and as ambassador to the U.N. 1979–1981. As a representative to the Contact Group (see entry in "Selected Organizations"), he took the lead in developing the basic plan for a Namibia settlement as outlined in Security Council Resolution 435.

Miller, David C., Jr.
From 1985 to 1986, Ambassador to Zimbabwe David Miller was temporarily recalled to Washington to direct the State Department's South Africa Working Group (SAWG), which was charged with developing a public diplomacy strategy for South Africa.

Minty, Abdul
Abdul Minty was a leading member of the international antiapartheid movement. In March 1979, he presented a report to the U.N. Special Committee Against Apartheid on nuclear collaboration with South Africa.

Mobutu, Sese Seko
President Mobutu of Zaire came to power in 1960 with the support of the United States after a civil war in the Congo, and he subsequently became Washington's strongest ally in the region. Throughout the civil war in Angola, Mobutu directed U.S. aid to FNLA leader Holden Roberto. In 1989, he hosted what U.S. officials heralded as a ground-breaking summit at Gbadolite between Angolan President dos Santos and UNITA chieftain Jonas Savimbi.

Mondale, Walter F.
Vice President Walter Mondale met with South African Prime Minister Vorster in Vienna on May 19, 1977, where he conveyed the Carter administration's new policy on southern Africa. He registered "basic and fundamental disagreement" with Vorster's view that separate development was not inherently discriminatory, and insisted that South Africa take steps toward "full political participation" by all its citizens.

Moose, Richard M.
Richard Moose served as assistant secretary of state for African affairs from July 1977 to January 1981.

Mugabe, Robert
Robert Mugabe was the leader of the Zimbabwe African National Union (ZANU) and a cochairman of the Patriotic Front in Zimbabwe. He emerged victorious in pre-independence elections and became the first president of the independent state in April 1980.

Muzorewa, Abel
Bishop Abel Muzorewa chaired the African National Council of Zimbabwe in 1974. In February 1978, he represented a group of nationalist leaders in an internal settlement agreement with Rhodesian Prime Minister Ian Smith. In April 1979, Muzorewa was voted prime minister in elections the United Nations and the Organization of African Unity would later call "null and void."

Neto, Agostinho
In November 1975, Agostinho Neto became the first president of the People's Republic of Angola. In June 1978, the MPLA leader wrote a letter to Jimmy Carter seeking to normalize relations with the United States. He died of pancreatic cancer in September 1979.

Newsom, David D.
David Newsom served as assistant secretary of state for African affairs from July 1969 to January 1974.

Nickel, Herman
Herman Nickel served as U.S. ambassador to South Africa 1982–1986. He was recalled to Washington in protest of South Africa's June 14, 1985, attack on Botswana.

Nixon, Richard M.
The administration of Richard Nixon initiated a policy shift toward South Africa that lifted the restrictions put into place by Presidents Kennedy and Johnson. This change followed a policy review conducted in response to National Security Study Memorandum 39 (NSSM 39) in 1969. Nixon attempted to balance U.S. economic and strategic interests in southern Africa with the political goal of dissociating the United States from colonial regimes and repressive racial policies.

Nkomo, Joshua
In 1961, Joshua Nkomo formed the Zimbabwe African People's Union (ZAPU). In 1976, he became cochairman of the Patriotic Front with Robert Mugabe. He later lost to Mugabe in his bid to become the independent country's first president.

Nyerere, Julius K.
As president of Tanzania, Julius Nyerere played an active role as a mediator in various southern African conflicts. He was outspoken in his criticism of the United States and its tendency to impose Cold War political schemas onto African disputes. He resigned in October 1985.

Palmer, Joseph, II
Joseph Palmer served as assistant secretary of state for African affairs from April 1966 to July 1969.

Perkins, Edward J.
A career diplomat, Edward Perkins was the first African-American ambassador to South Africa. He was appointed in November 1986 to replace Herman Nickel and served until May 1989. Perkins's appointment marked a shift away from constructive engagement, with which Nickel's tenure had been strongly identified.

Reagan, Ronald W.
As president 1981–1989, Ronald Reagan took a more benign attitude toward the South African regime than had most of his predecessors. Although he denounced apartheid as "repugnant," he often praised the Pretoria regime for improving the condition of blacks in the country, despite overwhelming evidence to the contrary. For Reagan, a major factor in South Africa's favor was its role as a barrier to Soviet infiltration of the region.

Roberto, Holden
A protégé of President Mobutu of Zaire, Holden Roberto became leader of the National Front for the Liberation of Angola (FNLA) in 1962. During the 1975–76 civil war, he received political and military support from the United States.

Rountree, William M.
William Rountree was appointed ambassador to South Africa in October 1965 to succeed Joseph Satterthwaite; he served until June 1970.

Roux, Abraham J. A.
Abraham Roux, one of the leading scientists in South Africa, served as director of the South African Atomic Energy Board. He was the architect of the construction program for the nuclear center at Pelindaba, near Pretoria.

Satterthwaite, Joseph C.
Joseph Satterthwaite became U.S. ambassador to the Union of South Africa in April 1961. He was reaccredited when the country became a republic in May of that year, and he served until November 1965.

Savimbi, Jonas
Jonas Savimbi is the leader of the National Union for the Total Independence of Angola (UNITA). His organization received substantial financial and moral support from the Reagan administration in the 1980s, which embraced him as a "freedom fighter." Following UNITA's loss in nationwide elections in September 1992, he initiated a new round of fighting in the country.

Schaufele, William E., Jr.
From December 1975 to July 1977, William Schaufele served as assistant secretary of state for African affairs. He participated in developing U.S. peace proposals for the independence of Zimbabwe.

Shultz, George P.
George Shultz served as secretary of state 1982–1989. During his tenure, he established an Advisory Committee on South Africa to recommend policies that would bring about peaceful change and promote democracy in the country. In 1987, he met with ANC leader Oliver Tambo in Washington, D.C.

Sithole, Ndabaningi
Reverend Ndabaningi Sithole became president of the Zimbabwe African National Union (ZANU) in 1964. In February 1978, he and other nationalist leaders entered into an internal settlement agreement with Prime Minister Ian Smith to form a transitional Rhodesian government.

Slabbert, Frederik Van Zyl
In 1979, Frederik Slabbert became leader of the Progressive Federal Party in South Africa, a position he held until 1986. In July 1987, he headed a group of Afrikaner whites and others in a much-publicized meeting with representatives of the ANC in Dakar, Senegal.

Slovo, Joe
Joe Slovo has been an active member of the South African Communist Party (SACP) since the 1940s, and in 1985 became the first white South African member of the ANC's National Executive Council. In exile since 1963, he returned home in 1990, and was named general secretary of the reconstituted Communist Party.

Smith, Ian
Ian Smith was prime minister of Rhodesia from 1965, when the country made its unilateral declaration of independence (UDI), until 1979, when he lost an election prior to the country's formal separation from Britain.

Solarz, Stephen J.
As chairman of the House Subcommittee on Africa 1979–1980, Stephen Solarz (D–N.Y.) was a strong critic of Reagan administration policies in southern Africa. In 1981, he helped defeat a measure to repeal the Clark Amendment.

Sullivan, Leon
In 1977, the Reverend Leon Sullivan authored a code of conduct (the Sullivan Principles) for U.S. firms operating in South Africa. He advocated desegregation of facilities, equal pay for equal work, and other principles aimed at elevating the position of blacks in the labor force.

Swing, William
William Swing replaced Edward Perkins as U.S. ambassador to South Africa, presenting his credentials in September 1989. He left this post in July 1992.

Tambo, Oliver
Oliver Tambo was a founding member of the ANC Youth League, established in 1944. In 1949, he became a member of the ANC National Executive Council. When the South

African government banned the ANC and the Pan Africanist Congress in 1960, he went into exile in Bechuanaland. In 1969, he became president of the ANC, serving until 1991, when he resigned for health reasons, and assumed the newly created position of chairman. Tambo died in 1993.

Tunney, John
Senator John Tunney (D–Calif.) introduced a provision amending the fiscal year 1976 Defense Appropriations Act to prohibit further U.S. involvement in Angola. President Ford reluctantly signed the bill in February 1976, complaining that the Tunney Amendment showed that members of Congress had "lost their guts."

Van der Westhuizen, P. W.
P. W. Van der Westhuizen was appointed chief of staff of the Directorate of Military Intelligence in 1978. He played a major role in Pretoria's destabilization activities in the region, including supplying weapons to UNITA and Mozambique National Resistance (MNR) forces.

Vance, Cyrus R.
Cyrus Vance was secretary of state 1977–1980. He worked with his British counterpart, David Owen, to formulate a settlement plan in Rhodesia, and took the lead in establishing the Contact Group, which sought to pave the way toward Namibian independence.

Verwoerd, Hendrik
Hendrik Verwoerd became prime minister of South Africa in 1958, and governed until his assasination in 1966. Regarded as the father of apartheid, he oversaw implementation of the doctrine of "separate development" for blacks, including the creation of separate tribal areas, or *bantustans*.

Vlok, Adriaan Johannes
Adriaan Vlok was appointed as South Africa's minister of law and order in December 1986. His ministry was responsible for suppressing revolts and detaining an estimated thirty thousand people, with as many as fifteen thousand being held at one time. He resigned following revelations of his involvement in covert attempts to undermine the anti-apartheid movement.

Vorster, John B.
When John Vorster was elected prime minister of South Africa in 1966, he was already identified with the country's strongest security legislation of the 1960s; he served until 1978, and as time passed he became even more extreme on racial issues. His decision to intervene, at the request of An-

golan rebel leaders and the United States, in Angola's civil war in late 1975 derailed his pursuit of improved regional relations. After resigning under a cloud in September 1978, he took over the post of president, which he left in June 1979.

Williams, G. Mennen

Mennen Williams served as assistant secretary of state for African affairs from February 1961 to March 1966.

Wisner, Frank G.

In the 1970s and 1980s, Frank Wisner served in a variety of State Department posts relating to southern Africa. In August 1979, he was sworn in as ambassador to Zambia, and served there until April 1982.

Wolpe, Howard

Howard Wolpe (Dem–Mich.) was elected to the House of Representatives in 1978. One of the leading congressional opponents of the apartheid system, he served as chairman of the House Subcommittee on Africa 1981–1990.

Young, Andrew

An outspoken critic of apartheid, Andrew Young served as ambassador to the United Nations 1977–1979. In May 1977, Young visited South Africa and further irritated the Vorster administration by espousing the use of economic boycott tactics employed by the American civil rights movement. Following a secret meeting with PLO representatives in New York, Young was asked to resign his post.

SELECTED ORGANIZATIONS

African National Congress (ANC)

The ANC was formed in South Africa in 1912 and banned following the Sharpeville Massacre of March 1960. In June 1961, ANC leaders decided to adopt armed struggle as a strategy to foster political change in South Africa. They created a military wing called *Umkhonto we Sizwe* (Spear of the Nation) and chose Nelson Mandela as its commander in chief. In July 1963, *Umkhonto*'s leaders were arrested in Rivonia and tried for sabotage and conspiring to overthrow the government. The Rivonia Trial lasted from 1963 to 1964 and resulted in the imprisonment of the top ANC leadership. ANC sabotage activities intensified in 1978 and have since continued to grow; the organization's popularity among black South Africans appears to have widened as a result of its new visibility. It was legalized in February 1990 as part of a series of reforms announced by President de Klerk that month.

Armaments Development and Production Corporation (ARMSCOR)

ARMSCOR, a state-supported company established in 1968, sits at the head of the South African arms industry and, as the country's sole weapons arbiter, dictates production considerations. It is empowered to direct the development, manufacture, purchase, and export of all weapons by South Africa. Its primary client is the South African military.

Atomic Energy Board

The South African Atomic Energy Board, established by the Atomic Energy Act of 1948, is responsible for regulating the production and sale of uranium as well as implementing research and development at the National Research Center at Pelindaba.

Atomic Energy Corporation of South Africa, Ltd. (AEC)

The AEC was established by the Nuclear Energy Act in 1982; it controls and coordinates all nuclear activities financed by the state.

Black People's Convention (BPC)

The BPC was formally launched in July 1972 for the purpose of establishing a confederate body to promote black educational, economic, political, and ecumenical development, and to provide solidarity and a political home for all black South Africans who were not willing to work within the framework of separate development. The BPC was declared unlawful and banned under the Internal Security Act in October 1977.

Congressional Black Caucus

The Black Caucus, founded in 1970, took the lead in channeling the wave of popular concerns over South Africa into political action in Congress. The caucus called for an escalating series of steps, from recalling the U.S. ambassador to supporting U.N. economic sanctions, in response to South Africa's crackdown on antiapartheid activists in October 1977.

Contact Group (Western Five)

The five western members of the U.N. Security Council— Canada, France, the Federal Republic of Germany, the United Kingdom, and the United States—form the Contact Group. In 1978, it mediated negotiations and developed the settlement proposal for resolution of the Namibia situation which became the basis for U.N. Security Council Resolution 435. The Contact Group was also active in promoting subsequent agreements concerning the implementation of Resolution 435, as well as in monitoring the transition process.

Control Data Corporation (CDC)
CDC of Minneapolis, Minnesota, supplied computer subsystems to a British firm for use in a large computer system being assembled for the South African Police. The system reportedly helped automate the administration of South Africa's "pass laws."

Directorate of National Intelligence
Formerly known as the Bureau of State Security (BOSS), later as the Department of National Security (DONS), South Africa's Directorate of National Intelligence (DNI) collects all intelligence that is understood to be "security-related"; it is also responsible for counterintelligence activities.

Edlow International Company
Edlow International of Washington, D.C., played a key role as broker between South Africa and uranium suppliers and enrichers in Switzerland, Belgium, and France, enabling South Africa to acquire almost one hundred tons of enriched uranium.

Electricity Supply Commission (ESCOM)
The Electricity Act of 1922 established the Electricity Supply Commission (ESCOM), a state-owned utility charged with generating electricity. ESCOM supplies 93 percent of the electricity used in South Africa and is responsible for developing nuclear energy facilities. In 1985, without the knowledge of the U.S. government, ESCOM recruited about twenty U.S. nuclear operators to help run the Koeberg nuclear power station.

Energy Research and Development Administration
Under the 1957 Agreement for Cooperation between the United States and South Africa for civil use of atomic energy, the U.S. Energy Research and Development Administration was required to contract with the South African Atomic Energy Board to reprocess nuclear fuel from the SAFARI-I reactor. They signed the contract on December 10, 1976.

Fluor Corporation
In February 1976, the Fluor Corporation, an engineering and construction firm, received a contract to design and supervise construction of a $2.5 billion coal gasification and liquefaction project–SASOL II–in South Africa. In 1983, along with the French nuclear company Framatome, Fluor won a maintenance contract for South Africa's Koeberg nuclear power plants.

Framatome
In 1976, Framatome, a French nuclear company, won a contract to supply two boiling-water reactors for South Africa's Koeberg I and II nuclear power plants. In 1983, it was awarded the maintenance service contract for the same plants.

Inkatha Freedom Party (IFP)
The Inkatha Cultural Movement was formed in 1977 as a regional, ethnic-based organization aimed at restoring the cultural and traditional customs of the Zulu-speaking people. Due to changing political conditions in 1990, which led to the legalization of liberation movements such as the ANC and PAC, the organization transformed itself into a national, multiracial, political party. Since this period, it has become known as the Inkatha Freedom Party (IFP). It is still headed by its founder and first president, Chief Mangosuthu Gatsha Buthelezi.

International Atomic Energy Agency (IAEA)
The IAEA came into existence under United Nations auspices following negotiations by an eighty-one-member conference in late 1954. South Africa became a member in 1957. The agency provides technical assistance to member states, acts as a repository for fissionable material, and develops and implements safeguards. The IAEA awarded several research contracts to South African institutions, and, as of the end of 1974, had provided over $100,000 worth of training assistance. In 1979, South Africa's credentials with the organization were rejected. It remains a member of the IAEA for safeguard purposes.

Mozambique National Resistance (MNR)/Resistencia Nacional Mozambicana (RENAMO)
The MNR/RENAMO was established in 1970 by the Rhodesian special forces with the support of South Africa. Initially called the Mozambique National Resistance, reflecting its Rhodesian origins, the rebel movement was later given a Lusophone name in order to lend it legitimacy as a supposedly indigenous organization.

National Accelerator Center
The National Accelerator Center is a nuclear research facility that was constructed in 1981 at Faure, east of Cape Town. According to a December 23, 1981, CIA report, the facility contains a cyclotron (a type of particle accelerator) capable of producing a powerful proton beam. CIA sources have claimed that the center could help develop a nuclear weapons program.

National Front for the Liberation of Angola (FNLA)
Formed in 1962, the FNLA was based in Zaire and enjoyed

strong support from President Mobutu. It is closely identified with the Bakongo tribes, which inhabit northern Angola. Though the Front has no strong ideological orientation, it received support from the United States during the Angolan civil war of 1975–1976.

National Intelligence Service
The South African NIS is charged with interpreting intelligence and formulating strategies for national security. The NIS reports to the president and the State Security Council.

National Union for the Total Independence of Angola (UNITA)
Jonas Savimbi established UNITA in Angola in 1966, following his resignation from the Angola Revolutionary Government in Exile (GRAE) in 1964. The organization draws its membership mainly from the Ovimbundu ethnic group, which inhabits central and southern Angola. It is dependent upon South Africa and the United States for arms and other military assistance.

Nuclear Fuels Corporation of South Africa (NUCOR)
NUCOR is a consortium comprising the Anglo American Corporation, Anglo Vaal Finance Corporation, General Mining and Finance Corporation, and Union Corporation. All South African uranium producers, with the exception of the Palaborwa Mining Company, currently sell their product through the Nuclear Fuels Corporation.

Pan Africanist Congress (PAC)
The PAC was formed in 1959 by a breakaway faction of the ANC Youth League, which advocated greater militancy and racial assertiveness. The PAC's leadership believed that the Pretoria regime could be brought down by passive disobedience, if undertaken on a large scale. Banned in 1960, the organization was legalized in February 1990 as part of a series of reforms announced by President de Klerk that month.

Popular Movement for the Liberation of Angola (MPLA)
The MPLA was founded in 1959 by intellectuals and working-class elements in Angola's major population centers. After several years of political activity in Portugal directed against Antonio Salazar and a stint in a Portuguese jail, Agostinho Neto returned to Luanda in that year and assumed a leading role in the organization. The ideological center of the MPLA is Marxist, and its major foreign supporters have been the Soviet Union and Cuba.

Secretary of State's Advisory Committee on South Africa
Pursuant to Executive Order 12532, Secretary of State George Shultz formed the Advisory Committee on South

Africa on December 19, 1985, to recommend a policy that would encourage peaceful change and equal rights in South Africa. The committee's January 1987 report concluded that constructive engagement had failed, and that Washington and its allies should impose coordinated economic sanctions to pressure Pretoria to negotiate with representative black leaders.

Separative Work Unit Corporation (SWUCO)
Maryland-based SWUCO, along with the Edlow International Company of Washington, D.C., helped South Africa acquire nearly one hundred tons of enriched uranium. The move violated U.S. government policy prohibiting uranium sales to South Africa because of Pretoria's refusal to sign the Nuclear Non-Proliferation Treaty.

South African–Angolan Joint Military Commission
The U.S.-sponsored Lusaka Accord of 1984 established the South African–Angolan Joint Military Commission to oversee the disengagement of South African and Angolan forces in the region and to facilitate communication between the two parties.

South African Council for Scientific and Industrial Research (CSIR)
Established in 1945, the government-run CSIR is the largest research organization in South Africa. The Reagan administration authorized CSIR to import a powerful Control Data Corporation computer despite reported Pentagon fears that it could be used to break secret U.S. codes and conduct nuclear research.

South African Defense Force (SADF)
The SADF was established by the Defense Act of 1957 and comprises four branches: the army, air force, navy, and medical services. In recent years the SADF has directed its operations against the South West Africa People's Organization (SWAPO) and the ANC, and has engaged in actions in Angola and raids into Botswana, Lesotho, Mozambique, Swaziland, Zambia, and Zimbabwe.

South Africa Working Group (SAWG)
National Security Decision Directive 187 established the SAWG in 1985 to coordinate the U.S. government's "public diplomacy" strategy toward South Africa. Like other public diplomacy plans, this was part of a concerted effort by the Reagan administration to win broader support for its policies and programs—in this case, those involving southern and South Africa.

South West Africa People's Organization (SWAPO)
SWAPO was established in 1959. During most of its existence it has sought a dialogue with South Africa, but in 1966 it adopted a policy of armed struggle against Pretoria's occupation of the territory. In 1973, the U.N. General Assembly granted SWAPO observer status as an "authentic" representative of the Namibian people, and in 1976 recognized it as the population's "sole and authentic" representative.

Space Research Corporation (SRC)
From 1976 through 1978, SRC of North Troy, Vermont, broke the U.S.- and U.N.-backed arms embargo by selling arms and technology to the South African government. Almost all of the equipment came from U.S. Army-owned plants and supply stocks.

State Security Council (SSC)
The South African State Security Council was created by legislation in 1972. It is chaired by the prime minister and includes the minister of foreign affairs, the minister of justice, the secretary for security intelligence (who oversees the Department of Military Intelligence and Department of National Security), the commander of the SADF, and the commandant of the South African Police.

TransAfrica
TransAfrica is a black lobbying group concerned with African and Caribbean affairs. Founded in 1977 and based in Washington, D.C., TransAfrica broadened the anti-apartheid activists' agenda from mere support for divestment to an attack on U.S. policy toward South Africa. By lobbying Congress to enact laws that would make it more costly for the South African government to maintain apartheid, TransAfrica became one of the leading organizations pressing for comprehensive and mandatory sanctions.

United Nations Transition Assistance Group (UNTAG)
U.N. Security Council Resolution 435 of 1978 established the UNTAG, a joint civilian and military force, to assist Special Representative Martti Ahtisaari in implementing the Resolution's Settlement Plan for Namibia.

United States Atomic Energy Commission (AEC)
The AEC issued a license in June 1961 authorizing the Allis-Chalmers Manufacturing Co. to export to South Africa a twenty-megawatt thermal materials-testing reactor utilizing 90 percent enriched uranium fuel. Known as SAFARI-I, the reactor is located at the National Nuclear Research Center at Pelindaba, near Pretoria.

United States Corporate Council on South Africa (USCCSA)
The USCCSA was formed following a White House meeting on South Africa with American corporate heads on September 16, 1985. Cochaired by Roger Smith of General Motors and Michael Blumenthal of Burroughs Corporation, USCCSA's mission was to coordinate American business efforts to resist divestment and "promote reform" in South Africa.

U.S. Nuclear, Inc.
In 1973, the Nuclear Regulatory Commission issued two licenses to U.S. Nuclear, Inc., of Oak Ridge, Tennessee, to export highly enriched uranium for use in the SAFARI-I reactor. In January 1975, the company received a new license authorizing an additional shipment; no later shipments are known to have occurred.

ACRONYMS AND ABBREVIATIONS

AALC = African-American Labor Center

AEC = U.S. Atomic Energy Commission

AEC = Atomic Energy Corporation of South Africa, Ltd.

AFL-CIO = American Federation of Labor–Congress of Industrial Organizations

AID = U.S. Agency for International Development

AMSAA = Army Material Systems Analysis Activity (U.S.)

ANC = African National Congress (South Africa)

ARMSCOR = Armaments Development and Production Corporation (South Africa)

ASC = American Security Council (U.S.)

AZAPO = Azanian People's Organization

BDF = Botswana Defense Force

BOSS = Bureau of State Security (South Africa)

BPC = Black People's Convention

CAAA = Comprehensive Anti-Apartheid Act of 1986

CCB = Civil Cooperation Bureau (South Africa)

CDC = Control Data Corporation (U.S.)

CIA = Central Intelligence Agency

CODESA = Congress for a Democratic South Africa

COSATU = Congress of South African Trade Unions

CSIR = Council for Scientific and Industrial Research (South Africa)

DIA = Defense Intelligence Agency (U.S.)

DNI = Directorate of National Intelligence (South Africa)

DOD = Department of Defense (U.S.)

DONS = Department of National Security (South Africa)

DOS = Department of State (U.S.)

EC = European Community

FAPLA = People's Armed Forces for the Liberation of Angola

ESCOM = Electricity Supply Commission (South Africa)

FBIS = Foreign Broadcast Information Service (U.S.)

FNLA = National Front for the Liberation of Angola

FRELIMO = Front for the Liberation of Mozambique

GRAE = Angola Revolutionary Government in Exile

IAEA = International Atomic Energy Agency

IBM = International Business Machines Corp.

ICJ = International Court of Justice (World Court)

ICL = International Computers, Ltd. (U.K.)

IFP = Inkatha Freedom Party

IMF = International Monetary Fund

IRBM = Intermediate-Range Ballistic Missile

MNR = Mozambique National Resistance (also RENAMO)

MPLA = Popular Movement for the Liberation of Angola

NARMIC = National Action/Research on the Military Industrial Complex (American Friends Service Committee)

NASA = National Aeronautics and Space Administration

NIS = National Intelligence Service (South Africa)

NP = National Party (South Africa)

NPT = Nuclear Non-Proliferation Treaty

NRC = Nuclear Regulatory Commission (U.S.)

NSAM = National Security Action Memorandum

NSC = National Security Council (U.S.)

NSDD = National Security Decision Directive

NSSM = National Security Study Memorandum

NUCOR = Nuclear Fuels Corporation of South Africa

NUM = National Union of Mineworkers (South Africa)

NUSAS = National Union of South African Students

OAU = Organization of African Unity

OECD = Organization for Economic Cooperation and Development

PAC = Pan Africanist Congress (South Africa)

PFP = Progressive Federal Party (South Africa)

PGM = Platinum-group metals

PLAN = People's Liberation Army of Namibia

PRC = People's Republic of China

RENAMO = Mozambique National Resistance (also MNR)

RSA = Republic of South Africa

SA = South Africa

SAAEB = South African Atomic Energy Board

SAAF = South African Air Force

SABC = South African Broadcasting Corporation

SACP = South African Communist Party

SADCC = Southern African Development Coordination Conference

SADF = South African Defense Force

SAG = South African Government

SAP = South African Police

SASO = South African Students Organization

SASOL = South African Coal, Oil and Gas Corporation, Ltd.

SAWG = South Africa Working Group (U.S. State Department)

SFRC = Senate Foreign Relations Committee

SPG = Special Planning Group (National Security Council)

SRBM = Short-Range Ballistic Missile

SRC = Space Research Corporation (U.S.)

SSC = State Security Council (South Africa)

SWAPO = South West Africa People's Organization

SWAPOL = South West African Police (of UNTAG)

SWATF = South West Africa Territory Force

SWUCO = Separative Work Unit Corporation (U.S.)

TAC = Total Arms Coverage

UDF = United Democratic Front (South Africa)

UNGA = United Nations General Assembly

UNHCR = United Nations High Commissioner for Refugees

UNIP = United National Independence Party (Zambia)

UNITA = National Union for the Total Independence of Angola

UNSC = United Nations Security Council

UNTAG = United Nations Transition Assistance Group

USCCSA = U.S. Corporate Council on South Africa

USG = United States Government

USIA = United States Information Agency

ZANU = Zimbabwe African National Union

ZAPU = Zimbabwe African People's Union

U.S. Policy Toward South Africa:
A Chronology of Events

SOURCE NOTES

This chronology, which describes key events relating to the evolution of U.S. policy toward southern and South Africa from 1962 to 1992, orients the flow of events and decisions represented in the documents by providing a narrative context. Each entry is followed by a citation for its sources. Documents are cited by title (in italics) and date. In some cases, Archive staff have provided a title (in brackets) that describes the document's contents. The vast majority of the documents appear in the Archive's microfiche collection, *South Africa: The Making of U.S. Policy, 1962–1989*; all are available for inspection at the National Security Archive. In most instances, books, periodicals, and reports are cited in an abbreviated form, often with references to specific sections or pages. For a listing of the abbreviated titles used in the citations, see the "Source Abbreviations" following the Chronology section on pages (pp. 45–46).

March 21, 1960: Sixty-nine blacks are killed and 180 injured in what becomes known as the Sharpeville Massacre, when white policemen fire upon a crowd of approximately twenty thousand demonstrators protesting the pass laws, which require them to carry passbooks at all times. (Lapping, p. 138; DOS Historian, p. v)

January 20, 1961: John F. Kennedy is inaugurated as the thirty-fifth president of the United States. (NYT 1/21/61)

January 21, 1961: Dean Rusk is appointed secretary of state. Rusk serves as secretary through the Kennedy and Johnson administrations, ending his tenure on January 20, 1969. (Principal Officers, p. 3)

March 22, 1961: National Security Action Memorandum 33 calls for a review of U.S. policy toward the Union of South Africa. (*Review of U.S. Policy Toward South Africa*, 3/22/61)

May 31, 1961: Following a referendum held among South Africa's white voters in late 1960, the Verwoerd administration declares the Union of South Africa to be a republic. In October 1961, the new republic withdraws from the British Commonwealth, severing South Africa's last constitutional tie to Britain. (Lapping, pp. 140–41; DOS Historian, p. v)

June 14, 1961: The United States licenses the export to South Africa of a light-water reactor using highly enriched uranium. The reactor, constructed by Allis-Chalmers Corporation, becomes known as SAFARI-I. (*Comments to NRC on Nuclear Exports License Application*, 1/19/77; House, p. 27)

June 1962: The South African government passes the Anti-Sabotage Bill, which, among other things, sanctions the death penalty for sabotage, prohibits the publishing or repeating of statements made by banned persons, allows for house arrest upon the decision of the Minister of Justice without court trial. (*Country Internal Defense Plan*, 12/18/62)

June 15, 1962: In an exchange of aides memoires between the United States and South Africa, the Kennedy administration expresses its willingness to give "prompt and sympathetic attention to reasonable requests for the purchase of military equipment required for defense against external aggression." (*Sale of Submarines to South Africa*, 9/16/63)

October 6, 1962: Secretary of State Dean Rusk and South African Foreign Minister Eric Louw meet for two hours in New York to discuss U.S.–South African relations. Secretary Rusk informs Louw that U.S. dealings with the rest of Africa are complicated by good relations between the United States and the Verwoerd administration, and that the policy of apartheid threatens the security of the entire continent. (*South Africa and South West Africa*, 3/10/64)

March 22, 1963: President Kennedy approves Secretary Rusk's March 16, 1963, proposal to allow the United States to sell three modern, conventional attack submarines to South Africa for $40 million apiece, and to provide training in their operation for key personnel. (*Sale to South Africa of Submarines and of Spare Parts for C-130's*, 8/28/63)

April 4, 1963: An internal State Department paper outlines the inconsistencies of U.S. arms policy toward South Africa and states that such policy has left the United States vulnerable to accusations "of talking against apartheid but supporting those who are responsible for its existence." The paper calls for terminating close military cooperation with South Africa in order to demonstrate U.S. opposition to apartheid. (*Arms Policy*, 4/10/63)

May 10, 1963: A CIA Special Report states that "subversive groups in the Republic of South Africa have recently displayed a growing capability to use sabotage and terrorism to harass the white community." However, the report claims, "they are not likely to confront the whites with a serious challenge for several years." (*Subversive Movements in South Africa*, 5/10/63)

July 11, 1963: South African security police raid the headquarters of *Umkhonto we Sizwe* in Rivonia, a white suburb of Johannesburg. The closely knit group, made up of members of the African National Congress, South African Communist Party, and others, had recently undertaken a series of symbolic sabotage attacks in Johannesburg and Port Elizabeth. *Umkhonto's* leaders, including Nelson Mandela, Walter Sisulu, and Govan Mbeki, are subsequently put on trial and sentenced to life imprisonment. (SATRO, p. 175)

In connection with the U.S. position on possible U.N. Security Council resolutions calling for severe measures against Portugal and the Republic of South Africa, Secretary of Defense Robert McNamara makes recommendations to the Department of State regarding U.S. military security. He proposes that the United States continue to object strongly to apartheid, but avoid supporting a U.N. resolution that calls for punitive measures against South Africa. (Document 4, Letter to Dean Rusk, 7/11/63)

July 17, 1963: Secretary of State Rusk and South African Ambassador Willem Naude meet to discuss the upcoming U.N. Security Council session and the U.S. position regarding an arms embargo against South Africa. Rusk informs the ambassador that the United States will consider imposing a voluntary embargo by the year's end, regardless of the Security Council resolution. (*South Africa and South West Africa*, 3/10/64; [*Concerning U.S. Government Intentions to Refrain from Sending Arms to South Africa after 1963*], 8/2/63)

July 20, 1963: In a ninety-five-minute discussion, South African Ambassador Naude briefs Secretary Rusk on South Africa's long-range program for developing self-government for nonwhites and for eventually granting independence to African states formed from "Bantu reserves." (*The South African Program of Grouping Independent Bantu States*, 7/20/63; *South Africa and South West Africa*, 3/10/64)

August 2, 1963: Before the U.N. Security Council, U.S. Ambassador to the United Nations Adlai Stevenson announces that the United States intends unilaterally to halt by December 31 the sale of all military goods to South Africa, excluding existing contracts on goods used for defense against external aggression. (*South Africa and South West Africa*, 3/10/64; *Statement by U.S. Representative to the U.N. Adlai E. Stevenson...*, 8/2/63)

August 7, 1963: U.N. Security Council Resolution S/5386 "strongly deprecates" South Africa's racial policies and calls upon Pretoria to abandon those policies and to free persons imprisoned for opposing apartheid. Furthermore, the resolution "solemnly calls upon all states to cease forthwith the sale of arms, ammunition of all types and military vehicles to South Africa." (DOS Historian, p. vi; *Background Paper on U.S. Policy Towards South Africa*, 3/24/64)

September 10, 1963: In a memo to President Kennedy, South African Foreign Minister Eric Louw states that "the U.S. and Britain could not count on continued South African assistance against communism, and that the Simonstown Agreement regarding use of the naval facilities might be dissolved in the light of British and American statements and attitudes, exhibited at the U.N. and elsewhere, towards South Africa's apartheid policy." (Document 5, Memorandum for the President, "Sale of Submarines to South Africa," 9/16/63; SATRO, p. 345)

September 23, 1963: President Kennedy approves Secretary of State Rusk's August 28 recommendation to continue, past the end of 1963, to license the sale of spare parts for C-130 aircraft sold to the South African government. (Document 6, Memorandum for Secretary Rusk and Secretary McNamara, 9/23/63)

November 20, 1963: Attorney General Robert Kennedy recommends to National Security Advisor McGeorge Bundy that the NSC Standing Group discuss what attitude and policy the United States should adopt toward the independence movements in Mozambique, South Africa, Angola, and Rhodesia. Kennedy suggests taking steps in the near future, "either through the CIA and/or making a concerted effort with students and intellectuals." ([*U.S. Attitude and Policy toward Individuals and Organizations Attempting to Gain Independence...*], 11/20/63)

November 22, 1963: President Kennedy is assassinated in Dallas, Texas. Vice President Lyndon Johnson is sworn in as the thirty-sixth president of the United States. (NYT 11/23/63)

January 1964: The South African government introduces the Bantu Laws Amendment Bill, termed in a National Security Council briefing paper "the most extreme apartheid legislation yet proposed." Its passage would "remove the last vestiges of job and residence security" for South Africa's non-white population by "reducing them to the status of migratory workers." (*South Africa and South West Africa*, 3/10/64)

January 17, 1964: Ambassador to South Africa Joseph Satterthwaite cables the Department of State raising questions about the potential for circumventing the U.S. arms embargo. Existing loopholes include sales of military equipment to South Africa via third countries, South African manufacture under U.S. license, and South African production within subsidiaries of U.S. firms. (*[Concerning Potential Loopholes in U.S. Embargo Policy]*, 1/17/64)

Late January 1964: The Odendaal Commission submits its report to the Verwoerd administration. The commission proposes a five-year development plan for South West Africa, which includes, as paraphrased by a March 10 NSC Briefing Paper, the following recommendations: the enforcement of apartheid "in an extreme degree" in the territory and the incorporation of the territory's administration into that of the Republic. (*South Africa and South West Africa*, 3/10/64)

February 12, 1964: The U.S. and British ambassadors in Cape Town present parallel aides memoires urging the South African government to postpone implementation of the Odendaal plan in South West Africa pending an International Court of Justice decision. (*Your Meeting with Ambassador Naude*, 3/18/64)

April 24, 1964: The U.S. government defines several major policies toward South Africa in National Security Action Memorandum 295. The memo authorizes increased diplomatic activity toward securing a deferral of the Odendaal Plan recommendations; continuing the present military sales policy; suspending action on South African applications for investment loans; planning alternative sites for NASA facilities currently based in South Africa; pressuring South Africa to accept the final decision of the International Court of Justice (ICJ) on the South West Africa case; and analyzing sanctions that could be applied against South Africa should it reject the ICJ decision. (Document 7, NSAM 295 "U.S. Policy Toward South Africa," 4/24/64)

February 10, 1965: The U.S. government authorizes the delivery of reactor fuel for South Africa's nuclear power plant, SAFARI-I. (*[Delivery of SAFARI-I Fuel Elements Authorized Today]*, 2/10/65)

June 1966: A draft amendment to the U.S.–South Africa atomic energy agreement extends the terms of the treaty until August 21, 1969. (*Renewal of United States–South Africa Atomic Energy Agreement*, 6/1/66)

Late June 1966: The CIA issues an Intelligence Memorandum regarding economic sanctions against South Africa. The report states that an "airtight embargo would be extremely difficult to enforce without a naval blockade of the southern African coast." Without such a blockade, the report argues, many countries, including Great Britain, will continue to do business with South Africa. The memo also notes that despite the current embargo, Pretoria is still able to obtain the military equipment it requires. (*Some Implications of Economic Sanctions Against South Africa*, 6/66)

September 6, 1966: Prime Minister Verwoerd is assassinated while attending a session of the South African Parliament. Minister for Justice John Vorster is named to replace him as prime minister and National Party leader. (*Assassination of Hendrik Verwoerd*, 9/6/66; SATRO, p. 211)

October 27, 1966: The U.N. General Assembly passes Resolution 2145, which terminates South Africa's mandate to govern South West Africa and establishes an Ad Hoc Committee for South West Africa, comprising fourteen member states, to develop proposals for the administration of the territory. (DOS Historian, p. vi)

March 27, 1967: An Action Memorandum is sent to the Secretary of State requesting authorization for a ten-year extension of the U.S.–South African atomic energy agreement. The memo argues that such an extension would promote bilateral cooperation in areas that would serve U.S. nonproliferation and nuclear safeguard objectives. The extension is granted on March 31. (*Circular 175 Request for Authority…*, 3/27/67; *Extension of Agreement with South Africa on Peaceful Uses of Nuclear Energy*, 3/31/67)

July 17, 1967: Following approval by President Johnson, representatives of the Department of State and the Atomic Energy Commission and South African Ambassador Harold Taswell sign the amendment to the U.S.–South African atomic energy agreement. (*[Amendment Extending Agreement on Peaceful Uses of Atomic Energy…]*, 7/21/67)

January 20, 1969: Richard M. Nixon is inaugurated as the thirty-seventh president of the United States. (NYT 1/21/69)

January 21, 1969: William P. Rogers is appointed secretary of state; his term begins the following day and runs until September 3, 1973. (Principal Officers, p. 3)

March 20, 1969: The U.N. Security Council passes Resolution 264 restating its demand that South Africa withdraw from Namibia and declaring as unjust the South African government's passage of the South West Africa Affairs Bill, by which it empowers itself to enforce the policies of apartheid in Namibia. (DOS Historian, p. 369)

April 10, 1969: National Security Advisor Henry Kissinger forwards National Security Study Memorandum 39 to the secretaries of State and Defense and the Director of Central Intelligence. The memo is a directive from the president to prepare a comprehensive review of U.S. policy toward southern Africa. (Document 36, "Southern Africa," 4/10/69)

April 16, 1969: The Fifth Summit Conference of East and Central African States, a group of fourteen countries, meets in Lusaka, Zambia, to issue the Lusaka Manifesto, a "remarkably articulate and remarkably restrained" document explaining the conference's hostility to the white minority regimes in southern Africa and expressing its support for the region's liberation movements. (Document 36, "Southern Africa," 4/10/69)

April 17–18, 1969: Senator Edward Kennedy (D–Mass.) and eleven other senators of both parties introduce identical bills on April 17 and 18, to terminate South Africa's sugar quota. (Document 36, "Southern Africa," 4/10/69)

April 21, 1969: Congressman Benjamin Rosenthal (D–N.Y.), with thirty-two cosigners, sends a letter to Secretary of State Rogers asking whether the Nixon administration will continue the practice of having all navy ships avoid South African harbors except in emergencies, and whether the policy long "under review" will be decided soon or delayed. (Document 36, "Southern Africa," 4/10/69)

July 8, 1969: David D. Newsom is appointed assistant secretary of state for African affairs, replacing Joseph Palmer. His tenure begins on July 17 and runs until January 13, 1974. (Principal Officers, p. 7)

December 9, 1969: The NSC Interdepartmental Group for Africa submits a revised "Study in Response to National Security Study Memorandum 39." (Document 36, "Southern Africa," 4/10/69)

July 20, 1970: Speaking before the South African House of Assembly, Prime Minister Vorster announces that South African nuclear scientists have developed a new and unique method of uranium enrichment, which will form the basis for a new pilot plant to be built under the auspices of the South African Atomic Energy Board. (IHT 7/22/70)

July 23, 1970: U.N. Security Council Resolution 282 is adopted in a vote of twelve to none, with abstentions by the

United States, France, and the United Kingdom. The resolution calls all countries to strengthen their commitment to the arms embargo against South Africa. (*U.N. Security Council Resolution 282 concerning Apartheid in South Africa, July 23, 1970,* 7/23/70)

July 24, 1970: John Hurd is appointed U.S. ambassador to South Africa, replacing William Rountree. His tenure begins on September 10 and ends on April 7, 1975. (Principal Officers, p. 96)

August 21, 1971: The Nixon administration reviews U.S. policy on contacts with South African Defense Force officers in the context of an overall review entitled "State-DOD Guidelines concerning Certain Aspects of Our Relations with the South African Military Establishment." (*USG Policy on Contacts with the South African Police and Military...,* 4/24/81)

December 12, 1971: The State Department's Bureau of African Affairs begins examining U.S. relations with African liberation movements—contacts that are considered a policy problem meriting early attention and planning. (*Policy Planning Memorandum—U.S. Relations with the African Liberation Movements,* 12/23/71)

July 11, 1973: Responding to congressional pressure, the National Aeronautics and Space Administration (NASA) announces its decision to phase out U.S. satellite-tracking stations located in South Africa beginning in mid 1974. (DOS Historian, p. vii)

September 21, 1973: Henry Kissinger is appointed secretary of state, replacing William Rogers. His term begins the following day and runs through the end of the Ford administration. (Principal Officers, p. 3)

December 12, 1973: The U.N. General Assembly adopts Resolution 311, recognizing the South West Africa People's Organization (SWAPO) as "the authentic representative of the Namibian people." The United States abstains. (DOS Historian, p. vi)

January 22, 1974: The U.S. government issues a license permitting the U.S. Nuclear Corporation of Oak Ridge, Tennessee, to export 12.5 kilograms of highly enriched uranium to South Africa. The license is amended on October 2, 1974, to allow the export of an additional 12.5 kilograms. (Danaher, p. 113)

February 27, 1974: Donald B. Easum is appointed assistant secretary of state for African affairs, replacing David Newsom. His tenure begins on March 18 and runs until March 26, 1975. (Principal Officers, p. 7)

April 25, 1974: In Portugal, the right-wing Caetano Marcelo dictatorship is overthrown by General Antonio Spinola, who favors decolonization in Guinea-Bissau, Mozambique, and Angola. The coup brings to an end almost five hundred years of colonial rule in Angola, with the years 1961–1974 the most bitter of all. After it became apparent that the wave of independence sweeping Africa in the late 1950s and early 1960s would not weaken Portugal's resolve to maintain its colonies, nationalist movements formed to fight for independence. Growing unrest turned to guerrilla warfare in 1961, which continued until independence. Despite the fact that fighting had been underway in Angola longer than in Portugal's other colonies, the insurgents had made no significant inroads on the military front, thanks in part to assistance provided to Portugal from other Western powers, including the United States. Ethnic and ideological differences among Angola's three main liberation movements—the MPLA, UNITA, and FNLA—would later cause widespread civil strife to develop in the country.

May 7, 1974: South African Defense Force (SADF) commander in chief Admiral H. H. Biermann meets with the U.S. Acting Secretary of the Navy William J. Middendorf at the Pentagon. (*USG Policy on Contacts with the South African Police and Military...*, 4/24/81)

May 22, 1974: The United States and South Africa sign an amendment to the U.S.–South African Agreement for Cooperation concerning Civil Uses of Atomic Energy. Although the current atomic energy agreement with South Africa does not expire until 1977, a State Department memo explains that "this new Amendment has been negotiated at this time in order that South Africa will be able to purchase enriched uranium for the first (of two) planned nuclear power stations scheduled to go into operation in 1982." (*Signing of Amendment to U.S.-S.A. Atomic Energy Agreement,* 5/21/74)

June 19, 1974: President Nixon meets with Portuguese president Spinola in the Azores to discuss, among other things, the situation in the Portuguese territories. The United States calls for a peaceful end to the African wars and for African self-determination. The same day, Secretary of State Henry Kissinger and Foreign Minister Mario Soares meet in Ottawa; Kissinger reiterates U.S. policy toward Portugal's decolonization efforts. (*Decolonization of Portuguese Africa,* 7/31/74)

August 9, 1974: President Nixon resigns. Vice President Gerald R. Ford is sworn in as thirty-eighth president of the United States. (NYT 8/10/74)

October 30, 1974: The United States, Great Britain, and France veto a draft U.N. Security Council resolution recommending the immediate expulsion of South Africa from the United Nations. (DOS Historian, p. vii)

November 12, 1974: The president of the U.N. General Assembly, acting upon a report from the Credentials Committee which the General Assembly has accepted, determines that the South African delegation to the General Assembly ought to be denied the right to participate in that body. The United States challenges the ruling, claiming that the General Assembly has no authority under the U.N. Charter to curtail the rights of any of its members. (DOS Historian, p. vii)

November 26, 1974: Secretary of State Henry Kissinger directs the U.S. delegation at the United Nations to vote against the U.N. Special Committee against Apartheid draft resolution on an arms embargo against South Africa, unless references to Chapter VII action are eliminated. (*Draft Resolution on Apartheid,* 11/26/74)

January 1975: With the approval of the 40 Committee (the sub-cabinet level group charged with reviewing major proposals for covert action), the CIA begins funding the FNLA and UNITA. The initial figure is $300,000, but it is later estimated that, by the end of 1975, the CIA has spent over $31 million on the Angolan conflict. (Document 38, Selection from the Pike Report Relating to Angola 2/76; *NY Times on US Aid to Angola,* 12/20/75)

January 15, 1975: The three liberation groups, the MPLA, FNLA, and UNITA, sign the Alvor Accord, which calls for Angolan independence by November 11, 1975. As of January 31, all three movements will participate in a Portuguese-supervised coalition government and prepare for a peaceful transfer of power. (*United States Policy on Angola,* 1/26/76; *Angolan Agreement,* 1/16/75)

January 28, 1975: General Antonio da Silva Cardoso is named High Commissioner in Angola, replacing Admiral Coutinho. (*United States Policy on Angola,* 1/26/76)

March 17, 1975: William G. Bowdler becomes U.S. ambassador to South Africa, replacing John Hurd; his tenure begins May 14, 1975, and runs until April 19, 1978. Nathaniel Davis replaces Donald Easum as assistant secretary of state for African affairs; he begins his tour on April 2 and leaves his post on December 18. (Principal Officers, pp. 7, 96)

April 7, 1975: Prime Minister Vorster announces the start-up of South Africa's first pilot plant for uranium enrichment at

Pelindaba. (*Sale of Uranium Made in U.S. to South Africa*, 4/16/75; *South African Uranium Enrichment Plant*, 4/17/75)

April 14, 1975: The *Washington Post* reports a story based on a press release by Representative Les Aspin (D–Wis.) that the U.S. Nuclear Corporation of Oak Ridge, Tennessee, has shipped ninety-seven pounds of enriched uranium—enough to make seven atomic bombs—to South Africa over the past year. (*Supply of Highly Enriched Uranium to South Africa*, 4/15/75; WP 4/14/75)

June 11, 1975: Acting Organization of African Unity Secretary-General Kamanda Wa Kamanda denounces the June 6 vetoes by the United States, Great Britain, and France of a U.N. Security Council Resolution calling for a mandatory arms embargo against South Africa. Kamanda warns that African liberation movements have no other choice but to "intensify the armed liberation struggle in the region until final victory," because the United Nations is unable to find a peaceful solution to the problem of Namibia. (*OAU Denounces Western UNSC Veto on Namibia*, 6/11/75)

July 1975: Fearful of a "communist" government on the Namibian border, South Africa begins channeling arms and supplies to FNLA and UNITA to help their struggle to overthrow the Soviet-supported MPLA. During this month, the United States also begins to fund antigovernment rebel groups in Angola. (DOS Bulletin, p. 16; *Your Breakfast Meeting December 18*, 12/17/75)

July 17, 1975: President Gerald Ford and the 40 Committee approve a $14 million covert program, later increased to $25 million in August and $32 million by November, to aid the FNLA and UNITA. (Document 37, Memorandum for the Senate Foreign Relations Committee, "U.S. Policy Toward Angola," 12/16/75; Document 38, Selection from the Pike Report Relating to Angola, 2/76)

August 21, 1975: The collapse of Angola's transitional government of three rival liberation movements leads the government of Portugal to suspend the Alvor Accord (see entry for January 15, 1975) and to adopt emergency measures. The suspension permits a Portuguese-controlled, centralized administration with new powers conferred upon the high commissioner. (*Security Council and Angola*, 8/22/75; *GOP Initiative in Angola*, 8/22/75; *Angola and UN*, 8/26/75)

Late August 1975: Assistant Secretary of State for African Affairs Nathaniel Davis resigns, making clear his opposition to Secretary of State Kissinger's policy of intervention in Angola. Davis had proposed that a diplomatic solution be found for Angola, but Kissinger rejected the option. (*Press Material*, 12/14/75)

September 1, 1975: The South African government convenes the Turnhalle constitutional conference in Windhoek, Namibia; the South West Africa People's Organization (SWAPO) and several other political factions in Namibia are barred from participating. The conference proposes an internal settlement aimed at achieving Namibian independence and recommends a constitution based on a separate white electorate and a federation of ethnic homelands. The proposals become the basis of the Vorster administration's thinking about Namibia, but the United States refuses to recognize the conference because of its rejection of important political groups (see entry for April 7, 1977). (DOS Historian, p. viii; *Namibia: Constitutional Conference Opens*, 9/2/75; AFP, pp. 1167–72)

October 8, 1975: Cuban troops arrive in Angola. A "reliable source" reports to the U.S. consul general that he spoke with the troops, most of them black Cubans who spoke Spanish, and was informed that they were volunteers who came to fight for the MPLA. (*Cuban Troops in Angola*, 10/10/75)

October 23, 1975: In an effort to aid the FNLA-UNITA alliance, the South African government sends heavily armed troops into Angola, including black Africans who served in the Portuguese colonial army and white Portuguese Angolans. As the army units push northward toward Luanda, the Soviets increase their arms shipments to the MPLA. South Africa later claims that its incursion was aimed at stopping the communists from gaining ground in Angola. (DOS Bulletin, p. 17; *Your Breakfast Meeting December 18*, 12/17/75)

November 8, 1975: The Portuguese government announces Portugal's withdrawal from Angola. Although Angola will gain its sovereignty, power will not be transferred to any one of the three liberation movements. Secretary of State Kissinger has declared that if the MPLA proclaims itself the legitimate government based on its purported control of the capital and twelve of the sixteen districts, the United States will not recognize its legitimacy. (*Angola Recognition*, 11/8/75)

November 10–11, 1975: Departing Angolan High Commissioner Cardoso proclaims the country's independence, ending Portuguese sovereignty in Angola. The MPLA proclaims itself the legitimate government in Luanda. The FNLA and UNITA establish a rival government, the Democratic Republic of Angola, in Huambo. (*United States Policy* on Angola, 1/26/76; *Briefing Material on Angola for Congressman Bowen*, 1/19/76; *Angolan Recognition Update*, 11/13/75)

November 25, 1975: Nigeria announces that it will recognize the MPLA as the legitimate government of Angola, citing South African involvement in Angola as the primary reason for recognition. In a December 3 cable to Secretary of State Henry Kissinger, Donald Easum warns that continuing silence by the United States on South African involvement in Angola would further discredit the United States in the eyes of many African countries and "provide ammunition for those who already accuse us of abetting South African intervention." (*Message to Nigerian Foreign Minister*, 11/29/75; *South African Involvement in Angola; MPLA Visit to Lagos*, 12/3/75)

December 11, 1975: William E. Schaufele, Jr., is appointed assistant secretary of state for African affairs, replacing Nathaniel Davis. His tenure begins on December 19 and runs until July 17, 1977. (Principal Officers, p. 7)

December 15, 1975: Deputy Assistant Secretary of State for African Affairs Edward W. Mulcahy and James Lee, president of Gulf Oil, meet to discuss Gulf Oil's dilemma in Cabinda, Angola. The MPLA is demanding that Gulf Oil pay $120 million in taxes and royalties due December and January to the Luanda Government or face confiscation of its facilities. Mulcahy informs Lee that if Gulf Oil pays, it will be contributing to the MPLA war effort against the coalition forces of the FNLA and UNITA. Lee requests that the U.S. government supply documentation stating that payment to the MPLA would not correspond with U.S. interests, thereby allowing Gulf Oil to cease operations in Cabinda without jeopardizing its relationship with any future Angolan regime. Once stability is established in Angola, Gulf Oil will make the required payment and resume operations. Secretary of State Kissinger approves of a plan that requests Gulf Oil to delay payment to the MPLA. (*Gulf Oil Operations in Cabinda*, 12/17/75; *Possible Payment by Gulf to the MPLA*, 12/15/75)

December 25, 1975: The United States launches a diplomatic campaign against countries that allow the Soviet Union to use their airspace and any facilities for airlifts to Angola. (*U.S. Position on Angola*, 12/24/75)

Late December 1975: Secretary of State Henry Kissinger praises the Central African Republic, Gabon, Ivory Coast, Liberia, and Senegal for their efforts to convince other African states of the danger of Soviet intervention in Angola.

He also assures them that despite discussions occurring in Congress about U.S. aid to Angola, funds are available to continue resisting Soviet intervention in Angola. (*Angola: Holding the Line*, 12/20/75; *U.S. Position on Angola*, 12/24/75)

January 2, 1976: State Department officials outline U.S. policy objectives during a briefing. They identify the Soviet incursion into Angola as the primary reason for U.S. covert military intervention. The briefing states that there is a real Soviet threat to southern Africa, and that to fail to intercede would compromise the United States' relations with black Africa, especially Zaire and Zambia, at whose request the United States has committed itself to the Angolan crisis. (NSSM 234, 1/2/76; *Possible Contingency Action Regarding Africa*, 1/10/76)

January 21, 1976: U.S. Ambassador James Spain meets with Tanzanian president Julius Nyerere to discuss the U.S. position in Angola. Nyerere, concerned about the Soviet and Cuban presence, believes that their withdrawal is linked with the withdrawal of South African troops, the waning of Western supplies to FNLA and UNITA forces, and the acceptance of a political structure in Angola in which the MPLA plays a major role. He asserts that once these steps have been taken, he can talk President Agostinho Neto of Angola into getting the Soviets and Cubans out. (*Continuing Dialogue with Chiefs of State*, 1/21/76)

January 25, 1976: South Africa begins withdrawing its troops from the interior of Angola toward the Namibian border. In a January 27 meeting, Foreign Minister Brand Fourie explains that the move is due to international and domestic political pressure and the lack of support from the West for anti-MPLA forces. (*Angola: Developments During Your Trip*, 1/26/76; *Staff Del Coughlin Visit to South Africa*, 1/28/76; CRS IB81063, 7/27/82)

February 7, 1976: Secretary of State Kissinger approves Gulf Oil's payment of $100 million to the government of Angola in taxes and royalties that were withheld during the months of the civil war. Payment is made to a Swiss bank, the Union Banque Suisse in Geneva, on March 8, 1976. (*Gulf Payments to the MPLA*, 2/8/76)

February 11, 1976: The Organization of African Unity recognizes the MPLA as the official government in Luanda. On February 22, Portugal also recognizes the MPLA. (*The United States and Angola, 1974–88: A Chronology*, 2/89)

April 1976: The Space Research Corporation of Vermont signs an arms sales contract with the South African government estimated at $50 million. (Danaher, p. 119; *U.N. Notes*, p. 9)

April 21, 1976: President Ford directs the NSC Interdepartmental Group for Africa to prepare National Security Study Memorandum 241, a study of U.S. policy toward southern Africa. According to a secret memo outlining the directive, the study should define U.S. interests in southern Africa, asses the questions of majority rule in Rhodesia and of settlement plans for Namibia, and analyze the implications of both situations for the future of U.S.–South African relations. The study is to be submitted to the NSC Senior Review Group by May 21. (*United States Policy in Southern Africa*, 4/21/76)

April 27, 1976: In Lusaka, Zambia, Secretary of State Kissinger issues a comprehensive statement on U.S. policy toward southern Africa. Kissinger says that "apartheid in South Africa remains an issue of great concern to those committed to racial justice and human dignity" but "no country, no people can claim perfection in the realm of human rights." Kissinger adds that U.S. policy toward South Africa is "based upon the premise that within a reasonable time we shall see a clear evolution toward equality of opportunity and basic human rights for all South Africans," and calls upon the government of South Africa to "make that premise a reality." (*A U.S. Policy Toward South Africa*, 1/87; *Address by the Honorable Henry Kissinger*, 4/27/76)

May 14, 1976: Secretary of State Kissinger meets with South African ambassador Pik Botha to discuss the role South Africa might play in finding a solution to the problems of Rhodesia and southern Africa. A State Department spokesman declares that the United States is trying to move the white and black populations of southern Africa toward greater coexistence, but that more meetings with South Africa will be required before progress can be predicted. (*Press Guidance on Secretary's Meeting with South African Ambassador Botha*, 5/18/76)

May 19, 1976: Prime Minister John Vorster announces that he is willing to accept an invitation from President Ford and Rhodesian Prime Minister Smith to discuss the "promotion of peace and understanding between people in Southern Africa." (*Vorster Welcomes Idea of Meeting with Ford*, 5/19/76)

June 5, 1976: The British and U.S. governments discuss developing a joint plan of action for implementing their "common policies" in Rhodesia. The British hope to convince Rhodesian Prime Minister Smith to agree to majority rule,

to hold elections leading to that within eighteen to twenty-four months, and to refrain from drawn-out negotiations. U.S. officials must in turn convince the Vorster administration to discontinue military aid to Smith and to impose economic sanctions on Rhodesia while denying Smith any opportunity to stall plans for majority rule. (*U.S.-U.K. Consultations on Rhodesia and South Africa*, 6/5/76)

June 16–19, 1976: Riots break out in the township of Soweto when police open fire on a group of students protesting South Africa's Bantu Education System. Tensions had been building over a period of five weeks as blacks responded with boycotts and demonstrations to a government order that half of all secondary-level courses be taught in Afrikaans. Within days of the shooting, protests spread to other black and colored townships; many protesters are killed. On June 18 and 19, the U.N. Security Council meets to consider the situation and adopts Resolution 392 condemning the South African government's violent response to the demonstrations and calling upon the Vorster administration to eliminate apartheid and racial discrimination. (Nelson, p. 59; DOS Historian, p. 567; *Statements by U.S. Representative Albert Sherer Concerning the Situation in South Africa...*, 6/19/76)

June 23–24, 1976: Prime Minister Vorster holds talks with Secretary of State Kissinger in Germany. During the discussions, Kissinger suggests that the United States is interested in working with South Africa to reach settlements in Namibia and Rhodesia. The talks end with an agreement to meet again later in the year. (*Conversation with Prime Minister Vorster*, 6/29/76)

June 30, 1976: President Ford signs into law the Clark Amendment, introduced by Senator Dick Clark (D–Iowa) as an extension of the Tunney Amendment. The Clark Amendment prohibits assistance of any kind with "the purpose, or which would have the effect, of promoting or augmenting, directly or indirectly, the capacity of any nation, group, organization, movement, or individual to conduct military or paramilitary operations in Angola unless the President determines such assistance is in the national security interest of the United States, and so reports to the Congress specifying the amount and the recipient of the aid." (*Angola and the Clark Amendment*, 10/20/82; *The United States and Angola, 1974–88: A Chronology*, 2/89)

September 7, 1976: Ambassador Bowdler relays the outcome of his recent discussions with Prime Minister Vorster in a cable to Secretary of State Kissinger. Vorster had told Bowdler that he wishes to include in his speeches a statement that the United States and South Africa are "drawing together" as a result of the talks. Bowdler responds that he believes that the statement could easily be misinterpreted and would detract from the present efforts toward negotiations. He advises Vorster to omit any mention of bilateral relations between the United States and South Africa. (*Prime Minister Vorster's Speeches on September 8 and 10, 9/7/76; Vorster Speeches, 9/7/76*)

September 9, 1976: Assistant Secretary of State William Schaufele, Jr., meets with Zambian President Kenneth Kaunda in Lusaka to discuss the outcome of Secretary Kissinger's discussions with Prime Minister Vorster. In a press conference the following morning, Schaufele states that the upcoming Kissinger-Vorster meeting has been set to achieve further progress on the Namibian and Rhodesian problems. (*Schaufele Lusaka Press Conference, 9/10/76*)

September 14, 1976: South African Prime Minister Vorster and Rhodesian Prime Minister Smith meet for over four hours on the Rhodesian issue. During "a full and frank exchange of views," Vorster conveys pertinent views of the U.S. and South African governments, based on his recent discussions with Secretary of State Kissinger. Smith is reportedly under extreme pressure from Washington and Pretoria to negotiate a transfer of power with the black nationalist opposition. (*Press Material, 9/15/76*)

September 15, 1976: Secretary of State Kissinger sends a message to British Prime Minister Harold Wilson concerning a Rhodesian plan that would have given blacks a majority on the interim government's Council of State. Prime Minister Vorster's objections to this change lead Kissinger to tell Wilson that the plan should allow for a white majority in the council. (*Message to the Prime Minister, 9/14/76*)

September 20, 1976: Secretary of State Kissinger sends a letter to Prime Minister Vorster telling him that he anticipates little objection from presidents of the frontline states—Angola, Botswana, Mozambique, Tanzania, and Zambia—to a proposal for a white chairman of the Council of State in Rhodesia; however, he feels that the proposal for a white minister for defense and law and order will be more difficult for them to accept. (*Message to Prime Minister Vorster, 9/20/76*)

September 21, 1976: Rhodesian Prime Minister Smith relays a message to Secretary of State Kissinger requesting "parity in the Council of Ministers, or, as an alternative, a white majority for the Council of State." Smith claims that without racial parity or a white majority it will be very diffi-

cult to obtain an agreement within the caucus. (*Message from Ian Smith, 9/21/76*)

September 21, 1976: Secretary of State Kissinger sends a message to Smith telling him that the U.S. government has no objections regarding the size of the Council of State, and that this issue needs to be addressed by the parties involved when they come together to discuss arrangements for the interim government. (*Follow-Up Items, 9/21/76*)

October 8, 1976: U.N. Secretary-General Kurt Waldheim and Secretary of State Kissinger review current developments regarding Rhodesia and Namibia during a forty-five-minute meeting at the United Nations. Kissinger's recent communications with African leaders, particularly with Kenneth Kaunda and Julius Nyerere, lead him to suggest that acceptable arrangements for a U.N. conference should be worked out, and to stress that if South Africa is "humiliated" during this proposed conference, it will choose to fight SWAPO for Namibia rather than negotiate. He adds that Cuba should not encourage SWAPO to fight because SWAPO's chances against the South African military are slim, and that this situation would lead the United States to intervene. Both Kissinger and Waldheim agree to persuade the parties involved to adopt "reasonable and flexible positions." (*Secretary's Meeting with U.N. Secretary General Waldheim, 10/12/76; Secretary's Meeting with U.N. Secretary General Waldheim October 8, 1976: Rhodesia and Namibia, 10/12/76*)

December 1976: The *New Haven Advocate* reveals that employees of two Connecticut arms manufacturers, the Colt Firearms division of Colt Industries and the Winchester Arms division of Olin Corporation, have arranged to ship rifles, shotguns, and ammunition to South Africa via "dummy" firms in the Canary Islands, Greece, West Germany, and other countries. (*Klare, p. 28*)

December 7, 1976: A draft resolution on "The Situation in Namibia Resulting from the Illegal Occupation by South Africa" is introduced to the U.N. General Assembly. The resolution, scheduled for a vote on December 10, reaffirms the right of the people of Namibia to "self-determination, freedom and national independence," recognizes SWAPO as the "sole and authentic representative of the Namibia people" and condemns South Africa for its "persistent refusal to withdraw from Namibia and for its maneuvers to consolidate its illegal occupation of the territory." The resolution also demands that South Africa release all Namibian political prisoners and prepare for U.N.-supervised elections, and it requests all states to stop selling military supplies to South Africa. (*31st UNGA: Fourth Committee: Namibia*, 12/8/76)

January 20, 1977: James Earl Carter is inaugurated as the thirty-ninth president of the United States. (NYT 1/21/77)

January 21, 1977: Cyrus Vance is appointed secretary of state. His term begins on January 23 and runs until April 28, 1980. (Principal Officers, p. 3)

February 16, 1977: The Carter administration declares its willingness to establish "normal" relations with Angola, contingent upon the removal of Cuban forces from the region. (*The United States and Angola, 1974–88: A Chronology*, 2/89)

March 1, 1977: Twelve major U.S. corporations doing business in South Africa announce support for a set of standards, known as the Sullivan Principles, to be used as guidelines for promoting equal employment rights for blacks and other nonwhite minorities in South Africa. The principles include a call for nonsegregation in places of work and dining facilities, as well as equal pay for equal and comparable work. (AFP, p. 1166; CRS1, p. 40)

April 7, 1977: The Contact Group—Canada, France, the United Kingdom, the United States, and West Germany—initiates new efforts to reach a settlement in Namibia through negotiations with the Vorster administration. It sends a memorandum to Vorster, stating that the Turnhalle conference proposals (see entry for September 1, 1975) are not suitable for successful implementation of U.N. Security Council Resolution 385, and warning that unless South Africa abides by international solutions, the Contact Group will be obliged to consider more serious measures against it. (DOS Historian, p. viii; AFP, pp. 1198–1203; *Namibia*, 7/77)

May 17, 1977: In a televised interview in Los Angeles, President Carter states that if South Africa does not end its rule of Namibia, the government will face "strong action" by the United States, West Germany, Great Britain, France, and Canada. Carter also adds that the United States is "not supporting South Africa" and is doing all it can to persuade the Vorster administration to abandon apartheid. (NYT 5/18/77)

May 20, 1977: Concluding one and a half days of meetings with Prime Minister Vorster, Vice President Mondale holds a press conference in Vienna to review U.S. policy toward southern and South Africa. Mondale warns South Africa in strong terms that continuing racial discrimination and denial of political rights to blacks will bring a "worsening of re-

lations" between South Africa and the United States as well as increased violence in southern Africa. In a separate meeting with the media, Prime Minister Vorster says that "a vital difference between the United States and South Africa stems from the fact that knowingly or unknowingly the United States wants to equate the position of the American Negro with the South African black man." (WP 5/21/77; AFP, pp. 1170–1174; *First Meeting Between Vice President Mondale and Prime Minister Vorster*, 5/20/77)

May 23, 1977: British Foreign Secretary David Owen says after a meeting with Vice President Walter Mondale that Great Britain solidly supports the new U.S. policy toward southern Africa, which puts equal stress on internal reform in South Africa and majority rule for Namibia. Speaking to reporters after their meeting in London, Owen describes the new U.S. policy as an "historic and massively important shift." (CSM 5/24/77; *Uncleared Draft Memorandum of Conversation: Mondale–Owen*, 5/23/77)

June 16, 1977: Richard M. Moose is appointed assistant secretary of state for African affairs, replacing William Schaufele, Jr. His tenure begins on July 6 and runs until January 16, 1981. (Principal Officers, p. 7)

June 16, 1977: In spite of Western objections, the Board of Governors of the International Atomic Energy Agency (IAEA) removes South Africa from its permanent position in the organization because of its continued exploitation of Namibian uranium. South Africa's credentials are also rejected at the IAEA General Conference ending its participation in this forum. (Spector, p. 223; Danaher, p. 124)

August 6, 1977: The Soviet government informs President Carter that a *Cosmos* satellite photograph reveals South African preparations to detonate a nuclear explosive in the Kalahari Desert. Carter orders an independent investigation, which subsequently confirms the Soviet findings. Later, the Carter administration warns South Africa against conducting a nuclear test. (WP 8/23/77; Spector, p. 221)

August 12, 1977: Secretary Vance holds talks in London with British Foreign Secretary David Owen and South African Foreign Minister Pik Botha in order to persuade the Vorster administration to accept Anglo-American strategies for the region, and to convince the frontline states to pressure Zimbabwean nationalists, particularly the Patriotic Front, to do likewise. (*Rhodesia: Approach to Host Governments*, 8/9/77)

August 14, 1977: President Carter, Secretary of State Vance, and National Security Advisor Brzezinski hold strategy talks on the South African nuclear situation. Carter orders a message to be sent to Soviet Premier Brezhnev on August 15, confirming that the United States also has sufficient evidence to suggest that South Africa is preparing for a nuclear test, which would have international consequences. (WP 8/28/77)

August 31, 1977: The rift within South Africa's government over the country's nuclear policy is revealed when Finance Minister Owen Horwood states in an address to the National Party Congress, "I think it is time we told Carter...that, if we did at any time wish to do other things with our nuclear potential, we will jolly well do so according to our own decisions and our own judgement." Later that day, however, Foreign Minister Pik Botha reiterates Vorster's pronouncement that "nuclear energy will be used solely for peaceful purposes." (WP 8/31/77)

September 13, 1977: South African Minister of Justice James Kruger announces that black consciousness movement leader Steve Biko, age thirty, has died in police detention in Pretoria—the forty-sixth detainee to die in custody since 1961. The following day, Kruger states that Biko died following a seven-day hunger strike while in detention. Kruger's statement sparks an outcry by both black and white South Africans. According to various press reports, Biko died from "multiple brain and body injuries." (CRS7, p. 31; Lapping, pp. 160–162)

October 19, 1977: The South African government moves to restrict certain publications, bans eighteen dissenting civil rights organizations, detains a number of black leaders, including the editor of *The World*, Percy Qoboza, and banishes six white supporters of black rights, including the editor of the *East London Daily Dispatch*, Donald Woods. (AFP, p. 1181; CRS7, p. 30)

October 27, 1977: According to the *Washington Post*, President Carter officially announces that "the United States will convert its [1963] voluntary ban on arms sales to South Africa into a broadened formal embargo, along with most members of the United Nations." This move, Carter says, "will demonstrate our deep and legitimate concern" about South Africa's suppression of black consciousness leaders and organizations. (WP 10/27/77; *Murrey Marder Article in Washington Post*, 10/28/77)

During a press conference following an evening interview with Walter Cronkite, South African Foreign Minister Pik Botha calls the U.S. decision to support an arms embargo against South Africa "totally unacceptable to the South African government." However, Botha admits that he believes the U.N. Security Council adoption of an arms embargo to be "inevitable." (*FONMIN Botha Terms USG Arms Embargo Decision "Unacceptable,"* 10/28/77)

October 31, 1977: The United States, Great Britain, and France veto three of four African-sponsored Security Council resolutions on South Africa. The resolutions seek to introduce an arms embargo, economic sanctions, and a determination on Chapter Seven of the U.N. Charter, which would characterize the situation in South Africa as being a threat to international peace and security. The Western Five members of the council introduce their own resolution for a mandatory arms embargo. (*West Vetoes African Resolutions on South Africa in Security Council October 31,* 11/1/77)

November 4, 1977: The U.N. Security Council adopts Resolution 418, instituting a mandatory arms embargo against South Africa. In a statement following the unanimous vote, U.S. Ambassador Andrew Young characterizes the resolution as a "genuine compromise," demonstrating the ability of all members of the Security Council to work together to reach an agreement. (Document 9, Cable for All African Diplomatic Posts, "Security Council Action on South Africa," 11/5/77)

November 9, 1977: In a statement made by South African Minister of Economic Affairs Chris Heunis, the South African government declares its authority to require those foreign businesses operating within South Africa to produce strategic minerals upon demand. (CRS7, p. 29)

November 21, 1977: A South African government doctor testifies that he and a colleague were forbidden from admitting black nationalist leader Steve Biko into a hospital five days before he died in police custody. (WP 11/22/77)

November 25, 1977: The U.S. government says that it would support a prohibition on the importation of gold from South Africa and a worldwide embargo on purchases of South African gold. This embargo would have a serious impact on sales of the South African "Krugerrand" gold coins. (*Embargo on Imports of Gold from South Africa,* 11/25/77)

December 2, 1977: The United States strongly denounces South Africa's verdict in the death of Steven Biko, saying the black leader was a "victim of flagrant neglect and official irresponsibility." State Department spokesman Hodding Carter presents the department's harsh statement in the wake of a ruling by Pretoria magistrate Marthius J. Prins that evidence did not show Biko's death "to be brought about by any act or omission involving an offense by any person." (WP 12/3/77)

December 14, 1977: The State Department announces that it has recommended that the Commerce Department approve export licenses for U.S. aircraft sales to South Africa. State Department spokesman John Trattner states that the United States has been assured that the aircraft will be used for civilian purposes, and that it will make efforts to verify this. On December 15, an article appears in the *Johannesburg Star* suggesting that the sale of six Cessna aircraft to private companies in South Africa violates U.N. Security Council Resolution 418, which prohibits the sale of military equipment to South Africa. (*U.N. Arms Embargo Committee Requests USG Comment on Cessna Sale to South Africa,* 9/1/78; *South Africa Sanctions: Sale of Cessnas to South Africa,* 9/9/78; WP 12/15/77)

May 3, 1978: William B. Edmondson is appointed U.S. ambassador to South Africa, replacing William Bowdler. His tenure begins on June 5 and runs until July 22, 1981. (Principal Officers, p. 96)

May 3–4, 1978: South African Defense Forces launch a major strike against SWAPO bases in Angola. This attack prompts Assistant Secretary Moose to call the South African ambassador and demand an explanation for the incursion into Angola. It is feared that South African belligerence against SWAPO forces in Angola may have serious repercussions on the Contact Group's peace initiatives with regard to the Namibian situation. (*South Africa Attack on SWAPO in Angola,* 5/5/78; *Namibia: South Africa's Raid into Angola— An Assessment,* 5/5/78; *The United States…,* 2/89)

May 6, 1978: The U.N. Security Council meets to discuss South Africa's attack on Angola and its use of Namibia as a "springboard" for its attacks. The UNSC adopts Resolution 428 condemning South Africa for its raids and continued occupation of Namibia. (*Security Council Meets to Consider South African Attack on Angola,* 5/6/78; *The United States and Angola, 1974–88: A Chronology,* 2/89)

June 9, 1978: U.S. Representative to the U.N. Andrew Young informs the Carter administration that the Western Five's diplomatic efforts to persuade South Africa to accept U.N. Security Council Resolution 385 have been ignored by South Africa. Pretoria's cooperation would have made it easier to enlist international support for a Namibian solution, but South Africa's actions have been aimed precisely at preventing any movement in that direction. (*Namibia: Additional SWAPO Response to Western Five Proposal,* 6/9/78)

June 25–29, 1978: Carter administration envoy Gerard Smith meets in Pretoria with Foreign Minister Pik Botha

and South African Atomic Energy Board Director Abraham Roux. The United States is hoping to convince South Africa to sign the Nuclear Non-Proliferation Treaty. In return, Botha and Roux demand access to U.S. uranium and nuclear technology, as well as help in getting reinstated on the Board of Governors of the International Atomic Energy Agency. (Danaher, p. 134)

July 27, 1978: The U.N. Security Council adopts two resolutions on Namibia. Resolution 431 establishes the U.N. Transition Assistance Group, to comprise seventy-five hundred troops and twelve hundred civilians from various countries who would monitor a Namibian cease-fire and elections. Resolution 432 declares that Walvis Bay must be reintegrated into Namibia, and that the South African government should do nothing to the port city "prejudicial to the independence of Namibia or the viability of its economy." (*Proposal to Respond to U.N. Secretary General's Request for Services, Supplies and Equipment to Help in the Struggle for Independence in Namibia,* 7/28/78)

August 1, 1978: At a Pretoria press conference, Foreign Minister Pik Botha announces South African government approval of a U.N. Security Council resolution authorizing Secretary-General Kurt Waldheim to send a special representative to Namibia to begin implementing a Western plan for the territory's independence. Botha says that South Africa "is willing to receive the U.N. special representative for Namibia," Martti Ahtisaari, and, based on his recommendations, will accept or reject the Western plan for the territory. The Western plan calls for U.N.-supervised elections, the installation of a U.N. peacekeeping force of several thousand troops, the appointment of a U.N. administrator to work with the current South African–appointed administrator, and the reduction of South Africa's military presence in the territory. (The Sun, 8/1/78)

August 6, 1978: A fifty-member U.N. transition team headed by Finnish diplomat Martti Ahtisaari, the United Nations' special representative to Namibia, arrives in Namibia to set in motion a U.N. operation to oversee elections and Namibia's transition to independence after almost sixty years as a territory under South African rule. (WP 8/7/78)

September 20, 1978: The South African government rejects the U.N. plan for establishing an independent Namibia and says it will follow its own course in loosening control over the disputed territory. Although South Africa originally agreed to the main provisions of the U.N. plan, Prime Minister Vorster says disputes over its implementation have led to an impasse that South Africa cannot allow to continue.

Vorster, however, resigns, taking the position of president. Initial reports attribute the move to health reasons, but later analyses indicate that Vorster was forced to step down following a scandal involving Department of Information use of funds for unauthorized political purposes. (WP 9/21/78)

September 28, 1978: Pieter W. Botha, South Africa's minister of defense, replaces John Vorster as prime minister. (CRS7, p. 22)

September 29, 1978: The U.N. Security Council approves Resolution 435 as the definitive framework for an internationally acceptable settlement in Namibia. The measure calls for the U.N. to supervise a cease-fire and elections as well as to frame a constitution. If accepted by all parties, the plan will take one year to implement. The South African government resists the plan because it calls for the removal of South African troops, and because South African military intelligence has reported that SWAPO will win a large majority of the vote. (*Security Council Approval of Establishment of UNTAG,* 9/29/78)

September 29, 1978: Secretary of State Vance delivers a speech before the U.N. Security Council in which he berates South Africa for superseding the Contact Group's Namibian proposal with plans of its own to sponsor elections in Namibia. According to Vance, "unilateral actions by South Africa, such as its decision to conduct elections in Namibia, cannot be recognized and will not result in a political process which has any international legitimacy." (AFP, pp. 1204–1205)

October 1978: The *New African* magazine publishes an article discussing General Motors' secret plans for cooperation with the South African military in cases of civil unrest. (*Arms Embargo Committee Note on General Motors' South African Operations,* 11/20/78)

October 19, 1978: Officials from the Western Five issue a joint statement in Pretoria, following a five-day visit to South Africa by Secretary of State Vance and other top representatives. They reiterate their view that there is no way to reconcile South Africa's planned elections in Namibia with its own proposal and the plan endorsed by the U.N. Security Council. The group claims that South Africa's "unilateral measure in relation to the electoral process will be regarded as null and void." (NYT 11/6/78; AFP, pp. 1206–1207)

November 10, 1978: The Evans Amendment to the Export-Import Bank Act of 1945 (P.L. 95-360) is enacted to restrict Ex-Im guarantees to the South African government and other South African customers. (U.N. Notes, p. 8)

November 30, 1978: South African Foreign Minister Pik Botha meets with President Carter and Secretary of State Vance in Washington, D.C. According to the *Washington Post,* Carter is "believed to have told Botha that the West will support limited economic sanctions against South Africa" if the South African government rejects U.N. supervision of elections in Namibia.

Vance urges South African Prime Minister P. W. Botha to respond "quickly and affirmatively" to an Angolan invitation to discuss the demilitarization of the Namibian-Angolan border. Vance feels that these discussions have considerable merit for the early implementation of U.N. Resolution 435. (CRS7, p. 21; *South African/Angolan Relations,* 12/1/78)

December 4–8, 1978: South Africa unilaterally holds elections for a constituent assembly in Namibia, outside the framework of the U.N. plan, which it had initially accepted, and without U.N. supervision. All but right-of-center political parties boycott the elections, which are declared null and void by the U.N. Security Council. (DOS Historian, p. ix)

December 21, 1978: The U.S. abstains on a vote in the U.N. General Assembly favoring sanctions against South Africa for its "defiance" of a U.N.-supervised election process in Namibia. The measure passes without a single negative vote. (CRS7, p. 20)

March 1979: The *St. Louis Post Dispatch* reveals that Control Data Corporation has manufactured and supplied equipment to International Computers, Ltd. (ICL), for use in the police forces. Control Data, the article explains, is a close business partner of ICL and is a major supplier of South African military and police agencies. (NARMIC, p. 29; SLPD 3/10/79)

March 7, 1979: Acting on the advice of a report generated by a special U.N. seminar on nuclear collaboration with South Africa held in London February 24–25, the U.N. Special Committee Against Apartheid recommends that the U.N. Security Council adopt a mandatory decision to "end all nuclear collaboration with South Africa." (*U.N. Anti-Apartheid Committee to Send Report on Nuclear Collaboration with South Africa to Security Council with Request for Action,* 3/13/79)

April 1979: One of South Africa's largest distributors of electronics and communications gear, United Electronics Corp., unveils a new mobile communications system, imported from the United States. The system, known as "Total Arms Coverage" or TAC, is made by the U.S. communications giant, RCA. Despite a potential police application,

RCA received a license from the Commerce Department to export the TAC system to South Africa. (NARMIC, p. 30)

April 12, 1979: Prime Minister P. W. Botha announces on national television the expulsion of three U.S. military attachés on charges of espionage, and the removal of the U.S. defense attaché aircraft, which he claims has been used systematically for aerial photography missions. The U.S. government reacts by requesting that the South African defense attaché and the air attaché leave the United States within one week. This is the most recent of several episodes that have eroded U.S. relations with South Africa. (*Current Foreign Relations...*, 4/18/79)

July 27, 1979: The Contact Group meets to discuss the demilitarization of the Angolan-Namibian border. The South African–Angolan proposal is determined to be difficult for the United Nations to implement. The U.N. calls upon the two nations to show goodwill and declares that a demilitarized zone in the form of a Maginot Line is a poor substitute for a "good faith" demilitarized zone. (*Contact Group Meeting with Urquhart*, 7/28/79; *Angola/Namibia Demilitarized Zone*, 7/14/79)

September 22, 1979: A U.S. *Vela* satellite records a light signal over the South Atlantic which U.S. officials believe may have come from a South African–generated nuclear explosion. This incident ultimately generates a storm of controversy over South Africa's nuclear program. The U.S. government later announces its conclusion that the light signal was not nuclear-generated but reports indicate that the opinion is not unanimous within the government. (*Press Panel Review of South Atlantic Event*, 2/7/80)

February 7, 1980: A State Department cable reports the results of the panel commissioned by the Carter administration to study the light signal sighted on September 22, 1979, over the Indian Ocean near South Africa. According to the panel, there is no clear indication as to whether the signal was caused by a nuclear explosion. The panel states that "the probability of the occurrence of a nuclear explosion with no corroborative data such as nuclear debris, is small." Further analysis is recommended to find corroborative evidence. (*Press Panel Review of South Atlantic Event*, 2/7/80)

April 1980: The Southern African Development Coordination Conference meets in Zambia. The nine member states (Angola, Botswana, Lesotho, Malawi, Mozambique, Swaziland, Tanzania, Zambia, and Zimbabwe) issue the Lusaka Declaration, which outlines a number of development goals, primarily reducing regional economic dependence on South Africa. (*South Africa: U.S. Foreign Assistance*, 3/9/90)

June 1980: Continued raids into Angola by South African forces prompt a demarche to the Pretoria regime by the Western Five ambassadors. The envoys call on South Africa to consider that further incursions could derail the Namibian negotiations and they stress the urgency of implementing UN Security Council Resolution 435. (*South African Incursions into Angola: Increased South African Military Activity in Namibia*, 6/17/80)

June 16, 1980: Space Research Corporation founder Gerald Bull and former president Rodgers Gregory are sentenced to six months in prison for selling artillery equipment to South Africa in violation of the arms embargo. A British press account later alleges that the equipment was used to test a nuclear device in September 1979 (see entry for September 22, 1979). (Danaher, p. 147)

July 15, 1980: According to the *Washington Post*, "a Defense Intelligence Agency [DIA] report has concluded that a mysterious flash over the South Atlantic last September probably was caused by a clandestine nuclear explosion." However, the *Post* reports that in a formal reply to questions on the DIA report, the Pentagon stated that since the experts disagree, "no clear conclusion exists." (WP 7/15/80; *South Africa: Defense Strategy in an Increasingly Hostile World*, 1/80)

September 24, 1980: The South African government accepts U.N. Secretary-General Waldheim's proposal to send a mission to Pretoria to hold talks on the implementation of the U.N. plan for Namibia. The Contact Group has voiced its support for the mission, and states that it will do everything to make sure that the meetings result in South Africa's acceptance of a date for implementing the U.N. plan. (*Current Foreign Relations...*, 9/24/80)

October 27, 1980: The U.N. Mission to Namibia returns to New York after six days of closed discussions with the South African government on implementation of the U.N. peace plan for Namibia. South Africa denies that it has accepted a time frame for the plan, although there are indications to the contrary. However, the strict conditions Pretoria has reportedly attached to its acceptance may not be acceptable to all parties involved. (*Namibia: U.N./South African Talks Completed*, 10/29/86)

November 25, 1980: U.N. Secretary-General Waldheim announces to the Security Council that a conference of parties to the Namibia negotiations will take place January 7–14, 1981, in Maputo, Mozambique. South Africa agrees to participate. However, the Botha administration believes that "acute mutual distrust and lack of confidence" pose a significant problem but that "if this obstacle can be overcome, the end of 1981 would be a realistic target date for the independence of Namibia." (*Current Foreign Relations...*, 11/26/80)

December 16, 1980: A U.S. *Vela* satellite detects a flash in the South Atlantic which the United States is concerned may have come from a South African–generated nuclear explosion. (*U.N. Request for Information on December 16, 1980 "Flash" in South Atlantic*, 2/19/81)

January 7–14, 1981: Pre-implementation negotiations on Namibian independence take place in Geneva under U.N. auspices, but they collapse without an agreement on a date for a cease-fire or for implementation of the U.N. proposals. The South African delegation claims that "trust and confidence" between the parties concerned must be established before implementation can begin. However, the negotiations do succeed in granting Namibian parties an opportunity to take part in the discussions. (*Current Foreign Relations...*, 1/21/81; FBIS, 1/15/81, p. U2)

January 20, 1981: Ronald Reagan is inaugurated as the fortieth president of the United States. (NYT 1/21/81)

March 3, 1981: President Reagan makes a televised speech in which he describes South Africa as a friendly country, a wartime ally, and a country of strategic importance to the free world.

With regard to the reported flash of December 16, 1980, the U.S. Mission to the United Nations is instructed to convey to the U.N. Disarmament Center the following message: "Infrared sensors on a U.S. satellite over the South Atlantic recorded a signal on December 15 [*sic*], 1980, but there is agreement among all agencies of the United States Government that it was not caused by a nuclear explosion." (FBIS, 3/5/81, p. U6; *U.N. Request for Information on December 16, 1980, "Flash" in South Atlantic*, 3/3/81)

March 9, 1981: Five senior South African military intelligence officers arrive in Washington, D.C., under what the Reagan administration describes as "misleading circumstances." They meet with representatives of the National Security Council and the Defense Intelligence Agency. Some of the meetings are allegedly arranged by President Reagan's former campaign manager John Sears, who is a registered foreign agent representing South Africa. The of-

ficials got their visas in South Africa after identifying themselves as civilian diplomats. On March 13, Ambassador Jeane Kirkpatrick meets with four of the officers in Washington at the invitation of the American Security Council, a private entity. The following day, the five officers are told to leave the country after U.S. officials determine that a U.S. ban on meetings with South African military personnel has been violated. (*Contingency Press Guidance on Visit to U.S. by High-Ranking South African Military Intelligence Officers*, 3/14/81; *Ambassador Lichtenstein's Report on Ambassador Jeane Kirkpatrick's Conversation with SADF Lt. Gen. Van der Westhuizen...*, 3/25/81; FBIS, 3/23/81, p. U2; Transcript, NBC News, 3/14/81)

March 14–15, 1981: Senior Deputy Assistant Secretary for African Affairs Lannon Walker meets privately with UNITA President Jonas Savimbi in Morocco. (*Visit of DAS Walker*, 3/13/81; *U.S. Statement about Savimbi Presence in Morocco*, 3/14/81)

March 17, 1981: The South African Air Force (SAAF) attacks a SWAPO base in Lubango, two hundred kilometers north of the Angolan-Namibia border. This is the deepest known attack in Angola by the SAAF since the SADF's 1975–76 incursion. (*South Africa: Military Contact in Angola and Mozambique*, 3/19/81)

March 19, 1981: President Reagan requests that Congress repeal the 1976 Clark Amendment in order to remove an "unnecessary restriction" on his foreign policy authority (see entry for August 9, 1985). Officials deny that any U.S. plans to aid UNITA exist. (DOS Bulletin, p. 18; *Angola: Repeal of the Clark Amendment*, 3/19/81)

April 4, 1981: A. J. Roux, chairman of the South African Uranium Enrichment Corporation, announces that South Africa is capable of producing enough uranium fuel to run its first nuclear power station economically. South Africa reports that it can now produce semi-enriched uranium, which it intends to use to fuel the SAFARI-I nuclear research reactor. According to one observer, because it is a relatively easy process to improve semi-enriched uranium to the fully enriched material needed for weapons capability, U.S. analysts later date South Africa's nuclear weapons capability to 1981. (FBIS, 5/4/81, p. U3; Spector, p. 222; WP 3/30/81)

April 15, 1981: Chester Crocker arrives in South Africa and meets with Foreign Minister Roelof Botha, Dr. Brand Fourie, General Magnus Malan, Adriaan Eksteen, and other South African officials in Johannesburg as part of a ten-country tour of Africa. During the discussions, Secretary Crocker invites Foreign Minister Pik Botha to the United States on behalf of Secretary of State Haig.

Frontline state leaders meet in Luanda and debate three main issues: the increasing, aggressive actions by South Africa; the continued refusal of the Botha administration to implement U.N. Security Council Resolution 435; and the repressive measures taken by the illegal regime in Namibia. (FBIS 4/15/81, p. U2; *South African Foreign Minister Botha Invitation*, 4/23/81; *Frontline African Leaders Issue Communiqué in Luanda...*, 4/16/81)

April 17, 1981: Chester Crocker arrives in Angola and tells Angolan government representatives that progress on a Namibian settlement is related to a Cuban troop withdrawal from Angola. This is the first public statement made by a senior U.S. government official linking the two situations. (DOS Bulletin, p. 18)

April 30, 1981: The United States, Great Britain, and France veto four U.N. resolutions calling for sanctions against South Africa. According to U.S. Ambassador to the United Nations Jeane Kirkpatrick, the United States believes that sanctions will not achieve independence for Namibia. The U.N. plan, she argues, "continues to provide a solid basis for a transition to an independent and stable Namibia." She said the United States supports a "peaceful negotiated solution to the Namibian problem." (*Current Foreign Relations...*, 5/6/81)

May 13, 1981: Following yesterday's House Foreign Affairs Committee vote (19–5) to retain the Clark Amendment, the Senate Foreign Relations Committee, in "an unusually chaotic session," votes to repeal the amendment while retaining prior congressional notification and other somewhat restrictive reporting requirements. (*SFRC Vote on (Modified) Repeal of the Clark Amendment*, 5/14/81)

May 13–16, 1981: South African Foreign Minister Pik Botha meets in Washington with President Reagan and Secretary of State Haig to discuss U.S.–South African nuclear cooperation, bilateral relations, and Namibia. (TransAfrica, pp. 5–7; *Scenario of Visit of South African Minister of Foreign Affairs...*, 5/12/81)

May 14, 1981: African Group Chairman Ambassador Rupia of Tanzania holds a press conference during which he deplores South African Foreign Minister Pik Botha's visit to the United States. Rupia says the invitation of Botha shows the "utmost contempt" for international opinion, adding that African nations consider it "an unfriendly act." (*Reaction to Botha Visit*, 5/15/81)

June 9, 1981: Chester A. Crocker is appointed assistant secretary of state for African affairs, replacing Richard Moose, whose term ended in January. (Principal Officers, p. 7)

June 30, 1981: The Reagan administration issues new guidelines allowing the sale of medical equipment and supplies to the South African military on a case-by-case basis. The new regulations also permit the sale of metal detectors used in combating sabotage. (Federal Register, 6/30/81, p. 33509)

July 22, 1981: The South African Defense Force publicly announces a "new approach" to the policy of "hot pursuit," confirming their readiness to become involved in cross-border military operations against Namibian guerrilla bases in Angola. (*Current Foreign Relations...*, 7/22/81)

August 31, 1981: The U.S. vetoes a U.N. Security Council resolution that condemns South Africa for an "unprovoked and persistent armed invasion" of Angola and for using Namibia as a staging ground in such attacks. The U.S. representative states that Washington voted against the resolution because it placed "all the blame on South Africa for the escalation of violence." (DOS Bulletin, p. 18; *SC Meeting on Angola*, 9/5/81)

September 1981: The board of governors of the International Atomic Energy Agency decides that South Africa should no longer be able to participate in the discussions and work of the Committee of Assurances of Supply. (*South Africa, Nuclear Weapons, and the IAEA*, 1/1/88)

October 1981: The Commerce Department grants a license to export a Sperry Univac 1100 Series computer to Atlas Aircraft Corp., a subsidiary of the South African Armaments Development and Manufacturing Corp. (ARMSCOR); the South African government owns a controlling interest in ARMSCOR. (NARMIC, p. 10; Africa News, 12/7/81)

October 20, 1981: Under the headline "CIA Link Feared in New Aid for Black Unions," a report in *The Star* claims that Nana Mahomo, director-designate of the African-American Labor Center's (AALC) new aid program to South African Union, might also have ties to the CIA, and states that the South African program bears strong resemblances to past CIA labor-related programs in other parts of Africa. The AALC denies the report. (*Local Paper Alleges Links Between CIA and American Labor in South Africa, Elsewhere*, 10/21/81; *Star Reports AALC Denial of CIA Links*, 10/22/81)

November 1–20, 1981: South Africa launches two separate but overlapping major military operations in Angola, code-named "Daisy." The U.S. believes these two operations demonstrate South Africa's determination to weaken SWAPO in anticipation of a possible Namibian settlement and to hinder Angola's effort to reinforce its southern defenses. (*South African Military Operations in Angola During November*, 12/7/81)

November 10, 1981: A Contact Group mission led by Chester Crocker completes another round of talks on negotiations for Namibian independence. The group held meetings with senior officials from Nigeria, the frontline states, South Africa, Kenya, and leaders of the main Namibian political parties and SWAPO. (*Current Foreign Relations...*, 11/10/81)

November 13, 1981: The South African press reports that the country's Electricity Supply Commission has acquired enough enriched uranium through the French consortium Framatome to last until the mid 1980s, when South Africa's enrichment facilities will meet the demand. *Die Burger* reports that further uranium shipments will ensure that the Koeberg nuclear power plants will be finished within the year. The enriched uranium may be coming from Italy, West Germany, the People's Republic of China, or Switzerland. (*Media Reports on Koeberg Fuel Supply*, 11/13/81; CRS2, p. 7)

November 28, 1981: The leader of UNITA, Jonas Savimbi, begins a private visit to the United States. (*Visit to U.S. of UNITA Leader Jonas Savimbi*, 11/28/81)

December 22, 1981: The Reagan administration approves the sale of a U.S.-made computer to the Atlas Aircraft Corporation, an ARMSCOR subsidiary, marking a reversal of Carter administration policy, which would have blocked the sale. The *Rand Daily Mail* reports that "the decision is seen as a test case for changes in the overall regulations to be announced by the end of this month." According to a State Department official, the United States permitted the sale because the Atlas Aircraft Corporation was not listed as a prohibited customer. (*Atlas Computer Sale Hits the Fan*, 12/22/81)

December 23, 1981: A CIA memo reports that a nuclear facility is under construction at Faure, twenty-five kilometers east of Cape Town. The facility contains a cyclotron, a type of particle accelerator, which, according to a South African publication, will be capable of producing a powerful proton beam. The installation can conduct basic nuclear research, produce radioisotopes, treat certain forms of cancer, and advance South Africa's nuclear weapons research. (*Africa Review*, 12/23/81)

January 6, 1982: A State Department cable reports an increase in bombings over the past year by the ANC against the South African government. In the past, the Botha administration has hidden much information about bombing attempts in order not to alarm the white population; however, security measures intended to clamp down on such attacks draw public attention to these events. (*Current Foreign Relations...*, 1/6/82)

March 1, 1982: The Commerce Department issues sweeping new regulations significantly relaxing controls—including foreign policy controls on trade with South Africa issued under the Export Administration Act of 1979—on exports to the South African police and military. (Document 10, Cable for CFR Collective, "Current Foreign Relations Issue No. 12," 3/24/82; NARMIC, p. 10)

March 4, 1982: Chester Crocker and Angolan Foreign Minister Paulo Jorge resume discussions in Paris on the Western Five's proposal for achieving Namibian independence through the withdrawal of foreign troops and the facilitation of the U.N. peace plans. (*Current Foreign Relations...*, 3/10/82; DOS Bulletin, p. 19)

March 26, 1982: The Commerce Department issues a license to Control Data Corporation to export a Cyber 170/750 computer to the Council for Scientific and Industrial Research, an organization run by the South African government. The computer reportedly could effectively be used for nuclear and cryptographic work. (Danaher, p. 164)

March 29, 1982: Herman Nickel is appointed ambassador to South Africa, replacing William Edmondson. His tenure begins on April 20, 1982, but he is recalled on June 15, 1985, following a South African raid into Botswana and the discovery of a South African commando operating near U.S. oil installations in Angola. (Principal Officers, p. 96; The Sun 7/24/85; WP 8/9/85)

April 13, 1982: The *Washington Post* reports that two American firms—the Edlow International Company of Washington, D.C., and the Separative Work Unit Corporation (SWUCO) of Rockville, Maryland—played a role in South Africa's acquisition of one hundred tons of enriched uranium. The firms' actions violate U.S. policy, which forbids uranium exports to South Africa because Pretoria has not signed the Nuclear Non-Proliferation Treaty. According to the *Post*, the uranium will be transferred to the nuclear power plants at Koeberg, near Cape Town, once it has been further processed in France. (CRS2, p. 3; *Africa in the U.S.*

Press, 4/13/82; [*Regarding South African Government's Acquisition of European Enriched Nuclear Fuel…*], 5/4/82)

April 26, 1982: The Commerce Department approves the sale to South Africa of twenty-five hundred 3500-volt shock batons designed for crowd control. The sale violates Section 502(b) of the Foreign Assistance Act, which prohibits exports to the police or military in countries with consistent human rights violations. The batons are shipped in August, but the sale is discovered only in September. Commerce Department officials say license approval was "an honest mistake," a "simple, unfortunate screw-up." (U.N. Notes, p. 11; Africa News 9/27/82; NYT 9/20/82)

May 5, 1982: The chairman of the South African Atomic Energy Board provides assurances through South Africa's ambassador in Washington, D.C., that because the SAFARI-I research reactor is subject to IAEA safeguards, any irradiation tests and material will also be subject to safeguards and inspection. (*Assurance Received May 5, 1982 from South African Embassy…*, 5/5/82; [*Department of State's Response to Senator Percy's Questions*], 5/13/82)

May 13, 1982: In response to a letter from Senator Charles Percy (R–Illinois), Commerce Secretary Malcolm Baldrige outlines the administration's decision to adopt a more "flexible" policy on dual-use nuclear technology exports to South Africa. (Danaher, p. 165; *Press Report on New U.S. Flexibility on Nuclear Policy Toward South Africa*, 5/20/82)

June 25, 1982: Secretary of State Haig resigns over policy disputes with the Reagan White House. He is eventually replaced by George P. Shultz. (NYT 6/26/82)

July 1982: TransAfrica, an African-American lobbying group, circulates a leaked copy of a State Department cable indicating South Africa's intention to seek an International Monetary Fund (IMF) loan. The State Department recommends that, to avoid criticism, South Africa delay its request until after the September IMF–World Bank annual convention. (CIP Report, 4/84)

July 21, 1982: The South African press reports that Israel and South Africa are tentatively making plans for an advanced fighter aircraft production program that would promote South Africa's Cheetah fighter plane. South African industrialists are reportedly offering high salaries to engineers who had worked on the recently canceled Israeli Lavi fighter program. (*Lavi Cancellation and Cheetah Update*, 9/10/87)

September 11, 1982: In a press conference, the chairman of the board of directors of Armaments Corporation of South Africa says that its G-5 tow and the G-6 SP Gun/Tow would be able to fire a nuclear round if necessary, but that South Africa does not intend to use weapons for that purpose. (*G-6 HMSP Gun/Howitzer*, 9/13/82)

September 27, 1982: CIA Director William Casey meets in South Africa with top government and military leaders to discuss the security situation in the region. Some press reports claim that Casey proposes a U.S.-backed cordon sanitaire to secure South Africa's borders. The visit is part of a several-country tour on which Casey meets intelligence chiefs in Nigeria, Zaire, Zambia, and Mozambique. (WP 11/3/82)

October 6, 1982: After several months of thawing relations between United States and Mozambique, as the latter government worked toward improving ties with Western countries, Foreign Minister Joaquim Alberto Chissano expresses his country's wish to improve relations with the United States during a meeting with Secretary of State Shultz. (*Current Foreign Relations…*, 11/3/82)

November 4, 1982: The International Monetary Fund approves a $1.1 billion loan to South Africa despite objections by many countries over the Botha administration's racial policies. U.S. Executive Director Richard D. Erb reiterates Washington's condemnation of apartheid but states that lending rules have to be applied impartially. The State Department responds to criticism by issuing a statement: "The U.S. position on the South African drawing indicates no change in our position to apartheid nor in our opposition to the use of force to resolve political differences in the region." (NYT 11/4/82)

December 8, 1982: Assistant Secretary of State Chester Crocker holds a second unannounced meeting in several weeks with Soviet Deputy Foreign Minister Leonid F. Ilichev regarding southern African affairs. On the same day, Foreign Minister Pik Botha and Defense Minister Magnus Malan meet in the Cape Verde Islands with representatives of the Angolan government. (WP 12/13/82)

December 19–20, 1982: The ANC sets off a series of bombs at South Africa's nuclear power plants at Koeberg, near Cape Town, in retaliation for the South African government's December 9 raid in Lesotho. The ANC calls the attack a "warning to foreign investors" as well as a commemoration to mark the twenty-first anniversary of the ANC's military wing. (*Aftermath of South African Raid on Lesotho*, 12/22/82)

December 20, 1982: By a vote of 129–0 with seventeen abstentions (including the United States), the U.N. General Assembly adopts Resolution 37/233-B. Affirming Security Council Resolutions 385 and 435 as the only legitimate basis for the Namibian settlement, the resolution rejects South African and U.S. attempts to link a Namibian settlement with "extraneous issues" such as a Cuban troop withdrawal from Angola. (DOS Bulletin, p. 19)

December 29, 1982: Irving Brown, director of the department of international affairs at the AFL-CIO, passes to Assistant Secretary of State Chester Crocker a list of proposed AFL-CIO projects in South Africa under U.S. government funding. The State Department subsequently provides a grant to the labor group for trade union assistance to South Africa as part of an effort to "counter 'communist influence' among trade unions abroad." (*USG-Funding for AFL-CIO Projects in S.A.*, 12/29/82; *DFAI Officials on USG-Funded AFL-CIO Activities*, 5/26/83)

January 25, 1983: The Reagan administration modifies U.S. limitations on exports to the South African and Namibian military and police forces. The new guidelines permit the export of certain nonstrategic industrial, chemical, petroleum, and transportation equipment without a license. This is the third relaxation of export restrictions in less than a year. (CRS1, p. 25; *Revision in U.S. Commodity List Controls on Exports to the South African Police and Military*, 1/22/83)

April 25, 1983: French Foreign Minister Claude Cheysson criticizes the U.S. linkage of Namibian independence with Cuban troop withdrawal from Angola. He says "it is not appropriate the Namibian people should serve as hostages" to be used in attaining other foreign policy goals. (NYT 4/6/83)

May 5, 1983: The House Committee on Banking, Finance, and Urban Affairs votes to pass the Patterson Amendment, which bars U.S. support for an International Monetary Fund loan to South Africa due to its policy of apartheid (see entry for November 4, 1982). (WP 5/6/83; NYT 5/6/83; *Transcript of Proceedings*, 5/5/83)

November 2, 1983: A referendum is held among South Africa's exclusively white electorate on a new constitution, which grants limited electoral power to colored and Asian South Africans but none to blacks. To the surprise of many observers, the white constituents vote to approve the new constitution by a ratio of 2–1. The right wing strongly opposes the constitution for betraying white rights, while the Left objects that it does not constitute a significant reform. Although the black majority is excluded from this constitu-

tional reform package, the Reagan administration concludes that the South African government is beginning to contemplate antiapartheid reforms. (*Current Foreign Relations…*, 9/14/83; *Current Foreign Relations…*, 11/9/83; DOS Historian, p. x)

December 15, 1983: In a letter addressed to Secretary-General Javier Pérez de Cuellar, Foreign Minister Pik Botha offers a cease-fire proposal and a conditional withdrawal from Angola beginning January 31. (*Press Reaction on SAG Cease-fire Offer*, 12/20/83)

December 19, 1983: SWAPO and the Angolan government reject South Africa's offer for conditional withdrawal. Nevertheless, the government of South Africa still intends to disengage its forces by January 31, 1984. (*Pik Botha's Public Reaction to Angolan Response to South African Withdrawal Offer*, 12/21/83; *Pik Botha's Reaction to Angolan Rejection of Withdrawal Offer*, 12/21/83)

December 31, 1983: Angolan President Jose Eduardo dos Santos sends a letter to U.N. Secretary-General Javier Pérez de Cuellar accepting South Africa's December 15 proposal for a truce between South Africa and Angola. (*State of Play in Southern Africa Negotiations*, 1/5/84)

January 31, 1984: Prime Minister P. W. Botha announces to Parliament South Africa's immediate disengagement from Angola. Botha implies in his speech the withdrawal is based on "assurances received from the United States Government." (*P. W. Botha's Speech on Angolan Disengagement*, 1/31/84)

February 14–16, 1984: Assistant Secretary of State Chester Crocker leads a U.S. delegation to Lusaka, Zambia, to negotiate an agreement between the governments of Angola and South Africa on the disengagement of South African forces from southern Angola. The resulting Lusaka Accord calls for a cease-fire and disengagement along the Angola-Namibia border, to be monitored by a joint South African–Angolan commission that will include a number of U.S. participants. (*Crocker/Platt Background Briefing*, 2/25/84; *South African Reaction to Possible Early Tripartite Meeting*, 2/9/84)

February 23, 1984: Due to the U.S. government's "symbolic" role as observer in the Lusaka Accords, at the request of both the South African and the Angolan governments, a U.S. Liaison Office, headed by William Twaddell, is set up in Windhoek, Namibia, to aid in monitoring the South African disengagement from Angola. Operations of the liaison office were subsequently suspended February 15, 1985, after

South Africa failed to withdraw completely following criticism about U.S. policy by some Africans and members of Congress. (*Update on Southern Africa Negotiations*, 3/13/84; *Update on the Southern Africa Negotiations*, 3/3/84; *Suspension of the U.S....*, 2/7/85)

March 16, 1984: P. W. Botha and Mozambican President Samora Machel meet on their countries' joint border to sign a formal nonaggression treaty. Known as the Nkomati Accord, the agreement contains a promise by South Africa to reduce its support for the Mozambican resistance movement, called RENAMO or MNR, and a corresponding pledge by the Mozambican government to end its support for ANC guerrilla operations against South Africa. (*Current Foreign Relations...*, 3/14/84; *Mozambique–South Africa Security Agreement*, 3/12/84; *South Africa–Mozambique Non-Aggression Treaty Signed*, 3/16/84; NYT 4/17/84)

March 19, 1984: The governments of Angola and Cuba issue a joint statement listing four conditions necessary for Cuban troop withdrawal from Angola: (1) "unilateral withdrawal of the racist troops of South Africa from Angolan territory"; (2) "scrupulous implementation" of U.N. Resolution 435 and the withdrawal of South African troops from Namibia; (3) "cessation of all types of direct aggression against" Angola by "South Africa, the United States, and its allies"; and (4) a withdrawal of support for "the counterrevolutionary organization UNITA and any other puppet group" by South Africa, the United States, and its allies. (*South African Reaction to the Havana Communiqué*, 3/20/84; *Angola/Cuba March 19 Communiqué*, 03/21/84)

April 16, 1984: A news account reports that a bomb exploded in northern Namibia killing the U.S. Liaison Office director, Dennis Keogh, and U.S. military representative Lt. Col. Kenneth Crabtree, who were involved in monitoring the cease-fire between South Africa and Angola. They are the first Americans reported killed in the seventeen-year struggle for Namibian independence. (NYT 4/16/84; *Suspension of the U.S. Liaison Office in Namibia*, 2/7/85)

September 3, 1984: Implementation of a new South African constitution establishing separate colored and Indian houses of Parliament but excluding black representation is marred by violence in several black townships near Johannesburg; twenty-nine people are killed. (*Current Foreign Relations...*, 9/5/84)

October 15, 1984: Deputy Assistant Secretary of State for African Affairs Frank Wisner, who has met several times in the last two years with Angolan officials, arrives in Luanda to discuss the Angolan response to proposals made in August by Assistant Secretary Chester Crocker. (NYT 10/16/84; *Southern Africa Negotiations Update*, 10/10/84)

October 31–November 1, 1984: Foreign Minister Botha and Assistant Secretary Crocker meet in Cape Verde to discuss South African disengagement from southern Angola and independence for Namibia. Crocker relays a proposal from the Angolan government which contains specific suggestions with regard to South African and Cuban troop withdrawals from Angola, the implementation of U.N. Resolution 435, and a cease-fire between South Africa and SWAPO. Crocker describes the talks as "positive for the progress of peace in southern Africa." (NYT 11/1/84; DOS Bulletin, p. 19)

November 21, 1984: Washington, D.C., Delegate Walter E. Fauntroy, U.S. Civil Rights Commission member Mary Frances Berry, and TransAfrica Executive Director Randall Robinson are arrested following a demonstration at the South African Embassy in Washington, D.C. (CRS1, p. 17)

November 22, 1984: Angolan President dos Santos makes public a letter he has written to the secretary-general of the United Nations offering a plan for a phased withdrawal of twenty thousand Cuban troops from the southern part of Angola over a three-year period. Dos Santos offers assurances that Cuban troops will be used only for security purposes in the north and northwest, especially for protection of Cabinda, and will not venture into southern areas. In a counteroffer, South Africa insists on the complete withdrawal of Cuban troops from Angola within twelve weeks in exchange for a reduction of South African forces in Namibia to fifteen hundred soldiers. (CRS5, p. 26; *Windhoek Newspaper Reports Angolan Offer on Cuban Troop Withdrawal*, 11/14/84)

January 4, 1985: According to a report by the Nuclear Control Institute, 70 percent of South African uranium is enriched in the United States for reexport to foreign utilities; fifteen U.S. companies purchase the remaining 30 percent. The report also details elaborate deals between U.S. uranium brokers and the State Department in violation of the Nuclear Non-Proliferation Act to help South Africa obtain enriched uranium for its own nuclear power program. (*Growing U.S. Uranium Trade with South Africa Promotes Pretoria's Atom Bomb Program, NCI Reports*, 1/4/85)

January 20, 1985: The *Washington Post* reports that U.S. officials believe that as many as forty American atomic operators employed by Electricity Supply Commission of South

Africa (ESCOM) are violating federal nuclear proliferation laws by working for South Africa's atomic power industry without authorization from the Secretary of Energy. The article, which quotes unnamed U.S. officials and congressional sources, say that ESCOM is suspected of recruiting Americans with tax-free salaries as high as 200,000 rand a year (roughly $150,000), free travel, and other benefits. Within a week Congress begins a full-blown investigation into the matter (*U.S. Citizens at Koeberg: Jan 21 Afternoon Press Coverage in South Africa*, 1/21/85, *Request for Complete Information Regarding U.S. Citizen Employment in the South Africa Nuclear Program*, 1/25/85)

January 25, 1985: Deputy Assistant Secretary of State for African Affairs Frank Wisner leaves Maputo, Mozambique, for South Africa after a four-day visit during which he discussed U.S. aid with Mozambican officials. His trip follows last week's announcement in Washington, D.C., that the Reagan administration is planning to seek authorization to send more than $1.1 million in "limited military assistance" to the government of President Samora Machel. (WP 1/26/85; *Developing Security Links with Mozambique*, 12/13/83)

January 27, 1985: The CIA publishes a research paper assessing Western dependence on platinum-group metals (PGMs) and the implications of a long-term supply cutoff, which would result if they were included in a trade embargo against South Africa. According to the paper, "South Africa and the Soviet Union produce over 90 percent of the world's reserves." (*Western Platinum Dependence: A Risk Assessment*, 1/85)

April 19, 1985: The CIA reports that the Soviet Union has not been giving the Mozambican government the help it needs to improve its faltering economy and to prevent the growing tide of the antigovernment RENAMO/MNR insurgency. President Samora Machel has therefore turned to the West for help, indicating a loss of confidence in the Soviets and their ability to support his administration. (*[Regarding Soviet Access and Interests in Mozambique]*, 4/19/85)

May 21, 1985: National Security Council staffmembers Walter Raymond, Jr., and Oliver North send an action memorandum to National Security Advisor Robert McFarlane announcing that Jonas Savimbi will host a meeting of anticommunist resistance groups in Jamba, Angola, in early June. According to the memo, "the purpose of the meeting…is to announce the formation of our Alliance for Liberation and Democracy," which they describe as "a fund-raising conduit for anti-communist resistance movements." Raymond and North suggest avoiding a "high administration profile" in Angola. (*Freedom Fighters International*, 5/21/85)

May 29, 1985: Following the Angolan government's discovery on May 21 of a commando team attempting to sabotage an oil installation owned in part by Gulf Oil Corporation in Cabinda, South Africa admits that it has undertaken "covert military reconnaissance forays" into northern Angola. (DOS Bulletin, pp. 19–20; *South Africa Admits Spying in Angola*, 5/23/85)

June 14, 1985: The South African Defense Force (SADF) raids what it claims are safehouses and offices in Gaborone, Botswana, used by the ANC to coordinate terrorist attacks against South Africa. The SADF asserts in particular that the ANC was responsible for two June 12 grenade attacks on colored members of Parliament in Cape Town. According to a U.S. Defense Intelligence Agency report, eleven to fifteen people are killed in the raid, including one Dutch citizen and two Botswanans. (*South Africa—Botswana: Cross-Border Raid June 14*, 6/17/85)

July 22, 1985: The South African Government proclaims a state of emergency in most parts of the country following nearly seven hundred deaths in township uprisings since August 1984; the unrest nevertheless continues. (*State of Emergency—Sit Rep*, 7/24/85)

August 8, 1985: A U.S. delegation, headed by National Security Advisor Robert McFarlane, meets a team headed by South African Foreign Minister Pik Botha at the U.S. Embassy in Vienna. The meeting, held in "unusual secrecy," reportedly had been requested by Pretoria a week earlier to discuss new proposals to deal with rising violence in South Africa and negative international opinion concerning events there. No details of the discussions are released. (WP 8/9/85)

August 9, 1985: President Reagan signs the repeal of the Clark Amendment of 1976, which prohibited U.S. aid to military or paramilitary operations in Angola. (*Angola and the Clark Amendment*, 9/13/85)

September 7, 1985: Responding to "increased tension in South Africa, and continued Soviet challenges to our important interests in the area," the White House issues National Security Decision Directive 187 restating "the broad objectives of U.S. political strategy toward South Africa" and outlining specific plans for fulfilling these objectives. President Reagan signs the document following a meeting on September 5 with his top national security advisors. (Document 14, NSDD 187, "United States Policy toward South Africa," 9/7/85; NYT 9/6/85)

September 9, 1985: The U.S. Embassy in Pretoria outlines a new public diplomacy policy in South Africa designed to address both the mistrust among the black South African community toward the Reagan administration and the continual resistance of the Afrikaner leadership toward external pressures to change. The policy supports measures urging the Botha administration to speed up its reform efforts while at the same time assuring U.S. support for those efforts.

Ronald Reagan signs Executive Order 12532 declaring South Africa to be "an unusual and extraordinary threat to the foreign policy and economy of the United States." The order places new restrictions on U.S. trade and financial transactions with South Africa and encourages U.S. firms operating in South Africa to adopt the Sullivan Principles of fair labor. The trade sanctions include an embargo on nuclear exports, covering those items permitted by the Non-Proliferation Act, but allow nuclear transfers, made in compliance with IAEA safeguards, intended for humanitarian purposes. The order does *not* include a ban on South African uranium imports, which, economically, would be the most detrimental nuclear-related sanction. (*Challenges and Risks of Public Diplomacy in S.A.*, 9/9/85; *Executive Order on South Africa*, 9/9/85; Spector, pp. 225, 321)

September 11, 1985: U.S. Ambassador Herman Nickel returns to South Africa after a three-month absence, bearing a message from President Reagan to President Botha urging the abolition of apartheid. (*Implementing Enhanced Embassy Public Outreach and Political Reporting Capacity*, 9/30/85; SAFN 10/85)

September 12, 1985: The House approves (308–77) legislation imposing new economic sanctions on South Africa, including a ban on all new American investment; the bill, which is identical to a measure passed in the Senate last month, goes to President Reagan. The president vetoes the bill on September 26, but two weeks later he imposes an import ban on the South Africa gold coin, the Krugerrand. (NYT 9/19/85)

September 17, 1985: The NSC releases a statement supporting UNITA's fight against the Soviet presence in Angola. The statement also denies any allegations made by the press concerning U.S. assistance to any Angolan party, including UNITA. (*Angola/U.S. Policy/Aid to UNITA*, 10/17/85)

October 1, 1985: Congress introduces a bill authorizing humanitarian assistance, in the sum of $27 million, for UNITA. (*H.R. 3472: To Authorize Humanitarian Assistance for the National Union for the Total Independence of Angola (UNITA)*, 10/1/85)

The *Pretoria News*, a daily that a Defense Department memo has termed "sometimes reliable," reports that documents captured from RENAMO/MNR suggest that conflicts exist between the group's supporters in the South African military and the Botha administration. Diaries captured when the MNR's Gorongoza headquarters was raided detail the South African Defense Forces' allegiance to the MNR as well as disagreements with Foreign Minister Pik Botha. A spokesman for the SADF is unwilling to confirm or deny the reports. (*Alleged MNR Diary*, 10/3/85)

October 2, 1985: David Miller, director of the South and Southern Africa Public Diplomacy Working Group, briefs the Special Planning Group—comprising National Security Advisor Robert McFarlane, Deputy Secretary of State John Whitehead, Secretary of Defense Caspar Weinberger, USIA Director Charles Wick, AID Administrator Peter McPherson, and White House Communications Director Pat Buchanan—on his Group's public diplomacy strategy for southern Africa. (*Meeting of the Special Planning Group...*, 10/1/85; [*NSC Approves the Public Diplomacy Strategy...*], 11/6/85)

October 12, 1985: Secretary of State George Shultz writes to House Minority Leader Robert Michel (R–Ill.), urging him to oppose legislation providing $27 million in nonlethal aid to the UNITA rebels in Angola. In light of recent positive developments toward a negotiated withdrawal of Cuban troops from Angola, Shultz argues that the aid is "ill timed." The Secretary's view is not shared by the Pentagon, the CIA, or the NSC, all of which strongly support aid to UNITA. (WP 10/23/85)

November 22, 1985: President Reagan says that his administration favors covert aid to insurgents attempting to overthrow the leftist government in Angola. Later, a State Department official reportedly explains that the president was referring to a recent secret policy decision to oppose public aid for insurgents and to look instead at the provision of funneling covert aid through the CIA. (NYT 11/23/85)

November 27, 1985: Assistant Secretary of State Chester Crocker meets with Angolan Interior Minister Manuel Duarte Rodrigues in Lusaka, Zambia, to discuss the Namibian situation and a political settlement of the Angolan civil war, including a Cuban troop withdrawal and the implementation of U.N. Security Council Resolution 435. (*Secretary's Press Conference...*, 12/6/85; WP 11/27/85; CRS5, p. 25; DOS Bulletin, p. 20)

December 3, 1985: Secretary of State Shultz announces the creation of a twelve-member advisory committee on South Africa to look at ways in which the United States can encourage an end to apartheid. The committee will be cochaired by Frank Gary, former chairman and chief executive officer of IBM, and William T. Coleman, transportation secretary during the Ford administration. (The Sun 12/20/85; *A U.S. Policy Toward South Africa: The Report of the Secretary of State's Advisory Committee on South Africa,* 1/87)

January 1986: A State Department memo on U.S. African policy emphasizes the need to end the legitimization of "terrorist, pro-Soviet groups" such as the ANC and the Azanian People's Organization as one of the key goals for U.S. policy in South Africa. The memo also proposes that the Reagan administration assist the development of "capitalistic, pluralistic, multi-party, multi-racial societies" in southern Africa with the consent of the South African government. (*U.S. African Policy: The Opportunity and Need for a Pro-Western Strategy,* 1/86)

January 23, 1986: In an article for the *New York Times,* Seymour Hersh reveals that the CIA under Reagan has supplied intelligence information to the white minority government concerning ANC and the movements of its leader, Oliver Tambo. In exchange, the Botha administration has provided information about Soviet shipping movements in the southern African region and the Cuban military presence in Angola. (NYT 1/23/86)

January 30, 1986: President Reagan promises covert financial support to UNITA leader Jonas Savimbi during Savimbi's visit to the White House. Reagan says that the United States could be "very helpful" to Savimbi's fight against the Soviet-backed Marxist Angolan government. (WP 1/31/86)

February 18, 1986: The Reagan administration informs Congress that it has decided to provide UNITA with antiaircraft and antitank missiles in order to prevent the Angolan government from achieving "a military solution" in its fight against the South Africa–backed rebels. The Angolan government responds by breaking off bilateral talks with Washington on a regional peace settlement. (NYT 2/19/86; DOS Bulletin, p. 21)

March 18, 1986: Angolan President Jose Eduardo dos Santos writes to U.N. Secretary-General Javier Pérez de Cuellar requesting that he assume responsibility for negotiations on the Namibian situation. Dos Santos states that Washington's "deliberate and systematic support" of South Africa and its bolstered military aid to UNITA have "jeopardized its credibility as a mediator." (DOS Bulletin, p. 20)

May 1986: South Africa attacks the capital cities of Botswana, Zambia, and Zimbabwe in another drive against the ANC. In its first reaction to the raids, the United States expresses "outrage." On May 20, the United States expels the South African defense attaché, claiming that South Africa's actions are a threat to the security of the region. The Botha administration reacts on May 24 by expelling the U.S. military attaché from Pretoria. (CRS4, p. 8)

May 21, 1986: Forty-four members of Congress introduce a bill calling for extensive new sanctions against South Africa, including a ban on new U.S. investments, which would be lifted if the white government released all black political prisoners and began "good faith negotiations" to end apartheid. (WP 5/22/86)

June 12, 1986: The Commonwealth Eminent Persons Group releases a report on its fact-finding mission to South Africa and on its attempts to persuade the South African government to negotiate with black opposition groups. The final report indirectly recommends imposing "economic measures" against South Africa. (CSM 6/13/86: *Confiscation of "Weekly Mail" Threatened,* 6/13/86)

South Africa declares a second, more intense nationwide state of emergency, a sign that the government intends to extend its crackdown on political opposition as long as it deems necessary. The state of emergency prohibits most forms of protest, including mass funerals, political meetings, calls for boycotts, strikes, and media coverage of unrest. Its laws give the security forces unprecedented powers to occupy the townships, search homes and offices, and detain people indefinitely—all in an attempt to forestall plans by opponents of apartheid to commemorate the Soweto uprising of June 16, 1976 (see entry for that date), which resulted in the deaths of several hundred blacks, including children, who were shot by the police.

Authorities have detained approximately twelve hundred people, and in succeeding days they enact new restrictive measures against the press and various political activities. A number of foreign governments, including the United States, condemn the action. (*A U.S. Policy Toward South Africa: The Report of the Secretary of State's Advisory Committee on South Africa,* 1/87; CRS6, pp. 13–15)

June 16, 1986: Millions of black South Africans strike to commemorate the anniversary of the 1976 Soweto uprising. 90 percent of the black population of Johannesburg, Port Elizabeth, and Pretoria, and 80 percent in Cape Town, participate in the action. The Botha administration further restricts news coverage by banning all reporters from black townships and prohibiting any reporting of police actions beyond the use of government-provided information. (CRS4, p. 6)

June 22, 1986: Assistant Secretary of State Chester Crocker states on ABC News that the South African government has "shot itself in both feet" by placing restrictions on the media and detaining antiapartheid activists. He also says that the measures "got in the way of any possibility for dialogue and polarize the issues further." According to Crocker, although the Reagan administration disapproves of Pretoria's actions, it will continue the constructive engagement policy and "firmly oppose" legislation proposing U.S. disinvestment. (*ABC News transcript*, 6/22/86)

July 14, 1986: Thousands of black South African students boycott classes in the wake of a new government ban on political activities in schools. In Soweto, the protest results in nearly vacant schools, and in the Cape Province only 30–50 percent of the students report to classes. However, according to official reports, attendance in other areas is 78 percent. (CRS4, p. 3)

July 16, 1986: A boycott staged by black South African trade unions is 90 percent effective in Port Elizabeth but much less successful in other parts of the country. Organized by the Congress of South African Trade Unions, the protest is hampered by recent government crackdowns on organized labor, which have included the detention of 250 union officials and restrictions on meetings. (CRS4, p. 3)

July 22, 1986: In a speech, President Reagan reiterates the main points of his constructive engagement policy on South Africa. He asks Congress and Western European countries to "resist this emotional clamor for punitive sanctions" against South Africa on the grounds that such sanctions would cause unemployment for black South Africans, hurt neighboring countries, and endanger access to strategic minerals by Western countries. He also calls on the Botha administration to set a "timetable" for eliminating apartheid laws, to end the ban on black opposition political groups, to release all political prisoners (including Nelson Mandela), and to open discourse with blacks on a new constitutional system. While criticizing the South African government's state of emergency, he also condemns the "calculated terror" of some elements within the ANC. The reaction of Congress and many black South African leaders to the speech is negative; Bishop Desmond Tutu calls the speech "nauseating" and says the West "can go to hell." Pretoria welcomes Reagan's speech, but Foreign Minister Pik Botha warns that if threats of sanctions continue, South Africa will "withdraw into the laager, as this will

be the only way to maintain the values which the West claims to hold." (CRS4, p. 2)

July 30, 1986: U.S. Ambassador to Zambia Paul Hare holds talks with three senior officials of the ANC aimed at "elevating the level" of dialogue between the United States and the outlawed organization. According to the Congressional Research Service, this is the first official meeting between the U.S. government and the exiled ANC. (The Sun 7/31/86; CRS6, p. 11)

August 3, 1986: The *New York Times* reports that, according to new Federal Reserve Board figures, after years of substantially increasing their lending in South Africa, U.S. banks have begun to cut back sharply on such loans. In the first three months of 1985, the period covered by the latest figures, the total amount owed by borrowers in South Africa to U.S. banks dropped by 10.8 percent, to less than $4.2 billion, from $4.7 billion. (NYT 8/3/86)

August 6, 1986: Reagan administration officials say that the White House wants to postpone the congressional drive for sanctions against South Africa until September, on the grounds that the European Community will take action against South Africa at that time. The United States, in the words of one official, wants "to coordinate with them." (NYT 8/7/86)

August 15, 1986: The Senate, ignoring objections by the Reagan administration, overwhelmingly approves the Comprehensive Anti-Apartheid Act—a set of tough economic sanctions against South Africa, banning new American investments in the country and restricting current business relations. (NYT 8/16/86)

September 4, 1986: President Reagan extends for one year the limited sanctions against South Africa set forth in his 1985 Executive Orders. (CRS7, p. 9)

October 1986: Ambassador-nominee Edward J. Perkins states during his Senate confirmation hearings that he would not use the term constructive engagement—which is associated with current Ambassador to South Africa Herman Nickel—to describe U.S. South Africa policy. Ambassador Perkins's appointment is confirmed, and his tenure begins on November 19. He is the first black U.S. ambassador to Pretoria. (NYT 11/19/86)

October 2, 1986: The Comprehensive Anti-Apartheid Act of 1986 is enacted after the Senate overrides President Reagan's veto of September 26 by a margin of 78–21; the House voted to override the veto (313–83) on September 29. The president issues a statement that his administration "will implement the law." Section 307 of the act allows South Africa to resume its nuclear exports if it ratifies the Nuclear Non-Proliferation Treaty or agrees to IAEA safeguards. Only certain forms of uranium are banned, allowing South Africa to continue importing uranium hexafluoride. (*Implementation of the Comprehensive Anti-Apartheid Act of 1986*, 12/12/86; Spector, p. 322; *Sanctions Against South Africa: Current Legislative Issues*, 1/21/87, p. 5)

October 9, 1986: The South African government declares the United Democratic Front (UDF) an "affected organization"; this permits the UDF to continue its activities but bans all foreign funding. (CRS6, p. 7)

October 21, 1986: The General Synod of the Dutch Reformed Church, to which the majority of the Afrikaner population belongs, withdraws its support of apartheid. (*A U.S. Policy Toward South Africa: The Report of the Secretary of State's Advisory Committee on South Africa*, 1/87)

October 27, 1986: President Reagan signs Executive Order 12571, which authorizes the U.S. government to implement the Comprehensive Anti-Apartheid Act of 1986. (*South Africa: U.S. Policy After Sanctions*, 1/19/90, p. 4)

December 1986: A U.S. Defense Intelligence Agency report on South Africa reveals that the Armaments Development and Production Corporation (ARMSCOR) relies on direct acquisition of foreign technology to help support its weapons manufacturing processes, and that it takes advantage of "loopholes" in trade with foreign countries to obtain dual-use technology in order to modernize the South African defense industry and its products. The report further states that American companies have been selling advanced products to civilian-owned South African companies, which in turn sell them to the government. U.S. firms have also been the primary sources of hardware for the Council for Scientific and Industrial Research, the South African government's largest research agency. The report suggests that an "effective total economic embargo" is needed to stop "covert sales" to South Africa. (*South Africa: The Effect of Economic Sanctions on the Defense Industry*, 12/86)

December 19, 1986: The South African government places restrictions on twelve Cape Town antiapartheid organizations, including the United Democratic Front. The restrictions prohibit the organizations from calling for the withdrawal of troops from black townships, the release of persons held in detention, and the legalization of the ANC.(CRS6, p.5)

January 1987: The Secretary of State's Advisory Committee releases a report on U.S. policy toward South Africa. The report claims that the constructive engagement policy has failed and recommends a different course of action, such as a coordinated effort by the United States and its allies to impose economic sanctions on South Africa so as to pressure the government into negotiating with black leaders. Not all the members of the committee agree on the issue of multilateral sanctions. (*A U.S. Policy Toward South Africa: The Report of the Secretary of State's Advisory Committee on South Africa*, 1/87; CRS3, p. 3)

January 14, 1987: In compliance with the 1986 Comprehensive Anti-Apartheid Act, President Reagan submits a report listing ten strategic minerals needed by the United States for economic and defense purposes which cannot be obtained in adequate quantities unless purchased from South African parastatals. (*South Africa: U.S. Policy After Sanctions*, 1/19/90, p. 4)

January 24, 1987: In Washington, D.C., Secretary of State George Shultz meets with ANC leader Oliver Tambo. Tambo calls upon the United States for "full support" of the ANC's nationalist aims and states that the administration's constructive engagement policy is not helpful in dismantling apartheid. Tambo asks for U.S. assistance in persuading other countries to adopt sanctions similar to those adopted by Congress. Shultz relays U.S. concerns regarding Soviet influence in the ANC and the group's increased use of violence; he also expresses U.S. concern over the ANC's program and warns against replacement of apartheid by "another form of unrepresentative government." The two officials conclude their meeting with a discussion of how to encourage white and black South African leaders to negotiate. (CRS3, p. 3)

February 20, 1987: The United States vetoes a U.N. Security Council Resolution calling for sanctions against South Africa along the lines of those instituted by the U.S. Comprehensive Anti-Apartheid Act. Secretary of State George Shultz defends the vote before the Senate Foreign Relations Committee, stating that "we have a lot of trouble as a matter of principle with mandatory sanctions as voted by the United Nations." (NYT 2/25/87)

April 2, 1987: In compliance with the Comprehensive Anti-Apartheid Act, the State Department releases a report to Congress canceling an international conference on sanctions against South Africa and withdrawing its decision to ask other countries to adopt sanctions similar to those adopted by the United States. The report indicates U.S. opposition to U.N. mandatory international sanctions and views the adoption of sanctions as a decision for sovereign nations to make individually. The report further reveals other countries' violations of the U.N. arms embargo against South Africa. According to the report, French, Italian, and Israeli defense companies have helped to maintain those arms provided to South Africa prior to the embargo, and companies in Great Britain, West Germany, and Switzerland are believed to have made "gray" sales, that is, transactions that are not formally sanctioned by governments. The report also informs Congress of U.S. efforts to negotiate multilateral measures to dismantle apartheid. (CAAA; CRS3, p. 1; CRS6, p. 1)

April 7, 1987: The U.S. and Angolan governments agree to resume negotiations for a regional settlement on the Angolan-Namibian situation, which were broken off in February 1986 following the decision by the United States to aid UNITA. The agreement follows talks between Assistant Secretary of State Chester Crocker and an Angolan delegation in Brazzaville, Congo. (DOS Bulletin, p. 21)

May 7, 1987: President Reagan issues National Security Decision Directive 272, which revises U.S. policy objectives in southern Africa. According to the Directive, these include: "the earliest possible end to apartheid in South Africa"; "reduction and elimination...of Soviet and Cuban military presence" in Angola and southern Africa; solidarity within the United States and with its western allies on southern Africa; increased regional stability; and continued reliable Western access to southern African mineral resources.

Reagan also issues National Security Decision Directive 273, which proposes U.S. responses to continued violence in South Africa. Recent repressive measures taken by the Botha administration have forced black South Africans to turn "from near-term revolutionary scenarios to a search for viable long-term strategies for challenging" the South African government. According to the directive, the imposition of sanctions, though perceived as supportive of South Africa's disenfranchised citizens, has severely weakened U.S.–South African relations. (*United States Objectives in Southern Africa*, 5/7/87; *National Security Decision Directive 273*, 5/7/87)

July 1987: The South African Defense Forces (SADF) invade southern Angola in an effort to shore up UNITA and to capture the strategic town of Cuito Cuanavale. In this invasion, which lasts for about eight months, South African and UNITA forces are defeated by a combination of People's Armed Forces for the Liberation of Angola (FAPLA) and Cuban troops. The military setbacks at Cuito highlight the

SADF's limitations. (*[Briefing Regarding Developments in the Military Situation in Angola since July 1987]*, 5/11/88; *[Excised] Thoughts on Military Situation in Angola*, 2/17/88)

July 11, 1987: President Reagan signs the Foreign Assistance Supplementary Appropriations Bill for fiscal year 1987, providing approximately $40 million for Southern African Development Coordination Conference projects. The bill stipulates that aid will be provided to any country that does not advocate "necklacing" (the practice of placing a gasoline-soaked tire around a victim's neck and setting it on fire) or allow terrorists to operate from its territory. (*South Africa: U.S. Policy After Sanctions*, 1/19/90, p. 12; Baker, p. 56)

July 14–15, 1987: Assistant Secretary of State Chester Crocker meets with Angolan officials in Luanda for negotiations on Namibian independence and a timetable for a Cuban troop withdrawal from Angola. (DOS Bulletin, p. 21)

August 5, 1987: Angola offers the United States a new peace plan, which includes the withdrawal of twenty thousand Cuban troops from below the Thirteenth Parallel in exchange for the following conditions: (1) withdrawal of South African forces from southern Angola; (2) an end to South African aggression toward Angola; (3) respect for Angola's political independence and territorial integrity; and (4) implementation of U.N. Resolution 435. (CRS5, p. 23)

August 9, 1987: The National Union of Mineworkers (NUM) organizes the largest workers' strike in South Africa since the 1946 miners' strike. More than 340,000 members of NUM participate in the action, aimed at securing contracts. (Lawyers' Committee, p. 23)

August 22, 1987: A communiqué signed by Jonas Savimbi, head of UNITA, reveals that UNITA plans to continue its prolonged attack against the Angolan government and strongly warns foreigners and international organizations attempting to distribute food to MPLA soldiers to leave; it adds that UNITA will not accept responsibility for anything that happens to those doing so. (*Angola Unita Engages Soviets, Cubans in Intense Fighting*, 8/22/87)

September 21, 1987: In the midst of a Nigerian-led effort to expel South Africa from the IAEA, President P. W. Botha circulates a statement at the thirty-first IAEA General Conference announcing that South Africa is prepared to "commence negotiations with each of the nuclear weapons states on the possibility of signing the Non-Proliferation Treaty" (NPT) and to consider negotiating safeguards on its installations in compliance with the NPT. (*South Africa, Nuclear Weapons, and the IAEA*, 1/1/88, p. 11; NYT, 10/22/87)

September 27, 1987: According to press reports today, the IAEA General Conference has decided to postpone until next year consideration of a recommendation by its board of governors to suspend South Africa's membership. Supporters of a suspension were unable to win a two-thirds' majority vote after the Soviet Union and its East European allies voted against the measure. (NYT 9/27/87)

October 28, 1987: U.N. Secretary-General Javier Pérez de Cuellar reports that South Africa is prepared to join a conference of all interested parties aimed at making peace in Namibia and Angola, but that it still insists that Cuban troops be withdrawn from Angola as a condition for granting independence to Namibia. (*South African Response to October 21 Angolan Letter*, 11/3/87)

October 30, 1987: The U.N. Security Council approves (14–0) Resolution 601, calling for the rapid implementation of U.N. Security Council Resolution 435 on Namibia. The United States abstains, maintaining that a withdrawal of Cuban troops from Angola is a precondition to the implementation of the U.N. peace plan. South Africa claims that the obstacle to implementation is the continued Soviet and Cuban presence in Angola. (DOS Bulletin, p. 21)

November 14, 1987: Defense Minister Magnus Malan announces that President P. W. Botha, Foreign Minister Pik Botha, Education Minister Frederik de Klerk, and Finance Minister Barend du Plessis have all visited southern Angola in recent days. President Botha is reportedly in the region to show his "empathy, involvement and personal responsibility" for South African military action in Angola. (*RSA: P. W. Botha, Cabinet Members Visit Southern Angola*, 11/14/87; IHT 11/16/87)

November 15, 1987: A spokesman for the Angolan Defense Forces tells the leaders of Angola, Zimbabwe, Zambia, Botswana, Tanzania, and Mozambique that South African equipment captured in Angola includes U.S.-made medicine, communications radios, and other military equipment, proving the involvement of the United States in the Angolan war. (*Angola: Dos Santos Condemns RSA as Frontline Leaders Meet*, 11/15/87)

December 10, 1987: The House passes the International Security and Development Coordination Act of 1987, sponsored by Representative Dante Fascell (D–Fla.), which requires that the president: (1) identify and possibly terminate U.S. military assistance to countries selling oil and petroleum to South Africa or otherwise circumventing sanctions; (2) try to persuade U.S. allies to apply sanctions against South Africa; and (3) submit a report on international sanctions against South Africa. (*South Africa: International Sanctions*, 6/16/88, p. 15)

December 22, 1987: The fiscal year 1988 Continuing Appropriations Resolution provides Southern African Development Coordination Conference (SADCC) projects with an additional $50 million in funds. The law stipulates that 50 percent of SADCC funds be used in the transportation sector while the rest may be used in other development sectors. The legislation places prohibitions on the use of funds in Angola and Mozambique. (*Southern Africa: U.S. Foreign Assistance*, 2/28/89, p. 12)

February 1, 1988: The State Department declares that both Angola and Cuba have agreed to a Cuban troop withdrawal from Angola as part of the terms for a still-unresolved regional settlement. The next day, a U.S. official is reported as stating that Washington will not approach South Africa for discussions until Angola arrives at a specific timetable for the withdrawal. In Paris, the Angolan ambassador denies any change in Angola's position on a withdrawal and claims that the crucial issue is not a timetable but whether South Africa will implement U.N. Security Council Resolution 435. (DOS Bulletin, p. 21; CRS5, pp. 22–23)

March 13, 1988: The Angolan government announces that it has presented U.S. officials with a new proposal for withdrawing Cuban troops from within its borders as part of the overall peace settlement in the region. Angola offers a specific timetable in exchange for the termination of U.S. and South African support for UNITA. (CSM 3/15/88; DOS Bulletin, p. 21)

March 14, 1988: Assistant Secretary of State Chester Crocker meets with South African Foreign Minister Pik Botha in Geneva to discuss a regional settlement. Afterward, Botha publicly criticizes proposals prepared by Cuba and Angola on the withdrawal of all Cuban forces from Angola as too vague. (*Cuban Media on Crocker-Botha Meeting*, 3/15/88; NYT 3/15/88; DOS Bulletin, p. 21; CSM 3/15/88)

April 14, 1988: The Organization of African Unity (OAU) sends a delegation to Washington, D.C., to seek an end to U.S. support for UNITA. According to the delegation, assistance to UNITA impedes U.S. efforts to mediate the southern African peace process. (CRS5, p. 22)

May 12–13, 1988: Following last week's four-party talks in London, Angolan and South African officials meet in Brazzaville to discuss a regional peace settlement. The Angolan delegation reportedly promises that the Peoples Armed Forces for the Liberation of Angola (FAPLA) will not go on the offensive and will not cross the Namibian border. Both sides agree to continue discussions in the near future. (*Angola–South Africa Talks in Brazzaville*, 5/11/88; NYT 5/13/88; SAFR 7/88; DOS Bulletin, p. 21)

May 20, 1988: Senator Ron Dellums (D–Calif.) introduces a House bill (H.R. 1580) containing amendments to the Comprehensive Anti-Apartheid Act. The amendments call upon President Reagan to confer with U.S. democratic allies in an effort to reach a multilateral sanctions agreement, and authorize him to restrict imports from foreign countries and individuals attempting to take advantage of international and U.S. sanctions against South Africa. (*South Africa: International Sanctions*, 6/10/88, p. 15)

June 1, 1988: At a meeting in Moscow between Assistant Secretary of State Chester Crocker and Soviet Deputy Foreign Minister Anatoly Adamishin, a September 29, 1988, deadline is set for an international accord on a southern Africa peace settlement, which would involve a Cuban troop withdrawal from Angola and independence for Namibia. The date marks the tenth anniversary of the adoption of U.N. Security Council Resolution 435. (CRS5, p. 21; NYT 6/1/88; NYT 6/6/88; DOS Bulletin, p. 21)

June 6, 1988: An estimated two million workers fail to report to their jobs for three days to protest a proposed Labour Relations Amendment Bill. Manpower Minister Pietie du Plessis calls on the Congress of South African Trade Unions (COSATU) and other unions to come forward with their objections to the bill and recommend changes. COSATU announces that it will accept the invitation. (SAFR 7/88)

June 22, 1988: An Angolan delegation led by Minister of State for Production Pedro de Castro van Dunem announces in Washington, D.C., that Angola is willing to negotiate the withdrawal of Cuban troops from its territory without first getting assurances that the United States will stop supporting UNITA. Angola still demands that South Africa withdraw its troops from Angola, stop giving aid to the guerrillas, and grant independence to Namibia. The statement follows meetings with National Security Advisor Colin Powell and Secretary of State George Shultz. (NYT 6/23/88)

June 24–25, 1988: A second round of talks involving Angola, South Africa, Cuba, and the United States takes place in Cairo. On June 25, the delegations issue a joint communiqué stating that they have agreed to meet concerning Angola and Namibia "at the experts level" in the United States

during the week of July 11. No further details are given. (CSM 6/24/88; *Africa*, 7/15/88; WP 6/26/88; WT 6/27/88)

June 29, 1988: South Africa says that a surprise ground and air attack against a South African Army unit defending the Calueque Dam and hydroelectric plant in southern Angola has jeopardized peace talks for the region. South Africa reportedly sends urgent messages to the United States and Angola asking whether any useful purpose will be served by further peace talks. (NYT 6/30/88; WT 6/30/88)

July 5, 1988: After receiving encouraging replies from Washington and Luanda following the attack on the Calueque Dam, South Africa reportedly decides to continue negotiations on a regional peace agreement. (WT 7/6/88)

July 11–13, 1988: The third round of regional peace negotiations takes place on Governors Island in New York City. At the conclusion of the meetings, Assistant Secretary of State Chester Crocker announces that all sides have agreed that South African troops will withdraw from Angola before the implementation of U.N. Security Council Resolution 435 and before a timetable is set for Cuban troop withdrawal. Major differences reportedly remain on a timetable for withdrawing Cuban troops and on the level of continued military support from the United States, the Soviet Union, and South Africa. (NYT 7/14/88)

July 20, 1988: South Africa, Angola, and Cuba announce that they have ratified the Governors Island principles for disengaging forces in Angola and Namibia. The principles call for implementing Security Council Resolution 435 as well as noninterference in Namibian internal affairs. Assistant Secretary of State Chester Crocker states that the agreement provides "a set of guidelines" for another meeting between the parties to be held on August 2 in Geneva, but warns that "hard bargaining" remains ahead. (WP 7/21/88; DOS Bulletin, p. 21)

July 22–23, 1988: High-level, secret military talks involving Angola, South Africa, and Cuba take place in Cape Verde. A Pentagon representative, James Woods, is also present. (WT 7/25/88; FT 7/25/88)

July 31–August 1, 1988: Assistant Secretary of State Chester Crocker and Soviet Deputy Foreign Minister Anatoly Adamishin hold meetings in Geneva in preparation for the next round of discussions on the southern African regional peace plan, scheduled to begin August 2. Concluding the talks, Adamishin notes a "positive momentum" toward resolving the conflict and predicts a settlement in the "nearest future." (NYT 8/2/88)

August 8, 1988: South Africa, Angola, and Cuba announce that they have agreed to observe an immediate cease-fire in Angola and Namibia. The cease-fire agreement sets September 1 as the deadline for the withdrawal of all South African troops from Angola. Their joint statement also marks November 1 as the date for starting implementation of U.N. Security Council Resolution 435, with elections to be held seven months later, contingent upon an agreement by September 1 on a timetable for withdrawing Cuban troops from Angola. (WP 8/31/88; NYT 8/9/88; DOS Bulletin, p. 21–22)

August 13, 1988: In Vienna, representatives of the United States, the Soviet Union, and Great Britain meet with South African Foreign Minister Pik Botha about South Africa's interest in signing the Nuclear Non-Proliferation Treaty. Botha announces that South Africa has the capability to make nuclear weapons but refuses to elaborate to reporters. (NYT 8/14/88)

August 15–16, 1988: Military officials from Angola, Cuba, and South Africa meet at Raucana on the Angola-Namibia border to form the Joint Military Monitoring Commission, which will ensure an end to regional hostilities and pave the way for implementing U.N. Security Council Resolution 435. The United States announces its willingness to assist the commission. (DOS Bulletin, p. 22; NYT 8/17/88)

August 27, 1988: South Africa, Angola, and Cuba announce that they have suspended talks for one week in order to discuss with their governments a possible compromise on a timetable for Cuban troop withdrawal. (WP 8/28/88)

August 30, 1988: South Africa announces that it has withdrawn its last troops from Angola into Namibia two days before the scheduled deadline set by the Geneva agreement. South Africa also states that SWAPO has agreed to a cease-fire and will keep its troops 120 miles north of Namibia's border. (WP 8/31/88; DOS Bulletin, p. 22)

September 7–9, 1988: Cuban, Angolan, and South African negotiators meet again in Brazzaville amid reports that fighting might resume if this round of talks fails. South Africa is reportedly pushing for an early withdrawal of Cuban troops from southern Angola. At the conclusion of the talks, all sides express optimism that another meeting could resolve the issue of a timetable for a Cuban withdrawal. The countries declare that the Geneva agreement has been met and affirm their adherence to a November 1 deadline for starting a seven-month U.N. plan leading to elections in Namibia. The joint statement also says that new proposals have been made, but that the details will not be

disclosed until the negotiators have consulted with their respective governments. (CSM 9/7/88; NYT 9/10/88; DOS Bulletin, p. 22)

September 22, 1988: U.N. Secretary-General Javier Pérez de Cuellar begins a round of meetings in Johannesburg with President P. W. Botha and other cabinet members in order to advance the regional peace agreement, including determination of who will pay an estimated $700 million for its implementation. In a joint press conference, Pérez de Cuellar announces that he has assured the South African government of U.N. impartiality with regard to the implementation of Resolution 435. Botha states that he has approved a U.N. proposal to send a technical assistance team to prepare for the U.N. Transition Assistance Group. (WP 9/23/88; DOS Bulletin, p. 22)

September 26–29, 1988: Representatives of the United States, Angola, Cuba, and South Africa meet in Brazzaville for four days of talks. The negotiators announce an agreement in principle to a twenty-four-month timetable for withdrawing all Cuban troops from Angola. The leader of the Angolan delegation declares, "we are at the door of a deal," while the South African negotiator says, "we are leaving basically in good spirits." No further details emerge. (NYT 9/30/88; DOS Bulletin, p. 22)

September 27, 1988: Thomas Joseph Dolce, a civilian employed as an operations research analyst for the U.S. Army Material Systems Analysis Activity, is charged with passing classified documents to a South African military attaché in Washington, D.C. Dolce claims to have acted for ideological rather than financial reasons. (*United States of America* v. *Thomas Joseph Dolce*, 9/27/88)

October 1, 1988: The Foreign Operations, Export Financing, and Related Programs Appropriation Act of 1989, which appropriates $50 million to Southern African Development Coordination Conference (SADCC) projects, is signed into law (see entry for December 22, 1987). The Act contains restrictions against use of the fund by Angola and Mozambique. (*Southern Africa: U.S. Foreign Assistance*, 2/28/89, p. 13)

November 1, 1988: South African officials say that they are prepared to be flexible about a U.S. proposal that will allow some Cuban troops to remain in Angola for one year after Namibian independence. Under the U.S. compromise proposal made during meetings held in New York, four thousand Cuban troops would withdraw before implementation of U.N. Security Council Resolution 435 begins in January.

The remaining Cuban troops would move north of Angola's Fifteenth Parallel by March 31, and above the Thirteenth Parallel by June 30, with Namibian elections set for August 1. According to the proposal, three quarters of the Cuban forces would withdraw from Angola in the twelve months after the election, and the remaining troops would depart by August 1991. (WP 11/2/88)

November 8, 1988: George Bush is elected president of the United States. (NYT 11/9/88)

December 1988: South Africa, Angola, and Cuba reach agreement on a peace accord that includes terms for withdrawal of South African and Cuban forces from Angola. *(The 1987–88 Combat in Southern Angola: Lessons Learned, 12/88)*

January 6, 1989: President-elect George Bush writes to UNITA leader Jonas Savimbi and commends as a "great diplomatic achievement" the tripartite agreement for the withdrawal of Cuban troops from Angola and the independence of Namibia. Bush promises that his administration will "continue all appropriate and effective assistance to UNITA." The letter, which appears to mark Bush's first foreign policy commitment, is considered a sign that the incoming administration intends to make southern Africa a new priority. (WP 1/8/89; WP 1/16/89)

January 20, 1989: George Bush is inaugurated as the forty-first president of the United States. (WP 1/21/89)

February 1, 1989: A Defense Intelligence Agency cable reports that the South African Defense Forces recently purchased an unknown number of Israeli-manufactured J79 engines, which it presumably is using to upgrade its Cheetah fighter planes. (*South Africa Reportedly Has Taken Delivery of J79 Jet Engines from Israel,* 2/1/89)

February 22, 1989: Representatives from South Africa's Armaments Development and Production Corporation (ARMSCOR) brief the military attachés assigned to Pretoria. The briefing includes a short history of South African Defense Forces purchases of 78 percent of ARMSCOR's production. The remainder is split between the South African Police Force, the prison service, the Republic of South Africa security community, and commercial export. It is reported that 600 million rand worth of equipment was sold outside of South Africa between 1977 and 1978. (*ARMSCOR—Overview of South African Armaments Corporation…,* 5/17/89)

June 21, 1989: The *Washington Post* reports that South Africa plans, with the help of Israel, to test-launch a new intermediate-range ballistic missile. In response, an ARMSCOR spokesman confirms that the company has over the last six years been developing a missile test range at Overberg, and that missiles are being fired in order to test their performance. (*[Regarding the Washington Post Reports That South Africa is Soon to Test Launch a New Intermediate Range Ballistic Missile with the Help of Israel],* 6/21/89)

June 22, 1989: According to an article in *The Star,* experts believe that South Africa has the technological capability to make ballistic missiles and nuclear bombs. However, the report also states that, for political and economic reasons, it would be counterproductive for South Africa to put nuclear warheads on ballistic missiles. Instead, it would be better to arm Israeli-built Jericho II intermediate-range ballistic missiles with conventional warheads and use them to fill gaps in the South African Air Force armory, for example, the lack of heavy bombers. (*Academics Ponder "Nuclear Option" for Missiles,* 6/22/89)

June 26, 1989: Despite the United Nations' rigid arms embargo, it is reported that South Africa exported over $420 million worth of military equipment last year (see entry for February 22, 1989). The large and aggressive overseas sales campaign launched by the Armaments Development and Production Corporation (ARMSCOR) has accounted for a significant percentage of its sales. ARMSCOR has participated in two international weapons exhibitions—in Chile in 1982, and in Turkey in May 1989. (*[Regarding South Africa's Circumvention of the U.N. Arms Embargo],* 6/26/89)

July 5, 1989: The Defense Intelligence Agency reports that a "probable SRBM [short-range ballistic missile] was launched in an easterly direction from South Africa's Arniston Missile Test Range." Press reports suggest that Israel has been assisting the South Africans with the project since the mid 1980s. South African military superiority is considered a significant deterrent to frontline state support for antiapartheid groups, cutting down external pressure for reform, and reassuring the white population. (*South Africa: Missile Activity,* 7/5/89; [*South Africa's Short-Range Ballistic Missile Program*], 8/89)

July 24, 1989: The Chilean Committee for Disarmament and Denuclearization charges that Chile is being used to "launder" South African weapons. This accusation comes soon after Chile has tested a South African–made G6 cannon within its borders. Chile's Cardoen Industries claims to have manufactured the cannon, but the committee says that the parts were made in Pretoria and merely assembled in Chile. (*South Africa Accused of Using Chile as a Front for Exporting Weapons*, 7/24/89)

September 6, 1989: Following a struggle within the ruling National Party and the resignation of State President P. W. Botha, Frederik W. de Klerk is chosen in parliamentary elections to lead South Africa. (NYT 9/21/89)

September 20, 1989: In his inauguration speech, new South African President de Klerk pledges to "work urgently" to dismantle Pretoria's discriminatory legislation, to continue the release of political prisoners, to give "urgent attention" to a bill of rights for all races, and to open negotiations with representatives of South Africa's black majority. "We are determined to turn our words into action," he asserts, appealing to the international community to "use your influence constructively to help us attain that goal.... Help me and the government to make a breakthrough to peace." (NYT 9/21/89)

March 2, 1990: The thirty-five member National Executive Council of ANC in Lusaka announces that Nelson Mandela has been elected deputy president, and that the organization will move its headquarters to Johannesburg. (*Foreign and Commonwealth: Background Brief*, 5/90–12/90)

April 27, 1990: President de Klerk grants temporary amnesty to five exiled ANC members to allow them to participate in talks with the government on obstacles to formal negotiations. (CRS3)

June 7, 1990: The South African government lifts the state of emergency everywhere except Natal province, where fighting between supporters of the ANC and Inkatha continues. (CRS3)

June 19, 1990: The South African Parliament repeals the Separate Amenities Act, which required the segregation of public facilities such as parks, hotels, swimming pools, beaches, libraries, toilets, and places of entertainment. (CRS3)

December 8, 1990: In a letter to the European Community, Nelson Mandela appeals to European leaders to maintain sanctions for another two or three months and to consider phasing them out only when the government meets certain key ANC demands. This marks a shift in the organization's position on sanctions. (WP 12/8/90)

December 14, 1990: Oliver Tambo, the ANC president, returns to South Africa after thirty years in exile. (NYT 12/14/90)

December 21, 1990: The European Community (EC) lifts investment sanctions on South Africa. The EC justifies its decision as a measure aimed at rewarding President de Klerk for his reform initiatives. (WT 12/21/90)

January 9, 1991: ANC leader Nelson Mandela calls for a multiparty congress to plan a new South African constitution. The congress is later referred to as the Congress for a Democratic South Africa. (WP 1/9/91)

January 29, 1991: Nelson Mandela and Chief Mangosuthu Buthelezi, leader of the Inkatha Freedom Party, sign a peace accord aimed at ending the violence in Natal. This is the first public meeting to be aimed at diminishing the political violence in black communities. (*The Natal Peace Accord*, 1/29/91)

February 2, 1991: South African President de Klerk announces the scrapping of the Group Areas Act (1950) and Land Acts (1913, 1936). The repeal of these laws, which have served as cornerstones of the apartheid system, raises hope for a peaceful resolution of the South African conflict. (NYT 2/3/91)

April 5, 1991: Nelson Mandela warns the South African government that his organization will halt crucial talks about a new constitution if measures are not taken to end violence in black townships. This ultimatum appears to signal the biggest rift between Mandela and President de Klerk since the ANC leader's release from prison. (WP 4/6/91)

April 19, 1991: The European Community, meeting in Luxembourg, agrees to lift its remaining economic sanctions against South Africa in response to Pretoria's continuing moves to dismantle apartheid. (NYT 4/15/91)

May 1, 1991: After sixteen years of civil war in Angola, the MPLA and UNITA agree to call a cease-fire before the end of the month and to hold the nation's first free elections in the second half of 1992. (NYT 5/1/91)

May 24, 1991: The last of fifty thousand Cuba troops leave Angola as part of the implementation plan agreed to in December 1988. (WT 5/24/91)

May 31, 1991: The MPLA government and UNITA sign a long-awaited peace agreement aimed at ending the sixteen-year civil war and preparing Angola for free elections and democracy. (NYT 5/31/91)

June 1, 1991: After a quarter century of bloodshed, Angola President Jose Eduardo dos Santos and Jonas Savimbi publicly shake hands as a gesture toward ending the civil war in Angola. (NYT 6/1/91)

September 14, 1991: The ANC, the Inkatha Freedom Party, the South African government, and members of the business community sign a National Peace Accord. This is the first such national initiative involving all the major South African political players. (*The National Peace Accord,* 9/14/91)

May 15–16, 1992: The Convention for a Democratic South Africa (CODESA II) convenes. Serious differences weigh down discussions on the procedure for writing South Africa's new constitution. A consensus on preliminary joint-rule formation could signal that the country has entered a decisive transitional phase toward democratization. However, disagreement over this issue and other key constitutional matters between the two major political players, the ANC and the government, leads to the collapse of the convention. (*Negotiation News,* 5/92)

July 15, 1992: The ANC, the South African government, Inkatha, and other homeland leaders, as well as representatives of the political parties participating in South Africa's tricameral Parliament request the U.N. Security Council to intervene in the political violence. (*Statement of the President of the ANC, Nelson Mandela at UN Security Council,* 7/15/92)

September 29–30, 1992: Nationwide elections take place in Angola, with the MPLA winning a plurality of the votes. UNITA's Jonas Savimbi rejects the results, but a U.N. special representative certifies that the balloting was generally free and fair. "[W]hile there were certainly some irregularities," the representative notes, "these appear to have been mainly due to human error and inexperience." She finds "no evidence of major, systematic or widespread fraud, or that the irregularities were of a magnitude to have a significant effect on the results." The State Department issues a statement concurring in the U.N.'s judgment. Because no candidate wins more than 50 percent of the vote, a second ballot must be scheduled; yet before that can happen, UNITA begins a new round of fighting that throws Angola once again into full-scale civil war. (Document 58, "Angola Elections," 10/19/92)

March 24, 1993: In a speech to Parliament, President de Klerk acknowledges the existence of South Africa's long-standing nuclear weapons program. He claims that six bombs were made, but all were dismantled in 1990. Independent observers later challenged some of de Klerk's facts, asserting that South Africa had the material for many more weapons. (Document 33, "The Nuclear Non-Proliferation Treaty and South Africa's Nuclear Capability," 3/24/93)

SOURCE ABBREVIATIONS

AFP = *American Foreign Policy. Basic Documents, 1977–1980.* Washington, D.C.: Department of State, 1983.

Baker = Baker, Pauline. *The United States and South Africa: The Reagan Years.* New York: Ford Foundation, 1989.

CAAA = Department of State. *The Comprehensive Anti-Apartheid Act of 1986: Implementing Regulations and Related Materials,* June 1, 1987.

CIP = Center for International Policy. *International Policy Report.* July 1982, March 1983, and April 1984.

CRS1 = Branaman, Brenda. Congressional Research Service. *South Africa: Issues for U.S. Policy.* IB80032. July 1, 1980 (updated June 5, 1983, Jan. 31, 1984, Feb. 4, 1985, and March 11, 1985).

CRS2 = Branaman, Brenda. Congressional Research Service. *South Africa: Issues for U.S. Policy.* IB88832. June 18, 1982.

CRS3 = Branaman, Brenda. *South Africa: Recent Developments.* IB85213. Jan. 5, 1987.

CRS4 = Branaman, Brenda. Congressional Research Service. *South Africa: Recent Developments.* IB86115. Sept. 2, 1986.

CRS5 = Copson, Raymond W. Congressional Research Service. *CRS Report for Congress: Angola/Namibia Peace Prospects, Background to the Current Problems, and Chronology.* IB88559. Aug. 16, 1988.

CRS6 = Branaman, Brenda. Congressional Research Service. *South Africa: Recent Developments.* IB87501. June 9, 1987.

CRS7 = Branaman, Brenda, and William N. Ralford. Congressional Research Service. *South Africa: Foreign Investment and Separate Development.* IB78078. Feb. 1, 1980.

CSM = *Christian Science Monitor.*

Danaher = Danaher, Kevin. *In Whose Interest?—A Guide to U.S.–South African Relations.* Washington, D.C.: Institute for Policy Studies, 1984.

DOS Bulletin = Department of State Bulletin, Feb. 1989.

DOS Historian = Department of State, Office of the Historian. *The United States and South Africa: U.S. Public Statements and Related Documents, 1948–1976.* Oct. 1985.

FBIS = Foreign Broadcast Information Service. *Daily Report, Middle East and Africa*. Department of Commerce, National Technical Information Service. Springfield, Va.: United States.

Federal Register = Federal Register. Office of the Federal Register. National Archives and Records Administration. Washington, D.C.: Government Printing Office.

FT = *Financial Times*.

House = United States Congress, House, Committee on International Relations, Subcommittee on International Resources, Food, and Energy. *Resource Development in South Africa and U.S. Policy*. 94th Congress, Second Session. May 25, June 8, and June 9, 1976.

IHT = *International Herald Tribune*.

Klare = Klare, Michael T. "Evading the Embargo." *Journal of International Affairs* 35, Spring/Summer 1981.

Lapping = Lapping, Brian. *Apartheid: A History*. New York: George Braziller, 1987.

Lawyers' Committee = Lawyers' Committee for Civil Rights Under Law. South Africa Project. *Annual Report: South Africa 1987: Choking Internal Resistance*. Washington, D.C., 1987.

NARMIC = National Action/Research on the Military Industrial Complex. *NARMIC Automating Apartheid: U.S. Computer Exports to South Africa and the Arms Embargo*. Philadelphia, AFSC 1982.

Nelson = Nelson, Harold D. *South Africa: A Country Study*, Washington, D.C.: Government Printing Office, 1981.

NYT = *New York Times*.

Principal Officers = Principal Officers of the Department of State and United States Chiefs of Mission, 1778–1986. U.S. Department of State, 1986.

SAFN = *South Africa Foundation News*.

SAFR = *South Africa Foundation Review*.

SATRO = Study Commission on U.S. Policy Toward Southern Africa. *South Africa: Time Running Out*. Berkeley, Calif.: University of California Press and the Foreign Policy Study Foundation, 1981.

SLPD = *St. Louis Post Dispatch*.

Spector = Spector, Leonard. *Going Nuclear*. Cambridge: Ballinger Publishing, 1987.

The Sun = *The Sun* (South Africa).

TransAfrica = TransAfrica. "New U.S. Policy on South Africa." *TransAfrica News Report*. Special Edition, August 1981.

U.N. Notes = *United Nations Center Against Apartheid, Notes, and Documents*. New York: United Nations.

WP = *Washington Post*.

WT = *Washington Times*.

PART II
U.S. POLICY TOWARD SANCTIONS

A CLASH OF PRIORITIES

Historically, the United States and South Africa have shared a number of interests that have brought the two countries relatively close together. Commercial and economic ties have been the predominant force— American business has pumped substantial investments into the South African economy—but mutual strategic interests have played their part as well. South Africa entered both world wars on the allied side, and during the Cold War Pretoria became an asset to the West in its active opposition to communism.

However, South Africa's policy of apartheid has made the country something of a liability to the United States, too, for it has raised moral qualms in the U.S. and throughout the rest of the world, complicating Washington's relationship with Pretoria. To cope with this dilemma, from 1960 onward, the United States developed a two-pronged policy toward South Africa: it publicly opposed apartheid on moral and political grounds, even as it maintained cordial relations on all strategic and economic concerns—notably cooperation on military and scientific ventures (among them deep-space tracking stations and arms sales). In effect, Washington wanted to have it both ways. Over the years, the United States has managed to steward most of its interests in South Africa—including preserving access to immense mineral resources and protected markets and investments there—but often at a high political cost at home and abroad.

Since 1960, the international community, particularly African governments in the United Nations, have called for economic sanctions and arms embargoes against South Africa. The incident that launched the international campaign against the apartheid regime was the Sharpeville massacre of March 21, 1960, when South African police fired into an enor-

mous crowd of black demonstrators. At first, the United States resisted demands for sanctions, but opinion in Washington was hardly unanimous. Noting continued pressure from African states, Assistant Secretary of State for African Affairs G. Mennen Williams concluded in a secret memo to Secretary of State Dean Rusk that "we have reached the point where we must take a more vigorous stand against apartheid. In African opinion we can no longer rest our case on a condemnation of apartheid" (Document 1). Williams's arguments sparked a philosophical debate in the State Department, as Dean Rusk's secret response on the use of sanctions makes clear (Document 2). While acknowledging that "we have the strongest objections to apartheid," Rusk nevertheless took the view that South Africa should not be singled out for harsher treatment than other countries:

> I believe it is worth reminding ourselves that there are other states where obnoxious practices of one sort or another exist—and in some of them in the most exaggerated form.... The question, it seems to me, is whether we ourselves precipitate sharp crises in our relations with other states over such issues or whether we try to maintain the structure of international relations in order to be able to work doggedly and persistently toward the decent world community which is our main objective.

This became a standard argument for future administrations interested in maintaining America's South Africa policy even as the passage of time made it more untenable.

PRESSING FOR AN ARMS EMBARGO

Williams countered Rusk a month later in another secret memo, in which he considered the practical effects of the African position on U.S. interests in Africa: "In my mind a complete arms ban is the least the U.S. can do to maintain our position of influence with the Africans and our ability to prevent more radical and violent action on their part" (Document 3).

This position was not shared by the Pentagon and Secretary of Defense Robert S. McNamara, who were concerned about any measures that would jeopardize U.S. military interests in Africa. In a July 1963 letter to Rusk, McNamara noted that "any position taken by our delegation will very likely alienate in some degree either Portugal and South Africa on the one hand, or the African bloc on the other" (Document 4). Speaking for the Joint Chiefs of Staff, he recommended stating Washington's "strong objections to apartheid" but hoped "it will be possible to avoid a vote in the U.N. in favor of economic sanctions, arms embargo, or expulsion in the cases of Portugal and South Africa."

Eventually, after lengthy maneuvers aimed at moderating the broad African demands, on August 7, 1963, the Kennedy administration agreed to support a limited resolution in the U.N. Security Council calling for member states to withhold arms that could facilitate the enforcement of apartheid policies in South Africa.

The August 1963 resolution meant that the United States would pursue a twofold arms policy toward South Africa: denying arms that could be used to enforce apartheid, while considering requests for military purchases that would be required for external defense. Consistent with this approach, the United States considered entering into new agreements with South Africa following the U.N. resolution. In August and September, for example, the Kennedy administration hashed out the question of whether to sell submarines to Pretoria. Among other things, the secretaries of state and defense highlighted the extreme political sensitivity of the issue in a memorandum to the president (Document 5). One week later, Kennedy approved McNamara's recommendation on the submarines—deciding at the same time that he would sell spare parts for C-130 aircraft to the South African government (Document 6).

The sensitivity of these sales exploded again in 1964, when the South African government announced the Odendaal Commission's recommendation on the controversial protectorate of South West Africa (Namibia), which caused the United States to consider further sanctions. If implemented, the Odendaal Plan would have had the effect of

> (1) extending apartheid in its most extreme form to South West Africa (Namibia), including shifting and separation of people to form 10 restrictive, racial "homelands", and (2) bringing about a shift in governing powers which is tantamount to annexation of the territory. [1]

Upon hearing of the South African government's decision to implement the commission's recommendations, the United States advised Pretoria to defer any actions. Anticipating a negative reaction from Pretoria, the administration issued a secret order, National Security Action Memorandum 295, directing the State Department ("as a matter of urgency"), the Defense Department, and the National Aeronautics and Space Administration (NASA) to plan a variety of appropriate measures—among them, postponing decisions on submarine sales, suspending action on loan applications, and relocating NASA and Defense Department facilities to other countries (Document 7). Three months later, a status report on NSAM 295 listed the steps taken and their results, including South Africa's issuance of a white paper in which "Prime Minister Verwoerd came round to full acceptance of our representations with regard to postponement" (Document 8).

After the Odendaal incident, U.S. policy reverted to its prior course, which would become the norm for the next three decades—consistently resisting calls from within and outside South Africa for economic sanctions while arguing that stable trade and investment were an important means of encouraging change in the policy of apartheid.

A NEW APPROACH?
For the next thirteen years this policy held sway without notable dissent within the U.S. government. And

once again it was internal events in South Africa that precipitated the next crisis in U.S. policy on sanctions. From the first months of 1977, South African authorities had been conducting a massive crackdown on opposition movements and black leaders—without eliciting any substantial response from the United States. However, in September 1977, black consciousness movement leader Steven Biko died after being detained and interrogated by police. After Biko's death, the government clamped down on further unrest by banning the South African Student's Organization, the Black People's Convention, and most other black consciousness organizations, as well as *The World,* the most widely read black publication in the country.

Not surprisingly, African states again took the lead in the United Nations by introducing broad resolutions calling for an arms embargo and economic sanctions against South Africa. Among other things, the resolutions aimed at cutting off all possible military or nuclear ties to Pretoria from the outside world. On October 31, the United States voted against the African resolutions, which also contained strong language labeling South African internal, Rhodesian, and Namibian policies a threat to international peace and security. In explaining the American action, U.S. Ambassador to the U.N. Andrew Young declared that the African states were making a serious error by attempting to go beyond the consensus that had developed in the world community. On October 31, 1977, the United States, Britain, and France cast three "triple vetoes" in the Security Council against the African resolutions. One State Department account summarized the impact of the Western action thus: "Triple vetoes deepened an atmosphere among Africans of frustration and disappointment with Western response to the current situation in South Africa."[2] The Africans were particularly dismayed because, prior to these catalyzing events, the Carter administration had announced that U.S. policy toward southern Africa had changed.

However, amid accusations that its antiapartheid policy was purely rhetorical, on November 4, 1977, the United States joined the world community by voting in support of U.N. Resolution 418, introduced by the Western Five, which condemned the system of apartheid and called for a mandatory arms embargo against South Africa. By replacing the voluntary arms embargo of 1963 with a stronger version, the resolution intensified the pressure on South Africa. In theory, the embargo provisions were far-reaching, covering direct imports of all arms and ammunition, as well as exports of licenses for internal arms production. The resolution also required regular reviews of existing licensing agreements.

Although the resolution was a compromise, with the African states pressing for far more stringent sanctions, Washington hailed its passage as a landmark. In a confidential cable transmitting guidance to "all African diplomatic posts," Secretary of State Cyrus Vance instructed U.S. officials to "seek to minimize negative fallout from UN debate" and "emphasize the fact that African and Western Council members were able to reach agreement on compromise resolution, which for the first time in history invoked Chapter VII sanctions against a member state" (Document 9). For his part, President Carter explained that the vote would demonstrate "our deep and legitimate concern" about South Africa's actions. However, he told a news conference that the United States stopped short of endorsing a far more damaging economic embargo in order to leave the door open for diplomacy.

"QUIET" DIPLOMACY

From the beginning, the Reagan administration envisioned maintaining a nonconfrontational approach toward South Africa with the goal of reversing Soviet gains in southern Africa and persuading Pretoria to reform its system. Its so-called constructive engagement emphasized dialogue and "quiet" diplomacy over public censure or strong measures, such as economic sanctions. Just how "constructive" this policy was intended to be was called into question in March

1982, when the Reagan administration relaxed controls on exports to the South African police and military, effectively reversing regulations laid down by the Carter administration (Document 10).

In 1984, political unrest erupted throughout South Africa, sparked by a combination of political and economic factors, including the government's abdication of responsibility for directly administering black townships, cuts in subsidies for basic necessities, rising unemployment, and intensified antiapartheid activities. In July 1985, authorities imposed a state of emergency in several strife-torn areas. By June 1986, the government saw it could not contain the uprising with partial measures, so it extended the state of emergency nationwide and granted police and security forces unlimited power to crush the movement. It has been estimated that between September 1984 and June 1986, twenty-five hundred people died, virtually all of them black, and about thirty thousand were detained.

Even in the face of these measures, Reagan policymakers clung to constructive engagement as the basic framework for U.S. policy. President Reagan himself went so far as to praise the Botha administration again and again for making substantial reforms. However, public concern about the Reagan administration's relations with South Africa eventually gave rise to a broad-based antiapartheid movement across the United States, marked by demonstrations in major cities and on college campuses. Its demands for tougher U.S. policies toward Pretoria resulted in boycotts of banks extending loans to South Africa, sales of stock in U.S. firms operating in South Africa, and pressure on American companies to withdraw their investments there.

In 1985, Congress, led by the Black Caucus, responded to both the antiapartheid movement and South Africa's limited state of emergency by introducing legislation calling for economic sanctions against South Africa. The House passed a sanctions bill in June 1985, followed soon after by the Senate; both bills provided for broad restrictions on trade and the complete disinvestment of U.S. companies. However, President Reagan preempted both bills by introducing a series of limited economic sanctions in Executive Order 12532, issued on September 9, 1985 (Document 11). In a statement accompanying the order, Reagan explained that he opposed sanctions and had issued the order only to forestall Congress from adopting even harsher measures, which he believed would have adverse effects on black South Africans and the economies of the region. As a result, neither side in South Africa was satisfied. Black leaders, led by Bishop Tutu, escalated their criticism of the administration—Tutu went so far as to call President Reagan a "racist." The United Democratic Front (UDF) publicity secretary, Murphy Morobe, called the order "hollow" and an "imperialist policy" designed to give the South African government more breathing space. The white government, on the other hand, expressed some relief that the executive order had preempted harsher legislation. Nevertheless, government politicians complained that Washington had proven to be an unreliable ally.

PUBLIC DIPLOMACY

Responding to increasing domestic and international pressure in the mid 1980s, the Reagan administration began a concerted push to ensure that any future sanctions would be coupled with new, more aggressive efforts to maintain close relations with the South African government. To succeed, White House officials saw the need for a full-fledged "public diplomacy" campaign aimed at cultivating positive images of constructive engagement and of the South African government itself.

This strategy grew out of concern about a variety of developments in southern Africa, including increased episodes of violent repression in South Africa and the perceived rise of Soviet influence in the region. Most important, a rising distrust of the United States, including among black South Africans, persuaded administration officials that they needed "to change the terms of the debate," in the words of a State

Department secret memorandum that described the "theoretical framework" of the program (Document 12).

The memo's author, Herman Nickel, disparaged "critics" who dismissed administration successes in South Africa (including Desmond Tutu, referred to as "a Nobel laureate of charismatic talents who plays the U.S. media like a violin") and attributed such opposition to a "perception gap" that Washington needed to address in order to sell its policies more effectively. Interestingly, Nickel saw the problem coming not only from people who thought that the United States was "soft on apartheid," but from "right-of-center constituencies" who needed to be convinced that U.S. policy was "not just do-good sentimentality."

In the memo, Nickel laid out several ways of "putting our message across," using both officials (from the president on down) and private-sector resources, such as private corporations, conservative groups, service clubs, and public figures. The idea was to "encourage" them to promote administration policies in various ways. He suggested, for example, that "academics, former government officials, politicians" could "write op-ed pieces and letters to the editors, appear on TV and other discussion panels." Presumably, as private individuals with no official ties to the administration, their views would substantiate the policy of constructive engagement.

Nickel thought it best to avoid "hostile audiences" during the campaign, since, he said, they would provide "lightning rods that will energize our opponents." Rather, he advised targeting "decision-makers who face pressure for 'divestiture'—State legislators, university trustees, trustees of pension funds, municipal leaders."

This would "probably best [be] achieved in quiet workshops," he added.

On September 5, 1985, the White House established a Special Working Group to implement the public diplomacy program. In an "urgent," confidential White House memorandum for the high-level Special Policy Group, National Security Advisor Robert McFarlane described the need to make "our

many audiences" in the United States and abroad understand the administration's "clear" principles on the subject:

> We seek to use the influence we have to end apartheid peacefully but rapidly, achieve peace in Namibia and in that context achieve a withdrawal of Cuban forces from Angola, end cross border violence in the region, and limit Soviet influence there (Document 13).

Two days later, the White House circulated National Security Decision Directive 187, "United States Policy Toward South Africa," which began:

> The United States and its allies have important political, commercial, and strategic interests in South Africa. These are being threatened by widespread violence and increased tension in South Africa, and continued Soviet challenges to our important interests in the area (Document 14).

The NSDD listed a number of steps to promote U.S. interests, including "oppose new, international mandatory economic sanctions against South Africa," and "explain…why punitive sanctions are counterproductive." Within a month, the White House's special working group proposed a more specific, three-step approach to implement the NSDD's public diplomacy elements:

> 1. An urgent, initial PR effort, closely coordinated with our efforts to prevent Congressional adoption of unhelpful legislation, to get an explanation for our policy to key leadership groups and audiences.
>
> 2. A medium-term program to strengthen Embassy Pretoria's ability to communicate effectively with audiences in South Africa through expanded political reporting, press and public outreach, and educational, human rights and economic aid to black South Africans.
>
> 3. A long-term effort to build a broader base of domestic support by involving key American citizens and institutions in contacts with South African

counterparts and programs for constructive, peaceful change in South Africa (Document 15).

In very short order, the program began to go into effect: President Reagan and members of the cabinet became involved, as did a string of government bureaucracies including the Agency for International Development, the Treasury Department, the United States Information Agency, the Commerce Department and the Defense Department. By the end of September 1985, Assistant Secretary of Defense Richard Armitage could report to Assistant Secretary of State Chester Crocker that his agency had already put the plan into operation (Document 16). Armitage went on to suggest that the battle for hearts and minds might also require "countering Soviet Disinformation."

At the administration's behest, new groups were created to help with the larger strategy of blunting public criticism. At a mid-September White House meeting, corporate chiefs discussed the idea of forming a U.S. Corporate Council on South Africa "to coordinate business efforts to resist divestment and promote reform" (Document 17). Crocker recommended to Secretary of State George Shultz that the State Department coordinate its own program with the council's.

The State Department also pressed to implement the idea of using private U.S. institutions to advance the administration's policies. A November 1985 confidential memo to Donald Gregg, Vice President George Bush's national security adviser, suggested that Bush raise the notion at a White House meeting of professional groups, which State hoped would include the American Bar Association and the American Medical Association (Document 18).

IMPOSING SANCTIONS

The strategy outlined in NSDD 187 marked a turning point in U.S. policy, for it emphasized the creation of a broader base of domestic support and targeted influential citizens and institutions at home and abroad. In the short run, however, the campaign fell flat: one year after Reagan's executive order instituting limited sanctions, Congress passed the Comprehensive Anti-Apartheid Act of 1986 (CAAA) and even overrode Reagan's veto. The Act amounted to a rejection of constructive engagement.

The CAAA prohibited U.S. trade and other economic relations with South Africa, and directed the president to persuade other industrialized democracies and South Africa's other trading partners to follow the American lead. However, as a classified State Department cable of April 1987 makes clear, the administration balked at implementing this provision of the Act (Section 401), arguing that the provision is "hortatory and not mandatory," and that "there would be no practical benefit at this time in invoking the cumbersome and complex procedures established in this section" (Document 19). Nevertheless, the executive branch conducted investigations to determine trade relations between its Western allies and South Africa.

The CAAA also required (in Title I) that the administration pursue greater contacts with the African National Congress and other antiapartheid groups. Previously, high-level official meetings with the ANC had been discouraged, primarily for fear of upsetting the South African government, but in January 1987 Secretary Shultz met with ANC President Oliver Tambo in the first public encounter between a U.S. cabinet official and a member of the outlawed organization. This signaled a shift in U.S. policy, which was underscored by the administration's reluctant decision to change its characterization of the ANC from a terrorist, communist-backed organization to a group with a legitimate voice in South Africa.

Another significant provision of the Act, Section 508, directed the president to determine the extent to which the international arms embargo was being violated and to report these findings to Congress. In one such report of March 1987, the State Department concluded that companies in Israel, France, Italy, Germany, the United Kingdom, the Netherlands, and Switzerland had continued to supply military items to Pretoria in violation of the U.N. embargo (Document 20). In the case of Israel, the report said, "we believe that the Israeli government was fully aware of most or all of the trade."

The basic purpose of economic sanctions was to push the South African government more quickly toward ending the apartheid system, and thus to bring a halt to unrest in the country. Instead of dismantling apartheid, though, Pretoria declared sanctions an act of interference in the country's domestic affairs. Ironically, as a result of this perceived threat, Pretoria saw the need to adopt a strategy that emphasized security measures rather than reform. For example, in May 1986, during a period when the South African government had been showing signs that it might begin power-sharing negotiations with democratic forces inside the country, the SADF mounted armed raids into neighboring states and, three weeks later, imposed a nationwide state of emergency. On the economic front, meanwhile, Pretoria helped businesses to evade the restrictions through "sanctions busting"—a variety of elaborate schemes that included rerouting trade through third countries, establishing offshore trading companies, and falsifying shipping documents—and, under a state of emergency, the regime intensified its repression of the antiapartheid movement. And in a final irony, considering its complaint about interference, Pretoria retaliated against the frontline states by cutting vital transportation links, choking trade routes, and otherwise attempting to destabilize their economies.

Much of the debate concerning sanctions has revolved around the very question of their effectiveness. South Africa's ability to flout restrictions on its economic activities has been an understandable source of anxiety for many proponents of sanctions. However, supporters generally agreed that the key to sanctions' effectiveness was a united multinational front to ensure that a total quarantine took hold. To that end, Congress included language in the CAAA directing the president to persuade other countries to adopt similar restrictions. The Reagan administration's refusal to take serious steps in that direction made it possible for Pretoria to sidestep the sanctions—and the resulting failure, the administration argued, demonstrated their ineffectiveness.

NOTES

1. Cyrus R. Vance, Cable for various posts, "Murrey Marder Article in Washington Post," October 28, 1977. This document is included in the National Security Archive's microfiche collection, *South Africa: The Making of U.S. Policy, 1962–1989* (Alexandria, Va.: Chadwyck-Healey, 1991).

2. Cable from U.S. Mission to the U.N. for the Secretary of State, "West Vetoes African Resolutions on South African [deleted] in Security Council October 31," November 1, 1977. This document is included as well in the National Security Archive's microfiche collection, *South Africa: The Making of U.S. Policy, 1962–1989.*

DOCUMENT 1: Undersecretary G. Mennen Williams, Memorandum for Secretary Dean Rusk, "U.S. Policy Towards South Africa," June 12, 1963.

PAGE 1 OF 2

C O C O O Ø 3

P P
Y

DEPARTMENT OF STATE

Assistant Secretary

SANITIZED VERSION

TO: The Secretary   NLK-76-312   June 12, 1963

THROUGH: M - Mr. Harriman

FROM   : AF - G. Mennen Williams

SUBJECT : U.S. Policy Towards South Africa

As I reflect on what has been happening in Africa during recent weeks, especially what took place at the Addis Ababa conference, I believe we are face to face with a new and decisive phase in the apartheid issue. We have reached the point where we must take a more vigorous stand against apartheid. In African opinion we can no longer rest our case on a condemnation of apartheid. We must be ready to back our condemnation with some form of meaningful action. This has been the message conveyed to us following the Addis meeting by Nyerere, Houphouet-Boigny and other responsible African leaders who are our friends. We confront this African pressure for action at a time when powerful forces in our own society are demanding action on racial inequalities at home. The two forces are inter-related and, as Addis showed, Africans are as aware of the inter-relationship as those who are opposing segregation in the United States.

One clear outcome of the Addis Ababa conference is the organization by the African countries of a better coordinated, more militant campaign of pressure on the South African Government and on Governments considered capable of influencing South African policy, especially the United States and the United Kingdom. There are no African "moderates" on the colonialism issue and apartheid is looked upon by Africans as another facet of colonialism. According to President Nyerere of Tanganyika, the "Liberation Committee" being set up in Dar es Salaam as the result of the Addis Ababa conference will have "military" as well as "political" functions. Thus, while consideration of the apartheid issue in the UN can now be considered as falling under Chapter VI (Pacific Settlement of Disputes of the Charter, it is moving in the direction of Chapter VII (Action with Respect to Threats to the Peace, etc).

The U.S. will be faced with the issue in the UN in July. The Addis Ababa conference, as you know, decided to send a delegation of four Foreign Ministers to New York "to inform the Security Council of the explosive situation existing in South Africa." (Liberia, Sierra Leone, Tunis, Madagascar.)

SECRET   The

DOCUMENT 1: Undersecretary G. Mennen Williams, Memorandum for Secretary Dean Rusk, "U.S. Policy Towards South Africa," June 12, 1963.

PAGE 2 OF 2

~~SECRET~~

- 2 -

The Security Council meetings will come at a time of greatly intensified domestic pressure for a stronger stand by the Administration on civil rights in the United States. Failure of the United States to take a stand on the racial issue on the international scene in the same forthright fashion as it has handled matters in Alabama and Mississippi would lead to unfortunate domestic, as well as international, repercussions.

In my view, the time has come to review our arms supply policy toward South Africa. I believe we should be thinking now in terms of a total arms embargo. Our present partial arms embargo policy is equivocal, is not an effective pressure on the South Africans, and is considered inadequate by the African countries and by many influential sources in the U.S. who are concerned about racial discrimination. While a total arms embargo would fall far short of the complete economic, diplomatic and arms embargo sanctions already recommended by the General Assembly and which will be even more vigorously urged by the African states as a result of the Addis Ababa conference, it is the only way we can convince both world and domestic opinion that we mean business in our disapproval of apartheid.

Recommendation:

That we examine the possibility of moving to a full embargo on the supply of arms to South Africa.

AF:AFI:CStrong/AFE:JMMacKnight
Pac;wab;6/12/63

~~SECRET~~

C　　C

O　　O

　P　P

　　Y

June 15, 1963

MEMORANDUM FOR:　M - Mr. Harriman
　　　　　　　　　　G - Mr. Johnson
　　　　　　　　　　AF - Mr. Williams
　　　　　　　　　　EUR - Mr. Tyler
　　　　　　　　　　S/P - Mr. Rostow

　　　　　　Through S/S

　　　　Mennen Williams memorandum to me of June 12 on U.S. policy toward South Africa raises again some far-reaching issues which ought to be considered within a broader framework of policy than that relating to the attitudes of the independent states of Africa.

　　　　At the heart of the issue is how we relate ourselves to those countries whose internal arrangements and practices are not only foreign to our own way of thinking but, in many cases, repugnant to us. Let us accept the general notion that the United States should use its influence steadily and persistently in the direction of the principles inscribed in the United Nations Charter as well as in our own basic commitments to constitutional processes, human rights, etc. It is another question, it seems to me, to extend such influence into the field of sanctions and into actions which, if consistently and conscientiously applied, would interrupt our relations with perhaps half of the existing community of states. Also involved is the position in which we would be if other states undertllk to apply sanctions against us because of practices of our own to which they take the strongest exception.

　　　　It is true that we have the strongest objections to apartheid in the Union of South Africa; we have said so repeatedly and have asserted our view to the point where our relations with the Union of South Africa are in a continuing state of tension. But I believe it is worth reminding ourselves that there are other states where obnoxious practices of one sort or another exist -- and in some of them in the most exaggerated form. I have in mind Bulgaria, Burma, China, Czechoslovakia, Ghana, Haiti, Hungary, Indonesia, Korea, Laos, Paraguay, Poland, Portugal, Rumania, Saudi Arabia, South Africa, Spain, Turkey, USSR, the UAR, Viet-Nam, and Yugoslavia. I have not listed some of the smaller African states whose

State　NLK-76-312

SKF　10/27/76

GROUP 2

- 2 -

internal practices reflect varying degrees of totalitarianism nor all of the Arab states whose attitudes in religious minorities or constitutional principles leave much to be desired. The question, it seems to me, is whether we ourselves precipitate sharp crises in our relations with other states over such issues or whether we try to maintain the structure of international relations in order to be able to work doggedly and persistently toward the decent world community which is our main objective. I will admit that apartheid presents a case of unusual difficulty but I would not put it ahead of the violations of human rights within the communist bloc or in certain countries governed on an authoritarian basis with which we have correct and sometimes even friendly relations.

I would draw a sharp distinction between our deep concern with respect to racial discrimination in the United States and the way in which we crusade on that very issue outside the United States. The United States is our responsibility; our failures are our failures; we live under a constitutional system in which we can do something about it. But no one has elected us to undertake such responsibilities in other countries. The President has reminded us that we are not interested in a Pax Americana. It seems to me, a fortiori, that we are not the self-elected gendarmes for the political and social problems of other states.

It would be hard to find a single state with which we have relations where it is not necessary for us to try to develop good relations despite important differences in points of view or in action. Specifically with regard to the Union of South Africa, I have felt that we cannot compromise our own attitudes toward apartheid, that we must use our influence wherever possible to modify their position on that matter, but that we must then also try to sustain good relations in other respects despite the severity of our differences on that particular issue. It has seemed to me, therefore, logical that we should not assist the Union of South Africa with means of enforcing its apartheid policy but that we should assist them in playing the kind of role which they have already played in two World Wars and which now is a part of a total confrontation affecting the life and death of our own nation.

- 3 -

A proposal for us to embark upon sanctions against the Union of South Africa must, it seems to me, be a part of a package of proposals for sanctions against other states in other situations where different but obnoxious situations obtain. And such proposals should include some concept of priorities -- that is, what are the situations which cause us the deepest concern?

I have no objection to the most intensive study of apartheid or other situations causing us concern. But I do think that we must give careful thought to the broader questions of 1) how we relate ourselves to the other 94% of the world's peoples whom we can influence but cannot control, and 2) where the interests of the American people lie with regard to actions designed to require someone else to act as we would like to have them act.

Dean Rusk

Attachment:
    Memorandum of June 12.

S:DRusk:jmr

DOCUMENT 3: Undersecretary G. Mennen Williams, Memorandum for Secretary Dean Rusk, "Arms Policy and South Africa," July 12, 1963.

PAGE 1 OF 3

DEPARTMENT OF STATE A/CDC/MR

REVIEWED BY *H Tanol it* DATE *9/20/95*

RDS☐ or XDS☐ EXT. DATE _____
TS AUTH. _____ REASON(S) _____
ENDORSE EXISTING MARKINGS☐
DECLASSIFIED☒ RELEASABLE☒
RELEASE DENIED☐ .
PA or FOI EXEMPTIONS _____

SECRET

This document consists of ⸺ pa&
No. ⸺ of ⸺ copies. Series A.

July 12, 1963

TO: The Secretary

THROUGH: S/S

FROM: AF – G. Mennen Williams

SUBJECT: Arms Policy and South Africa

As your memorandum of June 15 indicates, the policy question of a ban on arms to South Africa does indeed raise far reaching issues. These issues vitally affect the direct interests of the U.S. as well as our moral position. At this particular time also such a ban on arms shipments has a tactical importance.

In assessing the impact of imposing or failing to impose an arms ban, the problem must be put in context. That context is twofold. First, if there ever was any doubt, the Addis summit conference has indicated beyond peradventure that all African countries regard apartheid not only as obnoxious to human dignity but a threat to African freedom which under the leadership of their Committee of Nine at Dar es Salaam they intend to eliminate peacefully if possible, forcibly if necessary. Second, all countries will be judged friendly or unfriendly on the basis of their positive acts of opposition to apartheid. The time of good intentions is over and only concrete action will do.

The question of what practical concern this is for the U. S. involves what reaction the African countries may take with respect to those countries that do not actively aid their objectives or that oppose their means of achieving those objectives without offering a reasonable substitute.

In my mind a complete arms ban is the least the U.S. can do to maintain our position of influence with the Africans and our ability to prevent more radical and violent action on their part. Actually this does not differ in principle

AF:GM WILLIAMS:JNL   SECRET   from what we are

DOCUMENT 3: Undersecretary G. Mennen Williams, Memorandum for Secretary Dean Rusk, "Arms Policy and South Africa," July 12, 1963.

PAGE 2 OF 3

<u>SECRET</u>

-2-

from what we are already doing which is a conditional ban. Going to an all-out ban will merely be a difference in degree not in principle. However, this difference will be all important in our position in Africa as showing our good faith and determination to back our principles.

If we don't take significant action such as an arms ban the following damage to our position may be entailed.

1.   Loss of support in the UN on such questions as entry of Communist China in the UN (African votes were critical in the last session).

2.   Loss of military installations such as those in Morocco, Libya and Ethiopia (continued existence of foreign bases are political liabilities to African governments).

3.   Loss of scientific facilities such as those in Nigeria and Zanzibar.

4.   Loss of communications facilities such as those in Liberia and Nigeria.

5.   Loss of vital civil airline and MATS landing and overflight rights in Africa and corresponding increase in bloc aviation activities including Moscow to Havana.

6.   Weakening of our influence toward developing a moderate non-communist family of African nations. In this connection it is inevitable that if the African nations become convinced that the Free West will not help them solve their most important problems they will be forced to turn more and more toward bloc aid, which relies on disruption and violence.

7.   Incitement of our own racial tension by failing to respond positively to the archetype of racism in the world, apartheid.

It is true that an arms ban might jeopardize the use of certain tracking and naval facilities in South Africa but this would be a calculated risk and relatively small in comparison

to what else might be lost.

SECRET

DOCUMENT 3: Undersecretary G. Mennen Williams, Memorandum for Secretary Dean Rusk, "Arms Policy and South Africa," July 12, 1963.

PAGE 3 OF 3

C 516

SECRET

-3-

to what else might be lost. Commercial and business advantages can be affected either in South Africa or the rest of Africa. Unlike a few years ago, the U.S. now has larger interests outside South Africa than inside.

The moral issue needs little elaboration. Apartheid is obnoxious not only to all colored peoples who are the majority of the world's population but to all civilized people as well. Votes at the UN are ample evidence of this. If we refused an arms embargo, and another Sharpeville massacre occurred, we would stand condemned in the eyes of most of the world.

As to the tactical situation, it is clear that the Afro-Asians intend to push the issue of apartheid to the limit. For example, the Africans have decided to break diplomatic relations and some have already done so. Furthermore, a delegation of four Foreign Ministers, led by Mongi Slim, has been sent to New York to present the African case in the Security Council. They will most likely press for every sanction including explusion from the UN. Only if we can assume a strong moderate position such as an arms ban, can we successfully combat extreme measures and retain our moral position and influence.

In short, both right and self-interest dictate our adoption of an arms embargo posture and the sooner we take it the more effective our position will be.

AF:GMWilliams:jml

D005

7

THE SECRETARY OF DEFENSE
WASHINGTON

11 JUL 1963

R

Dear Dean:

In connection with the U.S. position on possible UN Security
Council resolutions calling for severe measures against Portugal
and the Republic of South Africa, we understand that these proposals
could include economic sanctions, arms embargo, and even expulsion
from the UN itself. We have given serious attention, from the standpoint of military security, to such resolutions, and this letter is
to indicate my conclusions and recommendations.

Any position taken by our delegation will very likely alienate
in some degree either Portugal and South Africa on the one hand, or
the African bloc on the other. As the attached memorandum from the
Joint Chiefs of Staff makes clear, we have significant military
interests, immediate and long-term, which could be jeopardized
either way. Insofar as Portugal is concerned, it remains true that
we have no fully satisfactory alternative to the Azores for tactical
air and troop movement operations in limited or general war in Europe,
the Middle East, or Africa; for ASW operations in the central Atlantic;
and for certain significant communications and intelligence requirements.

In the Republic of South Africa we presently operate only the
Atlantic Missile Range tracking station near Pretoria. As Ros
Gilpatric wrote to George Ball on 9 April 1963, this station has
contributed greatly to our missile development and other space
programs and will continue to be important after 1963, although
not vital. In addition, we must take into account the reaction of
our NATO allies, and the possible divisive effect upon the alliance,
should we give support to a strong African resolution on this subject.
Consequently, any course of action which we may envisage should be
coordinated in advance with at least the United Kingdom, France and
Belgium.

As the attachment indicates, the military assets we derive from
Portugal and South Africa must be weighed against those now available
to us in the "African bloc". The communications station at Kagnew,
Ethiopia, is of critical importance to a variety of communications
and intelligence objectives. As we have pointed out before, there
is no practical alternative to this facility. Wheelus Air Base in
Libya is particularly significant for air transport and training
operations for our fighter aircraft assigned to NATO; its replacement would be difficult and expensive. In Morocco, despite the

phase-out of the SAC bases, we have important communication facilities for which there is presently no substitute. Furthermore, in these countries and in the remainder of the North African and sub-Saharan area, we would attach long-term strategic importance to the preclusion of any Soviet Bloc foothold for military, political, and economic reasons.

Given these considerations, it should be our basic objective, to the extent that it is possible, to avoid prejudicing our relationship with either side in this dispute.

Thus, we recommend that the United States clearly state its strong objections to apartheid in the Union of South Africa and its criticism of the policies of Portugal in the Portuguese Territories. However, I hope it will be possible to avoid a vote in the UN in favor of economic sanctions, arms embargo, or expulsion in the cases of Portugal and South Africa. In any event, I believe the decisions on these issues should be based on general considerations of foreign policy.

I hope that you share the views I have expressed and that we can work on this basis toward a joint State-Defense recommendation to the President as to how we can meet this difficult problem without serious damage to our military position.

Sincerely,

BOB

Robert S. McNamara

1 Incl
  Cy JCSM-528-63
  dtd 10 Jul 63 *

Honorable Dean Rusk

Secretary of State

DOCUMENT 5: Secretary Dean Rusk and Secretary Robert McNamara, Memorandum for President John Kennedy, "Sale of Submarines to South Africa," September 16, 1963.

PAGE 1 OF 6

approved N.H. 4/23/65

MEMORANDUM FOR THE PRESIDENT

Subject: Sale of Submarines to South Africa

After you last considered this question, in the light of George Ball's Memorandum to you of August 28, you requested that the Departments of State and Defense consider, in particular, the following points:

If it is assumed that the decision is made ultimately to effect if possible the sale of the three submarines, then:

A. How can the possibility of effecting the sale be kept open during the UN General Assembly session, with the assumption being that the contractual arrangements would not be concluded until after its termination (after the first of the year)?

B. What would be the balance of payments benefits and when would these benefits probably be realized?

C. In view of the two preceding questions, should the possible sale of submarines be kept open?

1. Actions necessary to keep open the possibility of the sale, with contractual arrangements to be concluded after the first of the year.

Both the South African Ambassador in Washington and the South African Naval Chief of Staff in Pretoria have asked whether submarines could be sold under the "strategic exception" enunciated by Ambassador Stevenson in the Security Council on August 2, and if we were prepared to sell the submarines now (August 9 and 7 respectively).

CONFIDENTIAL

Dean Rusk

Robert S. McNamara

GROUP 4
Downgraded at 3 year intervals; declassified after 12 years

DOCUMENT 5: Secretary Dean Rusk and Secretary Robert McNamara, Memorandum for President John Kennedy, "Sale of Submarines to South Africa," September 16, 1963.

PAGE 2 OF 6

CONFIDENTIAL

-2-

The Naval Chief of Staff, indeed, inquired when the U. S. would send to South Africa the technical team, whose visit had long been anticipated.

It should also be noted that Foreign Minister Louw, in a statement in South Africa on September 10, said that the U. S. and Britain could not count on continued South African assistance against communism, and that the Simonstown Agreement regarding use of naval facilities might be dissolved in the light of British and American statements and attitudes, exhibited at the UN and elsewhere, towards South Africa's apartheid policy.

In light of the preceding and in view of uncertainties regarding technical specifications for the submarines in question and the terms and conditions of sale, in order to keep the possibilities of a sale open, we believe the following would be necessary:

(a) At a minimum, we would ask the South African Embassy here or the SAG in Pretoria if they still wished to purchase the submarines, while indicating that we could not undertake contract negotiations before the end of this year.

(b) At a maximum, we would suggest in addition to the above inquiry that we were prepared to send perhaps two qualified officials quietly to South Africa to discuss these matters with South African officials. These U. S. officials should not, in fact, be authorized to conclude negotiations but only to ascertain the degree of continuing interest of the South African Government in this sale and to obtain from the South African officials a clearer definition of their desires as to performance characteristics, financial terms, and production schedules.

CONFIDENTIAL

DOCUMENT 5: Secretary Dean Rusk and Secretary Robert McNamara, Memorandum for
President John Kennedy, "Sale of Submarines to South Africa," September 16, 1963.

PAGE 3 OF 6

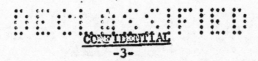

CONFIDENTIAL
-3-

(c) If the findings of the U. S. officials
resulting from their visit to South Africa indicate
it would be feasible for the U. S. to conclude
the sale, we could then consider whether additional
technical-level consultation could be undertaken,
either in the United States or in South Africa,
as a means of moving the sale along to conclusion.

2. <u>Balance of payments benefits</u>.

There are essentially two types of financing the
submarine sale, with two varying balance of payments
benefits. First, financing can be achieved through cash
with order, or time-deposit. In both cases, the balance
of payments benefits to the United States would be immediate, since the money would be transferred to U. S. banks
at once, although in the time-deposit arrangement the
payments to manufacturers would be made in accord with
the schedule worked out under the contract. In both
instances, the balance of payments benefits would be
between $75-90 million for the three submarines in the
year in which the contract is concluded. While these
immediate balance of payments benefits are possible, we
believe they are in fact unlikely, since it is unusual
to have all of the money transferred at one time.

The second type of financing consists of some form
of government-supported credit (i.e. Exim Bank guarantee
of commericial loan, Exim Bank loan, or "dependable undertaking" under Section 507 (b) of the Foreign Assistance
Act). In most of the government-supported arrangements,
the benefits to the U.S. balance of payments will depend
upon the payment schedule embodied in the contract and,
thus, will be spread out over a three-to-four year period
of time between signing the contract and delivering the
last of the submarines. The exception is a straight Exim
Bank loan, where the Bank can sell the South African government note on the International Market at a discount,
thus almost immediately benefiting the U. S. balance of
payments.

CONFIDENTIAL

[66]

DOCUMENT 5: Secretary Dean Rusk and Secretary Robert McNamara, Memorandum for
President John Kennedy, "Sale of Submarines to South Africa," September 16, 1963.

PAGE 4 OF 6

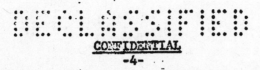

CONFIDENTIAL

-4-

The Department of State believes it politically
inadvisable to involve government credit, but we believe
you should be aware of the possible alternatives.

3. <u>Should the proposed sale be kept open?</u>

We believe that, in arriving at your decision, you
should consider two major points in favor and one opposed
to this course of action.

<u>Favorable</u>,

(a) We believe the U. S. is obligated to
advise the South Africans relatively soon regarding
the sale, given the August 7 and 9 inquiries in
Pretoria and Washington and our commitment to the
Ambassador to inform him of our decision. Unless
we do so shortly, they would be justified in
implying a negative decision, and it is then probable
that South Africa will purchase similar submarines
from European sources. We know that they explored
possibilities with the British and nearly concluded
a contract with the French, just prior to the U. S.
indications in early 1963 of the willingness to
sell the submarines. The potential loss to balance
of payments has been indicated in the preceding
paragraph. The efforts suggested in paragraph 1,
would at least help the U. S. ascertain whether
in fact South Africa would purchase U. S. or European
submarines.

(b) Moreover, we must remember that the South
Africans agreed to establish the missile and satellite tracking facilities because of an exchange
of Aide Memoires on June 15, 1962, which noted that
the U.S. was willing to give "prompt and sympathetic
attention to reasonable requests for the purchase
of military equipment required for defense against
external agression". Foreign Minister Louw's comments
of September 10 have some pertinence in this respect,
although they were not directed specifically at the
question of availability of arms but rather at the
general U. S. attitude toward South Africa.

CONFIDENTIAL

DOCUMENT 5: Secretary Dean Rusk and Secretary Robert McNamara, Memorandum for President John Kennedy, "Sale of Submarines to South Africa," September 16, 1963.

PAGE 5 OF 6

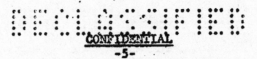

CONFIDENTIAL
-5-

Unfavorable,

On the other hand, we believe we must all recognize that the sending of perhaps two officials to South Africa to find out what the facts are with regard to South Africa's desire to purchase the submarines, and certainly subsequent technical discussions may well be exploited by South Africa to support its allegations that the U. S. really supports the South African Government and that the Security Council resolution really did not mean anything. Even though the South Africans did not so exploit the information, it could well leak. In either case, it will be difficult to justify to world public opinion, particularly African, what will be claimed to be an abrogation of U. S. policy enunciated in the Security Council on August 2. Despite the fact that we can explain the sale on the basis of Adlai Stevenson's statement of "strategic exception", it seems clear that African representatives at the UN appear to interpret Stevenson's statement to mean that we would not sell arms to South Africa after August 2, unless there should be a very substantial worsening of the international political scene justifying the provision of these arms in order to defend the free world. These considerations will, of course, continue to be operative even after the first of the year.

Conclusions

There are two lines of action which could be taken:

A. We could tell the South African government that we must defer consideration of the sale for a further period of time, and run the risk of losing the sale. This might impair our ability to continue to use the missile and satellite tracking facilities in South Africa but these, in turn, must be weighed against the importance of other base rights and facilities elsewhere in Africa. This course

CONFIDENTIAL

DOCUMENT 5: Secretary Dean Rusk and Secretary Robert McNamara, Memorandum for President John Kennedy, "Sale of Submarines to South Africa," September 16, 1963.

PAGE 6 OF 6

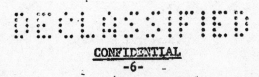

CONFIDENTIAL
-6-

of action, by which we quietly reiterate our policy of not supporting South African repression of its non-White majorities, would strengthen the pressure on that government to move ahead more rapidly on its domestic racial problems. The South African Ambassador on September 13 indicated clearly that his government was increasingly sensitive to U. S. views on the apartheid question. This course of action would also be consistent with our belief that continued pressure on South Africa is a principal available offset to African pressures for action against Portugal, and entirely in the spirit of our posture on apartheid as expressed repeatedly in the UN.

B. We can adopt the action suggested in paragraph 1 (a), (b), and (c) above. This means we would ask the South African government if they are interested in purchasing the submarines, even though a contract cannot be signed this year, and that we are prepared to send perhaps two officials now to explore matters quietly, on a preliminary basis.

Dean Rusk
Robert S. McNamara

Alternative B.

CONFIDENTIAL

DOCUMENT 6: National Security Assistant McGeorge Bundy, Memorandum for Secretary Dean Rusk and Secretary Robert McNamara, September 23, 1963.

PAGE 1 OF 1

THE WHITE HOUSE
WASHINGTON

September 23, 1963

~~SECRET~~

MEMORANDUM FOR: Secretary Rusk
Secretary McNamara

The President has approved the Secretary of State's recommendation of August 28 to continue after the end of this year to license the sale of spare parts of C-130s sold to the South African Government.

With respect to possible sale of submarines to South Africa the President has approved recommendation B of the joint State-Defense memorandum of September 16 but with these specific limitations:

(a) It should be made clear to the South Africans that any informal discussions held during the balance of this year are to be strictly confidential and involve no implied commitment to sell, and,

(b) The US can make no decision before the end of this year regarding sales and any eventual decision will be taken in the light of circumstances at the time the question is considered, under our policy stated in the UN Security Council in August.

DECLASSIFIED
F. O. 11652, SEC. 2(E), 5(D), 8(E) AND 11
U.S. Archivist . NLK-77-238
BY _____ NARS. DATE 2-28-78

McGeorge Bundy

~~SECRET~~

DOCUMENT 7: National Security Assistant McGeorge Bundy, Memorandum for Secretary Dean Rusk et al., National Security Action Memorandum 295, "U.S. Policy Toward South Africa," April 24, 1964.

PAGE 1 OF 2

~~SECRET~~ ~~FILE COPY~~ April 24, 1964

NATIONAL SECURITY ACTION MEMORANDUM NO. 295

MEMORANDUM TO: Secretary of State
                   Secretary of Defense
                   Secretary of the Treasury
                   Director, U. S. Information Agency
                   Administrator, National Aeronautics and Space
                                  Administration

SUBJECT: U. S. Policy Toward South Africa

    1. The State Department should as a matter of urgency develop a comprehensive program of diplomatic activity, based on the response of the South African Government to our two aide memoires, to the end of assuring that the implementation of the Odendaal report is deferred as long as possible and, hopefully, until the decision on the merits of the case in the International Court of Justice. In developing this program, the Department should consider all available diplomatic techniques, including the use of special emissaries, Presidential communications, etc. It should include modes of securing concerted or parallel action by other interested governments, particularly those in Western Europe.

    2. Existing policy regarding military sales to South Africa will be continued. Decision regarding possible sales of submarines or any variations in existing policy will be postponed and considered only in light of further developments, including those in the South West Africa - ICJ problem.

    3. US Government lending agencies will for the time being suspend action on applications for loans or investment guarantees with respect to South Africa. There should be no avoidable disclosure of this policy to interested parties, however, and agencies should continue to accept and process applications. No policy of warning private investors not to invest in South Africa will be undertaken pending further developments.

~~SECRET~~

DOCUMENT 7: National Security Assistant McGeorge Bundy, Memorandum for Secretary Dean Rusk et al., National Security Action Memorandum 295, "U.S. Policy Toward South Africa," April 24, 1964.

PAGE 2 OF 2

~~SECRET~~

- 2 -

4. The National Aeronautics and Space Administration and the Department of Defense should immediately undertake such planning for and construction of alternative stand-by facilities as would be required if it became necessary to evacuate the facilities in South Africa on six months' notice. In support of this, the Department of State will determine immediately the political acceptability of countries which the DOD and NASA may indicate as technically feasible and desirable. The Department of State will give priority to accomplishing required site surveys and negotiating necessary base agreements and assisting in needed land acquisition recommended by DOD and NASA. This program shall be carried out in such a manner as to avoid its coming to public notice as long as feasible, and in close consultation with the Department of State particularly so that the public aspects and the diplomatic aspects of our relations with South Africa may be coordinated.

5. The State Department will develop a program for actions during the months ahead, pending final ICJ decision in the South West Africa case, aiming to persuade the South African Government to acceptance of the Court's decision. In addition to use of available pressures, particular attention will be given to exploring possible bases for accommodation and understanding with more moderate members of the South African white community along the lines proposed by the State Department's memorandum of March 10th.

6. The State Department, in consultation with other interested agencies, will develop a program to explain privately to interested African countries the character and objectives of our program in order to try to obtain their understanding and cooperation.

7. The Department of State shall immediately undertake a comprehensive analysis of the various sanctions that could be considered if South Africa does not accept the ICJ decision on South West Africa. This analysis should include an estimate of the effectiveness on South Africa of the sanction if general compliance were obtained and of the prospects for obtaining such compliance.

McGeorge Bundy

Information copy:
    Secretary of Commerce

~~SECRET~~

July 30, 196

—— 1

STATUS REPORT ON NSAM NO. 295
of April 24, 1964 - South Africa

Following numbered paragraphs correspond to the seven numbered paragraphs of NSAM 295:

1. Defer Implementation of Odendaal Report in South West Africa

a. Action taken:

After negative South African Government responses to US and UK representations to Foreign Minister Muller on this subject in February, we convinced the British after some discussion that a second effort should be made with Prime Minister Verwoerd directly. Our approaches to the Prime Minister on March 19th brought a much more conciliatory, but not entirely clear South African response on March 27. Meanwhile Mr. Clarence Randall, whom we had briefed and enlisted before his private trip to South Africa, made strong personal representations to both Muller and Verwoerd in mid-March. Applicants in the International Court cases, Ethiopia and Liberia, were kept generally informed of progress and their Counsel was encouraged to refrain from seeking interim ICJ action.

b. Results:

In a Government White Paper and statement to Parliament on April 29, Prime Minister Verwoerd came round to full acceptance of our representations with regard to postponement. Citing South African technical reasons for delay, as we had suggested, he said inter alia and included in the White Paper the statement that the South African Government would "refrain from action which may be regarded - even theoretically - as detrimental or prejudicial to the alleged rights of the applicant states, or which may unnecessarily aggravate or extend the dispute before the Court". In effect, all controversial aspects of the Odendaal Report were postponed pending Court judgment and certain economic and social development projects not involving shifts of population or changes in administration were approved for action.

Ethiopian and Liberian Ambassadors expressed satisfaction with this achievement and indicated that interim Court action which might have precipitated a Security Council crisis this year would not be sought.

The larger problem of South African intentions after Court judgment is still very much with us. While agreeing to postponement of implementation of the Odendaal Report, Dr. Verwoerd nonetheless accepted it "in broad principle" and said "it will be implemented when the time is ripe". Thus, twelve to fourteen months' time was gained, but the issue will become even more critical by mid-summer 1965 when final Court decision on the merits is expected.

2. Policy

COPY LBJ LIBRARY

-2-

2. Policy Regarding Military Sales

Thus far during 1964 the South African Government has not initiated any official requests for arms or military equipment. Existing policy has been adhered to save for two technical exceptions under which it was decided to approve the sale of 100 helicopter firing heads (a safety device, not a weapon) and 12 sets of MK 32-5 torpedo tubes and 6 control panels as accessory equipment for torpedoes purchased by South Africa prior to inauguration of our arms embargo policy last August.

3. Suspension of Action on Applications for US Government Loans and Investment Guarantees

Implementation of this policy has involved refusal of only one application thus far and no others are presently pending. The application which was not approved was in the form of a request for a special political risk guarantee covering a proposed loan of approximately $7 million by Chase Manhattan Bank to the Palabora Mining Company of South Africa. The loan was to have been for purchase of mining machinery and equipment. The Palabora Company, an international consortium including Newmont and American Metals Climax of the United States, has since obtained alternate capital. The venture involves development of an extensive copper mine complex in the Republic of South Africa to begin production in 1966. There has been no repercussion from the South African Government as the result of the Ex-Im Bank action. A high functionary of the South African Industrial Development Corporation (IDC) did complain irately to one of our Embassy officers and vowed that in retribution the mining equipment would not be purchased in the United States. Ultimately about 95 percent is to be purchased in the United States, however, because letters of intent had already been signed for much of it and Palabora technicians insisted for the rest only US-manufactured machinery would be satisfactory.

Knowledge of the Palabora refusal has spread to some extent among American firms under contract for equipment as well as other US firms, some involved in the venture and some not. However, the general policy has been kept secret and no action beyond that indicated in the NSAM has been taken.

US private investment is continuing at a high rate in South Africa because of unusually favorable returns. Depending on future developments it may become necessary to review the policy of no warnings late this year or early in 1965.

4. Alternate Space Tracking Facilities

NASA and DOD are proceeding actively with plans and preparations for alternate space tracking facilities. NASA will locate various

alternate

-3-

alternate facilities in Malagasy, Spain and Ascension Island. Separate equipment will be installed and used in supplementary fashion pending any possible requirement to substitute entirely for present South African stations. NASA expects to complete its alternate sites by late 1965. Consent of the Spanish and Malagasy Governments has been obtained. The Ascension site is still subject to final negotiation with the British. DOD requires only stand-by land for a transfer of equipment which can be accomplished within six months. Malagasy is the prospective site for this. At some point later this year South African technicians will be able to deduce the purpose of alternate NASA facilities despite plausible and to some extent real additional reasons for their existence which NASA is fully prepared to make known. It is anticipated that the South African Government will not be likely to raise the issue with us in present circumstances so long as NASA and DOD continue normal operations in South Africa as planned. The questions of whether and when we should inform the South African Government about our alternate sites are still under consideration.

5. Program to Persuade South Africa to Comply with ICJ Decision and to Encourage Moderate Whites in South Africa

The substance and strategy of new diplomatic approaches to the South African Government concerning the future of South West Africa are currently in the process of inter-agency review as part of the final draft National Policy Paper on South Africa. This is scheduled for final inter-agency clearance by mid-August.

More effective liaison between interested private American groups and similar groups in South Africa has been assisted in response to inquiries to the Department of State from American groups

COPY IRL'T... BY

[75]

-4-

groups in the fields of business, labor, religion, youth and science.

6. <u>Program to Explain US Objectives to Interested African Countries</u>

Background and instructions have been provided USUN and all US diplomatic missions in Africa on our objectives concerning South West Africa and the Odendaal Report. These have been used as the basis for private conversations to bring about greater African understanding of the US position. To some extent this effort may have contributed to African willingness to go along with our current position on thorough and time-consuming study of sanctions in the UN Security Council.

7. <u>Analysis of Sanctions</u>

A comprehensive series of studies of sanctions and other possible enforcement measures, including estimates of their effectiveness, costs and prospects for compliance, has been launched in the State Department. First drafts on all topics are scheduled for completion between July 31 and August 15. These will be timely and useful both for the purposes envisaged in the NSAM and as supporting information for USUN participation in the Security Council Study Committee on enforcement measures.

Clearances: AF - Mr. Fredericks
            SCI - Mr. Dillery (subs)
            UNP - Mr. Kriebel (inf.)
            EUR/BNA Mr. Judd
            G/PM - Mr. Warren
            S/P - Mr. Duggan (subs.)

AF:AFE:PHooper:ams   7-30-64

SECRET

DOCUMENT 9: Secretary Cyrus Vance, Cable for All African Diplomatic Posts, "Security Council Action on South Africa," November 5, 1977.

PAGE 1 OF 3

DECLASSIFIED

Department of State

TELE

CONFIDENTIAL

CONFIDENTIAL

AN: D770409-0697

PAGE 01   STATE 264955
ORIGIN IO-14

INFO OCT-01 AF-10 EUR-12 ISO-00 TRSE-00 MMO-01 SIG-01
ACDA-12 MC-02 EB-08 COME-00 CIAE-00 DODE-00 PM-05
H-01 INR-07 L-03 NSAE-00 PA-01 PRS-01 SP-02
SS-15 NSCE-00 SSO-00 USIE-00 INRE-00 ERDA-05
NRC-05 OES-07 /113 R

DRAFTED BY IO/UNP:TNILES:YF
APPROVED BY AF:RMOOSE
IO:GSHELMAN
AF:WBEDMONDSON
IO/UNP:RLBARRY
-------------- 098106 051707Z /20
O 051620Z NOV 77
FM SECSTATE WASHDC
TO ALL AFRICAN DIPLOMATIC POSTS IMMEDIATE
INFO AMEMBASSY BONN IMMEDIATE
AMEMBASSY LONDON IMMEDIATE
AMEMBASSY PARIS IMMEDIATE
AMEMBASSY PRETORIA IMMEDIATE
AMEMBASSY OTTAWA IMMEDIATE
USMISSION USUN NEW YORK IMMEDIATE

C O N F I D E N T I A L STATE 264955

E.O. 11652: GDS

TAGS: PORG, PFOR, UN

SUBJECT: SECURITY COUNCIL ACTION ON SOUTH AFRICA

REF: (A) STATE 260818 (B) STATE 259771

1. SECURITY COUNCIL COMPLETED ACTION ON SOUTH AFRICAN
ISSUE, AT LEAST FOR TIME BEING, NOVEMBER 4 WITH ADOPTION
OF RESOLUTION 418 INSTITUTING MANDATORY ARMS EMBARGO ON
CONFIDENTIAL
CONFIDENTIAL

PAGE 02   STATE 264955

SOUTH AFRICA.

CONFIDENTIAL

DOCUMENT 9: Secretary Cyrus Vance, Cable for All African Diplomatic Posts, "Security Council Action on South Africa," November 5, 1977.

PAGE 2 OF 3

CONFIDENTIAL

2. DEPARTMENT APPRECIATES EXCELLENT WORK BY AFRICAN POSTS
IN BRINGING OUR POSITION TO ATTENTION OF HOST GOVERNMENTS
AND REQUESTING THEIR SUPPORT FOR COMPROMISE SOLUTION. WE
RECOGNIZE THAT EFFORTS OF AFRICAN POSTS IN CARRYING OUT
INSTRUCTIONS WERE COMPLICATED BY RAPIDLY-CHANGING SITUATION
IN NEW YORK AND DELAYS IN AVAILABILITY OF TEXTS OF VARIOUS
DOCUMENTS, BUT BELIEVE THESE EFFORTS CONTRIBUTED IMPORTANTLY
TO FAVORABLE OUTCOME.

3. IN VIEW FACT THAT SUPPORT OF AFRICAN STATES WILL BE
ESSENTIAL IN SECURING FURTHER SECURITY COUNCIL ACTION ON
RHODESIA AND ANY ACTION ON NAMIBIA, DEPARTMENT BELIEVES
WE SHOULD SEEK TO MINIMIZE NEGATIVE FALLOUT FROM UN DEBATE.
IN FURTHER DISCUSSIONS OF SECURITY COUNCIL ACTION WITH

OFFICIALS OF HOST GOVERNMENT, ACTION ADDRESSEES SHOULD
EMPHASIZE FACT THAT AFRICAN AND WESTERN COUNCIL MEMBERS
WERE ABLE TO REACH AGREEMENT ON COMPROMISE RESOLUTION,
WHICH FOR THE FIRST TIME IN HISTORY INVOKED CHAPTER VII
SANCTIONS AGAINST A MEMBER STATE. THIS ACTION BY US AND
OTHER WESTERN MEMBERS REPRESENTED MAJOR STEP TAKEN IN
COORDINATION WITH AFRICAN STATES.

4. IN DISCUSSING RESOLUTION POSTS SHOULD BE CAREFUL TO
AVOID INTERPRETING DOCUMENT, WHICH MAY IN PRACTICE BE
SUBJECT TO VARIOUS INTERPRETATIONS, BEYOND UNDERLINING
THAT ITS EFFECT IS TO IMPOSE A MANDATORY ARMS EMBARGO.
IN EVENT THAT AFRICAN OFFICIALS RAISE POSSIBILITY OF
FURTHER SANCTIONS, POSTS SHOULD AVOID COMMITMENT, POINTING
OUT THAT PRETORIA'S REACTION TO COUNCIL ACTION SHOULD BE
CAREFULLY STUDIED. IF QUESTION IS RAISED OF ESTABLISHMENT
CONFIDENTIAL
CONFIDENTIAL

PAGE 03   STATE 264955

OF SPECIAL COMMITTEE, AKIN TO EXISTING RHODESIAN SANCTIONS
COMMITTEE, TO MONITOR IMPLEMENTATION OF ARMS EMBARGO,
POSTS SHOULD STATE THAT WE DO NOT RPT NOT AT THIS TIME SEE
ANYNEED FOR SUCH A COMMITTEE. SECRETARY GENERAL HAS BEEN
REQUESTED IN RESOLUTION 418 TO REPORT TO THE COUNCIL NO
LATER THAN MAY 1, 1978 ON THE IMPLEMENTATION OF THE
RESOLUTION, AND THIS SHOULD BE SUFFICIENT TO MONITOR
COMPLIANCE WITH RESOLUTION.

5. POSTS SHOULD ALSO POINT OUT THAT UNITED STATES INTENDS

CONFIDENTIAL

DOCUMENT 9: Secretary Cyrus Vance, Cable for All African Diplomatic Posts, "Security Council Action on South Africa," November 5, 1977.

PAGE 3 OF 3

CONFIDENTIAL

TO GIVE IMMEDIATE EFFECT TO RESOLUTION WHICH IS LEGALLY
BINDING AND WILL BE IMPLEMENTED THROUGH THE NECESSARY
ADMINISTRATIVE ACTION. ALTHOUGH VOLUNTARY ARMS EMBARGO
HAS BEEN SCRUPULOUSLY OBSERVED TO DATE BY US, PURSUANT
TO NEW RESOLUTION WE WILL PERMIT NO MORE SALES OF SPARE
PARTS UNDER EXISTING CONTRACTS.

6. TEXT OF SECURITY COUNCIL RESOLUTION BEING TRANSMITTED
BY USUN. VANCE

CONFIDENTIAL

CONFIDENTIAL

DOCUMENT 10: Secretary George Shultz, Cable for CFR Collective, "Current Foreign Relations Issue No. 12," March 24, 1982 (relevant portion [paragraph 5] transcribed by the editors).

PAGE 1 OF 2

Department of State **TELEGRAM**

SECRET

AN: D820187-0474

SECRET

PAGE 01   STATE 078373
ORIGIN XREP-00

INFO OCT-00   ADS-00   /000 R

DRAFTED BY S/S-O:DASANDBERG:CL
APPROVED BY S/S-O:JOSTEMPEL
------------------266523 2422272 /34
R 2420632 MAR 82 ZEX
FM SECSTATE WASHDC
TO CFR COLLECTIVE
USICA WASHDC
SECDEF WASHDC 0000
USCINCSO QUARRY HTS CZ
USDOCOSOUTH NAPLES IT
USCINCEUR VAIHINGEN GE
USCINCRED MACDILL AFB
CINCLANT NORFOLK VA
CINCPAC HONOLULU HAWAII 0000
CINCUSAREUR HEIDLEBERG GE
CINCUSAFE RAMSTEIN AB
USNMR SHAPE BE

S E C R E T STATE 078373

CFR REPORT. INFORM CONSULS, CINC/SHAPE FOR POLANDS

E.O. 12065:ADS-4 3/24/82 (BREMER, L. PAUL, III)
TAGS: XX, US
SUBJECT:(U) CURRENT FOREIGN RELATIONS ISSUE NO. 12
--   MARCH 24, 1982

(U) TABLE OF CONTENTS

1. ARA - EL SALVADOR: FINAL WEEK OF
ELECTION CAMPAIGN
2. EUR - UNCERTAINTY FOR GOVERNING
COALITION IN WEST GERMANY
SECRET
SECRET
               — -

PAGE 02   STATE 078373

3. EUR - FRENCH DEPARTMENTAL COUNCIL

SECRET

DOCUMENT 10: Secretary George Shultz, Cable for CFR Collective, "Current Foreign Relations Issue No. 12," March 24, 1982 (relevant portion [paragraph 5] transcribed by the editors).

PAGE 2 OF 2

5. (U) AF—Revision of South African Trade Controls (GDS 3/24/88)

(U) Controls exercised under the Export Administration Act of 1979, including foreign policy controls on trade with South Africa, were revised and renewed March 1, 1982. The adjustments reflected in the new regulations make the South African trade controls less arbitrary from the perspective of US exporters while at the same time maintaining a strong symbolic and practical disassociation of the United States from the enforcement of apartheid in South Africa. The new regulations are in conformance with US obligations under the United Nations arms embargo of South Africa. They are at least as extensive as the military and apartheid-related trade controls maintained by the other major western nations.

(U) Under the regulations promulgated in 1978, there was a total ban on the export of any goods or technology to the South African military or police. Under the new regulations, there is a continued prohibition on the export of items controlled pursuant to the United Nations arms embargo on South Africa. Other proposed exports will be evaluated on a case-by-case basis and will be prohibited if the export would contribute significantly to military or police functions. A limited and carefully defined set of items (including food, non-military clothing and personal hygienic goods, certain industrial equipment and chemicals that are not used in the manufacture or maintenance of arms or related material; and certain office equipment) is exempted from this case-by-case review process and may be exported under general license.

(U) Under the old regulations governing non-military aircraft and computer sales to South Africa, exporters of aircraft were required to obtain written assurances from South African purchasers that the aircraft would not be used for police, military or paramilitary purposes. Under the new regulations, licences for the export of aircraft will be granted only on the condition that the aircraft will not be put to such use.

(C) Under the old regulations, all computer sales to South African government agencies were reviewed on a case-by-case basis to determine if the computer would be used to "enforce apartheid." The new regulations limit the computer control to the five government agencies (in addition to the military and police) that are primarily responsible for enforcing the apartheid system.

DOCUMENT 11: President Ronald Reagan, "Executive Order 12532—Prohibiting Trade and Certain Other Transactions Involving South Africa," September 9, 1985.

PAGE 1 OF 3

Executive Order 12532—Prohibiting Trade and Certain Other Transactions Involving South Africa
September 9, 1985

By the authority vested in me as President by the Constitution and laws of the United States of America, including the International Emergency Economic Powers Act (50 U.S.C. 1701 *et seq.*), the National Emergencies Act (50 U.S.C. 1601 *et seq.*), the Foreign Assistance Act (22 U.S.C. 2151 *et seq.*), the United Nations Participation Act (22 U.S.C. 287), the Arms Export Control Act (22 U.S.C. 2751 *et seq.*), the Export Administration Act (50 U.S.C. App. 2401 *et seq.*), the Atomic Energy Act (42 U.S.C. 2011 *et seq.*), the Foreign Service Act (22 U.S.C. 3901 *et seq.*), the Federal Advisory Committee Act (5 U.S.C. App. I), Section 301 of Title 3 of the United States Code, and considering the measures which the United Nations Security Council has decided on or recommended in Security Council Resolutions No. 418 of November 4, 1977, No. 558 of December 13, 1984, and No. 569 of July 26, 1985, and considering that the policy and practice of apartheid are repugnant to the moral and political values of democratic and free societies and run counter to United States policies to promote democratic governments throughout the world and respect for human rights, and the policy of the United States to influence peaceful change in South Africa, as well as the threat posed to United States interests by recent events in that country,

I, Ronald Reagan, President of the United States of America, find that the policies and actions of the Government of South Africa constitute an unusual and extraordinary threat to the foreign policy and economy of the United States and hereby declare a national emergency to deal with that threat.

Section 1. Except as otherwise provided in this section, the following transactions are prohibited effective October 11, 1985:

(a) The making or approval of any loans by financial institutions in the United States to the Government of South Africa or to entities owned or controlled by that Government. This prohibition shall enter into force on November 11, 1985. It shall not apply to (i) any loan or extension of credit for any educational, housing, or health facility which is available to all persons on a nondiscriminatory basis and which is located in a geographic area accessible to all population groups without any legal or administrative restriction; or (ii) any loan or extension of credit for which an agreement is entered into before the date of this Order.

The Secretary of the Treasury is hereby authorized to promulgate such rules and regulations as may be necessary to carry out this subsection. The initial rules and regulations shall be issued within sixty days. The Secretary of the Treasury may, in consultation with the Secretary of State, permit exceptions to this prohibition only if the Secretary of the Treasury determines that the loan or extension of credit will improve the welfare or expand the economic opportunities of persons in South Africa disadvantaged by the apartheid system, provided that no exception may be made for any apartheid enforcing entity.

(b) All exports of computers, computer software, or goods or technology intended to service computers to or for use by any of the following entities of the Government of South Africa:

(1) The military;

(2) The police;

(3) The prison system;

(4) The national security agencies;

(5) ARMSCOR and its subsidiaries or the weapons research activities of the Council for Scientific and Industrial Research;

(6) The administering authorities for the black passbook and similar controls;

(7) Any apartheid enforcing agency;

(8) Any local or regional government or "homeland" entity which performs any function of any entity described in paragraphs (1) through (7).

The Secretary of Commerce is hereby authorized to promulgate such rules and regulations as may be necessary to carry out this

DOCUMENT 11: President Ronald Reagan, "Executive Order 12532—Prohibiting Trade and Certain Other Transactions Involving South Africa," September 9, 1985.

PAGE 2 OF 3

subsection and to implement a system of end use verification to ensure that any computers exported directly or indirectly to South Africa will not be used by any entity set forth in this subsection.

(c)(1) Issuance of any license for the export to South Africa of goods or technology which are to be used in a nuclear production or utilization facility, or which, in the judgment of the Secretary of State, are likely to be diverted for use in such a facility; any authorization to engage, directly or indirectly, in the production of any special nuclear material in South Africa; any license for the export to South Africa of component parts or other items or substances especially relevant from the standpoint of export control because of their significance for nuclear explosive purposes; and any approval of retransfers to South Africa of any goods, technology, special nuclear material, components, items, or substances described in this section. The Secretaries of State, Energy, Commerce, and Treasury are hereby authorized to take such actions as may be necessary to carry out this subsection.

(2) Nothing in this section shall preclude assistance for International Atomic Energy Agency safeguards or IAEA programs generally available to its member states, or for technical programs for the purpose of reducing proliferation risks, such as for reducing the use of highly enriched uranium and activities envisaged by section 223 of the Nuclear Waste Policy Act (42 U.S.C. 10203) or for exports which the Secretary of State determines are necessary for humanitarian reasons to protect the public health and safety.

(d) The import into the United States of any arms, ammunition, or military vehicles produced in South Africa or of any manufacturing data for such articles. The Secretaries of State, Treasury, and Defense are hereby authorized to take such actions as may be necessary to carry out this subsection.

Sec. 2. (a) The majority of United States firms in South Africa have voluntarily adhered to fair labor principles which have benefitted those in South Africa who have been disadvantaged by the apartheid system. It is the policy of the United States to encourage strongly all United States firms in South Africa to follow this commendable example.

(b) Accordingly, no department or agency of the United States may intercede after December 31, 1985, with any foreign government regarding the export marketing activity in any country of any national of the United States employing more than 25 individuals in South Africa who does not adhere to the principles stated in subsection (c) with respect to that national's operations in South Africa. The Secretary of State shall promulgate regulations to further define the employers that will be subject to the requirements of this subsection and procedures to ensure that such nationals may register that they have adhered to the principles.

(c) The principles referred to in subsection (b) are as follows:

(1) Desegregating the races in each employment facility;

(2) Providing equal employment opportunity for all employees without regard to race or ethnic origin;

(3) Assuring that the pay system is applied to all employees without regard to race or ethnic origin;

(4) Establishing a minimum wage and salary structure based on the appropriate local minimum economic level which takes into account the needs of employees and their families;

(5) Increasing by appropriate means the number of persons in managerial, supervisory, administrative, clerical, and technical jobs who are disadvantaged by the apartheid system for the purpose of significantly increasing their representation in such jobs;

(6) Taking reasonable steps to improve the quality of employees' lives outside the work environment with respect to housing, transportation, schooling, recreation, and health;

(7) Implementing fair labor practices by recognizing the right of all employees, regardless of racial or other distinctions, to self-organization and to form, join, or assist labor organizations, freely and without penalty or reprisal, and recognizing the right to refrain from any such activity.

(d) United States nationals referred to in subsection (b) are encouraged to take rea-

DOCUMENT 11: President Ronald Reagan, "Executive Order 12532—Prohibiting Trade and Certain Other Transactions Involving South Africa," September 9, 1985.

PAGE 3 OF 3

sonable measures to extend the scope of their influence on activities outside the workplace, by measures such as supporting the right of all businesses, regardless of the racial character of their owners or employees, to locate in urban areas, by influencing other companies in South Africa to follow the standards specified in subsection (c) and by supporting the freedom of mobility of all workers, regardless of race, to seek employment opportunities wherever they exist, and by making provision for adequate housing for families of employees within the proximity of the employee's place of work.

Sec. 3. The Secretary of State and the head of any other department or agency of the United States carrying out activities in South Africa shall promptly take, to the extent permitted by law, the necessary steps to ensure that the labor practices described in section (2)(c) are applied to their South African employees.

Sec. 4. The Secretary of State and the head of any other department or agency of the United States carrying out activities in South Africa shall, to the maximum extent practicable and to the extent permitted by law, in procuring goods or services in South Africa, make affirmative efforts to assist business enterprises having more than 50 percent beneficial ownership by persons in South Africa disadvantaged by the apartheid system.

Sec. 5. (a) The Secretary of State and the United States Trade Representative are directed to consult with other parties to the General Agreement on Tariffs and Trade with a view toward adopting a prohibition on the import of Krugerrands.

(b) The Secretary of the Treasury is directed to conduct a study to be completed within sixty days regarding the feasibility of minting and issuing gold coins with a view toward expeditiously seeking legislative authority to accomplish the goal of issuing such coins.

Sec. 6. In carrying out their respective functions and responsibilities under this Order, the Secretary of the Treasury and the Secretary of Commerce shall consult with the Secretary of State. Each such Secretary shall consult, as appropriate, with other government agencies and private persons.

Sec. 7. The Secretary of State shall establish, pursuant to appropriate legal authority, an Advisory Committee on South Africa to provide recommendations on measures to encourage peaceful change in South Africa. The Advisory Committee shall provide its initial report within twelve months.

Sec. 8. The Secretary of State is directed to take the steps necessary pursuant to the Foreign Assistance Act and related legislation to (a) increase the amount of internal scholarships provided to South Africans disadvantaged by the apartheid system up to $8 million from funds made available for Fiscal Year 1986, and (b) increase the amount allocated for South Africa from funds made available for Fiscal Year 1986 in the Human Rights Fund up to $1.5 million. At least one-third of the latter amount shall be used for legal assistance for South Africans. Appropriate increases in the amounts made available for these purposes will be considered in future fiscal years.

Sec. 9. This Order is intended to express and implement the foreign policy of the United States. It is not intended to create any right or benefit, substantive or procedural, enforceable at law by a party against the United States, its agencies, its officers, or any person.

RONALD REAGAN

The White House,
September 9, 1985.

[*Filed with the Office of the Federal Register, 11:59 a.m., September 9, 1985*]

DOCUMENT 12: Ambassador Herman Nickel, Memorandum for Assistant Secretary of State Chester Crocker, "Our Public Diplomacy Initiative: The Theoretical Framework," August 26, 1985.

PAGE 1 OF 8

88 D138
By 4 939

United States Department of State

Washington, D.C. 20520

August 26, 1985

SECRET

TO: AF - Mr. Crocker

FROM: AF - Herman Nickel

SUBJECT: Our Public Diplomacy Initiative: The Theoretical
         Framework

DEPARTMENT OF STATE A/CDC/MR

REVIEWED by _____ DATE ___
( ) RELEASE   ( ) DECLASSIFY
( ) EXCISE   ( ) DECLASSIFY in PART
( ) DENY   ( ) Non-responsive info.
FOI, EO or PA exemptions _____
                              TS authority to:
( ) CLASSIFY as _____, OAI
( ) DOWNGRADE TS to ( ) S or ( ) C, OADR

The Problem

We have set as the broad objective of our southern African
public diplomacy effort the clarification and de-mythologizing
of our policy at home, in South Africa and elsewhere abroad.
Our major challenge is to change the terms of the public
debate, moving it beyond universal condemnation of apartheid
and ways of signaling American disapproval to the more
constructive question of how we can best use what influence we
have to help South Africans achieve a more just and stable
order--without fueling a tragic and destructive holocaust. To
change the terms of the debate, we need to engage a broader
range of American institutions to participate in the reform
process in South Africa and to move them with us in setting out
common principles and purposes, both here and in South Africa.

The Time Element

Our effort has both short-term and long-term aspects. The
likelihood of final Congressional action in the first half of
September means that the President faces a difficult decision
very soon. Our public diplomacy, therefore, must be organized
quickly so as to make it easier for the President to decide and
to provide persuasive answers to the questions of our eager
public at home, in South Africa and abroad. Looking beyond the
build-up to the decision and its immediate aftermath, we must
continue to build public understanding and support for the
President's decision and the continuity of our policy. There
is every possibility that violence and repression will continue
to be part of South Africa's future. The issue will not go
away and will trigger demands for additional action.
(Congressman Bill Gray has already served notice of this.)
This means that we will have to develop themes for the future
that will set out positive US involvement as "builders" and as
peacemakers, regionally and within South Africa itself, while
combatting misconceptions and misrepresentations of what we are
really about.

SECRET
OADR

DOCUMENT 12: Ambassador Herman Nickel, Memorandum for Assistant Secretary of State Chester Crocker, "Our Public Diplomacy Initiative: The Theoretical Framework," August 26, 1985.

PAGE 2 OF 8

<u>SECRET</u>

-2-

DECLASSIFIED

<u>Defining the Perception Gap</u>

Our critics have succeeded in putting across the simple, fallacious syllogism that, since apartheid is a crime against humanity, it must be punished and that economic sanctions are the best way of doing so. By implication, anyone who opposes punitive action condones the crime and is "soft on apartheid." Our protestations that our policy is designed to encourage the reform process and has in fact contributed to more change than South Africa has witnessed in decades is dismissed, because the stark images of repression have effectively blotted out the subtler story of reform. Moreover, every time we recite the evidence of change, we risk sounding like SAG apologists and invite our critics to cite all the remaining unresolved grievances--notably SAG's unwillingness to relinquish control and transfer power to the black majority. Anything less is dismissed as cosmetic and peripheral.

Some of our critics readily concede that the bills passed by Congress won't force the SAG to change course, but justify them as a tangible "message" of disapproval and disassociation, not only to satisfy important domestic constituencies, but also to let the black majority (and the rest of the world) know "where we stand." (This is also stated in terms of realpolitik as "getting on the winning side.")

Others believe and/or propagate exaggerated notions of the coercive leverage the United States could bring to bear to force apartheid to its knees. Among South African blacks, this feeds ever-present suspicions that, if only the mighty U.S. really wanted to, it could topple the apartheid system tomorrow and that the only reason it doesn't do so is its deep-down racist inhibitions. That is why anti-apartheid rhetoric and even practical programs to help the black victims of apartheid do little to wipe out black South African suspicions. The charges of our domestic critics that the Administration does not care about apartheid compound this problem.

References to South Africa as an "ally" and comments stressing the need to cope with rioting and terrorism rather than the causes of the unrest have further strengthened black perceptions that the President is "on the SAG's side." SABC references to the President as South Africa's "best friend" have reinforced this notion. Just as the charges of our domestic critics have an immediate feedback effect on South African black opinion, black South African attacks on CE become effective ammunition for our critics at home, especially when uttered by a Nobel laureate of charismatic talents who plays the U.S. media like a violin.

<u>SECRET</u>

DOCUMENT 12: Ambassador Herman Nickel, Memorandum for Assistant Secretary of State Chester Crocker, "Our Public Diplomacy Initiative: The Theoretical Framework," August 26, 1985.

PAGE 3 OF 8

<u>SECRET</u>

-3-

<u>Strategies</u>

A. Redefining the Moral Issue

We should proceed from the reality that South Africa is indeed a profound moral issue. Our job is to put across that we see it that way, too, and that we hold the moral high ground. In applied morality, it is not intentions which count--the road to hell is paved with them--but the foreseeable consequences of our actions. Mere expression of indignation is not a policy. Where that expression of indignation is translated into punitive steps, these become morally dubious if (1) they hurt most whom we are trying to help and (2) they make moving away from the evil we presume to punish more difficult. Is it justifiable to add to black suffering when there is no reasonable chance that it will accelerate peaceful change? Is it moral to contribute to further economic and political polarization (black anger and overexpectations on one hand and Boer truculence on the other)? Is it conscionable to stunt the growth of the South African economy (and thus the life potential of this and future generations of South Africans), especially in the light of the country's population explosion and its critical economic importance to the whole region? We must get across that washing our hands of the South African problem is a futile Pontius Pilate gesture and demolish the slogan that investing in South Africa is "investing in apartheid." (Investing in Alabama did not entrench Jim Crow--it helped destroy it.) We are a nation of builders--not destroyers.

B. Defining our National Interest in Southern African Stability

We must communicate that our approach to South Africa reflects not only American values but also important American interests. Right-of-center constituencies must understand why our concern for a more just order in South Africa (one resting on "the consent of the governed") is not just do-good sentimentality but a reflection of our hard-headed concern for stability in a key strategic region. By the same token, we must make clear to left-of-center constituencies that, when we speak of our national interest in South Africa, we do so in a way thoroughly consistent with our national values. To talk of strategic minerals, the Cape Route or the Soviet threat as if we relegated our moral opposition to apartheid to lower priority would be fatal with these constituencies. We must stress the need for regional security--and that we cannot play this role without being able to talk to all the players.

<u>SECRET</u>

DOCUMENT 12: Ambassador Herman Nickel, Memorandum for Assistant Secretary of State Chester Crocker, "Our Public Diplomacy Initiative: The Theoretical Framework," August 26, 1985.

PAGE 4 OF 8

SECRET

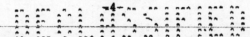

-4-

C. The Moral Nightmare of an Apocalyptic Scenario--Don't Play with Matches

Since change away from apartheid is inevitable, the critical question is <u>how</u> it comes. Our moral responsibility is to avoid anything that could fan the flames of a tragic holocaust. Only the Soviets thrive on conflict. We are peacemakers and have to play that role in South Africa, as we must do between South Africa and her neighbors. Regional security and the internal South African reform process go hand in hand.

D. We Believe in Self-Determination--South Africans have the Right to Work out their own Solutions

Just as our own racial problems had to be solved by Americans (and hardly overnight), so South Africans have the right to work out their own solutions. We cannot prescribe formulas for them, but we can urge them to start talking-- now--and to avoid action that will create obstacles to that process.

<u>Putting our Message Across</u>

<u>The role of the President</u>

The President is our most critical and valuable asset in our effort. Events have gone beyond the point where a routine Saturday radio broadcast is still an adequate instrument. A prime-time television address is the proper vehicle for the President to explain his views on the South African issue, in the context of his decision on the Congressional action (expectable by September 9). In keeping with the President's gifts at formulating issues simply and conveying sincerity and human decency, the speech:

-- Should be short, meaning about 7-10 minutes, 15 minutes at the outside.

-- Unequivocal in its total, unalterable rejection of apartheid, as something that runs against the grain of the President's <u>personal</u> as well as our American values.

-- A lucid explanation of his decision about the Congressional bill, <u>in terms of his anti-apartheid convictions</u>.

-- Emphasize that our talk is to help change South Africa, not punish it (especially that in "punishing" we hit the very

SECRET

DOCUMENT 12: Ambassador Herman Nickel, Memorandum for Assistant Secretary of State
Chester Crocker, "Our Public Diplomacy Initiative: The Theoretical Framework," August 26, 1985.

PAGE 5 OF 8

SECRET

-5-

people we want to help); that we are a nation of builders, not
destroyers, peacemakers and not match-throwers.

-- Sound a healing note: voice understanding for deep
feelings of our critics but plead not to let this issue divide
us when all decent Americans agree that apartheid is evil, but
also accept that a race war would be a tragedy in human terms
and in terms of our interests in stability in this important
region.

-- Reach out to the people of strife-torn South
Africa--express our compassion for the suffering and the just
aspirations of blacks; tell whites that we appreciate the
complexity of the problem but that the friendship we seek with
them also depends on their willingness to move towards a more
just South Africa in which racial domination gives way to
participation and cooperation by all.

-- Our understanding, from our own national experience,
that racial problems are not solved overnight and cannot be
solved by outsiders--that we must not delude ourselves that we
can determine the outcome of an internal political process in a
country 6,000+ miles away.

-- Our willingness, nevertheless, to do everything within
our power, however limited, to be builders (not destroyers),
peacemakers (not match-throwers)--emphasizing that this also
has a regional dimension and that peacemakers must be able to
talk to all sides, or become irrelevant.

-- An announcement that (besides sending our ambassador
back) the President will invite top leaders from business,
labor, education, religion to discuss practical ways of helping
South Africans build a more just society and to find peaceful
solutions. (The appointment of a Presidential Commission
remains an option worthy of further discussion).

-- End with an appeal for unity.

Administration Follow-Through

The Vice President, Secretary of State, and National
Security Adviser should follow through with press conferences
and/or backgrounders and, in due time, with speeches of their
own, in order to reinforce and further clarify the President's
message and addressing whatever questions may be raised in the
subsequent public debate. The Secretaries of Treasury and
Commerce may also be useful in this effort. Other State

SECRET

DOCUMENT 12: Ambassador Herman Nickel, Memorandum for Assistant Secretary of State Chester Crocker, "Our Public Diplomacy Initiative: The Theoretical Framework," August 26, 1985.

PAGE 6 OF 8

SECRET

-6-

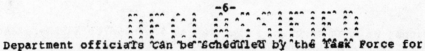

Department officials can be scheduled by the Task Force for media interviews, speeches, panel discussions, etc. throughout the country. There should be one-on-one sessions with key columnists and Washington correspondents. The Pretoria Embassy should call in correspondents filing for U.S. publications and networks.

Printed Materials

Going beyond the current State Department publications series, we will need to produce more attractive and readable materials; for example, a Q-and-A brochure that sets forth what Constructive Engagement is all about and answering our critics toughest questions.

P.V.O. and other Private Support

We should mobilize help from U.S. companies doing business in South Africa, notably the Sullivan Signatories, encouraging them to volunteer spokespersons who can tell the story of constructive contributions they have been making to community groups and on local television panels. Videos of such projects as the Pace School, housing projects and factory-floor integration would help.

Conservative groups are a valuable organizational resource. It is important to impress on them that the Administration is putting its case on the basis of our American belief in racial equality and peaceful solutions, not the subordination of these values to other considerations. (Strategic minerals are indeed of critical importance to us, but their production is jeopardized if South Africa cannot make peace with itself.) The U.S. needs a consensus, not further polarization on the South African issue. Service clubs, though they do not normally take political action, provide audiences that can be energized in support of the President's policy. We should identify public figures--academics, former government officials, politicians--who are prepared to take part in a process of public education on the South African issue and encourage them to write op-ed pieces and letters to the editors, appear on TV and other discussion panels.

We do not envisage concentrating on hostile audiences, such as university groups. We have no interest in providing lightning rods that will energize our opponents. Our main task is to persuade and activate the broad American center that has thus far been reluctant to become involved. With limited resources, we should avoid preaching to the converted, or those that will not be converted.

SECRET

DOCUMENT 12: Ambassador Herman Nickel, Memorandum for Assistant Secretary of State
Chester Crocker, "Our Public Diplomacy Initiative: The Theoretical Framework," August 26, 1985.

PAGE 7 OF 8

SECRET

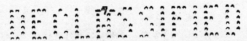

We need to focus special attention on decision-makers who
face pressure for "divestiture"--State legislators, university
trustees, trustees of pension funds, municipal leaders. They
will need information to strengthen their hand and resolve.
This is probably best achieved in quiet workshops.

Foreign Outreach

With the President's speech as the kick-off, our campaign
must also be used to combat misperceptions and
misrepresentations of our policy in South Africa, black Africa
and elsewhere.

A. South Africa

South African coverage of the President's speech will
require reinforcement and follow-through by way of:

-- VOA coverage.

-- Special embassy briefings (by ambassador, if
   possible) for key S.A. journalists, notably black
   editors.

-- Op-ed pieces or TV appearances by credible S.A.
   figures (Paton, Suzman, Schlemmer, Buthelezi, etc.)
   for U.S. media.

-- Announcement of new USG programs for the black
   community.

B. Black African Countries

Follow-through may include:

-- World net broadcasts

-- Meetings with Front Line African presidents in the
   context of the UNGA.

-- Calls on heads of state and governments by US
   ambassadors.

-- VOA broadcasts.

C. Western Allies

Since most of our major allies are concerned that the
disinvestment campaign should not spread to their

SECRET

DOCUMENT 12: Ambassador Herman Nickel, Memorandum for Assistant Secretary of State Chester Crocker, "Our Public Diplomacy Initiative: The Theoretical Framework," August 26, 1985.

PAGE 8 OF 8

SECRET

countries, they should be encouraged to restate their own opposition to disinvestment and sanctions, as a matter of mutual reinforcement. Continued opposition to punitive economic measures by key allies strengthens our position in our domestic debate.

AF:HNickel:bb
08/26/85 632-3218 2934E

SECRET

DOCUMENT 13: National Security Advisor Robert McFarlane, Memorandum for the Special Policy Group Principals, "Establishment of a Special South and Southern African Public Diplomacy Working Group," September 5, 1985.

PAGE 1 OF 2

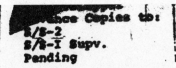

UNITED STATES SENSITIVE 00X6157

THE WHITE HOUSE   *SSWG*   SYSTEM II
90880

WASHINGTON

CONFIDENTIAL

September 5, 1985

DIST 9/6

URGE[N]

S
D
P
M
AF
PA
S/S
S/S-I

MEMORANDUM FOR THE SPG PRINCIPALS

SUBJECT: Establishment of a Special South and Southern
African Public Diplomacy Working Group (C)

As the result of consideration by the NSC regarding United States
policy in South and southern Africa, it is necessary to undertake
an immediate effort to design and implement a public diplomacy
program in the United States and abroad to gain understanding and
support for the Administration's policy toward southern Africa,
with emphasis on South Africa. (C)

The principles this Administration stands for in South and
southern Africa are clear. We seek to use the influence we have
to end apartheid peacefully but rapidly, achieve peace in Namibia
and in that context achieve a withdrawal of Cuban forces from
Angola, end cross border violence in the region, and limit Soviet
influence there. Because of our history, deep commitment to
racial justice and our national interests, we should play a role
in achieving racial understanding, justice, equality, and political participation by all in South Africa. Our international
prestige permits us to play a key role in advancing peace in the
region. To make a difference in these areas, this Administration
is determined to be involved and make a contribution. Our many
audiences need to understand this message. (C)

The public diplomacy strategy should have:

    -- a short term component which, in its first phase, will
develop themes, plan and carry out a domestic and international
public diplomacy strategy designed to explain our policy toward
the area;

    -- a component, particularly in the short term, to communi-
cate effectively with South African audiences; and

    -- a longer phase to build a broader base of understanding at
home and abroad, to involve more of our citizens and our institutions in promoting peaceful change in South Africa. (C)

The short term component coincides with final Congressional
action on a South African sanctions bill, continued anti-
apartheid demonstrations, and consideration of disinvestment
legislation by state and local governments. The longer range
phase would last at least through the end of 1986. (C)

Received in S/S-S

CONFIDENTIAL

DOCUMENT 13: National Security Advisor Robert McFarlane, Memorandum for the Special Policy Group Principals, "Establishment of a Special South and Southern African Public Diplomacy Working Group," September 5, 1985.

PAGE 2 OF 2

 CONFIDENTIAL

The effort will be undertaken under the authority of the Special Planning Group (SPG), which was designated under NSDD 77, and managed by the International Political Committee (IPC). (C)

I would like to note the fact that Secretary Shultz has named Ambassador Dave Miller to head the interagency South and Southern African Working Group. I ask the Secretary of State to obtain resources, staff and funds for this extremely important public diplomacy effort. All agencies represented on the SPG are requested to make available personnel and provide resources for this effort. Under the direction of the IPC, the Working Group should develop an integrated public diplomacy strategy to cover both our short and longer term objectives and report back to the SPG within three weeks. (C)

FOR THE PRESIDENT:

Robert C. McFarlane

DOCUMENT 14: National Security Decision Directive 187, "United States Policy Toward South Africa," September 7, 1985.

PAGE 1 OF 3

THE WHITE HOUSE
WASHINGTON

September 7, 1985

National Security Decision
Directive Number 187

UNITED STATES POLICY TOWARD SOUTH AFRICA

The United States and its allies have important political,
commercial, and strategic interests in South Africa. These are
being threatened by widespread violence and increased tension in
South Africa, and continued Soviet challenges to our important
interests in the area. At the same time, there has been growing
Congressional and public criticism of our policy despite our
active engagement and strong record of accomplishment during the
past four years. It is, therefore, now necessary to re-emphasize
the broad objectives of U.S. political strategy toward South
Africa which are:

-- Use U.S. influence to promote peaceful change away from
apartheid, to a system which provides justice and opportunity
for all with a government based on the consent of all its people;

-- Use U.S. influence to reduce the prospect of
revolutionary violence and the opportunities for expansion of
Soviet influence;

-- Encourage peace and coexistance between South Africa and
its neighbors, promoting policies which can enhance regional
stability and foster the benefits of democracy to all peoples of
South Africa and the region.

In order to achieve these objectives, the U.S. will remain
actively involved and pursue a comprehensive and coordinated
strategy toward South Africa. This strategy will consist of the
following specific elements:

-- Maintain close diplomatic communications including
Presidential messages, when appropriate, and quiet diplomacy,
to influence the actions of that government;

-- Make it clear to South Africa that our present
relationship can be sustained only in a framework of cooperation,
continued internal reform toward ending apartheid and with a
system of rule based on the consent of all governed;

-- Urge and apply pressure on South Africa to pursue the
course of reform energetically and without delay, to begin
genuine negotiations with the country's black leadership, and
take steps to redress black grievances;

SECRET
DECLASSIFY ON: OADR

Declassified/Released on 5-12-91
under provisions of E.O. 12356
by S. Tilley, National Security Council

(FS1-1435)

SECRET

[95]

DOCUMENT 14: National Security Decision Directive 187, "United States Policy Toward South Africa," September 7, 1985.

PAGE 2 OF 3

2

-- Expand contacts with representative black organizations
in South Africa and encourage them to pursue change by nonviolent
means;

-- Increase funding for education, labor, business, self-help
and human rights programs in South Africa aimed at improving
conditions for black Africans, and black awareness of U.S.
initiatives and policies;

-- Urge U.S. business entities in South Africa to continue
and to consolidate programs to improve the welfare of black
South African employees, to assist black-owned companies and to
use their influence to argue for change away from apartheid;

-- Combine the resources of the White House and the
Departments of State, Treasury and Commerce to oppose or
satisfactorily limit the imposition of new legislative sanctions
against South Africa;

-- Pursue negotiating possibilities offered by the
South African Government, including high level meetings,
as appropriate, to discuss internal developments; seek to
establish and maintain a cooperative framework for a relationship
based upon realistic appraisals of both achievable goals and U.S.
influence;

-- Review the possibilities of joint diplomatic efforts
with key Western allies to foster progress toward internal reform
and away from apartheid;

-- Continue U.S. efforts to work with South Africa and the IAEA
to safeguard South African nuclear facilities and obtain South
African adherence to the non-proliferation treaty.

Recent South African Government actions require more
forthright public diplomacy to create better public and media
understanding of our policies, especially our opposition to
apartheid and our encouragement of reform, and to broaden
both domestic and international support for them. Our
Public Diplomacy and Public Affairs strategy shall consist of
the following elements:

-- I, the Vice President, and other senior Administration
officials will make public statements or speeches when appropriate reflecting high-level concern over developments in South
Africa, explaining our principled opposition to apartheid, and
underscoring our commitment to promote peaceful, non-violent
change away from that system;

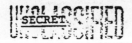

SECRET

DOCUMENT 14: National Security Decision Directive 187, "United States Policy Toward South Africa," September 7, 1985.

PAGE 3 OF 3

-- Mobilize a coordinated State Department-led public affairs strategy involving senior officials throughout government, including the White House Public Liaison Office, to explain and seek public understanding and support of our policies and of why punitive sanctions are counterproductive;

-- Under the leadership of USIA, engage in renewed and vigorous public diplomacy abroad to defend our policy and our long-term goals and carefully explain the explosive and unacceptable alternatives to peaceful change and continued U.S. engagement in South Africa;

-- In the United Nations and other international fora, actively promote understanding of U.S. policy; oppose new, international mandatory economic sanctions against South Africa;

-- Mobilize and coordinate U.S. mission outreach and USIA Visitor Programs in South Africa to promote human rights and constitutional reforms broadly acceptable to the parties inside South Africa; seek to move these key issues from the discussion to the agenda stage;

-- Work with non-governmental groups, including the National Endowment for Democracy and key private groups representing labor, business, and religious groups to help strengthen the democratic forces in South Africa.

DOCUMENT 15: State Department Memorandum, "Sustaining a Public Diplomacy Program on South Africa," October 1, 1985.

PAGE 1 OF 4

88 D138
By 4939

E11

R

United States Department of State
Washington, D.C. 20520

Secret/Sensitive

SUBJECT: Sustaining a Public Diplomacy Program on South Africa

As directed by your memorandum of September 5, a special working group has been established at the State Department to coordinate a strategy for gaining better public understanding and support of US policy toward South and southern Africa. It proposed a three-phase program in support of the objectives of NSDD-187:

1. An urgent, initial PR effort, closely coordinated with our efforts to prevent Congressional adoption of unhelpful legislation, to get an explanation of our policy to key leadership groups and audiences.

2. A medium-term program to strengthen Embassy Pretoria's ability to communicate effectively with audiences in South Africa through expanded political reporting, press and public outreach, and educational, human rights, and economic aid to black South Africans.

3. A long-term effort to build a broader base of domestic support by involving key American citizens and institutions in contacts with South African counterparts and programs for constructive, peaceful change in South Africa.

As noted in my interim report of September 16, we have already moved to implement the first phase through six major programs:

-- high-level briefings for key US leadership groups;

-- meetings with key media by senior US officials;

-- reaching out to media outlets outside Washington through a carefully crafted speaker program using US ambassadors to African countries;

-- working with targeted US institutions to help develop policies to deflect pressures for disinvestment;

-- carrying the message to important European and African governments and publics; and

-- increase activities within South Africa to gain more understanding of our policy among both whites and blacks.

DOCUMENT 15: State Department Memorandum, "Sustaining a Public Diplomacy Program on South Africa," October 1, 1985.

PAGE 2 OF 4

DECLASSIFIED

This strategy was discussed at a meeting of the IPC September 20. Other agencies were asked to comment. None have registered a disagreement. Through the Special Working Group, the State Department, USIA, and AID have developed a coordinated action plan detailed below to move into the medium- and long-term phases of this effort. Ambassador Miller will provide a briefing on these plans October 3 to a meeting of the SPG which will take up the issue of our longer-term objectives and the resources which will be required to accomplish them.

It is now clear that the Working Group should continue for at least one year. Funding and positions for a staff of seven professionals and two secretaries are being provided by USIA, DoD, and State.

The key to the success of this effort, however, lies in South Africa. It will be hard to win a public debate in the United States unless black leaders in that country moderate their public criticism and are drawn into cooperation with us on a range of programs which address shared interests and provide them with a reason for supporting our engagement. It is imperative that we do a better job in reaching out within South Africa with both more contact with the press and programs to provide more educational, human rights, and economic aid to black South Africans.

Measured against the capacity of developments in that country to damage US interests, our Embassy in South Africa is thinly stretched. We have dispatched on temporary duty one additional, senior press attache and an additional deputy political counselor whose primary responsibility will be liaison with black opposition groups. We are considering re-opening a consulate at Port Elizabeth, a center of recent and anticipated black unrest. Five additional positions are being considered to upgrade Embassy ability to meet two key demands: political reporting and analysis and administrative support.

USIA is responding to the call for enhanced programming activities within South Africa by improving outreach efforts to black journalists, entrepeneurs, industrial relations officers, trade unionists, and teachers. More exchange programs will be offered to disadvantaged South Africans from those fields. There will be an increase in the number of American lecturers in South African universities, and USIA plans to begin an undergraduate-level scholarship program in the US for South

DOCUMENT 15: State Department Memorandum, "Sustaining a Public Diplomacy Program on South Africa," October 1, 1985.

PAGE 3 OF 4

DECLASSIFIED

Over the long term, institutional linkages will be encouraged through grants to US universities seeking to exchange faculty and administrators with South African counterparts. The total exchange program for South Africa will double this next year, both in terms of numbers (297 grantees) and budget ($3,313,116). USIS staff in South Africa is expected to increase from 13 to 18 Americans and from 30 to 41 local employees. USIS South Africa's operating budget will increase from $1.993 million to $2.974 million to support an enhanced program.

Illustrative of the private-sector groups which will be used to forge more contacts with South African institutions is the National Endowment for Democracy.

AID proposes to step up programs in South Africa to benefit those disadvantaged by apartheid, an essential part of the strategy of constructive engagement. In order to comply with the President's Executive Order of September 9, which included a commitment by the President that $8 million would be spent on educational aid, it will be necessary to increase AID's FY 1986 budget for South Africa from $14 million to $17 million. Two additional local-hire positions will be needed to administer increased programs. AID believes a supplemental appropriation may be necessary. If so, it plans to ask for an additional $15 million in aid to black-ruled countries near South Africa which could be harmed by sanctions.

AID's proposals for in-country programs include:

Scholarships: $4 million to bring 116 black South African students to 50 US universities in 1984. Increase to $x million.

Bursaries: New program signed September 26 to give $x million for back scholarships to universities inside South Africa. Students will choose whether to attend all-black universities or those universities attempting to desegregate.

Human rights: Fund will provide $1 million to support legal and humanitarian actions by South African human rights groups.

Additional programs will train black labor leaders and small business entrepeneurs to take advantage of the gradual reduction of apartheid barriers to black activity; support self-help efforts by black communities; and provide block-grant support to multiracial institutions in South Africa which work effectively for peaceful change.

DOCUMENT 15: State Department Memorandum, "Sustaining a Public Diplomacy Program on South Africa," October 1, 1985.

PAGE 4 OF 4

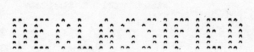

Though not a member of the working group, Commerce supports this strategy and recommends developing initiatives to encourage greater US contact with black business leaders in South Africa, including stepped-up US private and official purchases from non-white business groups.

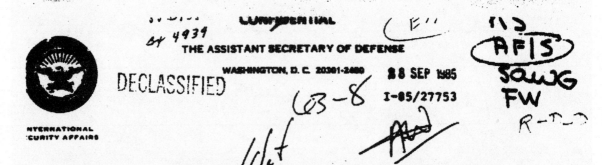

84 4939

CONFIDENTIAL

THE ASSISTANT SECRETARY OF DEFENSE

WASHINGTON, D.C. 20301-2400

DECLASSIFIED

28 SEP 1985

I-85/27753

INTERNATIONAL SECURITY AFFAIRS

MEMORANDUM FOR ASSISTANT SECRETARY OF STATE CHESTER A. CROCKER

SUBJECT: South Africa Public Diplomacy (U)

(U) I have reviewed the efforts/accomplishments of Dave Miller's South Africa Working Group (SAWG) and am impressed with the fine job they have done in crafting an immediate public diplomacy counter offensive. This effort has my full support. I will be happy to speak before appropriate audiences in support of the effort and look forward to SAWG ideas on building the speech.

(U) I have asked the Assistant Secretary of Defense for Public Affairs, Robert Sims, to detail a Public Affairs officer (0-5) to serve as executive assistant to the SAWG. It is our understanding that this assignment will be for an initial period of six months. Further, my Africa Region has contacted the Policy Support office, which is the Pentagon organization charged with NSDD 77 Public Diplomacy efforts, and asked them to develop detailed suggestions concerning your proposed PA strategy. (The point of contact there is Mr. Irwin Kern; he will be contacting you separately with comments from their perspective.)

(C) Three initial suggestions: first, if not yet considered, we recommend engaging State's Soviet Active Measures Working Group on those aspects which fall within its responsibilities; second, Julius Becton's Africa Famine Relief task force has a JCS paper on countering Soviet Disinformation in Africa which might be useful in the same context (we are putting an officer there to help);

(U) My points of contact on this are Jim Woods (697-2864) and Berry McConnell (697-8824).

RICHARD L. ARMITAGE
Assistant Secretary of Defense
(International Security Affairs)

DECLASSIFIED

CONFIDENTIAL

DOCUMENT 17: Assistant Secretary Chester Crocker, Action Memorandum for Secretary George Shultz, "U.S. Corporate Council on South Africa," October 24, 1985.

PAGE 1 OF 2

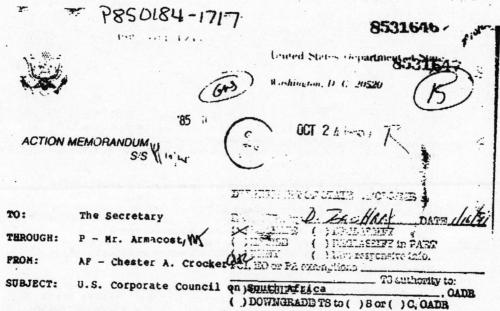

P85 0184-1717

8531646

United States Department of State

Washington, D.C. 20520

'85

OCT 24

ACTION MEMORANDUM
S/S

TO: The Secretary

THROUGH: P - Mr. Armacost,

FROM: AF - Chester A. Crocker

SUBJECT: U.S. Corporate Council on South Africa

ISSUE FOR DECISION

Whether to send the attached letters (Tab 1) to Roger Smith and Mike Blumenthal commending formation of a U.S. Corporate Council on South Africa and suggesting that its efforts be coordinated with the Department's public diplomacy program on South Africa.

ESSENTIAL FACTORS

One of the key suggestions made at your September 16 White House meeting on South Africa with U.S. corporate CEO's was that a "U.S. Corporate Council on South Africa" be formed to coordinate business efforts to resist divestment and promote reform.

The Council has now been formally launched. Co-chairmen will be Roger Smith of General Motors and Mike Blumenthal of Burroughs.

One of the Council's first actions has been to place full-page advertisements in major U.S. newspapers aligning it firmly with South African business groups in urging Pretoria to move more rapidly away from apartheid (Tab 2). Roger Smith, the driving force behind the Council, asked that the ad be brought to your attention. He and Blumenthal are grateful for your support and anxious to coordinate their efforts with our public diplomacy effort on South Africa.

DOCUMENT 17: Assistant Secretary Chester Crocker, Action Memorandum for Secretary George Shultz, "U.S. Corporate Council on South Africa," October 24, 1985.

PAGE 2 OF 2

- 2 -

Smith appeared on television October 21 to discuss the Council. In response to his request, we provided him with copies of our October 18 press statement commending the Council's initiative (Tab 3).

Also raised at the September 16 meeting (by James Burke of Johnson & Johnson) was a proposal that U.S. corporations operating in South Africa spend $100 million on a 2- to 3-year program of increased affirmative action and community outreach there. This dovetails well with our encouragement of U.S. institutions to commit resources to constructive, long-term programs to increase educational and economic opportunities for black South Africans.

The Corporate Council may be the best body to coordinate any such business effort. The letters at Tab 1 praise Smith and Blumenthal for getting the Council off the ground, remind them of the $100 million "offer," and suggest that we work closely with them through the Special Working Group on South and southern Africa Public Diplomacy.

RECOMMENDATION

That you sign the attached letters.

Attachments:
1. Letters to Roger Smith and Mike Blumenthal
2. Advertisement by U.S. Corporate Council on SA
3. Department press statement

DOCUMENT 18: Executive Secretary Nicholas Platt, Memorandum for Vice President's National Security Advisor Donald Gregg, "Public Diplomacy on South Africa: Involving U.S. Professional Groups in Dialogue and Change," November 5, 1985.

PAGE 1 OF 2

P860037-2226

'85 NOV -5 PM 22

S/S 8532349
United States Department of State

Washington, D.C. 20520

November 5, 1985

MEMORANDUM FOR MR. DONALD GREGG
THE WHITE HOUSE

Copies to
S
D
P
S/S
S/S-S
Tmb
AF
INR
PA
S/P
rf
(Chs)

Subject: Public Diplomacy on South Africa: Involving U.S.
          Professional Groups in Dialogue and Change

An important aspect of our strategy for increasing public support for U.S. policy toward South Africa is to expand the number of Americans who take a participatory interest in this issue. By broadening the base of those debating how to deal with apartheid, we dilute immoderate views and gain appreciation for the complex factors which our policy must address. At the same time, by encouraging Americans to grapple with the underlying problems of black poverty, illiteracy and discrimination, we may persuade them to view change in South Africa as a process which requires a sustained and positive U.S. involvement, rather than a situation calling for symbolic, one-time gestures, or a negative approach.

As part of this strategy, we would like to encourage U.S. institutions to forge links with counterpart organizations among the various racial groups in South Africa to work together for change. In addition to university-to-university, church-to-church, and business-to-business links, we have in mind encouraging professional organizations such as the ABA, AMA, and others to explore such contacts. By exchanging personnel, ideas, and experience, members of both the U.S. and South African organizations would gain a better understanding of the process of change, and our appropriate role in it, while at the same time strengthening moderate forces in South Africa.

Ambassador David Miller of the South Africa Working Group raised informally with you the idea of a meeting in the Roosevelt Room at which Vice President Bush might raise this idea with representatives of professional groups. I encourage this approach. We have asked our Embassy in South Africa to suggest credible institutions or groups in South Africa with which they might be paired. The following are representative of the U.S. groups we have in mind:

-- American Bar Association
-- American Society for Public Administration
-- American Council of Young Political Leaders
-- American Council for Advancement of Human Rights
-- American Medical Association
-- American Society for Training and Development
-- American Association of Black Women Entrepreneurs
-- The Young Presidents Organization

CONFIDENTIAL
OADR

DOCUMENT 18: Executive Secretary Nicholas Platt, Memorandum for Vice President's National Security Advisor Donald Gregg, "Public Diplomacy on South Africa: Involving U.S. Professional Groups in Dialogue and Change," November 5, 1985.

PAGE 2 OF 2

CONFIDENTIAL
-2-

The Vice President's message would be a challenge to these groups to become involved in active and constructive change away from apartheid toward the values we and they support. We sense a strong public desire to hear this kind of positive message from the Administration on South Africa, and recommend that the Vice President take the lead in presenting it to these key citizen groups.

Nicholas Platt
Executive Secretary

Drafted: SA/WG:KMcCormick
10/30/85, 632-6545, 0152Z

Clearance:

AF - CACrocker f. CAC
AF - FWisner
AF/S - JDavidow JD
P - GHelman GH

CONFIDENTIAL

DOCUMENT 19: Secretary George Shultz, Cable for All OECD Capitals, "Text of Report to Congress on U.S. Multilateral Measures to Dismantle Apartheid," April 4, 1987.

PAGE 1 OF 5

BELLAMY VERNELL P   08/04/88 094300   PRINTER: VL
87 STATE 100300
                    UNCLASSIFIED

UNCLASSIFIED
PAGE 01   STATE 100300
ORIGIN AF-00
INFO LOG-00   COPY-71 ADS-00 FUB-00 OIC-02 EB-08   P-01
      IO-19   HA-09   L-03   PA-02   SP-02   OIG-01 /048 P
DRAFTED BY: AF/S:FDBENJAMINSON W2331F
APPROVED BY: AF/S:EGLANPHER
AF/S:AWILLS   L/AF:LCLARIZIO
AF/P:NMORGAN
------------------------------115333 040555Z /22

P 040325Z APR 87 ZEX
FM SECSTATE WASHDC
TO ALL OECD CAPITALS PRIORITY
NAMIBIA COLLECTIVE
AMCONSUL DURBAN PRIORITY
UNCLAS STATE 100300
CAPE TOWN ALSO FOR EMBASSY
E.O. 12356: N/A
TAGS: PREL, SF
SUBJECT: TEXT OF REPORT TO CONGRESS ON U.S. MULTILATERAL
MEASURES TO DISMANTLE APARTHEID
1. FOLLOWING IS TEXT OF REPORT TO CONGRESS MANDATED
UNDER SECTION 401(B)(2)(A) OF THE COMPREHENSIVE
ANTI-APARTHEID ACT OF 1986. REPORT WAS SENT TO CONGRESS
ON APRIL 2. POSTS ARE WELCOME TO DISTRIBUTE THE REPORT
AS THEY FEEL APPROPRIATE.
2. BEGIN TEXT. REPORT PURSUANT TO SECTION 401(B)(2)(A)
OF THE COMPREHENSIVE ANTI-APARTHEID ACT OF 1986: U.S.
EFFORTS TO NEGOTIATE MULTILATERAL MEASURES TO DISMANTLE
APARTHEID. SECTION 401(B)(2)(A) OF THE COMPREHENSIVE
ANTI-APARTHEID ACT OF OCTOBER 2, 1986 (P.L. 99-440), AS
AMENDED, PROVIDES THAT THE PRESIDENT SHALL SUBMIT A
UNCLASSIFIED
UNCLASSIFIED
PAGE 02   STATE 100300
REPORT TO CONGRESS CONTAINING A DESCRIPTION OF U.S.
EFFORTS TO NEGOTIATE MULTILATERAL MEASURES TO BRING ABOUT
THE COMPLETE DISMANTLING OF APARTHEID. IN EXECUTIVE
ORDER 12571 OF OCTOBER 27, 1986, THE PRESIDENT DIRECTED
THE SECRETARY OF STATE TO IMPLEMENT THIS REQUIREMENT.
THE FOLLOWING INFORMATION IS SUBMITTED PURSUANT TO THESE

REQUIREMENTS. A SEPARATE REPORT WILL BE FURNISHED
PURSUANT TO SECTION 401(B)(2)(B) AND SECTION 506(A) OF
THE ACT ON THE RELATIONS BETWEEN OTHER INDUSTRIALIZED
DEMOCRACIES AND SOUTH AFRICA AND ON ECONOMIC AND OTHER
MEASURES ADOPTED BY OTHER COUNTRIES TO INFLUENCE THE
DISMANTLING OF APARTHEID.
     THE UNITED STATES HAS BEEN AND CONTINUES TO BE
ENGAGED IN SUBSTANTIVE DISCUSSIONS WITH BOTH ITS OECD
PARTNERS AND WITH OTHER NATIONS CONCERNING POSSIBLE
MULTILATERAL STEPS TO BRING ABOUT AN END TO APARTHEID.
                    UNCLASSIFIED   /   PAGE   1

DOCUMENT 19: Secretary George Shultz, Cable for All OECD Capitals, "Text of Report to Congress on U.S. Multilateral Measures to Dismantle Apartheid," April 4, 1987.

PAGE 2 OF 5

BELLAMY VERNELL P   08/04/88 094300   PRINTER: VL
87 STATE 100300
                    UNCLASSIFIED
WE HAVE COMMITTED OURSELVES TO A CONTINUING DIPLOMATIC
EFFORT -- BOTH BILATERALLY AND MUTILATERALLY -- TO HELP
CREATE A POLITICAL FRAMEWORK IN WHICH NEGOTIATIONS CAN
BEGIN IN SOUTH AFRICA. THIS DIPLOMATIC EFFORT HAS
INCLUDED NUMEROUS HIGH-LEVEL EXCHANGES BOTH HERE AND
ABROAD. FOR EXAMPLE, BOTH SECRETARY OF STATE SHULTZ AND
UNDER SECRETARY OF STATE ARMACOST RECENTLY TRAVELLED TO
AFRICA, AT WHICH TIMES THEY ENGAGED IN SERIOUS
DISCUSSIONS CONCERNING OUR SOUTH AFRICAN POLICY.
   IN OUR CONTINUING DIPLOMATIC EFFORTS WITH OUR
ALLIES AND THE KEY PARTIES IN SOUTH AND SOUTHERN AFRICA,
U.S. OFFICIALS HAVE FOCUSED PARTICULAR ATTENTION ON THE
QUESTION OF HOW TO ACHIEVE A RESUMPTION OF GENUINE REFORM
EFFORTS AND, MOST IMPORTANTLY, AN OPENING FOR NEGOTIATION
BETWEEN THE SOUTH AFRICAN GOVERNMENT AND OPPOSITION
UNCLASSIFIED
UNCLASSIFIED
PAGE 03   STATE 100300
LEADERS. IN OUR EXPANDED CONTACTS ACROSS THE SOUTH
AFRICAN POLITICAL SPECTRUM, WE SEEK TO UNDERSCORE THE
FUTILITY OF VIOLENCE IN THE SOUTH AFRICAN CONTEXT AND TO
CHALLENGE KEY PARTIES TO REVIEW WHAT CONTRIBUTION EACH

CAN MAKE TO CREATE A CLIMATE CONDUCIVE TO THE BEGINNING
OF NEGOTIATIONS. THESE THEMES HAVE BEEN AT THE CORE OF
THE CONTINUING DIALOGUE OF THE SECRETARY, OTHER SENIOR
DEPARTMENT OFFICIALS, AND AMBASSADOR PERKINS AND HIS
COLLEAGUES WITH KEY PARTIES IN SOUTH AFRICA. BELIEVING
AS WE DO THAT NEGOTIATION IS THE BEST AND QUICKEST ROUTE
TO BUILDING A POST-APARTHEID SOUTH AFRICA, WE HAVE
MAINTAINED ACTIVE EXCHANGES WITH OUR ALLIES ABOUT HOW WE
AND THEY CAN BEST ENCOURAGE SOUTH AFRICANS TO FOCUS ON A
POSITIVE, DEMOCRATIC POST-APARTHEID FUTURE. IN THIS
REGARD, OUR ALLIED DIPLOMACY HAS BEEN PARTICULARLY
FOCUSED ON IDENTIFYING THE KEY CONDITIONS THAT WOULD
CREATE A BETTER CLIMATE FOR NEGOTIATION AND WHAT EACH OF
US CAN DO TO HELP BRING ABOUT THOSE CONDITIONS, AS WELL
AS THE KEY QUESTION OF HOW TO ENSURE THAT THE POLITICAL
AND ECONOMIC SYSTEM THAT SUCCEEDS APARTHEID WILL MEET THE
DEMOCRATIC ASPIRATIONS OF ALL SOUTH AFRICANS.
   IN RECENT MONTHS, SENIOR STATE DEPARTMENT
OFFICIALS HAVE TRAVELLED TO LONDON, BONN, PARIS, ROME,
BRUSSELS, THE HAGUE, TOKYO, AND LISBON FOR CONSULTATIONS
WITH KEY ALLIES ON POLICY TOWARD SOUTH AND SOUTHERN
AFRICA. SIMILAR CONSULTATIONS HAVE BEEN HELD IN
WASHINGTON WITH SENIOR OFFICIALS OF THE CANADIAN AND
ISRAELI GOVERNMENTS, AMONG OTHERS. THE ISSUE OF
APPROPRIATE INTERNATIONAL MEASURES, INCLUDING SANCTIONS,
HAS BEEN AN IMPORTANT PART OF THESE DISCUSSIONS. AID
ADMINISTRATOR PETER MCPHERSON ATTENDED THE SOUTHERN
AFRICAN DEVELOPMENT COORDINATION CONFERENCE (SADCC)
ANNUAL MEETING IN BOTSWANA IN FEBRUARY. HE UNVEILED THE
                UNCLASSIFIED   /

PAGE   2

DOCUMENT 19: Secretary George Shultz, Cable for All OECD Capitals, "Text of Report to Congress on U.S. Multilateral Measures to Dismantle Apartheid," April 4, 1987.

PAGE 3 OF 5

BELLAMY VERNELL P   08/04/88 094300   PRINTER: VL
87 STATE 100300
                         UNCLASSIFIED

ADMINISTRATION'S PROPOSED MULTI-YEAR AID PACKAGE TO
SOUTHERN AFRICA, AND DISCUSSED MULTILATERAL POLICY WITH
UNCLASSIFIED
UNCLASSIFIED
PAGE 04   STATE 100300
THE FRONT-LINE STATES (FLS) AND WITH OECD REPRESENTATIVES
AT THE CONFERENCE. THE STATE DEPARTMENT HAS ALSO
CONSULTED CLOSELY WITH THE DIPLOMATIC CORPS HERE IN
WASHINGTON REGARDING THESE ISSUES.
    ON THESE VARIOUS OCCASIONS, ADMINISTRATION
REPRESENTATIVES HAVE EXPLAINED BOTH U.S. SANCTIONS AND
ASSISTANCE MEASURES, INCLUDING THOSE MEASURES COVERED IN
THE COMPREHENSIVE ANTI-APARTHEID ACT. WE HAVE EXPLAINED
THAT THE PRESIDENT HAS DIRECTED ALL AFFECTED AGENCIES TO
TAKE ALL STEPS NECESSARY, CONSISTENT WITH THE
CONSTITUTION, TO IMPLEMENT THE REQUIREMENTS OF THE ACT.
WE HAVE MADE CLEAR OUR COMMITMENT TO IMPLEMENT THESE
REQUIREMENTS FULLY AND FAITHFULLY.
    DURING THESE DISCUSSIONS, WE HAVE ALSO OUTLINED
OUR AID PROGRAMS IN SOUTH AFRICA AND IN THE REGION.
THESE INCLUDE THE INITIATIVE FOR REGIONAL ECONOMIC
PROGRESS ANNOUNCED AT THE SADCC CONFERENCE IN FEBRUARY.
IN INCREASING ASSISTANCE TO THE BLACK-RULED STATES OF
SOUTHERN AFRICA, THE U.S. AND ITS OECD ALLIES ARE WORKING
TO CREATE A SOUND, COORDINATED BASIS FOR A POST-APARTHEID
REGION -- A SOUTHERN AFRICA WHERE CONTINUED ECONOMIC
PROGRESS CONTRIBUTES TO AN ENVIRONMENT IN WHICH DEMOCRACY
AND RESPECT FOR FUNDAMENTAL HUMAN RIGHTS CAN FLOURISH.
IN DEVELOPING ITS "INITIATIVE FOR ECONOMIC PROGRESS" IN
SOUTHERN AFRICA, THE ADMINISTRATION CONSULTED CLOSELY
WITH THE EUROPEANS AND JAPANESE ON ASSISTANCE PROGRAMS
ALREADY IN PLACE, AND ON AREAS WHERE ENHANCED DONOR
EFFORTS --BOTH INDIVIDUAL AND COLLECTIVE-- COULD BEAR
FRUIT. THE AREAS SINGLED OUT FOR INCREASED U.S.
INVOLVEMENT --SUPPORT FOR PRIVATE SECTOR-ORIENTED POLICY
REFORMS, PROMOTION OF INTERREGIONAL TRADE AND INVESTMENT,
UNCLASSIFIED
UNCLASSIFIED
PAGE 05   STATE 100300

AND BACKING OF CERTAIN PRIORITY REGIONAL TRANSPORT
PROJECTS-- COMPLEMENT THE PROGRAMS AND PROJECTS OF OTHER
WESTERN DONORS IN A CONCERTED APPROACH TO THE REGION'S
DEVELOPMENT NEEDS.
    WE HAVE ALSO EXPLAINED OUR COMMITMENT TO ASSISTING
SOUTH AFRICANS DISADVANTAGED BY APARTHEID, AND ENCOURAGED
OUR ALLIES TO MAKE FURTHER EFFORTS IN THIS AREA. AMONG
ALL NATIONS, THE UNITED STATES HAS PIONEERED THE
ESTABLISHMENT OF POSITIVE MEASURES IN SOUTH AFRICA. WE
REGARD OUR GROWING AID PROGRAMS AS A NECESSARY COMPLEMENT
TO RESTRICTIVE MEASURES AIMED AGAINST APARTHEID. OUR
POSITIVE PROGRAMS CONTINUE TO SET THE PACE AMONG ALL
              UNCLASSIFIED   /   PAGE   3

DOCUMENT 19: Secretary George Shultz, Cable for All OECD Capitals, "Text of Report to Congress on U.S. Multilateral Measures to Dismantle Apartheid," April 4, 1987.

PAGE 4 OF 5

BELLAMY VERNELL P   08/04/88 094300   PRINTER: VL
87 STATE 100300
                    UNCLASSIFIED
NATIONS. IT IS OUR GOAL TO HELP VICTIMS OF APARTHEID TO
ATTAIN AN INCREASED SHARE OF THEIR NATION'S ECONOMIC
REWARDS AND PREPARE THEMSELVES FOR THE INEVITABLE DAY
WHEN THEY PARTICIPATE FULLY IN THE GOVERNANCE OF THEIR
COUNTRY.
    SECTION 401 OF THE ACT ALSO AUTHORIZES THE
PRESIDENT TO NEGOTIATE CERTAIN INTERNATIONAL AGREEMENTS
THAT COULD RESULT IN MODIFICATIONS OF THE ACT IF THEY ARE
APPROVED BY JOINT RESOLUTION. IT PROVIDES THAT SUCH
AGREEMENTS SHOULD BE NEGOTIATED WITHIN SIX MONTHS. IT
ALSO RECOMMENDS THAT AN INTERNATIONAL CONFERENCE BE
CONVENED FOR THIS PURPOSE. THE LEGISLATIVE HISTORY OF
SECTION 401 CONFIRMS THAT THIS PROVISION IS PORTATORY AND
NOT MANDATORY (EXCEPT WITH REGARD TO THE REPORTING
REQUIREMENTS) AND THAT IT WAS LARGELY DESIGNED TO
ESTABLISH A SPECIFIC PROCEDURE TO MODIFY THE ACT IF THE
PRESIDENT CHOSE TO RELY ON THE AUTHORITY CONTAINED IN
THIS SECTION.
    THE PRESIDENT HAS THE INHERENT AUTHORITY UNDER THE

CONSTITUTION TO NEGOTIATE INTERNATIONAL AGREEMENTS AND
COULD CONSEQUENTLY NEGOTIATE AGREEMENTS DEALING WITH
UNCLASSIFIED
UNCLASSIFIED
PAGE 06   STATE 100300
SOUTH AFRICA WITHOUT INVOKING THE AUTHORITY IN SECTION
401. IT IS ALSO CLEAR THAT THE PRESIDENT COULD PROPOSE
LEGISLATION TO REPEAL OR MODIFY THE MEASURES CONTAINED IN
THE ACT WITHOUT RELYING ON THE PROVISIONS ESTABLISHED FOR
THIS PURPOSE IN SECTION 401. SECTION 401 IN EFFECT
ESTABLISHES AN EXPEDITED CONGRESSIONAL PROCEDURE FOR THE
CONSIDERATION OF A JOINT RESOLUTION THAT COULD RESULT IN
SUCH CHANGES TO THE ACT.
    THE ADMINISTRATION HAS GIVEN CAREFUL CONSIDERATION
TO THE RECOMMENDATIONS MADE IN SECTION 401. WE TOOK INTO
ACCOUNT THE STATED PURPOSES OF THIS PROVISION AND THE
AGREEMENTS CONTEMPLATED AS WELL AS THE PRACTICAL
DIFFICULTIES INHERENT IN PROPOSING AND NEGOTIATING SUCH
AGREEMENTS (A CONCERN VOICED ON THE SENATE FLOOR AT THE
TIME THE PROVISION WAS CONSIDERED). THE DEPARTMENT TOOK
INTO ACCOUNT THE STRICT STANDARDS ESTABLISHED FOR SUCH
AGREEMENTS (I.E., REQUIREMENTS BASED ON THE NET ECONOMIC
EFFECT OF CERTAIN SANCTIONS). WE HAVE CONCLUDED THAT
THERE WOULD BE NO PRACTICAL BENEFIT AT THIS TIME IN
INVOKING THE CUMBERSOME AND COMPLEX PROCEDURES
ESTABLISHED IN THIS SECTION.
    ACCORDINGLY, THE IMPORTANT ISSUE REMAINS THE
IDENTIFICATION OF THOSE BILATERAL AND MULTILATERAL
MEASURES WHICH ARE LIKELY TO INFLUENCE THE SOUTH AFRICAN
GOVERNMENT TO ABANDON APARTHEID. IN ADDITION TO THE
BILATERAL DISCUSSIONS REFERRED TO ABOVE, WE HAVE
ADDRESSED WHAT MEASURES WOULD BE APPROPRIATE IN THE U.N.
                  UNCLASSIFIED   PAGE   4

DOCUMENT 19: Secretary George Shultz, Cable for All OECD Capitals, "Text of Report to Congress on U.S. Multilateral Measures to Dismantle Apartheid," April 4, 1987.

PAGE 5 OF 5

BELLAMY VERNELL P   08/04/88 094300   PRINTER: VL
87 STATE 100300
                          UNCLASSIFIED

CONTEXT. FOR EXAMPLE, ON OCTOBER 28, 1986, WE VOTED IN
FAVOR OF A SECURITY COUNCIL RESOLUTION TO STRENGTHEN THE
ARMS EMBARGO. WE DECIDED THAT THE MEASURES CONTEMPLATED
UNCLASSIFIED
UNCLASSIFIED
PAGE 07   STATE 100300
IN THAT U.N. RESOLUTION WERE CAREFULLY FOCUSED ON
IMPROVING ENFORCEMENT OF THIS SIGNIFICANT EMBARGO AND A
CONSENSUS DEVELOPED AMONG OUR ALLIES TO SUPPORT THE
RESOLUTION.
    ON THE OTHER HAND, WE VOTED AGAINST ADDITIONAL
MANDATORY INTERNATIONAL SANCTIONS AGAINST SOUTH AFRICA IN
THE U.N. SECURITY COUNCIL. IN TAKING THIS DECISION, WE
WERE ALIGNED WITH BOTH THE UNITED KINGDOM AND THE FEDERAL
REPUBLIC OF GERMANY. DURING THE PAST YEAR, NATIONAL
SANCTIONS IMPOSED BY MANY COUNTRIES (INCLUDING THE U.S.)
HAVE BEEN STRENGTHENED. NEVERTHELESS, WE CONTINUE TO
BELIEVE THAT IT WOULD BE A MISTAKE TO AGREE TO THE
IMPOSITION OF MANDATORY MULTILATERAL SANCTIONS BY THE
U.N. SECURITY COUNCIL. THIS WOULD GIVE ANY OF THE
PERMANENT MEMBERS OF THE COUNCIL -- INCLUDING THE USSR --
UNACCEPTABLE INFLUENCE OVER U.S. POLICY TOWARD SOUTH
AFRICA IN THE EVENT THAT CIRCUMSTANCES WERE TO CHANGE IN
SOUTH AFRICA. SUCH A STEP WOULD CONTRADICT LONGSTANDING
U.S. PRACTICE AND WOULD DEPRIVE US OF THE DIPLOMATIC
FLEXIBILITY NECESSARY TO DEAL EFFECTIVELY WITH A RAPIDLY
EVOLVING SITUATION IN SOUTH AND SOUTHERN AFRICA. AS A
MATTER OF PRINCIPLE, WE ALSO BELIEVE THAT SANCTIONS
AGAINST SOUTH AFRICA ARE PROPERLY A SOVEREIGN
RESPONSIBILITY AND THAT DECISIONS AS TO WHETHER TO IMPOSE
THEM SHOULD BE MADE BY EACH NATION ACCORDING TO ITS OWN
EXPERIENCE AND ESTIMATE OF WHAT ACTIONS WILL BE EFFECTIVE.
    WE CONTINUE TO TAKE MEASURES IN INTERNATIONAL
FORUMS THAT UNDERSCORE THE SERIOUSNESS OF OUR REJECTION
OF THE APARTHEID SYSTEM. WE RECENTLY INTRODUCED A
RESOLUTION TO THE 43RD SESSION OF THE U.N. HUMAN RIGHTS
COMMISSION IN GENEVA WHICH STATES, IN PART, OUR

RECOGNITION THAT "APARTHEID IS A GROSS VIOLATION OF THE
FUNDAMENTAL HUMAN RIGHTS OF THE PEOPLE OF SOUTH AFRICA
UNCLASSIFIED
UNCLASSIFIED
PAGE 08   STATE 100300
AND ...VIOLATES THE BASIC PRINCIPLES OF THE UNIVERSAL
DECLARATION OF HUMAN RIGHTS". WE CONTINUE TO TAKE A FIRM
STANCE, PUBLICLY AND IN PRIVATE, WITH THE SOUTH AFRICAN
GOVERNMENT OVER ITS HUMAN RIGHTS POLICIES AND PRACTICES.
WE WILL CONTINUE TO USE OUR INFLUENCE WITH OUR ALLIES TO
ENSURE THAT APPROPRIATE MEANS ARE IDENTIFIED TO HELP
BRING ABOUT AN END TO APARTHEID. END TEXT. SHULTZ
UNCLASSIFIED

PAGE   5

DOCUMENT 20: State Department, "Report to Congress Pursuant to Section 508 of the
Comprehensive Anti-Apartheid Act of 1986: Compliance with the U.N. Arms Embargo,"
March 1987.

PAGE 1 OF 3

A001

R

REPORT TO CONGRESS PURSUANT TO SECTION 508 OF THE
COMPREHENSIVE ANTI-APARTHEID ACT OF 1986:
COMPLIANCE WITH THE U.N. ARMS EMBARGO

Section 508 of the Comprehensive Anti-Apartheid Act of 1986
(P.L. 99-440) provides that the President shall conduct a study
on the extent to which the international arms embargo on the
sale and export of arms and military technology to South Africa
is being violated. It also requires that a report be submitted
to Congress setting forth the findings of the study, including
an identification of the countries engaged in such sales and
exports. In Executive Order 12571, the President directed the
Secretary of State to implement the requirements relating to
Section 508 of the Act.

The arms embargo referred to in the Comprehensive
Anti-Apartheid Act was adopted by the Security Council on
November 4, 1977. Resolution 418 of that date was adopted
pursuant to Chapter VII of the U.N. Charter. Consequently, the
requirements of the resolution are mandatory upon member states.

The Security Council determined that the acquisition of
arms and related materiel by South Africa constitutes a threat
to the maintenance of international peace and security. It
therefore decided that all states must cease forthwith any
provision to South Africa of arms and related materiel of all
types. Resolution 418 provides that this includes the sale or
transfer of weapons and ammunition, military vehicles and
equipment, paramilitary police equipment, and spare parts. It
also requires states to cease the provision of all types of
equipment for such items and grants of licensing arrangements
for the manufacture or maintenance of such items. The Security
Council also decided that all states shall refrain from any
cooperation in the manufacture and development of nuclear
weapons.

The mandatory arms embargo is applicable to direct
transfers by governments as well as private transfers of arms.
States are required to take whatever measures are necessary to
prohibit commercial exports of arms to South Africa.

In a separate paragraph, the Security Council called upon
states to review all existing contractual arrangements and
licenses involving South Africa relating to the manufacture and
maintenance of arms, ammunition, and military equipment and
vehicles, with a view to terminating the arrangements. Unlike
the other provisions referred to in the preceding paragraph,
this particular provision does not constitute a binding
decision of the Security Council.

It should be emphasized that this limited exception deals
only with preexisting arrangements relating to the manufacture
and maintenance of arms, ammunition, and military equipment.
It does not authorize deliveries of arms under preexisting
contracts. This interpretation of Security Council Resolution
418 was shared by the United States, the United Nations Legal

DOCUMENT 20: State Department, "Report to Congress Pursuant to Section 508 of the Comprehensive Anti-Apartheid Act of 1986: Compliance with the U.N. Arms Embargo," March 1987.

PAGE 2 OF 3

-2-

Counsel, and all members of the Security Council at the time the resolution was adopted. It is, furthermore, the position of the United States that new agreements relating to the manufacture and maintenance of arms, ammunition, and military equipment (as well as extensions or renewals of preexisting agreements upon their termination) are subject to the mandatory ban. It appears, however, that some states may take a different view on the extension of preexisting contracts.

The United States has strictly enforced the mandatory arms embargo, and no exceptions have been authorized with respect to any prohibited sale or export. In addition, the U.S. also prohibits all exports from the U.S. to the military or police in South Africa (with two minor exceptions for medical supplies and devices to be used in preventing unlawful interferences with international civil aviation). This prohibition is based on significant U.S. policy considerations and prior statutory requirements, but is not required by Resolution 418. The U.S. is not required under the U.N. arms embargo or U.S. law to monitor compliance by other states.

The Key Judgments of the study conducted by the Department of State are:

1. South Africa has reacted to the international arms embargo by developing a large and sophisticated indigenous arms industry. It imports weapon systems and sub-systems when it cannot manufacture the item itself and cannot arrange a license-manufacturing arrangement in South Africa (or the cost of doing so would be extremely inefficient compared to the cost of available imports).

2. South African defense industries' clear preference is to maintain overall control of items manufactured in South Africa and to limit foreign involvement to technical advice and the provision of sub-systems either already complete or for licensed manufacture.

3. Most of the major weapon systems in the South African inventory were present prior to the 1977 arms embargo (French-designed armored vehicles, Israeli-designed patrol boats, Italian- and French-designed combat aircraft). These items have been maintained and in many cases upgraded since the embargo, usually with the assistance of the original manufacturer.

4. Because most of the weapon systems that South Africa imports now are small and difficult to detect, or are sub-systems, or are of licensed manufacture, we cannot estimate the volume or dollar value of the imports. Thus, we cannot assign a percentage of the market that originates with an individual nation.

DOCUMENT 20: State Department, "Report to Congress Pursuant to Section 508 of the Comprehensive Anti-Apartheid Act of 1986: Compliance with the U.N. Arms Embargo," March 1987.

PAGE 3 OF 3

-3-

5. Due to the nature of the South African imports and the efforts at concealment made by both importers and exporters, intelligence on non-compliance with the arms embargo is difficult to obtain. As a result, we have a partial, incomplete, and somewhat random picture. It is also difficult to substantiate through reliable intelligence means many of the allegations that are publicly made.

6. Given what we do know, we believe that South Africa obtains weapon systems and sub-systems from a wide variety of sources worldwide. There are three notable patterns in this worldwide supply network:

--We believe companies in France, Italy, and Israel have continued to be involved in the maintenance and upgrade of major systems provided before the 1977 embargo.

--Prior to the Israeli government's decision on March 18 not to sign new military contracts and to let existing contracts expire, Israel appears to have sold military systems and sub-systems and provided technical assistance on a regular basis. Although Israel does not require end-use certificates and some cut-outs may have been used, we believe that the Israeli government was fully aware of most or all of the trade. (There is no evidence that Israel has transferred U.S. manufactured or licensed end-items, but in the absence of an inspection of Israeli made or licensed weapons in South African hands, we cannot say whether Israel has reverse-engineered U.S. weapons or transferred U.S. technology into Israeli weapons that are similar to U.S. systems.)

--Companies in Germany, the United Kingdom, the Netherlands, and Switzerland have on occasion exported articles covered by the embargo without government permission or have engaged in sales to South Africa in the gray area between civilian and military applications.

PART III

NUCLEAR COLLABORATION BETWEEN THE UNITED STATES AND SOUTH AFRICA

On April 14, 1975, the *Washington Post* carried a front-page story entitled "South Africa Gets A-Bomb Type U.S. Uranium."[1] Based on a press release by then-Congressman Les Aspin (D–Wisc.), the story indicated that the United States had sent ninety-seven pounds of highly enriched uranium—enough to make seven atomic bombs—to South Africa over the past year. The article also noted that, for many reasons, South Africa had failed to sign the Nuclear Non-Proliferation Treaty of 1968 (NPT). One motive was to leave themselves the option of developing their own atomic weapons.

Responding to the article, the U.S. government asserted that "such supply is under an inter-governmental agreement for cooperation since 1957 guaranteeing its peaceful use…[and] that material subject to agreement will not be used for any nuclear explosive device."[2] However, Washington did not claim that such an agreement could prevent South Africa from diverting the uranium for use in developing a nuclear device. Almost two decades later, the South African government would finally acknowledge that it did indeed build several atomic weapons following a decision, made as early as 1974, to embark on that course. Whether the United States was privy to such information is not known, but for years experts had speculated that U.S.–South African cooperation on nuclear matters could certainly make it possible for Pretoria to join the nuclear club.

A CLOSE RELATIONSHIP

Collaboration is one of the continuing themes in the story of South Africa's nuclear program, which has benefited from ties not only with the United States but also with a number of other countries, including France and West Germany. Historically, however, the United States has been Pretoria's most important for-

eign source of nuclear expertise. U.S. technicians and scientists have visited South African nuclear facilities to provide technical assistance and training, and South Africans have, in turn, come to the United States to receive training and practical experience. In addition, U.S. companies have, with export licenses granted by Washington, sold special nuclear materials and technologies to South Africa. All of this assistance came despite Pretoria's steadfast refusal for years to sign the NPT and to submit to full international safeguards inspections.

Beginning with the Atomic Energy Act of 1954, which authorized a broad program of international cooperation in peaceful nuclear applications, the U.S. government was authorized to export special nuclear materials and reactors to South Africa. Three years later, the U.S.–South African Agreement of Cooperation concerning the Civil Uses of Atomic Energy of 1957 was signed, and has since defined the limits of the relationship. Among other things, the 1957 agreement allowed South Africa to purchase a U.S.-designed research reactor—SAFARI-I—which was subsequently fueled and refueled with highly enriched U.S. uranium. SAFARI-I soon became the principal training facility for South African nuclear scientists and technicians.

In 1974, the two sides extended the agreement to the year 2007 and expanded its scope. According to a State Department document, "this amendment provide[d] for transfers to South Africa of increased quantities of enriched uranium (U-235) to fuel two nuclear power reactors" (Document 21). The following year, Washington stepped back from the arrangement when the Ford administration suspended shipments of highly enriched uranium for SAFARI-I over the issue of inspections of South African facilities.[3]

In the summer of 1977, suspicions arose that South Africa possessed a nuclear bomb after Soviet satellites detected what the Kremlin believed was a nuclear test facility in the Kalahari Desert. Moscow relayed the data to the United States in August, prompting President Carter to order an independent investigation. The review subsequently confirmed the Soviet findings. The Kalahari discovery alarmed the international community, particularly South Africa's neighbors, who felt directly threatened by this development. Observers of southern Africa concluded that Pretoria sought a nuclear capability because of its increased isolation stemming from, among other things, its apartheid policies.4

The Carter administration expressed its "concerns" about the Kalahari discovery to South African officials (Document 22); the demarche reportedly included a warning not to use the facility. According to secret talking points prepared by the State Department, the South African government assured U.S. officials on August 24 that it did not intend to develop nuclear weapons (Document 23). The talking points indicated that Washington "would view with the utmost gravity any further actions which would be inconsistent with South Africa's assurances." The Vorster administration offered no explanation of the nature of the facility, however.5

THE UNITED NATIONS STEPS IN
International concerns led to a series of resolutions in the U.N. in an attempt, among other things, to cut back on further foreign collaboration with South Africa's nuclear program. State Department cable traffic shows that Washington objected strongly to this provision:

> While we are profoundly concerned about South African nuclear developments, we believe that international action at this stage should concentrate on efforts to win South African adherence to the Non-Proliferation Treaty and immediate agreement to place all its nuclear facilities under international safeguards (Document 24).

The United States vetoed that section of the proposed resolution. In November 1977, however, Washington and its allies joined in voting for U.N. Resolution 418, which left out more stringent demands made by African states but did call for a mandatory arms embargo against South Africa (see Document 9).

However, the embargo had no practical effect when it came to nuclear collaboration. Countries that collaborated with South Africa in nuclear matters, including the United States, claimed that their support was intended for "peaceful purposes," and that the technology and plants they provided could not be put to military uses. However, the close connection between civil and military nuclear technologies has since been widely recognized. The process for enriching uranium to create nuclear fuel for commercial use can be developed further to provide material for nuclear weapons. In addition, extensive research supposedly conducted for civil purposes in South Africa has directly and indirectly fed the country's military capability.

Questions about that capability came up again on September 22, 1979, when a U.S. *Vela* satellite detected a double flash in the South Atlantic, indicating the possibility of a nuclear blast. Again, Carter convened a panel of scientific experts to conduct a thorough technical review of all available data. The panel concluded that while it could not rule out the possibility that the signal was of nuclear origin, it was more likely the consequence of a collision between the satellite and a small meteor (Document 25).6

Other U.S. government agencies investigating the event—including the Defense Intelligence Agency (DIA), the CIA, and the State Department's Bureau of Intelligence and Research (INR)—saw the evidence differently. In an Interagency Intelligence Memorandum prepared for the Director of Central Intelligence, the participating agencies noted:

> Technical information and analyses suggest that:
>
> —An explosion was produced by a nuclear device detonated in the atmosphere near the earth's surface

—It had a yield equivalent to less than 3 kilotons

—It took place within a broad area, primarily oceans, that was generally cloudy (Document 26).

Although the foreword to the document equivocated that "on the basis of available information, we cannot determine with certainty the nature and origin of the event on 22 September 1979," the authors indicated in another part of the document that, as requested by the National Security Council, they conducted their analysis "based on the assumption that the event...was a nuclear explosion." Noting that their purpose was to "estimate what countries may have been responsible for, or involved in, the event," the conclusions differed somewhat. For its part, the INR declared that while the arguments were inconclusive about Pretoria's role, "South Africa is the most likely candidate for responsibility."

REVIVING THE PARTNERSHIP

On assuming power, the Reagan administration made clear where it stood regarding the nuclear relationship with South Africa: a draft set of State Department talking points in April 1981 began with the statement, "The United States places a high priority on the resumption of nuclear cooperation with South Africa" (Document 27). The previous year, the Carter administration had embargoed all nuclear fuel deliveries until Pretoria agreed to subject all its nuclear facilities to IAEA safeguards. While adhering to this law, the new U.S. administration made an effort to find alternative sources of supply, from France among other countries.

Following a May 1981 meeting between Secretary of State Alexander Haig and South African Foreign Minister Pik Botha, the Reagan administration took further steps to expand the relationship. A State Department cable later that year reflected "US willingness to provide assistance in the area of research reactor LEU [low enriched uranium] fuel fabrication technology" and a desire to explore "possible follow-on cooperation [that] could include training of S.A. fuel experts" (Document 28).

When Congress and others outside the administration called on the White House to justify its policy of permitting increases in exports of nuclear material, computers, and high-technology items to South Africa, Reagan officials continued to draw a distinction between civil and military applications. In a May 1982 letter to Senator Charles Percy (R–Ill.), Commerce Secretary Malcolm Baldrige defended a proposal to export Helium-3 for "nuclear safety–related testing," even though it was identified on the "Nuclear Referral List" as a commodity that, in Baldrige's words, "could be used for nuclear explosive purposes" (Document 29). He insisted that the deal would not contradict U.S. policy, noting that "this Administration has adopted a more flexible policy with respect to approvals of exports of dual-use commodities...."

In 1985, the issue of nuclear cooperation with South Africa erupted into public view when Representative Edward Markey (D–Mass.), chairman of the House Subcommittee on Energy Conservation and Power, initiated an investigation into the illegal employment of U.S. citizens as nuclear reactor operators by the Electricity Supply Commission of South Africa (ESCOM). A February 1985 secret memorandum from the executive director for operations of the U.S. Nuclear Regulatory Commission showed that "in September 1983 the Executive Branch authorized activities involving assistance to the safeguarded Koeberg Nuclear Power Plant in South Africa" (Document 30). Apparently, though, some cases of Americans working on the South African nuclear program were in violation of the Atomic Energy Act of 1954, which, the memorandum noted, "requires that certain assistance to foreign nuclear programs must be authorized by the Secretary of Energy unless specifically authorized under an agreement for cooperation."

In 1989, a more chilling development took place that had direct implications for regional security. In July, the DIA prepared a Special Assessment entitled "South Africa: Missile Activity," which began, "A probable SRBM [Short-Range Ballistic Missile] was launched from South Africa's Arniston Missile Test Range on 5 July" (Document 31). The missile reportedly would have given South Africa the capability to launch a nuclear warhead against a target at least nine hundred miles away—as far north as Angola and Tanzania. The revelation understandably provoked alarm among the frontline states.

As noted, South Africa has received substantial assistance for its nuclear program from other countries besides the United States. According to the DIA assessment, Israel may have played a role in developing the SRBM: "Israel's connection to the project has been rumored since the mid-1980s." The Israeli government denied these allegations, but important evidence of Jerusalem's covert military collaboration with South Africa surfaced in November 1989 when a member of the government-owned Israel Aircraft Industries (IAI) was implicated in a sting operation conducted by the U.S. Customs Services (Document 32). In that case, two Americans and three South Africans were charged with trying to export U.S.-origin missile technology to South Africa, using IAI as a facilitator, in violation of U.S. laws, including the Arms Export Control Act and the Comprehensive Anti-Apartheid Act of 1986.

On March 24, 1993, in a speech to Parliament, President F. W. de Klerk finally admitted what the world had long suspected: that "[a]t one stage, South Africa did, indeed, develop a limited nuclear deterrent capability," consisting, he said, of six nuclear fission devices (Document 33). According to de Klerk, Pretoria had decided to develop atomic weapons as early as 1974 with the objective of producing seven bombs.[7] Ultimately, he said, six weapons were built; all were dismantled in 1990 once the government had determined that changes in "the global political situation," including the end of the cold war and the December 1988 signing of the tripartite agreement on Angola and Namibia, had made such a deterrent obsolete.[8]

The U.S. government welcomed de Klerk's March 1993 disclosure, noting that "the candid revelations of South Africa's past nuclear weapons activities...are major positive steps to demonstrate to the international community that South Africa has truly dismantled its nuclear weapons capability and is complying with the treaty."[9] However, de Klerk's revelations were not spontaneous; they followed demands for full disclosure of South Africa's secret weapons program by the ANC and the international community in the wake of reports by the International Atomic Energy Agency (IAEA) that the country had "produced several hundred kilograms of highly enriched uranium (HEU) [which] indirectly confirms that South Africa has an active and secret nuclear development program, since no South African nuclear facility requires uranium enriched to levels above 45 percent."[10] Furthermore, many observers have concluded that Pretoria's decision to reveal its nuclear program was motivated not by a desire to clear up any doubts about its nuclear intentions, but by concerns that its arsenal might fall into the hands of a black- or ANC-controlled successor government. However, the ANC has repeatedly stated that it has no ambitions to develop nuclear weapons.

To a certain extent, the United States contributed to South Africa's ability to produce atomic weapons by regularly aiding its nuclear program even while trying to bring pressure on Pretoria to adhere to international safeguarding standards, and especially to sign the Nuclear Non-Proliferation Treaty (which South Africa finally did in July 1991). Generally speaking, the U.S. approach to nuclear matters concerning Israel, Pakistan, and other allies has usually been swayed by foreign policy goals that compete with its public stance on discouraging proliferation.[11] In the case of South Africa, Washington's strategic objectives of containing communism and preserving a profitable commercial and economic foothold in the country frequently outweighed its commitment to rein in the nuclear ambitions of the apartheid regime.

NOTES

1. Secretary Kissinger, cable to U.S. Embassy Pretoria, "Supply of Highly Enriched Uranium to South Africa," April 15, 1975. This document is available at the National Security Archive.

2. Ibid.

3. Leonard S. Spector, *Going Nuclear* (Cambridge, Mass.: Ballinger, 1987), pp. 223–24, 319.

4. Ibid., p. 222. U.S. Officials later determined that South Africa did not have the ability in 1977 to produce a nuclear bomb; they now believe that Pretoria attained that ability in 1981. Nevertheless, as Spector notes, the Kalahari incident did offer "compelling evidence" of South Africa's intentions.

5. South African scholar Renfrew Christie notes that in 1987 South Africa apparently reactivated the test site, but no similar demarche was forthcoming from the Reagan administration. Renfrew Christie, "South Africa's Nuclear History" (Paper presented at the Nuclear History Program Conference in Nice, France, June 23–27, 1993), pp. 54–55. The paper is available at the National Security Archive.

6. Ibid., p. 51. Renfrew Christie notes that "on all forty-one previous occasions when the *Vela* registered a double flash, a nuclear explosion was independently shown to have occurred."

7. De Klerk's numbers appear to be consistent with the information provided by then-Congressman Les Aspin as reported in "South Africa Confirms Nuclear Arms Program," *Washington Post*, March 25, 1993.

8. Independent observers challenged de Klerk's claims. For example, according to the Washington, D.C.–based Natural Resources Defense Council, South Africa "has on hand some 600 to 950 kg of high-enriched uranium (HEU), with a best estimate of 770 kg HEU. This amount could be used to construct 15 (range 12 to 19) Hiroshima-type fission bombs." See Thomas Cochran, "Highly Enriched Uranium Production for South African Nuclear Weapons" (Draft), August 2, 1993, p. 1.

9. "South Africa Confirms Nuclear Arms Program," *Washington Post*, March 25, 1993.

10. "ANC Deeply Concerned about Nuclear Program," FBIS-AFR-92-246, December 22, 1992.

11. For a discussion of Washington's conflicting aims, see Virginia Foran's introductory essay, "Strategic Non-Proliferation: Balancing Interests and Ideals," in the National Security Archive's microfiche collection, *U.S. Nuclear Non-Proliferation Policy, 1945–1991* (Alexandria, Va.: Chadwyck-Healey, 1991), pp. 23–31.

DOCUMENT 21: State Department, "Statement Regarding the Amendment to the Agreement for Cooperation Between the Government of the United States of America and the Government of the Republic of
South Africa Concerning Civil Uses of Atomic Energy Signed at Washington on May 22, 1974," July 23, 1974.

PAGE 1 OF 4

L 0016
R

Statement Regarding
the Amendment to the Agreement for Cooperation
Between the Government of the United States of America
and the Government of the Republic of South Africa
Concerning Civil Uses of Atomic Energy
Signed at Washington on May 22, 1974

Explanation of Agreement

This Amendment provides for transfers to South Africa
of increased quantities of enriched uranium (U-235) to fuel
two nuclear power reactors. Article I of the Amendment
extends the Agreement, which would have expired in 1977,
into the year 2007. The provisions of the Amendment are in
accord with U.S. Atomic Energy Commission policy governing
foreign supply of enriched uranium which was revised in 1971.

Article II allows the U.S. Atomic Energy Commission to
enter into toll enrichment contracts, subject to the availability of enrichment capacity, to supply U-235 on a long-
term basis for fueling power reactors. The Article also
continues provision for transfer to South Africa of relatively
small quantities of U-235 for fueling research and testing
reactors, as well as plutonium for fueling purposes. Paragraphs E through J of Article II set forth conditions governing
material supply from the United States and its use within
South Africa. Article III amends the formulation of the U-235
ceiling to accord with the USAEC's current supply policy
respecting long-term power requirements. (The ceiling now
represents merely an upper limit on transfers for power

DOCUMENT 21: State Department, "Statement Regarding the Amendment to the Agreement for Cooperation Between the Government of the United States of America and the Government of the Republic of South Africa Concerning Civil Uses of Atomic Energy Signed at Washington on May 22, 1974," July 23, 1974.

PAGE 2 OF 4

- 2 -

purposes, rather than an advance allocation against diffusion plant capacity.] Article IV provides necessary editorial and updating changes in the article which currently provides United States safeguards rights in the comprehensive form standard in the Agreements for Cooperation. Pursuant to Article V, the "peaceful uses" guarantee given by South Africa extends to material, equipment and devices transferred under the Agreement, and to produced special nuclear material.

Background Information on Negotiations

Formal consideration of the Amendment began in 1973. The Amendment was needed for two basic reasons: (a) to update the Agreement for Cooperation to reflect current U.S. Atomic Energy Commission policies governing long-term supply of enriched uranium, which is effected through subsequent toll enrichment services contracts; and (b) to permit South Africa to contract with the U.S. Atomic Energy Commission on a timely basis for enrichment services necessary to meet South Africa's expanding requirements for nuclear power fuel.

Effect of Agreement

The Amendment will continue the close cooperation that has existed between South Africa and the United States in developing peaceful uses of atomic energy. It will permit

DOCUMENT 21: State Department, "Statement Regarding the Amendment to the Agreement for Cooperation Between the Government of the United States of America and the Government of the Republic of South Africa Concerning Civil Uses of Atomic Energy Signed at Washington on May 22, 1974," July 23, 1974.

PAGE 3 OF 4

-3-

South Africa to meet part of its expanding energy requirements by enabling the South African nuclear power industry to contract in the United States for its nuclear fuel needs.

DOCUMENT 21: State Department, "Statement Regarding the Amendment to the Agreement for Cooperation Between the Government of the United States of America and the Government of the Republic of South Africa Concerning Civil Uses of Atomic Energy Signed at Washington on May 22, 1974," July 23, 1974.

PAGE 4 OF 4

Drafted by SCI/AE:R. L. Huff:hm
July 23, 1974/ext. 22432

Clearances: USAEC:DIP - Miss Thomas
               SCI/AE - Mr. Brewster

DOCUMENT 22: U.S. Embassy Pretoria, Cable for Secretary Cyrus Vance, "Soviet Demarche on Nuclear Weapons Development by SAG," August 10, 1977.

PAGE 1 OF 1

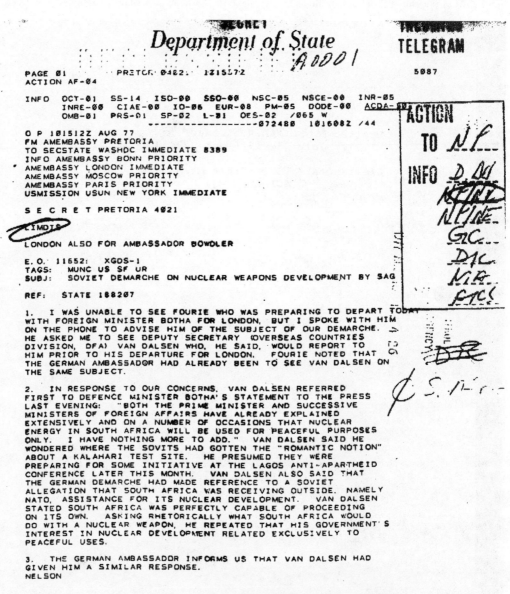

SECRET

Department of State

TELEGRAM

A0001

PAGE 01   PRETOR 0402   121557Z   5087
ACTION AF-04

INFO OCT-01 SS-14 ISO-00 SSO-00 NSC-05 NSCE-00 INR-05
      INRE-00 CIAE-00 IO-06 EUR-08 PM-05 DODE-00 ACDA-00
      OMB-01 PRS-01 SP-02 L-31 OES-02 /065 W
      ------------------------072480 101608Z /44

O P 101512Z AUG 77
FM AMEMBASSY PRETORIA
TO SECSTATE WASHDC IMMEDIATE 8389
INFO AMEMBASSY BONN PRIORITY
AMEMBASSY LONDON IMMEDIATE
AMEMBASSY MOSCOW PRIORITY
AMEMBASSY PARIS PRIORITY
USMISSION USUN NEW YORK IMMEDIATE

S E C R E T PRETORIA 4021

LIMDIS

LONDON ALSO FOR AMBASSADOR BOWDLER

E.O. 11652: XGDS-1
TAGS: MUNC US SF UR
SUBJ: SOVIET DEMARCHE ON NUCLEAR WEAPONS DEVELOPMENT BY SAG

REF: STATE 188207

1. I WAS UNABLE TO SEE FOURIE WHO WAS PREPARING TO DEPART TODAY
WITH FOREIGN MINISTER BOTHA FOR LONDON, BUT I SPOKE WITH HIM
ON THE PHONE TO ADVISE HIM OF THE SUBJECT OF OUR DEMARCHE. HE
HE ASKED ME TO SEE DEPUTY SECRETARY (OVERSEAS COUNTRIES
DIVISION, DFA) VAN DALSEN WHO, HE SAID, WOULD REPORT TO
HIM PRIOR TO HIS DEPARTURE FOR LONDON. FOURIE NOTED THAT
THE GERMAN AMBASSADOR HAD ALREADY BEEN TO SEE VAN DALSEN ON
THE SAME SUBJECT.

2. IN RESPONSE TO OUR CONCERNS, VAN DALSEN REFERRED
FIRST TO DEFENCE MINISTER BOTHA'S STATEMENT TO THE PRESS
LAST EVENING: "BOTH THE PRIME MINISTER AND SUCCESSIVE
MINISTERS OF FOREIGN AFFAIRS HAVE ALREADY EXPLAINED
EXTENSIVELY AND ON A NUMBER OF OCCASIONS THAT NUCLEAR
ENERGY IN SOUTH AFRICA WILL BE USED FOR PEACEFUL PURPOSES
ONLY. I HAVE NOTHING MORE TO ADD." VAN DALSEN SAID HE
WONDERED WHERE THE SOVITS HAD GOTTEN THE "ROMANTIC NOTION"
ABOUT A KALAHARI TEST SITE. HE PRESUMED THEY WERE
PREPARING FOR SOME INITIATIVE AT THE LAGOS ANTI-APARTHEID
CONFERENCE LATER THIS MONTH. VAN DALSEN ALSO SAID THAT
THE GERMAN DEMARCHE HAD MADE REFERENCE TO A SOVIET
ALLEGATION THAT SOUTH AFRICA WAS RECEIVING OUTSIDE. NAMELY
NATO, ASSISTANCE FOR ITS NUCLEAR DEVELOPMENT. VAN DALSEN
STATED SOUTH AFRICA WAS PERFECTLY CAPABLE OF PROCEEDING
ON ITS OWN. ASKING RHETORICALLY WHAT SOUTH AFRICA WOULD
DO WITH A NUCLEAR WEAPON, HE REPEATED THAT HIS GOVERNMENT'S
INTEREST IN NUCLEAR DEVELOPMENT RELATED EXCLUSIVELY TO
PEACEFUL USES.

3. THE GERMAN AMBASSADOR INFORMS US THAT VAN DALSEN HAD
GIVEN HIM A SIMILAR RESPONSE.
NELSON

DEPARTMENT OF STATE A/CDC/MR

REVIEWED by____N.TS_____ DATE__JUL 10 1991
(✓) RELEASE   (✓) DECLASSIFY
( ) EXCISE   ( ) DECLASSIFY in PART
( ) DENY   ( ) Non-responsive info.
FOI, EO or PA exemptions _____
                                    TS authority to:
                                    _____, OADR
( ) CLASSIFY as _____
( ) DOWNGRADE TS to ( ) S or ( ) C, OADR

SECRET

DOCUMENT 23: Leslie H. Gelb, Memorandum for Secretary Cyrus Vance, "Your Meeting with Gromyko: South African Nuclear Issue," September 21, 1977.

PAGE 1 OF 4

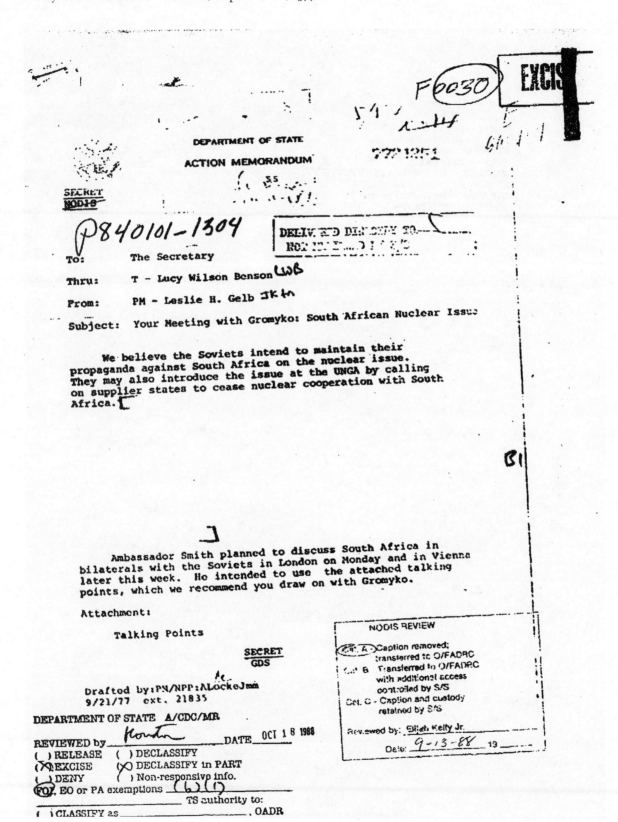

DEPARTMENT OF STATE

ACTION MEMORANDUM

F6030 EXCIS

SECRET
NODIS

P840101-1304

DELIVERED DIRECTLY TO
NODIS ...

To: The Secretary

Thru: T - Lucy Wilson Benson LWB

From: PM - Leslie H. Gelb JKfn

Subject: Your Meeting with Gromyko: South African Nuclear Issue

We believe the Soviets intend to maintain their propaganda against South Africa on the nuclear issue. They may also introduce the issue at the UNGA by calling on supplier states to cease nuclear cooperation with South Africa. [

]

Ambassador Smith planned to discuss South Africa in bilaterals with the Soviets in London on Monday and in Vienna later this week. He intended to use the attached talking points, which we recommend you draw on with Gromyko.

Attachment:

Talking Points

SECRET
GDS

Drafted by:PM/NPP:ALockeJmm
9/21/77 ext. 21835

DEPARTMENT OF STATE A/CDC/MR

REVIEWED by Houston   DATE OCT 18 1988
( ) RELEASE   ( ) DECLASSIFY
(X) EXCISE   (X) DECLASSIFY in PART
( ) DENY   ( ) Non-responsive info.
(X) FOI, EO or PA exemptions (b)(1)
_____ TS authority to:
( ) CLASSIFY as _____, OADR

NODIS REVIEW

Cat. A - Caption removed;
transferred to O/FADRC
Cat. B - Transferred to O/FADRC
with additional access
controlled by S/S
Cat. C - Caption and custody
retained by S/S

Reviewed by: Elijah Kelly Jr.

Date 9-13-88 19____

[125]

DOCUMENT 23: Leslie H. Gelb, Memorandum for Secretary Cyrus Vance, "Your Meeting with Gromyko: South African Nuclear Issue," September 21, 1977.

PAGE 2 OF 4

SECRET

-2-

Clearances:

AF - Mr. Edmondson
S/AS - Mr. Kelly
OES/NET - Mr. Nosenzo
S/MS - Mr. Shulman
EUR/SOV - Mr. Garrison
IO/UNP - Mr. Barry

SECRET

DOCUMENT 23: Leslie H. Gelb, Memorandum for Secretary Cyrus Vance, "Your Meeting with Gromyko: South African Nuclear Issue," September 21, 1977.

PAGE 3 OF 4

SECRET

PROPOSED TALKING POINTS:
SOUTH AFRICA NUCLEAR ISSUE

You are aware of the public assurances offered by the South African Government on August 24 that it does not intend to develop nuclear explosives.

-- We believe that their assurances were an important step toward defusing a volatile situation.

B1

-- Notwithstanding South Africa's recent assurances and any reinforcing actions they take, we will continue to monitor South African nuclear activities, including those at the Kalahari site. We would view with the utmost gravity any further actions which would be inconsistent with South Africa's assurances.

-- The South African Government is fully aware of our opposition to its conducting any nuclear weapons-related activities, and we believe that you and we are each in a

SECRET

DOCUMENT 23: Leslie H. Gelb, Memorandum for Secretary Cyrus Vance, "Your Meeting with Gromyko: South African Nuclear Issue," September 21, 1977.

PAGE 4 OF 4

SECRET

-2-

position to verify that such activities in fact do not occur.

-- We will, of course, be in continuing consultation with you on this subject.

-- It is our view that the quiet cooperation in which we have engaged will be an important contribution to this effort, and is a significant development in its own right.

SECRET

DOCUMENT 24: Secretary Cyrus Vance, Cable for All African Diplomatic Posts, "October 31 Security Council Discussion of South Africa," November 1, 1977.

PAGE 1 OF 5

Department of State

CONFIDENTIAL

CONFIDENTIAL

AN: D770401-0325

PAGE 01   STATE 260818
ORIGIN IO-14

INFO   OCT-01 ISO-00 AF-10 ARA-10 EA-10 EUR-12 NEA-10
CIAE-00 DODE-00 PM-05 H-01 INR-07 L-03 NSAE-00
PA-01 PRS-01 SP-02 SS-15 NSCE-00 SSO-00 USIE-00
INRE-00 DHA-05 SIG-01 /108 R

DRAFTED BY IO/UNP:TNILES:ST
APPROVED BY IO:CWMAYNES
AF:MR. HARROP (IN SUBSTANCE)
IO:GBHELMAN
------------------037095 0105012 /21
O 010412Z NOV 77
FM SECSTATE WASHDC
TO ALL AFRICAN DIPLOMATIC POSTS IMMEDIATE
AMEMBASSY BUCHAREST
AMEMBASSY CARACAS
AMEMBASSY ISLAMABAD
AMEMBASSY NEW DELHI
AMEMBASSY PANAMA
INFO AMEMBASSY BONN IMMEDIATE
AMEMBASSY LONDON
AMEMBASSY MOSCOW
AMEMBASSY OTTAWA
AMEMBASSY PARIS
USMISSION USUN NEW YORK

C O N F I D E N T I A L STATE 260818

E.O. 11652:   GDS

TAGS: PORG, PFOR, SA

SUBJECT: OCTOBER 31 SECURITY COUNCIL DISCUSSION OF
SOUTH AFRICA

REF: STATE 295771
CONFIDENTIAL
CONFIDENTIAL

PAGE 02   STATE 260818

1. AT THE UNITED NATIONS TODAY, DESPITE EFFORTS BY

CONFIDENTIAL

87- DOS...KM...

DOCUMENT 24: Secretary Cyrus Vance, Cable for All African Diplomatic Posts, "October 31 Security Council Discussion of South Africa," November 1, 1977.

PAGE 2 OF 5

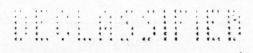

CONFIDENTIAL

WESTERN FIVE, THE FOUR AFRICAN RESOLUTIONS (TEXTS IN
STATE 259799)WERE BROUGHT TO A VOTE. FIRST RESOLUTION
WAS ADOPTED15-0-0. OTHER THREE RESOLUTIONS WERE DEFEATED
10-5-0 WITH ALL WESTERN MEMBERS VOTING AGAINST. IN
EXPLANATION OF VOTES, AMBASSADOR YOUNG POINTED OUT THAT
AFRICAN STATES WERE MAKING SERIOUS ERROR BY ATTEMPTING
TO PUSH MATTERS BEYOND CONSENSUS WHICH HAD DEVELOPED IN
WORLD COMMUNITY. USUN WILL REPORT AMBASSADOR YOUNG'S
REMARKS IN GREATER DETAIL WHICH SHOULD BE USED AS
APPROPRIATE IN BRIEFING HOST GOVERNMENT OFFICIALS AND
LOCAL MEDIA (SEE INSTRUCTION BELOW).

2. FOLLOWING FOUR-HOUR RECESS, COUNCIL RESUMED SESSION
WITH FRG AND CANADA JOINING WITH INDIAN PERMREP (AND
COUNCIL PRESIDENT) JAIPAL IN PROPOSING DRAFT RESOLUTION
PREVIOUSLY DEVELOPED BY JAIPAL (FOR TEXT SEE SEPTEL FROM

USUN). ALTHOUGH WESTERN DELEGATIONS WOULD HAVE PREFERRED
PUSHING MATTER TO A VOTE OR OBTAINING AGREEMENT ON EARLY

COUNCIL SESSION, COUNCIL WAS ADJOURNED WITH AGREEMENT
ONLY TO HOLD INFORMAL CONSULTATIONS NOVEMBER 1 LOOKING
TOWARD AN EARLY FORMAL SESSION.

3. AS POSTS WILL RECOGNIZE, TODAY'S ACTION IN SECURITY
COUNCIL COULD BE USED TO PUT UNITED STATES AND WESTERN
POWERS ON THE DEFENSIVE SINCE THERE WAS GENERAL ASSUMPTION
THAT A CHAPTER VII ACTION BACKED BY THE WEST AGAINST SOUTH
AFRICA WOULD EMERGE FROM THIS COUNCIL SESSION. DEPARTMENT
BELIEVES THAT IT IS ESSENTIAL THAT AFRICAN POSTS TAKE
STEPS TO MAKE SURE THAT BOTH HOST GOVERNMENTS AND LOCAL
CONFIDENTIAL
CONFIDENTIAL

PAGE 03   STATE 260818

MEDIA HAVE CLEAR UNDERSTANDING OF WHAT ACTUALLY HAPPENED
IN NEW YORK TODAY.

4. CONSEQUENTLY, AFRICAN POSTS SHOULD APPROACH HOST
GOVERNMENTS AT HIGHEST POSLE LEVEL TO MAKE FOLLOWING
PRESENTATION:

(A) AS PRESIDENT CARTER MADE CLEAR AT HIS OCTOBER 27
PRESS CONFERENCE, THE UNITED STATES IS PREPARED TO SUPPORT
A CHAPTER VII ARMS EMBARGO AGAINST SOUTH AFRICA WHICH
REPRESENTS A DEPARTURE FROM A 17-YEAR POLICY:

CONFIDENTIAL

DOCUMENT 24: Secretary Cyrus Vance, Cable for All African Diplomatic Posts, "October 31 Security Council Discussion of South Africa," November 1, 1977.

PAGE 3 OF 5

CONFIDENTIAL

(B) WE CONSIDER THIS TO BE AN APPROPRIATE RESPONSE BY THE SECURITY COUNCIL TO RECENT MEASURES TAKEN BY SOUTH AFRICA. WE BELIEVE THAT A CONSENSUS EXISTS IN THE SECURITY COUNCIL TO TAKE THIS STEP;

(C) THE AFRICAN MEMBERS IN THE SECURITY COUNCIL PUT FORWARD FOUR RESOLUTIONS, THREE OF WHICH CONTAINED MEASURES WHICH, IN THE VIEWS OF THE U. S. AND THE OTHER WESTERN MEMBERS OF THE SECURITY COUNCIL, WENT BEYOND THE EXISTING INTERNATIONAL CONSENSUS. THE FIRST RESOLUTION WAS ADOPTED UNANIMOUSLY.

(D) THE SECOND RESOLUTION FOUND THAT SOUTH AFRICAN POLICIES IN RHODESIA, NAMIBIA AND INTERNALLY CONSTITUTED A THREAT TO THE PEACE. SINCE WE HAVE SOME GROUNDS FOR HOPING THAT SOUTH AFRICA WILL COOPERATE IN BRINGING ABOUT A PROMPT TRANSITION TO MAJORITY RULE IN RHODESIA AND NAMIBIA, WE DO NOT BELIEVE THEIR POLICIES IN THESE AREAS CURRENTLY SHOULD BE DENOMINATED AS A THREAT TO THE PEACE. ALTHOUGH NO ACTION IS MANDATED, RESOLUTION THREATENS SOUTH AFRICA WITH FULL RANGE OF SANCTIONS, INCLUDING USE OF MILITARY FORCE, IF POLICIES ARE NOT CHANGED. WE DO NOT SEE HOW THREATS OF THIS TYPE COULD BE HELPFUL.

CONFIDENTIAL
CONFIDENTIAL

PAGE 04   STATE 260838

(E) THE THIRD AFRICAN RESOLUTION PROVIDING FOR A MANDATORY ARMS EMBARGO CALLS FOR A SWEEPING BAN ON ALL KINDS OF TIES WITH SOUTH AFRICA WHICH COULD POSSIBLY HAVE MILITARY UTILITY INCLUDING "DIRECT AND INDIRECT ASSISTANCE" BY CORPORATIONS TO THE SOUTH AFRICAN GOVERNMENT. SUCH A BAN COULD EMBRACE MANY SALES OF PRODUCTS FOR CIVILIAN BUYERS WHICH WE DO NOT NOW THINK IT DESIRABLE TO INTERDICT. SINCE WE, TOO, SUPPORT MANDATORY ARMS EMBARGO, IT WAS NOT EASY FOR US TO OPPOSE THIS RESOLUTION. HOWEVER, THIS RESOLUTION'S CALL FOR SWEEPING ECONOMIC SANCTIONS WAS BEYOND EXISTING CONSENSUS. MOREOVER, IT ALSO CALLS FOR A MANDATORY CUT-OFF ON ANY COOPERATION WITH SOUTH AFRICA IN THE NUCLEAR FIELD. WHILE WE ARE PROFOUNDLY CONCERNED ABOUT SOUTH AFRICAN NUCLEAR DEVELOPMENTS, WE BELIEVE THAT INTERNATIONAL ACTION AT THIS STAGE SHOULD CONCENTRATE ON EFFORTS TO WIN SOUTH AFRICAN ADHERENCE TO THE NON-PROLIFERATION

CONFIDENTIAL

DOCUMENT 24: Secretary Cyrus Vance, Cable for All African Diplomatic Posts, "October 31 Security Council Discussion of South Africa," November 1, 1977.

PAGE 4 OF 5

CONFIDENTIAL

TREATY AND IMMEDIATE AGREEMENT TO PLACE ALL ITS NUCLEAR
FACILITIES UNDER INTERNATIONAL SAFEGUARDS. A CUT-OFF OF
ALL NUCLEAR COOPERATION MIGHT CONVINCE SOUTH AFRICA THAT IT
HAS NOTHING TO LOSE BY PROCEEDING TO DEVELOP NUCLEAR
EXPLOSIVES. AS AMBASSADOR YOUNG STRESSED IN HIS SPEECH
TODAY, WE TAKE SOUTH AFRICA'S ASSURANCES SERIOUSLY,
"AND WOULD RESPOND VIGOROUSLY IN CONCERT WITH OTHERS
SHOULD IT APPEAR THAT SOUTH AFRICA DOES NOT INTEND TO
HONOR THEM", I.E., RECENT SAG ASSURANCES ON PEACEFUL USES.

(F) FOURTH AFRICAN RESOLUTION CALLS FOR A SWEEPING
CUTBACK IN ECONOMIC TIES WITH SOUTH AFRICA, INCLUDING
A BAN ON NEW INVESTMENTS, A CESSATION OF LOANS AND AN
END TO MEASURES TO FACILITATE TRADE. WE BELIEVE THAT IN
DEALING WITH THE UNFOLDING CRISES IN SOUTH AFRICA, WE
MUST PROCEED IN ACCORDANCE WITH THE DEVELOPING CONSENSUS.
CONFIDENTIAL
CONFIDENTIAL

PAGE 05   STATE 260818

IT IS IMPORTANT TO AVOID EXTREME PROPOSALS WHICH GIVE
SOUTH AFRICA THE HOPE THAT IT CAN DIVIDE OR DISCOUNT
THE OUTSIDE WORLD. AT THE SAME TIME WE ARE REVIEWING
OUR ECONOMIC RELATIONS WITH SOUTH AFRICA.

5. FOLLOWING ABOVE PRESENTATION, EMBASSY SHOULD STRESS
OUR DESIRE TO WORK WITH AFRICAN GROUP AT THE UN TO WIN
PROMPT ADOPTION OF A RESOLUTION WHICH IMPOSES A MANDATORY
ARMS EMBARGO AGAINST SOUTH AFRICA. EMBASSY SHOULD PASS
COPY OF NEW FRG/CANADA DRAFT (TEXT BEING REPEATED BY USUN)
AND STRESS OUR VIEW THAT IT REPRESENTS APPROPRIATE FIRST
STEP IN INTERNATIONAL RESPONSE TO LATEST SOUTH AFRICAN
MOVES.

6. EMBASSY REPRESENTATIVE SHOULD FURTHER COMMENT:

(A) THIS RESOLUTION, AS ADOPTED, WOULD REPRESENT FIRST
TIME CHAPTER VII ACTION HAS BEEN TAKEN AGAINST A UN
MEMBER; (RHODESIA IS NEITHER A MEMBER NOR A STATE).

(B) FAILURE OF UN TO TAKE ACTION AT THIS POINT COULD
BE MISINTERPRETED, BOTH IN SOUTH AFRICA AND ELSEWHERE,
AS INDICATION THAT INTERNATIONAL COMMUNITY CANNOT AGREE
TO ACT AGAINST SOUTH AFRICA. IN FACT, THERE IS GENERAL
AGREEMENT THAT A MANDATORY ARMS EMBARGO IS NEEDED, AND
ONLY VORSTER CAN TAKE COMFORT FROM A FAILURE TO ACT ON

CONFIDENTIAL

DOCUMENT 24: Secretary Cyrus Vance, Cable for All African Diplomatic Posts, "October 31 Security Council Discussion of South Africa," November 1, 1977.

PAGE 5 OF 5

DECLASSIFIED

CONFIDENTIAL

THIS CONSENSUS.

(C) MANDATORY ARMS EMBARGO WOULD NOT PRECLUDE FURTHER MEASURES.

(D) WHILE IT IS UP TO AFRICAN STATES TO DECIDE ON COMPROMISE DRAFT RESOLUTION, WE BELIEVE IT MERITS CAREFUL CONSIDERATION AS APPROACH ON WHICH CONSENSUS EXISTS.

CONFIDENTIAL
CONFIDENTIAL

PAGE 06   STATE 260818

7. PUBLIC AFFAIRS OFFICERS AT ALL AFRICAN POSTS SHOULD USE POINTS ABOVE IN BACKGROUNDING LOCAL PRESS. USUN WILL BE SUPPLYING SEPTELS CONTAINING ADDITIONAL INFORMA-TION WHICH CAN BE USED WITH THE MEDIA.

8. FOR ISLAMABAD, PANAMA, CARACAS AND BUCHAREST: SUPPORT OF OTHER NON-PERMANENT MEMBERS MAY BE KEY ELEMENT IN DETERMINING WHETHER COMPROMISE TEXT WILL BE ADOPTED. AMBASSADORS SHOULD REQUEST EARLIEST POSSIBLE MEETING AT APPROPRIATE LEVEL IN FOREIGN MINISTRY TO MAKE PRESENTATION ALONG LINES ABOVE AND REQUEST SUPPORT FOR COMPROMISE TEXT.

9. FOR USUN: SUGGEST YOU COORDINATE WITH FRG, UK, FRENCH AND CANADIAN MISSIONS WITH EYE TO SIMILAR APPROACHES BY THEIR AMBASSADORS IN AFRICAN POSTS. FRENCH COULD BE EXTREMELY HELPFUL HERE IF THEY WISHED.   VANCE

CONFIDENTIAL

CONFIDENTIAL

DOCUMENT 25: Secretary Cyrus Vance, Cable for U.S. Embassy Paris, "Press Panel Review of South Atlantic Event," February 7, 1980.

PAGE 1 OF 6

 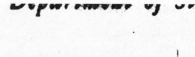

CONFIDENTIAL

CONFIDENTIAL

PAGE 01   STATE 034128
ORIGIN OES-09

AN: D8020670102

INFO OCT-00 AF-10 EUR-12 EA-10 ADS-00 ACDA-12 CIAE 00
INR-10 IO-14 L-03 NSAE-00 NSC-05 EB-08 NRC-02
DODE-00 H-01 DOE-17 SS-15 SP-02 CEQ-01 PM-05
SAS-02 PA-01 ICA-11 /150 R

DRAFTED BY OES/NEP:MGUHIN:DJR
APPROVED BY OES:TRPICKERING
NSC:HOWEN   INR/STA:JSIEGEL
OSTP:JMARCUM PM/NPP:GSUCHAN
DOE:JDEUTCH IO/INP:SESCUDERO
OSD:WSLOCOMBE, DMURPHY
CIA:JINGLEY S/P:RGALLUCCI
ACDA/NP:RROCHLIN
S/AS:ALOCKE OES/N:LVNOSENZO
AF/S:LMACFARLANE
--------------------125827 0802542 /658
P O 0720062 FEB 80
FM SECSTATE WASHDC
TO AMEMBASSY PARIS PRIORITY
AMEMBASSY LONDON PRIORITY
AMEMBASSY BONN PRIORITY
AMEMBASSY TOKYO PRIORITY
AMEMBASSY OTTAWA PRIORITY
AMEMBASSY CANBERRA PRIORITY
AMCONSUL CAPE TOWN PRIORITY
AMEMBASSY WELLINGTON PRIORITY
INFO AMEMBASSY PRETORIA IMMEDIATE

C O N F I D E N T I A L STATE 034128

CAPE TOWN FOR EMBASSY

E.O. 12065 RDS 02/05/86 (PICKERING, THOMAS R.) OES

TAGS: PARM, MNUC,
CONFIDENTIAL
CONFIDENTIAL

PAGE 02   STATE 034128

SUBJECT: (C) PRESS PANEL REVIEW OF SOUTH ATLANTIC EVENT

CONFIDENTIAL

DOCUMENT 25: Secretary Cyrus Vance, Cable for U.S. Embassy Paris, "Press Panel Review of South Atlantic Event," February 7, 1980.

PAGE 2 OF 6

CONFIDENTIAL

REF: (A) STATE 9603, (B) TOKYO 889

1. (C) ENTIRE TEXT.

2. FOLLOWING UP INFORMATION PROVIDED REF A, WE HOPE TO
RELEASE PUBLIC STATEMENT ON PRESS PANEL'S REVIEW OF
SEPTEMBER 22 EVENT IN THE NEAR FUTURE, DRAWING ON POINTS
BELOW. PRESS PANEL REVIEW HAS ALREADY BEEN SUBJECT TO SOME
MEDIA ATTENTION IN US, AND RECENT ARTICLE IN SCIENCE
FORWARDED BY SEPTEL. WE WISH TO KEEP HOST GOVERNMENTS AND
UG WALDHEIM APPRISED ON THIS MATTER, BUT ASK THAT INFORMA-
TION WE PROVIDE BE HELD IN CONFIDENCE UNTIL WE HAVE ISSUED
RELEASE. ACTION ADDRESSEES SHOULD DRAW ON ABOVE AND
POINTS BELOW (TO EXTENT THEY ADD TO PREVIOUSLY AUTHORIZED
POINTS) AT EARLIEST APPROPRIATE OPPORTUNITY TO BRING HOST
GOVERNMENTS AND WALDHEIM UP-TO-DATE. IN YOUR PRESENTATION
YOU SHOULD ENSURE THAT OUR TECHNICAL UNCERTAINTY AND
PANEL'S INABILITY TO DETERMINE WHETHER NUCLEAR EXPLOSION
WAS THE SOURCE OF THE SIGNAL SHOULD NOT BE MISCONSTRUED
AS A FINDING THAT A NUCLEAR EXPLOSION DID NOT TAKE PLACE.
THE MOST WE CAN SAY IS THAT WE ARE UNABLE TO PROVE, ON THE

BASIS OF PRESENTLY AVAILABLE DATA AND ANALYSIS, THAT SUCH
AN EXPLOSION DID TAKE PLACE. AS NOTED BELOW, WE WILL
CONTINUE THE SEARCH FOR CORROBORATIVE EVIDENCE AND CANNOT
RULE OUT THE POSSIBILITY THAT IT WILL BE FOUND.

(A) TO ASSIST IN EVALUATION OF THE NATURE AND PROBABLE
SOURCE OF THE LIGHT SIGNAL RECORDED BY A VELA SATELLITE
OVER THE SOUTH ATLANTIC ON SEPTEMBER 22, 1979, A PANEL OF
CONFIDENTIAL
CONFIDENTIAL

PAGE 03   STATE 034128

NON-GOVERNMENT SCIENTISTS WAS CONVENED BY THE WHITE HOUSE
UNDER THE GUIDANCE OF DR. FRANK PRESS, SCIENCE ADVISER TO
THE PRESIDENT AND DIRECTOR OF THE OFFICE OF SCIENCE AND
TECHNOLOGY POLICY. THE PANEL WAS CHAIRED BY DR. JACK
RUINA OF THE MASSACHUSETTS INSTITUTE OF TECHNOLOGY AND
INCLUDED EIGHT OTHER DISTINGUISHED SCIENTISTS WITH
SPECIFIC EXPERTISE IN RELEVANT SCIENTIFIC AND TECHNICAL
FIELDS.

(B) THE PANEL WAS ASKED TO CONDUCT A THOROUGH TECHNICAL
REVIEW OF WHETHER OR NOT THE SEPTEMBER 22 LIGHT SIGNAL WAS

CONFIDENTIAL

DOCUMENT 25: Secretary Cyrus Vance, Cable for U.S. Embassy Paris, "Press Panel Review of South Atlantic Event," February 7, 1980.

PAGE 3 OF 6

CONFIDENTIAL

CONFIDENTIAL

GENERATED BY A NUCLEAR EXPLOSION AND, MORE SPECIFICALLY, TO (1) REVIEW ALL AVAILABLE DATA FROM BOTH CLASSIFIED AND UNCLASSIFIED SOURCES THAT COULD HELP IDENTIFY THE SOURCE OF THE SIGNAL AND SUGGEST ANY ADDITIONAL SOURCES OF DATA THAT MIGHT BE HELPFUL IN THIS REGARD; (2) EVALUATE THE POSSIBILITY THAT THE SIGNAL IN QUESTION WAS A "FALSE ALARM" RESULTING FROM TECHNICAL MALFUNCTION SUCH AS INTERFERENCE FROM OTHER ELECTRICAL COMPONENTS ON THE SATELLITE PLATFORM; AND (3) EVALUATE THE POSSIBILITY THAT THE SIGNAL RECORDED BY THE SATELLITE WAS OF NATURAL ORIGIN, POSSIBLY RESULTING FROM THE COINCIDENCE OF TWO OR MORE NATURAL PHENOMENA AND ATTEMPT TO ESTABLISH QUANTITATIVE LIMITS ON THE PROBABILITY OF SUCH AN OCCURRENCE.

(C) THE PANEL BEGAN ITS STUDY ON NOVEMBER 1, 1979. DURING THE COURSE OF ITS WORK THE PANEL RECEIVED NUMEROUS BRIEFINGS BY US GOVERNMENT AGENCIES AND OUTSIDE CON- TRACTORS; STUDIED PERFORMANCE DATA, CIRCUITRY AND HARDWARE INVOLVED IN THE VELA SATELLITE PROGRAM; INITIATED AND REVIEWED RESULTS OF STATISTICAL ANALYSES OF THE HUNDREDS OF THOUSANDS OF LIGHT SIGNALS THAT HAVE BEEN RECORDED PREVIOUSLY BY VELA SATELLITES AND OF COMPUTER MODELING OF NATURAL PHENOMENA THAT MIGHT HAVE GENERATED THE SEPTEMBER 22 SIGNAL; AND REVIEWED ALL AVAILABLE DATA THAT MIGHTTEND TO CORROBORATE WHETHER THAT SIGNAL WAS GENERATED BY A
CONFIDENTIAL
CONFIDENTIAL

PAGE 04   STATE 034128

NUCLEAR EXPLOSION.

(D) RESULTS OF THE PANELS REVIEW ARE SUMMARIZED BELOW.

(E) DESPITE THE EXTENSIVE ANALYSIS OF ALL AVAILABLE DATA

AND THE SEARCH FOR POSSIBLE ADDITIONAL EVIDENCE CONCERNING THE NATURE AND PROBABLE SOURCE OF THE SEPTEMBER 22 LIGHT SIGNAL, THE PANEL WAS UNABLE TO DETERMINE WHETHER THIS SIGNAL WAS GENERATED BY A NUCLEAR EXPLOSION OR BY SOME OTHER PHENOMENON.

(F) IN OVER TEN YEARS OF OPERATION, THE VELA SATELLITES HAVE BEEN "TRIGGERED" HUNDREDS OF THOUSANDS OF TIMES, MOSTLY BY SIGNALS ATTRIBUTED TO LIGHTNING OR TO COSMIC RAY PARTICLES.

(G) THE SIGNAL OF SEPTEMBER 22, 1979 DOES HAVE THE GENERAL
CONFIDENTIAL

Document 25: Secretary Cyrus Vance, Cable for U.S. Embassy Paris, "Press Panel Review of South Atlantic Event," February 7, 1980.

PAGE 4 OF 6

CONFIDENTIAL

CHARACTER OF SIGNALS GENERATED BY NUCLEAR EXPLOSIONS. IT RESEMBLES A NUCLEAR EXPLOSION SIGNAL MORE THAN ANY SIGNAL PREVIOUSLY RECORDED EXCEPT FROM THOSE KNOWN THROUGH CORROBORATING INFORMATION TO HAVE BEEN FROM NUCLEAR EXPLOSIONS. HOWEVER, A DETAILED COMPARISON OF THE SIGNAL WITH THOSE FROM KNOWN NUCLEAR EXPLOSIONS RAISED SOME DOUBT ABOUT WHETHER THE SIGNAL WAS OF NUCLEAR ORIGIN. ALSO, TO DATE, WE HAVE NO INFORMATION CLEARLY CORROBORAT- ING THE OCCURRENCE OF A NUCLEAR EXPLOSION ON SEPTEMBER 22, 1979. IT SHOULD BE NOTED THAT PREVIOUS SIGNALS RECORDED BY VELA SATELLITES FROM NUCLEAR EXPLOSIONS WERE CONFIRMED BY OTHER INFORMATION TO HAVE BEEN OF NUCLEAR ORIGIN.

(H) THE PANEL FOUND THAT AN IONOSPHERIC DISTURBANCE PRO- VIDED THE ONLY SUGGESTIVE ADDITIONAL EVIDENCE FOR A
CONFIDENTIAL
CONFIDENTIAL

PAGE 05   STATE 034128

NUCLEAR EVENT. THERE WERE AMBIGUITIES IN INTERPRETATION OF THIS DISTURBANCE, AND THE INFORMATION WAS NOT PERSUASIVE AT THIS TIME AS CORROBORATIVE EVIDENCE FOR A NUCLEAR EVENT.

(I) THE PANEL RULED OUT THE POSSIBILITY THAT THE SIGNAL WAS CAUSED BY A SATELLITE MALFUNCTION.

(J) IT ALSO REVIEWED A NUMBER OF NATURAL PHENOMENA WHICH MIGHT HAVE CAUSED THE SIGNAL AND, WITH ONE EXCEPTION NOTED BELOW, RULED THEM OUT. NATURAL PHENOMENA RULED OUT INCLUDED SUNLIGHT REFLECTED FROM THE VELA SATELLITE ITSELF OR FROM A DISTANT SATELLITE; AN ASTRONOMICAL FLARE FROM A STELLAR OBJECT SUCH AS THE SUN; LIGHT FROM A METEOR RE-ENTRY INTO THE ATMOSPHERE; LIGHTNING PHENOMENA INCLUD- ING SO-CALLED SUPER-BOLTS; COSMIC RAYS; AND THE ACCIDENTAL COINCIDENCE OF TWO OR MORE OF THESE PHENOMENA.

(K) THE PANEL CONSIDERED THAT THE ONE POSSIBLE EXCEPTION IS THE REFLECTION OF SUNLIGHT FROM A SMALL OBJECT PASSING NEAR THE SATELLITE. IN FACT, PREVIOUS LIGHT SIGNALS RECORDED BY VELA SATELLITES INCLUDED SIGNALS WHICH HAD

SOME OF THE SPECIAL CHARACTERISTICS OF THOSE FROM NUCLEAR EXPLOSIONS, SUCH AS A DOUBLE PULSE OF LIGHT. HOWEVER, THESE SIGNALS WERE DETERMINED NOT TO BE OF NUCLEAR ORIGIN, OWING TO DIFFERENCES IN THE DURATION AND INTENSITY OF THE

CONFIDENTIAL

DOCUMENT 25: Secretary Cyrus Vance, Cable for U.S. Embassy Paris, "Press Panel Review of South Atlantic Event," February 7, 1980.

PAGE 5 OF 6

CONFIDENTIAL

SIGNAL, AND SOME WERE TENTATIVELY ATTRIBUTED TO SMALL METEOROIDS PASSING NEAR THE SATELLITE. ANALYSES BY COMPUTER MODELING SHOWED THAT SUNLIGHT REFLECTED FROM A SMALL METEOROID OR PIECE OF SPACE DEBRIS COULD POSSIBLY GENERATE A LIGHT SIGNAL SUCH AS THE ONE RECORDED ON SEPTEMBER 22.

(L) THE PANEL NOTED THAT THE PROBABILITY OF THE OCCURRENCE OF A NUCLEAR EXPLOSION WITH NO CORROBORATIVE DATA SUCH AS
CONFIDENTIAL
CONFIDENTIAL

PAGE 06   STATE 034128

NUCLEAR DEBRIS IS SMALL. THE PANEL NOTED THAT THE PROBABILITY THAT THIS WAS THE FIRST INSTANCE OF A SIGNAL FROM A METEOROID OR OTHER PHYSICAL PHENOMENON WITH THE RIGHT PROPERTIES AFTER TEN YEARS OF OBSERVATION IS ALSO SMALL. THE PANEL WAS UNABLE TO ASSIGN RELATIVE PROBABILITIES TO WHETHER THE SIGNAL WAS GENERATED BY A NUCLEAR EXPLOSION OR A NATURAL PHENOMENON.

(M) THE PANEL RECOMMENDED FURTHER ANALYSIS WHICH WILL BE UNDERTAKEN AND MAY RESULT IN IMPROVING OUR UNDERSTANDING OF THE SEPTEMBER 22 SIGNAL. THESE INCLUDE:

(1) A MORE THOROUGH STATISTICAL ANALYSIS OF ALL PREVIOUS SIGNALS RECORDED BY VELA SATELLITES TO IMPROVE UNDERSTANDING OF THEIR PHYSICAL ORIGIN AND OF THE LIKELIHOOD OF A "FALSE ALARM"; AND

(2) A THOROUGH REVIEW OF ALL RELEVANT METEOROID DATA TO ASSESS FURTHER THE PROBABILITY THAT LIGHT REFLECTED FROM A METEOROID OR PIECE OF SPACE DEBRIS WAS THE CAUSE OF THE SIGNAL RECORDED ON SEPTEMBER 22.

(N) IN ACCORDANCE WITH A FURTHER RECOMMENDATION OF THE PANEL, THE SEARCH FOR CORROBORATIVE INFORMATION WILL CONTINUE. WE CANNOT RULE OUT THE POSSIBILITYTHATSUCH EVIDENCE WILL BE FOUND IF A NUCLEAR EXPLOSION OCCURRED.

3. FOR TOKYO: ABOVE ANSWERS SOME QUESTIONS POSED REF 9. IN ADDITION YOU MAY INFORM GOJ THAT PRESS PANEL COMPLETED ITS REVIEW IN EARLY JANUARY. YOU SHOULDALSOMAKECLEAR TO GOJ THAT, WHILE PANEL CONDUCTED EXTENSIVE REVIEW, NO DETAILED REPORT AS SUCH HAS BEENCOMPILED. INSTEAD, PANEL

CONFIDENTIAL
CONFIDENTIAL

DOCUMENT 25: Secretary Cyrus Vance, Cable for U.S. Embassy Paris, "Press Panel Review of South Atlantic Event," February 7, 1980.

PAGE 6 OF 6

CONFIDENTIAL

CONFIDENTIAL

PAGE 07   STATE   034128

HAS PROVIDED AN ASSESSMENT WHICH IS SUMMARIZED IN THE POINTS ABOVE AND REF A. YOU MAY ALSO ADVISE GOJ THAT WE HAVE INFORMED THE GAG AS WELL AS OTHER INTERESTED GOVERN- MENTS (FRANCE, UK, FRG, CANADA, AUSTRALIA, AND NEW ZEALAND) AND SG WALDHEIM ON CONFIDENTIAL BASIS.

4. FOR USUN: IN BRINGING WALDHEIM UP TO DATE, YOU SHOULD MAKE CLEAR THAT THE ABOVE POINTS SUMMARIZE ESSENTIALLY ALL SIGNIFICANT ASPECTS OF THE PANEL'S REVIEW AND THAT WE DO NOT EXPECT OUR PUBLIC RELEASE TO GO BEYOND THESE POINTS. (WE WILL OF COURSE PROVIDE COPY OF PUBLIC RELEASE TO HIM.) WE WISH TO AVOID ANY IMPRESSION, IF THERE IS ONE, THAT THERE WILL BE A LARGER REPORT FOR HIS USE IN PREPARING HIS OWN REPORT.   VANCE

CONFIDENTIAL

CONFIDENTIAL

DOCUMENT 26: Director of Central Intelligence, Interagency Intelligence Memorandum, "The 22 September 1979 Event," December 1979.

PAGE 1 OF 10

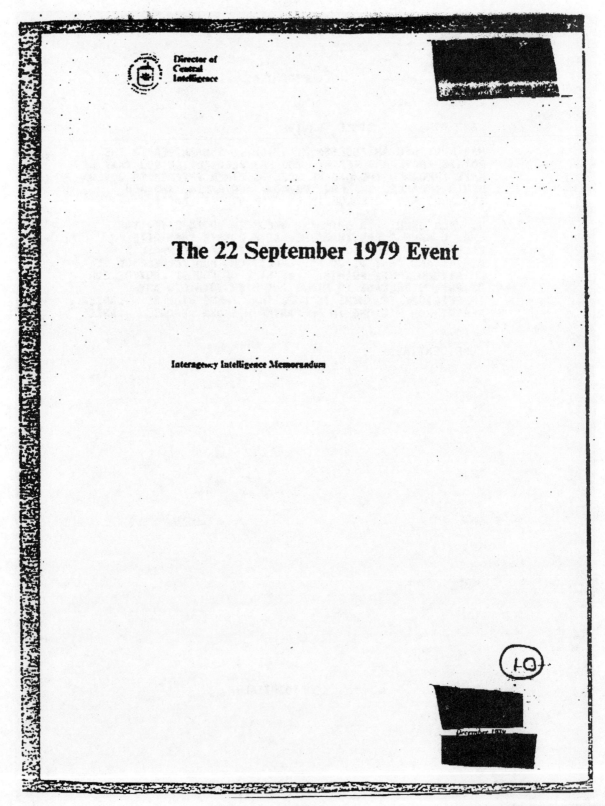

Director of
Central
Intelligence

The 22 September 1979 Event

Interagency Intelligence Memorandum

December 1979

DOCUMENT 26: Director of Central Intelligence, Interagency Intelligence Memorandum, "The 22 September 1979 Event," December 1979.

PAGE 2 OF 10

FOREWORD

On the basis of available information, we cannot determine with certainty the nature and origin of the event on 22 September 1979 ██

This memorandum was prepared under the auspices of the National Intelligence Officer for Nuclear Proliferation in response to a National Security Council request. It was coordinated at the working level with NFIB representatives in the Interagency Intelligence Working Group on Nuclear Proliferation. █████

DOCUMENT 26: Director of Central Intelligence, Interagency Intelligence Memorandum, "The 22 September 1979 Event," December 1979.

PAGE 3 OF 10

KEY JUDGMENTS

DOCUMENT 26: Director of Central Intelligence, Interagency Intelligence Memorandum, "The 22 September 1979 Event," December 1979.

PAGE 4 OF 10

DISCUSSION

1. As requested by the National Security Council, this assessment is based on the assumption that the event detected over a portion of the southern hemisphere (see map on page 12) by optical sensors on a Vela satellite at about 0100 GMT on 22 September 1979 was a nuclear explosion. Given the assumption that a nuclear explosion occurred, the purpose of this paper is to estimate what countries may have been responsible for, or involved in, the event.

2. Technical information and analyses suggest that:

— An explosion was produced by a nuclear device detonated in the atmosphere near the earth's surface.

— It had a yield equivalent to less than 3 kilotons.

— It took place within a broad area, primarily oceans, that was generally cloud.

3. Various types of nuclear devices could have yielded the equivalent of less than 3 kilotons of high explosive. Such yields could have been obtained either by careful design of a weapon with that yield, through intentional reduction of yield of a higher yield device, or by partial failure of a higher yield device. In practical terms, the testing of a nuclear device at sea would not have needed to involve more than two or three ships or aircraft, including several dozen crewmen and technicians. Equipped with appropriate magnetic instruments, they could have located the test within a few hours, detonated the device, obtained required data within minutes after the explosion, and dispersed within another few hours.

5. The Defense Intelligence Agency believes, however, that if an atmospheric test were in the technical interest of the USSR, an anonymous test near an unwitting proxy state such as South Africa could have provided an attractive evasion method. The Department of Energy believes that, while the Soviets have had the capability to test clandestinely, they have recently had no technical reason or motivation to do so. The Department further concludes that such a test could have been seen as exposing Soviet motivations by disrupting peace efforts and other independent moderate elements in southern Africa.

6. An unintended firing and near-surface detonation of a nuclear weapon during a military exercise could also have produced the signals that were detected. The multiple safety measures that would have had to be negated, however, and the absence of any known weapons carriers in the area on 22 September would have made such an event quite unlikely. The explosion of a nuclear weapon aboard a weapons carrier would have been even less likely, because the yield of an accidental detonation almost certainly would not have been sufficient to produce the detected signals. Moreover, no nuclear weapons carriers are known to have been missing and no one associated

DOCUMENT 26: Director of Central Intelligence, Interagency Intelligence Memorandum, "The 22 September 1979 Event," December 1979.

PAGE 5 OF 10

search-and-rescue operations have been noted. Finally, it is very unlikely that any known subnational entity could have conducted a nuclear explosion or would have been motivated to do so.[3] So the following assessment considers the capabilities and motivations of only those five "non-nuclear-weapon states" that might have attempted to test secretly in a remote ocean area of the southern hemisphere during September 1979.

A Secret Test by South Africa

8. In late 1977 the Vorster government apparently suspended preparations to test. Strong US pressure and other international reactions appeared to have deflected South Africa at least temporarily from testing. The setback probably compelled Vorster and the key officials in the nuclear weapons program to review their whole approach toward weapons development and testing. Statements made by the Vorster government at that time did not permanently foreclose future options for testing. Rather than completely stopping their weapons program, the South Africans could then have decided to prepare for a future nuclear test more securely. In any case nuclear testing was almost certainly not feasible until late 1978 at the earliest, when sufficient quantities of highly enriched uranium could have been expected to become available. In short, the Vorster administration may well have deferred any decisions on whether or when to test.

9. *Botha's Policy.* Arguments that nuclear testing could make an important contribution to technical confidence in and, to the extent it was disclosed,

foreign respect for South Africa's military strength in all likelihood would have resonated with Prime Minister Botha and other South African officials. Botha had overseen a substantial buildup of South Africa's defense forces in the late 1960s and 1970s, following a decision in the early 1960s to achieve self-sufficiency in arms. Because of his personal convictions as well as his official responsibilities, he has advocated more than any other Cabinet officer the military components of South Africa's strategy for coping with possible external threats. He has regarded the West as unwilling to support South Africa against foreign threats that he has perceived to be growing. Moreover, he has probably sympathized with views that nuclear weapons might ultimately be needed. However, he probably has not foreseen any imminent military requirement for nuclear weapons or any political advantages to disclosing particular elements of South Africa's nuclear weapons capabilities at this time. Nevertheless, he may have been persuaded that undeclared but undenied nuclear weapons would have an important psychological deterrent effect that South Africa could better achieve through testing.

11. If P. W. Botha had decided in favor of a nuclear test, he would have evaluated alternative options for conducting it in terms of their expected effectiveness, risks, and costs. To minimize adverse foreign reactions, he would have had to assess both the chances and the consequences of discovery. While an atmospheric test over unfrequented international waters presumably would have been seen to entail some risk of being found in violation of the Limited Test Ban Treaty, to which South Africa is a party, it also would have offered a relatively quick, safe, and easy way for South African weapons designers to prove a nuclear device without creating unambiguous evidence that South Africa was responsible for a nuclear explosion. In contrast, an atmospheric or underground test in South Africa probably would have entailed higher risks of

6

DOCUMENT 26: Director of Central Intelligence, Interagency Intelligence Memorandum, "The 22 September 1979 Event," December 1979.

PAGE 6 OF 10

prior detection and ultimate proof by foreign intelligence because it probably would have required site preparations and left tangible indications of a nuclear explosion. Botha's security advisers might have warned him that, if South Africa were discovered to have violated the LTBT, it might suffer more serious sanctions than if it tested underground. On the other hand, they would have raised the possibility of another international uproar and more serious threats if new underground test preparations were detected, and the likelihood of more serious sanctions if South Africa proceeded to test under such circumstances. Thus, Botha probably would have decided to minimize the risks of prior detection and certain attribution by testing secretly at sea rather than within South Africa

12. As Defense Minister since 1966, P. W. Botha very likely supported the development of a nuclear weapons program, including military preparations for nuclear testing. As Prime Minister, Botha has retained the Defense portfolio and has continued to keep closer counsel with senior military officers than with other government officials. We have no specific evidence that senior military officers perceive any imminent, or an eventually important, role for nuclear weapons

DOCUMENT 26: Director of Central Intelligence, Interagency Intelligence Memorandum, "The 22 September 1979 Event," December 1979.

PAGE 7 OF 10

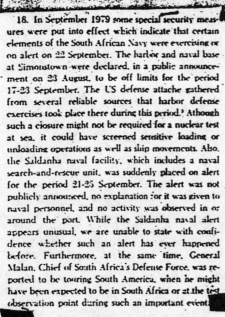

18. In September 1979 some special security measures were put into effect which indicate that certain elements of the South African Navy were exercising or on alert on 22 September. The harbor and naval base at Simonstown were declared, in a public announcement on 23 August, to be off limits for the period 17-23 September. The US defense attache gathered from several reliable sources that harbor defense exercises took place there during this period.[?] Although such a closure might not be required for a nuclear test at sea, it could have screened sensitive loading or unloading operations as well as ship movements. Also, the Saldanha naval facility, which includes a naval search-and-rescue unit, was suddenly placed on alert for the period 21-25 September. The alert was not publicly announced, no explanation for it was given to naval personnel, and no activity was observed in or around the port. While the Saldanha naval alert appears unusual, we are unable to state with confidence whether such an alert has ever happened before. Furthermore, at the same time, General Malan, Chief of South Africa's Defense Force, was reported to be touring South America, when he might have been expected to be in South Africa or at the test observation point during such an important event.

19. Prime Minister Botha has avoided public comment on the issue since the US disclosure of the Vela indications. However, on 25 September—three days after the nuclear event—he told a provincial congress of the ruling National Party that "South Africa's enemies might find out we have military weapons they do not know about." His enigmatic remark prompted speculation in the South African press that he had undeclared nuclear weapons in mind.

20. On 24 October—before the US disclosures of the technical indications of a test—the Prime Minister, addressing an anniversary dinner attended by past and present members of the AEB as well as members of the local diplomatic corps, reportedly paid tribute to the South African nuclear scientists who had been engaged in secret work of a strategic nature. He reportedly said that, for security reasons, their names could not be mentioned and that they would never gain the recognition in South Africa or abroad that they deserved.

21. *South African Responses to Nuclear Test Allegations.* South African official commentary since the United States disclosed the Vela indications of a nuclear event have been consistent with Pretoria's longstanding practice of cloaking its nuclear intentions in ambiguity—intimating a weapons capability without saying anything that would prove a case for tightening international sanctions against South Africa.

22. Only one official has categorically denied South Africa's involvement. On 26 October, immediately following the announcement in Washington of the Vela indications, Jacobus de Villiers, President of South Africa's Atomic Energy Board, told the press, "If there was anything of the sort, my first reaction would be that some other power might have undertaken a test, but it was definitely not South Africa." De Villiers, who had been directly involved in weapons design work at the Pelindaba nuclear research center before his promotion to President of the AEB in July 1979, almost certainly would be witting if South Africa had conducted a test explosion—and prepared to parry press queries if such a test were detected. On 6 November, De Villiers issued a report of periodic atmospheric samplings that had been conducted by the AEB; the report concluded, "It is considered most unlikely that an atmospheric nuclear test has recently been conducted in this region."

23. On 25 October the Commander of the South African Navy made allegations we believe to be false

8

DOCUMENT 26: Director of Central Intelligence, Interagency Intelligence Memorandum, "The 22 September 1979 Event," December 1979.

PAGE 8 OF 10

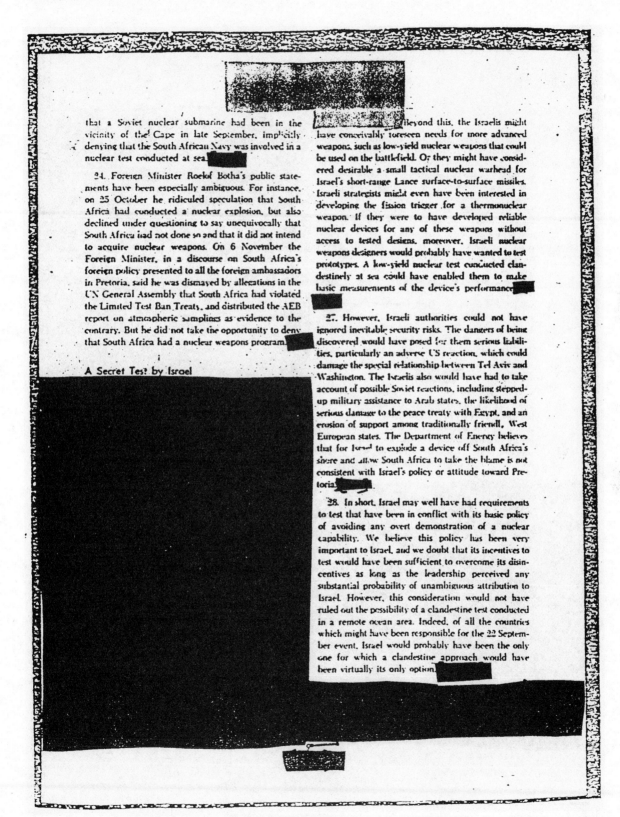

that a Soviet nuclear submarine had been in the vicinity of the Cape in late September, implicitly denying that the South African Navy was involved in a nuclear test conducted at sea.

24. Foreign Minister Roelof Botha's public statements have been especially ambiguous. For instance, on 25 October he ridiculed speculation that South Africa had conducted a nuclear explosion, but also declined under questioning to say unequivocally that South Africa had not done so and that it did not intend to acquire nuclear weapons. On 6 November the Foreign Minister, in a discourse on South Africa's foreign policy presented to all the foreign ambassadors in Pretoria, said he was dismayed by allegations in the UN General Assembly that South Africa had violated the Limited Test Ban Treaty, and distributed the AEB report on atmospheric samplings as evidence to the contrary. But he did not take the opportunity to deny that South Africa had a nuclear weapons program.

A Secret Test by Israel

Beyond this, the Israelis might have conceivably foreseen needs for more advanced weapons, such as low-yield nuclear weapons that could be used on the battlefield. Or they might have considered desirable a small tactical nuclear warhead for Israel's short-range Lance surface-to-surface missiles. Israeli strategists might even have been interested in developing the fission trigger for a thermonuclear weapon. If they were to have developed reliable nuclear devices for any of these weapons without access to tested designs, moreover, Israeli nuclear weapons designers would probably have wanted to test prototypes. A low-yield nuclear test conducted clandestinely at sea could have enabled them to make basic measurements of the device's performance.

27. However, Israeli authorities could not have ignored inevitable security risks. The dangers of being discovered would have posed for them serious liabilities, particularly an adverse US reaction, which could damage the special relationship between Tel Aviv and Washington. The Israelis also would have had to take account of possible Soviet reactions, including stepped-up military assistance to Arab states, the likelihood of serious damage to the peace treaty with Egypt, and an erosion of support among traditionally friendly West European states. The Department of Energy believes that for Israel to explode a device off South Africa's shore and allow South Africa to take the blame is not consistent with Israel's policy or attitude toward Pretoria.

28. In short, Israel may well have had requirements to test that have been in conflict with its basic policy of avoiding any overt demonstration of a nuclear capability. We believe this policy has been very important to Israel, and we doubt that its incentives to test would have been sufficient to overcome its disincentives as long as the leadership perceived any substantial probability of unambiguous attribution to Israel. However, this consideration would not have ruled out the possibility of a clandestine test conducted in a remote ocean area. Indeed, of all the countries which might have been responsible for the 22 September event, Israel would probably have been the only one for which a clandestine approach would have been virtually its only option.

DOCUMENT 26: Director of Central Intelligence, Interagency Intelligence Memorandum, "The 22 September 1979 Event," December 1979.

PAGE 9 OF 10

A Secret Test by South Africa and Israel

29. If the South Africans had considered testing Israeli designs in exchange for Israeli technical assistance, the benefits of cooperation would have been carefully weighed by both parties against the security risks inherent in such joint operations. On the one hand, the Israelis would have calculated that South Africa, as a pariah state in need of reliable friends, would have had every reason to preserve security and to remain silent in the face of inevitable speculation about its complicity with Tel Aviv. The Israelis also could have counted as a high probability that responsibility for any nuclear test in the area under investigation would be attributed to South Africa. On the other hand, unless the Israelis had offered advanced weapons technology, South African weapons developers would probably have preferred to test their own design, before incurring security risks in testing a foreign design. The Defense Intelligence Agency believes that South Africa would probably have had enough confidence in Israeli security to consider conducting a joint test ████

30. Israelis have not only participated in certain South African nuclear research activities over the last few years, but they have also offered and transferred various sorts of advanced nonnuclear weapons technology to South Africa. So clandestine arrangements between South Africa and Israel for joint testing operations might have been negotiable. ████

10

DOCUMENT 26: Director of Central Intelligence, Interagency Intelligence Memorandum, "The 22 September 1979 Event," December 1979.

PAGE 10 OF 10

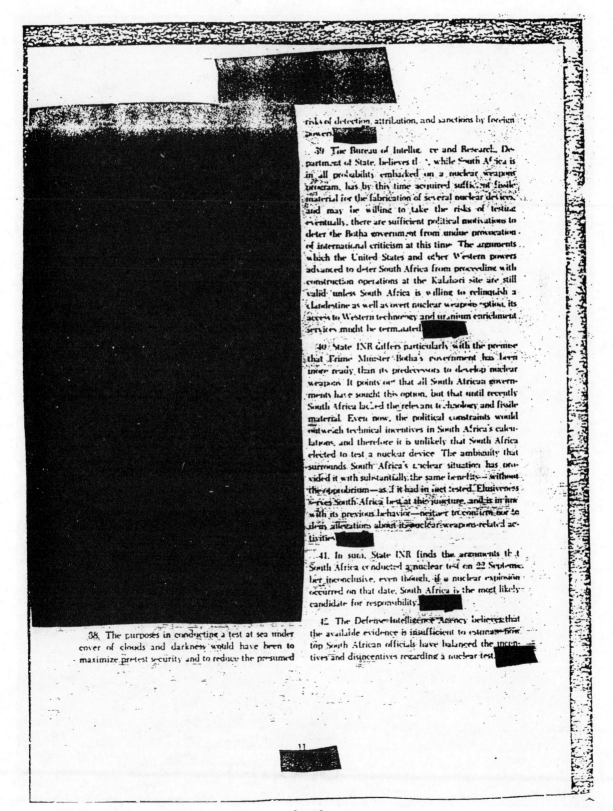

risks of detection, attribution, and sanctions by foreign powers.

39. The Bureau of Intelligence and Research, Department of State, believes that, while South Africa is in all probability embarked on a nuclear weapons program, has by this time acquired sufficient fissile material for the fabrication of several nuclear devices, and may be willing to take the risks of testing eventually, there are sufficient political motivations to deter the Botha government from undue provocation of international criticism at this time. The arguments which the United States and other Western powers advanced to deter South Africa from proceeding with construction operations at the Kalahari site are still valid unless South Africa is willing to relinquish a clandestine as well as overt nuclear weapons option, its access to Western technology and uranium enrichment services might be terminated.

40. State INR differs particularly with the premise that Prime Minister Botha's government has been more ready than its predecessors to develop nuclear weapons. It points out that all South African governments have sought this option, but that until recently South Africa lacked the relevant technology and fissile material. Even now, the political constraints would outweigh technical incentives in South Africa's calculations, and therefore it is unlikely that South Africa elected to test a nuclear device. The ambiguity that surrounds South Africa's nuclear situation has provided it with substantially the same benefits — without the opprobrium — as if it had in fact tested. Elusiveness serves South Africa best at this juncture, and is in line with its previous behavior — neither to confirm nor to deny allegations about its nuclear weapons-related activities.

41. In sum, State INR finds the arguments that South Africa conducted a nuclear test on 22 September inconclusive, even though, if a nuclear explosion occurred on that date, South Africa is the most likely candidate for responsibility.

42. The Defense Intelligence Agency believes that the available evidence is insufficient to estimate how top South African officials have balanced the incentives and disincentives regarding a nuclear test.

38. The purposes in conducting a test at sea under cover of clouds and darkness would have been to maximize pretest security and to reduce the presumed

11

DOCUMENT 27: State Department, Draft Talking Points, "South Africa—Nuclear Issue," April 3, 1981, with Attached Background Paper.

PAGE 1 OF 4

Obsolete
AF DRAFT
4/3/81

SECRET

A 0041

R

SOUTH AFRICA - NUCLEAR ISSUE

Talking Points

-- The United States places a high priority on the resumption of nuclear cooperation with South Africa and the provision of fuel for the Koeburg reactors. Our delegation in Paris presented you with a detailed proposal addressing the question of an interim supply arrangement with France; possible ways of dealing with ESCOM liability under its enrichment contract with DOE; and the Safari fuel supply situation.

-- It is my understanding that while the South African Government had previously indicated that it would consider NPT adherence and implementation of full scope safeguards, that your government now wished to reconsider this position.

-- In this regard you raised the possibilities of terminating the DOE contract and initiating a direct supply agreement with France or implementing the U.S. proposal on the contract concerning French supply for the initial core and one reload followed by resumption of U.S. supply under the DOE contract.

-- As you are aware, DOE has indicated that if ESCOM will agree to a firm date of August 31, 1981 for constructive delivery of enriched uranium under the contract, DOE will agree to accept delivery of fuel material on or before May 31, 1981. However, this proposal is contingent on the overall approach outlined to you by our delegation in Paris.

-- I would be interested in your analysis of the meetings in Paris and what you believe should be the next steps in our discussions.

SECRET

DOCUMENT 27: State Department, Draft Talking Points, "South Africa—Nuclear Issue," April 3, 1981, with Attached Background Paper.

PAGE 2 OF 4

SOUTH AFRICA NUCLEAR ISSUE

Background Paper

US Proposal

On March 30, 1981 the United States informed South Africa that the U.S. would interpose no objections to the proposal that France supply up to the initial core and first reload for each of the Koeberg reactors provided it contained these essential elements:

-- that before reactor fuel is shipped, South Africa would have adhered to the NPT and have brought an INFIRC/153 safeguards agreement into force; and

-- that a safeguards development program consisting of measures similar to that at the centrifuge facilities in the Netherlands and Japan would be instituted at the Valindaba enrichment facility promptly following South African acceptance of the arrangement and lasting until IAEA safeguards are applied under an NPT safeguards agreement.

Contract Relief

If South Africa would agree to this proposal whereby France would substitute for the U.S. in the delivery of the initial core and first reload, the U.S. made the following proposal to resolve the duplication of fuel supply and in order to continue the DOE contracts without any termination charges:

-- South Africa delivers feed to the U.S. in accordance with the DOE contracts;

-- South Africa stores the material at DOE for modest storage charges;

-- But DOE would not require payment of the invoices for separative work and storage costs until final action is taken on the export license.

-- When final action is taken, only then is South Africa obligated to pay for DOE invoices for separative work and storage fees;

-- Assuming the nuclear issues are resolved, South Africa and DOE resume scheduled contract deliveries.

-- Recognizing that this approach leaves South Africa with a surplus of enriched uranium the following opportunities exist to handle this material:

DOCUMENT 27: State Department, Draft Talking Points, "South Africa—Nuclear Issue," April 3, 1981, with Attached Background Paper.

PAGE 3 OF 4

- 2 -

-- The existing type of contracts for Koeberg 1 and 2 could be converted to the more flexible type of contract DOE now offers.

-- Beginning six years after converting to this new more flexible contract, South Africa would be able to start to use up the surplus product produced by DOE which was in storage with us.

-- South Africa would not need to purchase additional DOE enrichment services until all of this excess product was utilized.

-- South Africa would always have the option to sell the product on the commercial market in the U.S. for use in the U.S. or abroad.

SAG Position

The South African delegation indicated that because of changed circumstances the SAG did not wish to adhere to the NPT or implement full-scope safeguards at Valindaba. Instead, the SAG sought US neutrality toward a separate GOF-SAG fuel supply agreement.

Such an approach may suggest that South Africa is only concerned with the early supply to Koeberg before South Africa brings its commercial enrichment plant on stream in 1985. It is unclear whether South Africa has the necessary fuel fabrication capability at this time.

French Position

The GOF has indicated that because of the effect on other African countries, France would continue to insist that any interim French supply to Koeberg would be based on the proposed U.S. terms. However, the French indicated to the United States that if South Africa were to accept full-scope safeguards, but not NPT, the French would review their position.

Alternative U.S. Positions

In the event that the SAG does not meet the U.S. conditions for supply, the U.S. may wish to review the following options:

DOCUMENT 27: State Department, Draft Talking Points, "South Africa—Nuclear Issue," April 3, 1981, with Attached Background Paper.

PAGE 4 OF 4

- 3 -

(a) <u>Terminate the Agreement for Cooperation</u> between the U.S. and SAG by mutual agreement followed by DOE termination of the two LTFC contracts. Under Article IX of the LTFC Contract, these actions would release South Africa from all obligations under the contract at no charge.

(b) <u>Payment of the penalty charges by South Africa</u> for either partial or complete termination of the LTFC contracts which South Africa may do on a unilateral basis. (Complete termination charges equal $77 million, partial termination for the first cores of both reactors equal $31.6 million).

(c) <u>Grant South Africa relief from the terms of the DOE contract</u> on as narrowly defined a basis as possible in order to minimize the risks of having to provide similar relief to all customers. The U.S. could establish a new policy under which the Secretary of Energy, through a waiver, could relieve customers of all or a portion of the requisite termination charges when the Secretary of State advises that foreign policy dictates that an export license cannot or should not be granted and then only when contractual relief would further our foreign policy interests. The degree of contract relief could apply, with the concurrence of both the State Department and DOE, to the termination of the first two Koeburg cores whose delivery is not judged as desirable or practical at this time. Alternatively, the waiver could apply to termination charges for cancelling the entire contract if we judge such a waiver of our rights to such charges to be desirable.

<u>Alternative SAG Position</u>

<u>Litigation in the U.S. against DOE for breach of contract</u> may be considered by the SAG if it determines not to meet the U.S. requirements for an export license and not to deliver fuel by May 1, 1981 under the DOE contract. The objective would be to overturn the required termination charges.

The U.S. position is that the ESCOM-DOE contract and the export license requirements are separate issues. DOE is required by the contract to deliver fuel FOB to the DOE plant in the United States. It is not required to assure delivery to ESCOM in South Africa. The export license must meet certain political criteria which are separate from the terms of the ESCOM-DOE contract. Thus ESCOM's decision not to deliver the feedstock would be a unilateral termination invoking the requisite termination charges.

DOCUMENT 28: Secretary Alexander Haig, Cable for U.S. Embassy Pretoria, "Safari Research Reactor Fuel Conversion to Low Enriched Uranium," December 14, 1981.

PAGE 1 OF 2

Department of State **TELEG**

Referral: ACDA

R

CONFIDENTIAL

CONFIDENTIAL

AN: 0810595-0009

PAGE 01   STATE 330209
ORIGIN ACDA-12

INFO OCT-00 ADS-00 INR-10 EUR-12 SS-10 AF-10 CIAE-00
EB-08 DODE-00 H-01 IO-15 NSC-05 NSAE-00 L-03
DOE-10 PM-09 SAL-01 OES-09 SP-02 NRC-02 /119 R

DRAFTED BY ACDA/NWC/NST:OJSHEAKS
APPROVED BY ACDA/NWC/NST:JMENZEL
STATE/OES:ASESSOMS
AF/S:DDLOUHY
DOE/IP:SCEJA
------------------334347 142231Z /

P 142148Z DEC 81
FM SECSTATE WASHDC
TO AMEMBASSY PRETORIA PRIORITY
INFO AMEMBASSY VIENNA PRIORITY
AMCONSUL CAPE TOWN

ARMS CONTROL AND DISARMAMENT AGENCY
( ) Release ( ) Excise ( ) Deny
( ) Declassify ( ) Declassify in part
FOIA, PA, E.O. Exemptions _____
Downgrade TS to ( )S or ( )C, OADR
Classify _____ OADR
Class/Declass Auth _____ Date 4-13-91

CONFIDENTIAL STATE 330209

USIAEA

E.O. 12065: GDS 12/14/87 (MENZEL, JOERG) ACDA/NWC/NST

TAGS: PARM, TNUC, SF

SUBJ::SAFARI RESEARCH REACTOR FUEL CONVERSION TO LOW ENRICHED URANIUM

REF: PRETORIA 6904

1. (CONFIDENTIAL ENTIRE TEXT

2. DURING RECENT VISIT BY US SAFEGUARDS DELEGATION TO SOUTH AFRICA SOUTH AFRICANS RAISED POSSIBLE US ASSISTANCE IN CONVERTING THE SAFARI RESEARCH REACTOR TO USE OF LOW ENRICH-ED URANIUM (LEU, LESS THAN 20 U-235 FUEL). SAFARI IS
CONFIDENTIAL
CONFIDENTIAL

PAGE 02   STATE 330209

CURRENTLY OPERATING AT ABOUT 5 MW WITH INDIGENOUSLY

CONFIDENTIAL

DOCUMENT 28: Secretary Alexander Haig, Cable for U.S. Embassy Pretoria, "Safari Research Reactor Fuel Conversion to Low Enriched Uranium," December 14, 1981.

PAGE 2 OF 2

CONFIDENTIAL

PRODUCED HIGH ENRICHED FUEL (HEU, 45 U-235).

3. REDUCING THE ENRICHMENT REQUIREMENTS FOR SAFARI WOULD
HAVE IMPORTANT BENEFITS TO US NONPROLIFERATION POLICY
GOALS. FIRST, THE ARGUMENT FOR OPERATION OF THE SOUTH
AFRICAN PILO" ENRICHMENT PLANTS IN AN HEU PRODUCTION MODE
WOULD BE ELIMINATED. AND, SHOULD SOUTH AFRICA AGREE TO THE
APPLICATION OF SAFEGUARDS AT THE PILOT PLANT, LIMITING THE
PLANT PRODUCT TO LEU WOULD FACILITATE THE APPLICATION OF
SAFEGUARDS AND WOULD ENHANCE THEIR EFFECTIVENESS. SECOND,

SOUTH AFRICA WOULD JOIN THE CONSIDERABLE INTERNATIONAL
EFFORT TO ELIMINATE THE NEED WORLDWIDE FOR PRODUCTION,
TRANSPORTATION, AND USE OF HEU IN RESEARCH REACTORS.
THESE BENEFITS WARRANT US ASSISTANCE TO AID SOUTH AFRICAN
DEVELOPMENT OF ADVANCED LEU RESEARCH REACTOR FUEL
FABRICATION CAPABILITY.

4. THE SAFARI REACTOR HAS BEEN EXAMINED BY ARGONNE
NATIONAL LABORATORY (ANL) RESEARCH REACTOR EXPERTS.
ADVANCED LEU FUEL TYPES, SUCH AS URANIUM SILICIDES ARE NOW
BEING DEVELOPED AND DEMONSTRATED IN THE REDUCED ENRICHMENT
IN RESEARCH AND TEST REACTOR (RERTR) PROGRAM AT ANL AND
OAK RIDGE NATIONAL LABORATORY (ORNL).

5. EMBASSY IS REQUESTED TO APPROACH APPROPRIATE SOUTH
AFRICAN OFFICIALS TO EXPRESS US WILLINGNESS TO PROVIDE
ASSISTANCE IN THE AREA OF RESEARCH REACTOR LEU FUEL
FABRICATION TECHNOLOGY. US SUGGESTS THAT S.A. EXPERTS
VISIT RELEVANT FUEL FABRICATION FACILITIES AT ANL ON
JANUARY 11-12 AND ORNL ON JANUARY 13-14 TO BECOME
ACQUAINTED WITH THE RERTR PROGRAM AND TO EXPLORE POSSIBLE
CONFIDENTIAL
CONFIDENTIAL

PAGE 03   STATE 330209

COOPERATIVE PROGRAMS WHICH COULD BE BENEFICIAL TO SAFARI
CONVERSION. (ANL IS DEVELOPING THE URANIUM SILICIDE FUEL
TECHNOLOGY, AND ORNL IS DEVELOPING URANIUM OXIDE
DISPERSION FUEL TECHNOLOGY AND IS EXTENSIVELY INVOLVED IN
THE IRRADIATION AND POST-IRRADIATION EXAMINATION OF ALL
ADVANCED FUEL TYPES.) O.J. SHEAKS (ACDA) WILL ESCORT SAG
EXPERTS AT ANL. SAG TEAM COULD REVIEW NEXT STEPS WITH
USG OFFICIALS IN WASHINGTON ON JANUARY 15. POSSIBLE
FOLLOW-ON COOPERATION COULD INCLUDE TRAINING OF S.A. FUEL
EXPERTS AT ANL AND/OR ORNL.   HAIG

CONFIDENTIAL

DOCUMENT 29: Secretary Malcolm Baldrige, Letter to Honorable Charles H. Percy, May 12, 1982.

PAGE 1 OF 5

MAY 12 1982

Release in full ①

Honorable Charles H. Percy
Chairman, Subcommittee on Energy, Nuclear
    Proliferation, and Government Processes
Committee on Governmental Affairs
United States Senate
Washington, D.C. 20510

Dear Chuck,

Thank you for your letter concerning the proposed export of
95 grams of Helium-3 to the Atomic Energy Board of the
Republic of South Africa.

Section 309(c) of the Nuclear Non-Proliferation Act of 1978
requires the Department of Commerce to control for nuclear
nonproliferation reasons items that could be of significance
for nuclear explosive purposes, if used for purposes other
than for which the export is intended. The regulatory
implementation of this section takes into consideration
factors such as the status of the recipient country under the
Non-Proliferation Treaty, the mechanisms available to ensure
strict adherence to the stated end-use, and the ability of
the recipient to ensure safe operation of its nuclear
facilities.

I have requested the Secretary of Energy to respond to your
first three questions due to the fact that nuclear explosive
information is the responsibility of the Department of
Energy. Enclosed are our responses to the other questions
which you have raised. The information has been provided in
both a confidential version and a non-confidential version,
as you requested. The information furnished herewith is
subject to the provisions of Section 12(c) of the Export
Administration Act of 1979, 50 U.S.C. App. 2411(c), and its
unauthorized disclosure is prohibited by law.

                          Sincerely,

                          (sgd) MAB

                          Secretary of Commerce

This Document is Automati.
Declassified When Classified
Enclosures Are Removed

Enclosure

Prepared:BJohnson(EA) 5-10-82, Revised:ELevy(US/IT) 5-11-82
Wang #6402g Control #205099s Return File Copy to Denysyk
cc:ES(2),SEC,HR,D/S,OCA,GC,PC,CHRN,AS/TA,AGC,Jerome,Johnson
    Levy

CONFIDENTI 87 DOC 06 KM

DOCUMENT 29: Secretary Malcolm Baldrige, Letter to Honorable Charles H. Percy, May 12, 1982.

PAGE 2 OF 5

Partial Denial
b(3)(B) or b(1)

(2)

~~CONFIDENTIAL~~

CONFIDENTIAL VERSION
Responses to Questions on U.S. Nuclear Export Policy

1) Can He-3 be used directly in a nuclear explosive device?

2) Can He-3 be used in any manner in a nuclear explosive?

3) If He-3 can be used in a nuclear explosive, what kind?

(To be answered by the Secretary of Energy.)

4) For what purpose does South Africa want He-3?

(3)

5 USC 552(b)(3)
5 USC 552(b)(1)

5) What assurances will the United States receive that this material will be put to use in the manner South Africa has stated?

(1)

5 USC 552(b)(1)

5 USC 552(b)(3)

6) What other nations use He-3 in their civil nuclear programs?

He-3 is used for safety-related testing activities in Sweden, Belgium, and France.

7) Are there alternatives to using He-3 in civil nuclear programs?

Because of its unique properties, He-3 has been selected for similar testing programs in a number of countries. As such, it is not clear that a viable replacement for He-3 could be found for this application.

8) What statutory requirements are there for the export of nuclear material like He-3?

Exports of certain materials like He-3 are controlled under the provisions of Part 378 of the Export Administration Regulations (EAR). These controls are administered by the Department of Commerce and apply to all commodities identified on the "Nuclear Referral List" as well as to any other item under Commerce jurisdiction of significance for nuclear explosive purposes which could be used for purposes other than for which the export is intended. Licensing procedures for these items are established pursuant to Section 309(c) of the Nuclear Non-Proliferation Act of 1978 and Section 17(d) of the Export Administration Act of 1979 and appear in Supplement 1 to Part 378 of the EAR.

CLASSIFIED BY *CR Stoiber/OES/NES/State*

DOCUMENT 29: Secretary Malcolm Baldrige, Letter to Honorable Charles H. Percy, May 12, 1982.

PAGE 3 OF 5

-2-

9) What other nuclear materials fall under the same export requirements as He-3 and do any of these have a nuclear explosive application?

All materials identified on the "Nuclear Referral List", or materials which if used for other than the intended end-use could be used for nuclear explosive purposes, fall under the same export requirements as He-3. All commodities on the "Nuclear Referral List" have been idenitified as being of significance for nuclear explosive purposes. This list includes such items as certain computer equipment, specially designed compressors and blowers, nuclear reactor equipment, boron, certain radioisotopes, and others.

10) What is the United States' policy on nuclear cooperation with South Africa?

The United States' policy with respect to nuclear cooperation with South Africa continues to require adherence by the South African government to the Non-Proliferation Treaty and acceptance of full-scope safeguards as a condition to US supply of nuclear facilities and fuel controlled under the Atomic Energy Act. However, this Administration has adopted a more flexible policy with respect to approvals of exports of dual-use commodities and other materials and equipment which have nuclear-related uses in areas such as health and safety activities.

11) Does the export of He-3 represent a contradiction to and departure from this policy?

As indicated in the response to Question 10, this export, for use in nuclear safety-related testing, does not represent a contradiction to or departure from U.S. policy.

12) Please provide a list and a description of all nuclear end-use materials and equipment shipped to South Africa under U.S. export licenses in the past two years.

Since May 1980 the following equipment has been licensed for export to South Africa pursuant to the procedures described in the response to Question 8:

      One (1) set of vibration test equipment
      One (1) hot isostatic press
      Nine (9) sets of computers or computer-related equipment
      One (1) multi-channel analyzer
      One (1) set of hydrogen recombiners

87   DOC   06   KM

DOCUMENT 29: Secretary Malcolm Baldrige, Letter to Honorable Charles H. Percy, May 12, 1982.

PAGE 4 OF 5

Full Release

③

NON-CONFIDENTIAL VERSION
Responses to Questions on U.S. Nuclear Export Policy

1) Can He-3 be used directly in a nuclear explosive device?

2) Can He-3 be used in any manner in a nuclear explosive?

3) If He-3 can be used in a nuclear explosive, what kind?

(To be answered by the Secretary of Energy.)

4) For what purpose does South Africa want He-3?

Disclosure of this information is limited by the provisions of Section 12(c) of the Export Administration Act of 1979. It may only be released publicly if the full Committee determines that not doing so would be contrary to the national interest.

5) What assurances will the United States receive that this material will be put to use in the manner South Africa has stated?

The United States will require assurances that this material will be put to use in the manner that South Africa has stated.

6) What other nations use He-3 in their civil nuclear programs?

He-3 is used for safety-related testing activities in Sweden, Belgium, and France.

7) Are there alternatives to using He-3 in civil nuclear programs?

Because of its unique properties, He-3 has been selected for similar testing programs in a number of countries. As such, it is not clear that a viable replacement for He-3 could be found for this application.

8) What statutory requirements are there for the export of nuclear material like He-3?

Exports of certain materials like He-3 are controlled under the provisions of Part 378 of the Export Administration Regulations (EAR). These controls are administered by the Department of Commerce and apply to all commodities identified on the "Nuclear Referral List" as well as to any other item under Commerce jurisdiction of significance for nuclear explosive purposes which could be used for purposes other than for which the export is intended. Licensing procedures for these items are established pursuant to Section 309(c) of the Nuclear Non-Proliferation Act of 1978 and Section 17(d) of the Export Administration Act of 1979 and appear in Supplement 1 to Part 378 of the EAR.

87   DOC   06   KM

DOCUMENT 29: Secretary Malcolm Baldrige, Letter to Honorable Charles H. Percy, May 12, 1982.

PAGE 5 OF 5

-2-

9) What other nuclear materials fall under the same export requirements as He-3 and do any of these have a nuclear explosive application?

All materials identified on the "Nuclear Referral List", or materials which if used for other than the intended end-use could be used for nuclear explosive purposes, fall under the same export requirements as He-3. All commodities on the "Nuclear Referral List" have been idenitified as being of significance for nuclear explosive purposes. This list includes such items as certain computer equipment, specially designed compressors and blowers, nuclear reactor equipment, boron, certain radioisotopes, and others.

10) What is the United States' policy on nuclear cooperation with South Africa?

The United States' policy with respect to nuclear cooperation with South Africa continues to require adherence by the South African government to the Non-Proliferation Treaty and acceptance of full-scope safeguards as a condition to US supply of nuclear facilities and fuel controlled under the Atomic Energy Act. However, this Administration has adopted a more flexible policy with respect to approvals of exports of dual-use commodities and other materials and equipment which have nuclear-related uses in areas such as health and safety activities.

11) Does the export of He-3 represent a contradiction to and departure from this policy?

As indicated in the response to Question 10, this export, for use in nuclear safety-related testing, does not represent a contradiction to or departure from U.S. policy.

12) Please provide a list and a description of all nuclear end-use materials and equipment shipped to South Africa under U.S. export licenses in the past two years.

Since May 1980 the following equipment has been licensed for export to South Africa pursuant to the procedures described in the response to Question 8:

    One (1) set of vibration test equipment
    One (1) hot isostatic press
    Nine (9) sets of computers or computer-related equipment
    One (1) multi-channel analyzer
    One (1) set of hydrogen recombiners

DOCUMENT 30: William J. Dircks, Memorandum for the Nuclear Regulatory Commission, "U.S. Citizens at the Koeberg Nuclear Power Plant in South Africa," February 26, 1985.

PAGE 1 OF 6

SECRET

IP-85-27
6   A

Information in this record was deleted
in accordance with the Freedom of Information
Act, exemptions ____
FOIA- 87-3

Document No. ____
This document consists of ____ pages
No. ____ of ____ copies, Series ____

February 26, 1985

SECY-85-69

For: The Commission

From: William J. Dircks
                Executive Director for Operations

(U) Subject: U.S. CITIZENS AT THE KOEBERG NUCLEAR POWER
                PLANT IN SOUTH AFRICA

(U) Purpose: To (1) provide the Commission information requested at a
                February 1 Commission meeting on the above subject, and
                (2) forward for Commission review questions and answers that
                may be of use in upcoming Congressional hearings.

(U) Background: 10 CFR Part 810, which implements Section 57.b of the Atomic
                Energy Act of 1954, as amended, requires that certain
                assistance to foreign nuclear programs must be authorized by
                the Secretary of Energy unless specifically authorized under
                an agreement for cooperation. In February 1983, the
                Department of Energy issued an amended Part 810 that, among
                other things, requires case-by-case review of all such
                assistance to non-nuclear weapons states not parties to the
                NPT, except those accepting fullscope safeguards or for
                which the Treaty of Tlatelolco is currently in force. (Such
                reviews are also required for Iran, Iraq, Libya, Syria, and
                Afghanistan.) Prior to that time, specific authorization
                for power reactor-related assistance to South Africa was not
                required. The final rule excluded from coverage any
                activities prior to September 17, 1982.

(U)   The Commission will recall that in September 1983 the
                Executive Branch authorized activities involving assistance
                to the safeguarded Koeberg Nuclear Power Plant in South
                Africa. Action on these long-pending requests had been
                awaiting development of a comprehensive policy regarding
                nuclear exports to South Africa. However, since that time
                only one additional activity covered by Part 810, the
                extension of a previously existing contract, has been

CONTACT:
W. Upshaw, IPEI
49-24724

Multiple Sources

OADR

James R. Shea, Dir., IP

NATIONAL SECURITY INFORMATION
Un____

SECRET

~~SECRET~~

The Commission   2

authorized by DOE (in April 1984). Several additional Part
810 authorization requests for Koeberg continue to be held
in an indefinite pending status because DOE has been unable
to obtain Department of State concurrence.

(S) Discussion:

(U)

However, the staff's inquiries have disclosed that in
September 1984, NRC officials were made aware of possible
South African recruitment efforts in the U.S. when Region 2
was requested orally by the South African utility ESCOM to
verify if certain individuals were NRC-licensed reactor
operators. With concurrence of IP staff, Region 2 responded
to ESCOM on September 20, 1984, quoting data from the public
record (Appendix A). Later, on October 26, 1984, during a
visit to the Catawba nuclear power plant in Region 2,
Chairman Palladino also recalls being told that Duke Power
Company was losing people to the South African nuclear
program (See Appendix B for an extract from the transcript
of the February 1 Commission meeting at which the South
African matters were discussed).

DOCUMENT 30: William J. Dircks, Memorandum for the Nuclear Regulatory Commission, "U.S. Citizens at the Koeberg Nuclear Power Plant in South Africa," February 26, 1985.

PAGE 3 OF 6

The Commission   3

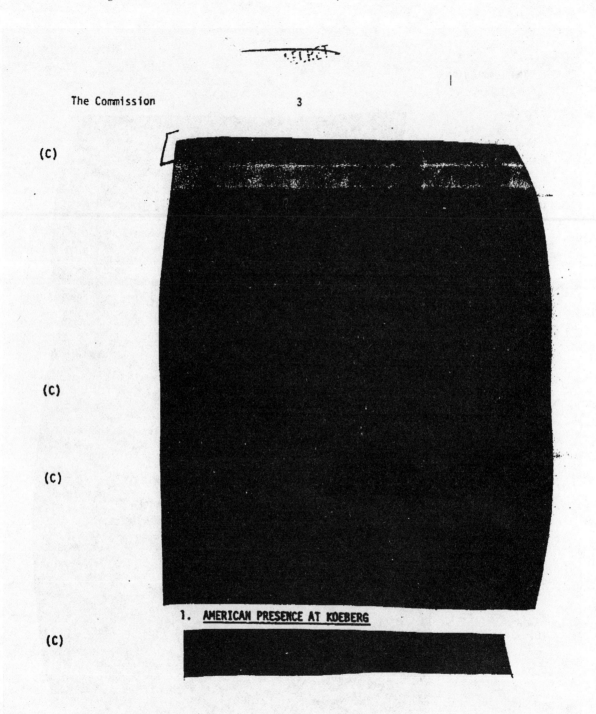

(C)

(C)

(C)

1. **AMERICAN PRESENCE AT KOEBERG**

(C)

DOCUMENT 30: William J. Dircks, Memorandum for the Nuclear Regulatory Commission, "U.S. Citizens at the Koeberg Nuclear Power Plant in South Africa," February 26, 1985.

PAGE 4 OF 6

The Commission

4

(C)

(C)

(C)

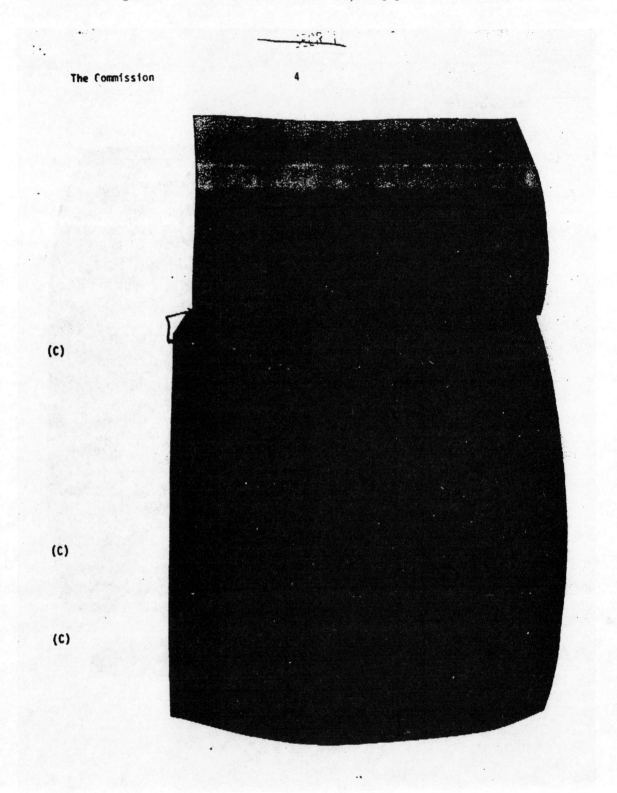

DOCUMENT 30: William J. Dircks, Memorandum for the Nuclear Regulatory Commission, "U.S. Citizens at the Koeberg Nuclear Power Plant in South Africa," February 26, 1985.

PAGE 5 OF 6

The Commission   5

(C)

After informing the Commission, the staff, on February 8, informed DOE that NRC had "no objection" to the State Department's recommendation that the then-pending and future Part 810 applications by American individuals to work at Koeberg be denied.

(C)

NRC's Current Involvement

(U)   At the present time, NRC's involvement in this matter is limited to the review of the Part 810 cases at hand. However, in an effort to prevent future inadvertent violations of Part 810, the staff has prepared, in cooperation with DOE, a notice to inform all NRC reactor licensees, licensed reactor operators and appropriate NRC officials of the Part 810 requirements (Appendix D).

(U)   As a separate but related matter, the South African Atomic Energy Corporation has offered a position in its licensing branch to an NRC employee[   ] While NRC has not been directly involved in the arrangements for this employment, the staff has obtained a copy (Appendix E) of a letter from DOE to the NRC employee in which he is informed in an advisory opinion that his proposed employment is not subject to the provisions of Part 810.

(U)   Finally, the staff has learned that one current NRC employee (a regional inspector) and a recent applicant for a position at NRC were formerly employed by ESCOM in South Africa. The NRC inspector was employed under contracts which apparently predate the February 1983 amendments to 10 CFR Part 810, but we are not sure of the situation with regard to the recent applicant, whose work for ESCOM was between 1981 and 1984. Copies of the correspondence in NRC files regarding these two individuals are attached at Appendix F. The staff plans to inform DOE of these two individuals and will cooperate in any follow-up activities that DOE might request.

The Commission   6

Request from Representative Markey

(U)   On January 25, Representative Markey wrote to Chairman Palladino requesting information on NRC's involvement in and knowledge of these matters. The staff has forwarded separately a proposed response to Representative Markey.

Q's and A's

(U)   Attached at Appendix G are draft Q's and A's on this South Africa matter which the Commission may wish to use as appropriate during forthcoming Congressional hearings.

(C)   Conclusion:

(U)   The responsible official at DOE has also agreed to brief the Commission on this matter should the Commission so request.

William J. Dircks
Executive Director for Operations

Appendices:
A. 9/20/84 Region II/ESCOM (U)
B. Unclassified Portion of February
    Commission Meeting (U)
C. 2/1/85 SNEC Minutes (C)
D. Notice to NRC Reactor Licensees
    on Part 810 (U)
E. 12/20/84 Thorne/Norris (U)
F. Correspondence re NRC employees
    previously employed by ESCOM (U)
G. Q's and A's (U)

DISTRIBUTION:
Commissioners
OGC
OPE
EDO
ELD
REGIONAL OFFICES
SECY

DOCUMENT 31: Defense Intelligence Agency, Special Assessment, "SOUTH AFRICA: Missile Activity," July 5, 1989.

PAGE 1 OF 2

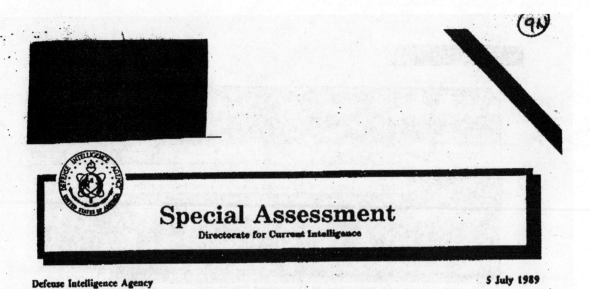

Special Assessment

Directorate for Current Intelligence

Defense Intelligence Agency

5 July 1989

SOUTH AFRICA: Missile Activity (U)

Major Points

A probable SRBM was launched from South Africa's Arniston Missile Test Range on 5 July.

(5 July) a probable SRBM was launched in an easterly direction from South Africa's Arniston Missile Test Range.

(Continued on Reverse)

DOCUMENT 31: Defense Intelligence Agency, Special Assessment, "SOUTH AFRICA: Missile Activity," July 5, 1989.

PAGE 2 OF 2

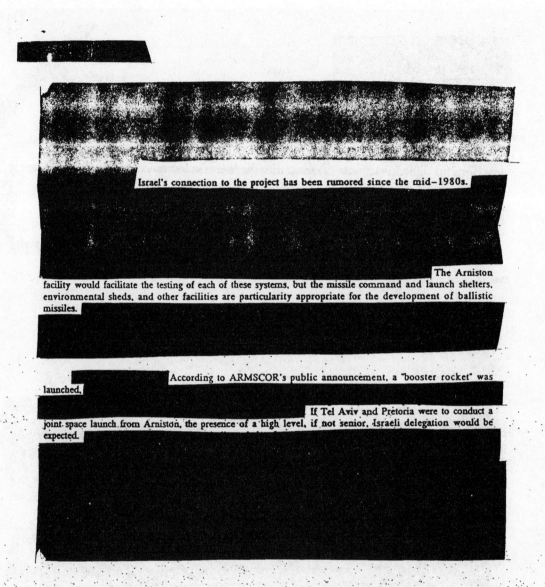

Israel's connection to the project has been rumored since the mid–1980s.

The Arniston facility would facilitate the testing of each of these systems, but the missile command and launch shelters, environmental sheds, and other facilities are particularity appropriate for the development of ballistic missiles.

According to ARMSCOR's public announcement, a "booster rocket" was launched,

If Tel Aviv and Pretoria were to conduct a joint space launch from Arniston, the presence of a high level, if not senior, Israeli delegation would be expected.

2

DOCUMENT 32: Secretary James Baker, Cable for U.S. Embassy Tel Aviv, "Israel Aircraft Industries and Indictment for Illegal Exports to South Africa," November 22, 1989.

PAGE 1 OF 1

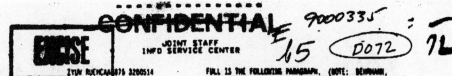

CONFIDENTIAL 9000335

JOINT STAFF
INFO SERVICE CENTER

15 (D072) 72

IMMEDIATE
C 2205132 NOV 89
FM SECSTATE WASHDC
TO AMEMBASSY TEL AVIV IMMEDIATE 9711
INFO AMEMBASSY PRETORIA IMMEDIATE 6341

C O N F I D E N T I A L

LIMITED OFFICIAL USE STATE 373875

E.O 12356: N/A
TAGS: MASS, IS, SA
SUBJECT: ISRAEL AIRCRAFT INDUSTRIES AND INDICTMENT FOR ILLEGAL EXPORTS TO SOUTH AFRICA

1. THE NEW YORK TIMES REPORTED ON NOVEMBER 15 THAT THREE SOUTH AFRICANS AND TWO AMERICANS WERE TO BE CHARGED WITH TRYING TO EXPORT US-ORIGIN MISSILE TECHNOLOGY ILLEGALLY TO SOUTH AFRICA. THE PRESS REPORT, WHICH WAS BASED ON AN AFFIDAVIT BY A U.S. CUSTOMS AGENT, REFERRED TO ALLEGATIONS BY ONE OF THE SUSPECTS THAT ISRAEL AIRCRAFT INDUSTRIES (IAI) HAD OFFERED TO ACT AS A MIDDLEMAN IN THE PROPOSED TRANSACTION. AT THE NOON PRESS BRIEFING ON NOVEMBER 16, THE DEPARTMENT REFERRED ALL QUESTIONS ON THIS MATTER TO THE DEPARTMENT OF JUSTICE.

2. THE FIVE SUSPECTS WERE INDICTED ON NOVEMBER 16 IN THE DISTRICT OF COLUMBIA FOR VIOLATIONS OF VARIOUS LAWS INCLUDING THE ARMS EXPORT CONTROL ACT AND THE COMPREHENSIVE ANTI-APARTHEID ACT.

3. THE AFFIDAVIT SUBMITTED IN SUPPORT OF THE INDICTMENT OUTLINES A SERIES OF ATTEMPTS BY THE INDICTEES TO EXPORT GYROSCOPES MANUFACTURED BY NORTHROP CORPORATION TO ARMSCOR IN SOUTH AFRICA. THE GYROSCOPES, WHICH THE INDICTMENT ALLEGES WERE TO TOTAL SOME FIFTY MILLION DOLLARS IN VALUE, WERE TO BE USED IN MISSILES DESIGNED TO DEFEAT THE SOVIET T-80 MAIN BATTLE TANK.

4. U.S. CUSTOMS OFFICIALS LEARNED OF THE SCHEME AT AN EARLY STAGE AND SET UP AN UNDERCOVER OPERATION TO INVESTIGATE THE SUSPECTS. SEVERAL POSSIBLE METHODS OF ROUTING THE GYROSCOPES THROUGH THIRD COUNTRIES (INCLUDING ISRAEL) TO SOUTH AFRICA WERE DISCUSSED, BUT THE ONLY EQUIPMENT EVER DELIVERED BY NORTHROP, WHICH WAS ACTING IN COOPERATION WITH CUSTOMS, WAS APPARENTLY GOING TO BE SMUGGLED DIRECTLY TO SOUTH AFRICA.

5. ONE PARAGRAPH OF THE AFFIDAVIT, WHICH CONCERNS THE ALLEGED OFFER BY IAI TO FACILITATE THE EXPORTS, IS OF PARTICULAR INTEREST TO THE DEPARTMENT. IT IS QUOTED IN-

FULL IN THE FOLLOWING PARAGRAPH. (NOTE: BENJAMIN, MENTIONED IN PARA 6, IS ONE OF THE INDICTEES).

6. BEGIN TEXT: ON OCTOBER 12, 1988, JOHN KEVO, MANAGER, INTERNATIONAL CONTRACTS, NORTHROP CORPORATION, NORWOOD MASSACHUSETTS, CONTACTED THE SAC/DC-VIRGINIA'S (UNDERCOVER OPERATION) REGARDING AN INQUIRY HE HAD RECEIVED FROM ISRAEL AIRCRAFT INDUSTRIES, LTD., (IAI), TEL AVIV, ISRAEL. KEVO, WHO IS AWARE OF THE ATTEMPT BY SOUTH AFRICA TO OBTAIN THE GYROSCOPES, STATED THAT IAI'S REQUEST IS NEARLY IDENTICAL TO THE GYROSCOPES THAT WERE CURRENTLY BEING SOUGHT BY THE SOUTH AFRICANS THROUGH THE SAC/DC-VIRGINIA'S UNDERCOVER OPERATION. IAI HAD PREVIOUSLY BEEN IDENTIFIED BY BENJAMIN IN AUGUST, 1988 AS A FIRM WHICH WOULD ASSIST IN ACQUIRING THE GYROSCOPES FOR DIVERSION TO SOUTH AFRICA. BENJAMIN REPORTEDLY MET WITH THE OWNER OF IAI WHILE HE WAS IN ISRAEL. ACCORDING TO BENJAMIN, IAI WOULD HELP THE SOUTH AFRICANS OBTAIN THE GYROSCOPES, BUT THE PRICE WOULD BE VERY HIGH. END TEXT

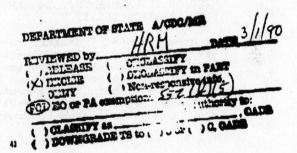

DEPARTMENT OF STATE A/CDC/MR

REVIEWED BY _____ HRM DATE 3/1/90

( ) RELEASE ( ) DECLASSIFY
(X) EXCISE ( ) DECLASSIFY in PART
( ) DENY ( ) Non-responsive info.
(FOI) EO or PA exemptions: _____

( ) CLASSIFY as _____
( ) DOWNGRADE TS to ( ) S ( ) C, OADR

43

JOINT STAFF
ACTION   (U,8,7,8)
INFO MIDS(1) WNCC:DDO(1) J5(2) J5-MEAF-J(1)
      J5-MEAA-J(1) SECDEF-M(1) OSSA-PA(1) OSSA-NM(1)
      USDP:NESA(3) USDP:AFR(1) USDP:OSAA(4) USDP:PBREQ(1)
      USDP:IEEA(1) USDP:LIC(1) USDP:AFR POL(1)
      USDP:POLPLAN(1) DI-1(1) NMIC(1) CS(1) NMS(1)
      JS1-58(1) JS1-5A(1) DAT-6(1) DIO-GPF(1) DE-4(1)
      DB-8C(3) DB-8B(1) DB-8D(4) DX-5B(1) DIA(1) DIO-AF(1)
      DIO-NESA(1)
      +OCSA WASHINGTON DC
      +CNO WASHINGTON DC
      +CSAF WASHINGTON DC
      +PTC WASH DC
      +USCINCEUR VAIHINGEN GE
      +USEUCOM AIDES VAIHINGEN GE
      +CMC CC WASHINGTON DC
      +USCINCSOC INTEL OPS CEN MACDILL AFB FL
      +USCINCCENT MACDILL AFB FL
      +MAC INTEL CEN SCOTT AFB IL//IN//
      +CJTF FIVE//J20//
      +CJTF FOUR
      +SAFE

DOCUMENT 33: President F. W. de Klerk, Speech to Parliament, "The Nuclear Non-Proliferation Treaty and South Africa's Nuclear Capability," March 24, 1993.

PAGE 1 OF 7

EMBASSY OF SOUTH AFRICA
3051 MASSACHUSETTS AVENUE, N. W.
WASHINGTON, D. C. 20008
(202) 232-4400

(COPY OF SPEECH BY PRESIDENT DE KLERK TO JOINT SESSION OF PARLIAMENT ON MARCH 24, 1993 REGARDING THE NUCLEAR NON-PROLIFERATION TREATY AND SOUTH AFRICA'S NUCLEAR CAPABILITY)

QUOTE

SPEECH BY THE STATE PRESIDENT, MR F W DE KLERK, TO A JOINT SESSION OF PARLIAMENT, 24 MARCH 1993; NUCLEAR NON-PROLIFERATION TREATY

Mr Speaker, when I decided last week to call a joint session, it was my intention to concentrate on the announce-ment to Parliament of important information with regard to the Nuclear Non-proliferation Treaty and related matters. Since then certain developments have compelled me to cover a much wider area. I am, however, still commencing with announcements relating to South Africa's nuclear capability.

THE NUCLEAR NON-PROLIFERATION TREATY AND RELATED MATTERS

Honourable Members will recall that when I delivered my first opening address on 2 February 1990, I emphasised, among other things, the normalisation of South Africa's international relations. An important aspect of this was, and is, the significant contribution that South Africa can and will have to make towards peace, stability and progress

DOCUMENT 33: President F. W. de Klerk, Speech to Parliament, "The Nuclear Non-Proliferation Treaty and South Africa's Nuclear Capability," March 24, 1993.

PAGE 2 OF 7

in Southern Africa. With this objective in mind the Government has - in addition to many other initiatives in a variety of other spheres - taken far-reaching and drastic decisions with regard to the non-proliferation of all weapons of mass destruction. This includes nuclear, as well as chemical and biological weapons.

The Government acceded to the Nuclear Non-proliferation Treaty (NPT) on 10 July 1991. We became a founder signatory of the United Nations Convention on the Prohibition of the Development, Production, Stockpiling and Use of Chemical Weapons and on their Destruction on 14 January 1993. It is also participating in the current review of the Convention on Biological and Toxin Weapons.

I wish to concentrate today on the Nuclear Non-proliferation Treaty and would like to convey important information to Parliament, the public and the international community. It is important that the integrity of the Republic of South Africa with regard to its commitments to the Nuclear Non-proliferation Treaty should be placed above any doubt.

When a country accedes to the NPT, it undertakes, as from the date of accession, not to manufacture or otherwise acquire nuclear weapons. It also undertakes to enter into a Safeguards Agreement, in terms of which a comprehensive inventory of all the nuclear material and nuclear facilities as they exist for the country as a whole at the time that agreement enters into force, be submitted to the International Atomic Energy Agency. Such facilities and material are then subject to international inspection and verification. The IAEA also conducts regular inspections to verify the inventory and to ensure that these materials and facilities are used for peaceful purposes only.

Since its accession to the NPT, South Africa has strictly adhered to the conditions of the NPT and has maintained a policy of transparency and professional co-operation with the IAEA. This positive approach has led to South Africa's resuming its seat at the IAEA General Conference, since September 1991, without opposition, after an absence of 12 years.

The process of verifying the completeness of South Africa's declaration of nuclear materials and facilities has proceeded so successfully that the IAEA was in the position to report to the Board of Governors in September 1992 that it was satisfied that South Africa's inventory of nuclear materials and facilities was complete and that all such facilities and materials had been submitted to acceptable controls.

However, mainly because of the events in Iraq, which violated the conditions of the NPT by launching a clandestine nuclear weapons programme, certain countries have

DOCUMENT 33: President F. W. de Klerk, Speech to Parliament, "The Nuclear Non-Proliferation Treaty and South Africa's Nuclear Capability," March 24, 1993.

PAGE 3 OF 7

called the effectiveness of the IAEA verification rgime into question. Some countries have also alleged that South Africa still has covert aspirations in this regard and that it has not fully disclosed its stockpile of enriched uranium.

Such allegations are regularly taken up by both the local and the international press, and are beginning to take on the dimensions of a campaign. South Africa's present nuclear programme which is directed towards commerciali- sation including the export of high technology products is in the process placed under suspicion and is harmed. Our country cannot afford this. Accordingly, I wish today to confirm unequivocally that South Africa is adhering strictly to the requirements of the NPT and that it will continue to do so.

I would, however, like to go further. Any doubt about the Government's intentions with regard to nuclear matters, must, for once and all, be removed. For this reason, the Government has decided to provide full information on South Africa's past nuclear programme despite the fact that the NPT does not require this.

At one stage, South Africa did, indeed, develop a limited nuclear deterrent capability.

The decision to develop this limited capability was taken as early as 1974, against the background of a Soviet expansio- nist threat in Southern Africa, as well as prevailing uncertainty concerning the designs of the Warsaw Pact members.

The build up of the Cuban forces in Angola from 1975 onwards reinforced the perception that a deterrent was necessary - as did South Africa's relative international isolation and the fact that it could not rely on outside assistance, should it be attacked.

Details relating to the limited deterrent capability, and the strategy in this regard, which were at that time developed, are as follows:

- The objective was the provision of 7 nuclear fission devices, which was considered the minimum for testing purposes and for the maintenance thereafter of credible deterrent capability.

- When the decision was taken to terminate the programme, only 6 devices had been completed.

- No advanced nuclear explosives, such as thermo-nuclear explosives. were manufactured.

DOCUMENT 33: President F. W. de Klerk, Speech to Parliament, "The Nuclear Non-Proliferation Treaty and South Africa's Nuclear Capability," March 24, 1993.

PAGE 4 OF 7

- The programme was under the direct control of the Head of Government, who decided that it should be managed and implemented by Armscor.

- Knowledge of the existence of the programme was limited to a number of Ministers on a "need-to-know" basis.

- The strategy was that, if the situation in Southern Africa were to deteriorate seriously, a confidential indication of the deterrent capability, would be given to one or more of the major powers, for example the United States, in an attempt to persuade them to intervene.

- It was never the intention to use the devices and from the outset the emphasis was on deterrence.

This was the situation when I became State President in 1989. As a former Minister of the AEC I was also informed about this.

On my assumption of office as State President it was already evident to me, and also to my colleagues who were also informed, that it was in our national interest that a total reverse - also in respect of our nuclear policy - was called for.

During 1989, the global political situation changed dramatically:

- A cease-fire in Angola was agreed.

- On 22 December 1988, a tripartite agreement was signed at the United Nations with Cuba and Angola which provided for the independence of Namibia and the withdrawal of 50 000 Cuban troops from Angola.

- The Cold War had come to an end and developments leading to the destruction of the Berlin Wall and the break-up of the Soviet-bloc had become the order of the day.

- The prospects of moving away from a confrontational relationship with the international community in general and with our neighbours in Africa, in particular, to one of co-operation and development were good.

In these circumstances a nuclear deterrent had become, not only superfluous, but in fact an obstacle to the development of South Africa's international relations.

World opinion had also become increasingly opposed to nuclear weapons, and significant advantages for South Africa could be forthcoming should it accede to the NPT. Although it already had an advanced nuclear technology base and nuclear industry, accession would facilitate the international exchanges of the new technology for its future development. It could also be of benefit to our neighbouring states and in due course to Africa as a whole.

DOCUMENT 33: President F. W. de Klerk, Speech to Parliament, "The Nuclear Non-Proliferation Treaty and South Africa's Nuclear Capability," March 24, 1993.

PAGE 5 OF 7

Within this factual framework, and with consideration to all of the other innovative policy objectives which by then had already began to take on form, it was decided towards the end of 1989, that the pilot enrichment plant at Pelindaba should be closed and decommissioned.

Early in 1990, final effect was given to decisions that:

- all the nuclear devices should be dismantled and destroyed;

- all the nuclear material in Armscor's possession be recast and returned to the AEC where it should be stored according to internationally accepted measures;

- Armscor's facilities should be decontaminated and be used only for non-nuclear commercial purposes;

- after which South Africa should accede to the Non-Proliferation Treaty, thereby submitting all its nuclear materials and facilities to international safeguards.

The implementation of these decisions and instructions proceeded according to plan. The process of dismantling took place under the strict, joint control of the AEC and ARMSCOR. As a further control measure, an eminent professor of nuclear physics, Prof W L Mouton, was appointed as independent auditor to oversee the process. It was his task to satisfy himself that every gram of nuclear material had been accounted for and all the hardware and design information was destroyed. This has been done.

South Africa acceded to the Non-Proliferation Treaty on 10 July 1991 and signed, according to the requirements of the Treaty, a Safeguards Agreement with the IAEA on 16 September 1991 with immediate force and effect.

On 30 October 1991, in accordance with the Safeguards Agreement with the IAEA, South Africa submitted a complete inventory of all nuclear materials and facilities under its jurisdiction which contained such materials on 30 September 1991, since which date all such materials and facilities are subject to international safeguards.

South Africa's hands are clean and we are concealing nothing. Permission has now been granted by the Government, with a view to international inspection, for full access to facilities and records of facilities. which in the past were used for the preparation of a nuclear deterrent capability.

I sincerely trust that this unprecedented act, namely the voluntary dismantling of a nuclear deterrent capability, and the voluntary revelation of all relevant information will confirm this Government's effort to assure transparency. I trust also that South Africa's initiative will inspire other countries to take the same steps.

DOCUMENT 33: President F.W. de Klerk, Speech to Parliament, "The Nuclear Non-Proliferation Treaty and South Africa's Nuclear Capability," March 24, 1993.

PAGE 6 OF 7

In conclusion, I wish to emphasize that at no time did South Africa acquire nuclear weapons technology or materials from another country, nor has it provided any to any other country, or co-operated with another country in this regard. Our expertise, technology and nuclear materials were fully protected and dealt with strictly according to international standards and agreements. South Africa has never conducted a clandestine nuclear test.

There may be a perception that the decision to abandon the programme means that the investment in the whole enterprise had been wasted. This is not the case.

The enrichment technology developed by the AEC as well as the nuclear materials which were produced, constitute an important asset for South Africa. They will contribute significantly to the ultimate success of the AEC's peaceful commercialisation programme.

The operation of the pilot enrichment plant allowed South Africa to continue operation of the AEC's research reactor, which is also used for the production of radioactive isotopes for medical purposes, during a period when the international community refused to provide nuclear fuel for its operation.

The nuclear material that was used for the devices has been recovered and will be used to enlarge the production of these and other isotopes. SAFARI-I is amongst the very few reactors which can meet this need.

Furthermore, the application of the enrichment technology to the establishment of the semi-commercial enrichment plant provided South Africa with the ability to provide all the nuclear fuel requirements of the Koeberg nuclear power station, and to guarantee this supply at a time when the delivery of nuclear fuel for Koeberg from overseas was denied.

In addition to this, South Africa's accession to the NPT has already led to the lifting of nuclear sanctions by the United States of America. Exchanges of visits with states in Africa have also taken place with a view to agreements on the use of medical isotopes and training programmes. We have become a member of the African Regional Co-operative Agreement (AFRA), an organization within the IAEA which co-ordinates peaceful, nuclear projects and co-operation between African states in the nuclear field.

The prospects for further co-operation will be enhanced by the establishment of a nuclear weapons free zone in Africa. The Government has already publicly committed itself to this, and believes that it can make a significant contribution to the establishment of peace and security in Southern Africa.

DOCUMENT 33: President F. W. de Klerk, Speech to Parliament, "The Nuclear Non-Proliferation Treaty and South Africa's Nuclear Capability," March 24, 1993.

PAGE 7 OF 7

South Africa will soon be taking an active part in the
trans-continental discussions on this all-important issue.
We will be supported by the fact that South Africa acquired
a nuclear capability, and, in recognition of its new
relationship with Africa and the broader international
community, abandoned it.

Without accession to the NPT none of this would have been
possible. I trust that the book on this chapter of the past
can now be closed, and that a new one of international
co-operation and trust can now be opened.

UNQUOTE

DATUMTYDGROEP
19930324/1320

EINDE

PART IV

THE UNITED STATES AND THE REGION

THE SUBVERSIVE THREAT

U.S. policy toward South Africa over the years has generally followed a pattern defined by the Cold War rivalry with the Soviet Union. South Africa's strategic location and abundant resources have lured president after president to try to protect U.S. influence with Pretoria and to keep the Soviets out—even if that meant supporting, or appearing to support, the apartheid regime. As early as the Kennedy administration, Washington devoted a good deal of energy to rooting out potential sources of destabilization in the region which could threaten the Pretoria government and, by extension, America's predominance compared with Moscow. However, opponents of apartheid have argued that, along the way, concentrating so intently on the Soviets has damaged U.S. interests vis-à-vis other African countries and the world (see Document 1), and harmed the well-being of South Africa's black majority.

One of the means U.S. administrations used to protect their interests was to keep an eye on internal threats to the regime, both real and potential. Even in the early 1960s, U.S. intelligence regularly followed developments among South Africa's dissident and underground movements. A CIA Special Report on "Subversive Movements in South Africa" dated May 10, 1963, is indicative of this type of "reportage" (Document 34).

However, through the 1960s, the threat from such groups as the ANC, and even its "action arm," "Spear of the Nation," seems to have generated very little concern in Washington; instead, "their basic weaknesses when pitted against the power of the South African state" were emphasized. Not to be caught unawares by "subversives," though, Washington wanted to be prepared in the event that things heated up: a

"Country Internal Defense Plan" was drawn up in late 1962, which included descriptions of different opposition groups and acts of sabotage they had undertaken, as well as actions U.S. personnel should take in response to a possible insurgency (Document 35). The plan focused on the need to counter "communist inspired, supported or directed subversion or insurgency" as well as "other types...inimical to U.S. national security interests vis-à-vis South Africa." Interestingly, the basic U.S. position, as stated in the document, was that "[t]he U.S. does not wish to assume a stance against revolution, *per se*, as an historical means of change."

Yet recent reports about U.S. cooperation with South African authorities in clamping down on certain groups call this apparent lack of concern into question. One incident involved a young Nelson Mandela, described in Document 35 as the leader of a "Congress Alliance Committee...organized...to perform sabotage." The report noted that in late July 1962, South African police arrested Mandela while he was driving from Durban to Johannesburg disguised as a chauffeur. In July 1986, though, the *Johannesburg Star* published a story quoting a "retired senior police officer" who claimed that an unnamed American diplomat once drunkenly boasted at a party that he had been responsible for Mandela's arrest. According to the account, the diplomat told listeners that at the time "he was anxious to supply his government with Pretoria's Bantustan plans, and the information he needed was available from a Colonel Bester, then head of the Natal Police." The diplomat allegedly went on, "In exchange for the information, he told Colonel Bester the date, time and route Mandela would be taking."[1]

Whatever the validity of this account, the record

definitely shows that U.S. officials kept close tabs on Mandela and other dissidents over the years, lest they ever pose a credible threat to American interests in South Africa.

KISSINGER AND THE COMMUNIST THREAT

Despite these efforts, an enormous threat did emerge—though from a very different quarter. On April 25, 1974, a military coup took place in Portugal; although relatively short-lived, it succeeded in dismantling the former world power's colonial holdings in Africa, including Angola and Mozambique. This Portuguese withdrawal facilitated the rise to power of pro-Soviet, nationalist movements in the newly decolonized countries, which radically changed the region's political landscape: black Africa was strengthened, and the white minority regime in South Africa seemed far more vulnerable. The United States reacted to these destabilizing developments with understandable alarm; from then on, Washington accorded southern Africa a far more prominent place on its foreign policy agenda.

A major player behind this reassessment was Henry Kissinger. Early in the first Nixon administration, the then–national security advisor signed National Security Study Memorandum 39, which set in motion "a comprehensive review of U.S. policy toward Southern Africa" including consideration of "the full range of basic strategies and policy options open to the United States" (Document 36). The culmination was a seminal document, produced in December 1969, that laid out U.S. interests in the region, discussed current policy, and presented a detailed list of six options (a lengthy extract of the study is appended to Document 36). The United States eventually picked the second choice, known as the "tar-baby option," which posited that

> We can, by selective relaxation of our stance toward the white regimes, encourage some modification of their current racial and colonial policies and through more substantial economic

assistance to the black states…help to draw the two groups together and exert some influence on both for peaceful change (Document 36).

Among the "pros" listed for this option were that it would help "broaden relations between black states and white"; "preserve U.S. economic, scientific and strategic interests in the white states"; "help lift [the whites'] present siege mentality"; and "offer the black states an alternative to the recognized risks of mounting communist influence." The "cons," however, included the possibility that the whites would see U.S. actions as a "vindication of their policies"; the fact that relaxing sanctions unilaterally "would be a highly visible violation of our international obligations"; and the conclusion that "there is virtually no evidence that change [in South Africa's racial system] might be forthcoming…as a result of any approach on our part." Despite these obstacles, the administration went ahead with this option.

THE UNITED STATES GOES UNDERGROUND IN ANGOLA

After the events of 1974–75, Kissinger became increasingly concerned about Soviet ideological and military expansion in the region, and the waning of Western influence that likely would follow.[2] To counter this prospect, he proposed to President Ford, against the recommendation of an interagency task force on Angola, a policy of covert intervention in that country. In June 1975, Ford approved Kissinger's plan, which pursued the following "limited objectives":

> (1) preventing the MPLA and its Soviet and Cuban backers from achieving a quick military take-over of Angola; and (2) sufficiently redressing the balance among Angola's political movements to facilitate a political solution in which the MPLA does not dominate UNITA and FNLA (Document 37).

Covert intervention was supposed to force the Soviet Union to cut back its involvement; instead, it led Moscow to boost its support for the MPLA government and, moreover, led Fidel Castro to respond to the MPLA's plea for help in countering external aggression by sending thousands of troops. During this period, in the wake of disclosures of presidential abuse of power in the course of the Vietnam War and the Watergate scandal, Congress had begun to take steps to reassert its role in the policymaking process, including holding extensive hearings on the conduct of the intelligence community. U.S. covert activities in Angola shortly became one such subject of congressional inquiry. In 1976, the House Select Committee on Intelligence, chaired by Otis Pike (D–N.Y.), held hearings on U.S. intelligence programs abroad. The committee's report, which was later leaked to the press, unearthed significant details on the CIA's operations in Angola (Document 38). Compared to Director of Central Intelligence William Colby's dismissal of the Angolan factions— "They are all for some fuzzy kind of social system, you know, without really much articulation, but some sort of let's not be exploited by the capitalist nations"³ — the report was a model of factual clarity:

> The CIA has informed the Committee that since January 1975, it had expended over $31 million in military hardware, transportation costs, and cash payments by the end of 1975. The Committee has reason to believe that the actual U.S. investment is much higher. Information supplied to the Committee also suggests that the military intervention of the Soviet Union and Cuba is in large part a reaction to U.S. efforts to break a political stalemate, in favor of its clients (Document 38).

The resulting congressional opposition to U.S. covert action in Angola was codified in the Clark Amendment, named for Senator Dick Clark (D–Iowa), which prohibited all aid, overt or covert, to any of the factions in the country.

RHODESIA: THE DIPLOMATIC APPROACH

While the Clark Amendment represented a major setback for Kissinger, the new restrictions did little to change his belief that the balance of forces in southern Africa in the mid 1970s had been undergoing a major shift in favor of the Soviet Union. Intent on reversing that tide, and faced with the need to salvage U.S. policy toward the region, he devoted his energies to the situation in Rhodesia.

Following the August 1975 collapse of constitutional talks at Victoria Falls between Rhodesian Prime Minister Ian Smith and the African National Council of Zimbabwe, Kissinger embarked in 1976 on a more assertive initiative aimed at stabilizing Rhodesia. Again, he kept his eye on Moscow, hoping that his strategy would preempt the Soviets and the Cubans in a way that Africans would view favorably and U.S. public opinion would support. (Critical to this approach was the need to address black African aspirations.) Kissinger enlisted backing for a negotiated settlement from both the frontline states— Angola, Botswana, Mozambique, Tanzania, Zambia—and the South Africans. His initial strategy, spelled out in a State Department Action Memorandum dated April 1, 1976, included

> Support...repeal [of] the Byrd Amendment [which is] look[ed] upon as a symbol of basic American support for the white Rhodesian regime....[M]ake it clear [to Smith] that he can count on no help from the U.S. in his fight to maintain white rule....[E]ncourage[Vorster] to increase his political and economic pressure to persuade Smith that further resistance to a negotiated settlement is futile....Inform [African leaders] Kaunda, Nyerere, Khama and Machel of our intended actions....(Document 39).

The progression of documents included in this reader provides a fascinating overview of Kissinger's "shuttle diplomacy," particularly his contacts with South African Prime Minister Vorster (Document 40) and Smith (Document 41). The white Rhodesians wanted assurances that, among other things, a transfer of power would leave "Europeans" in control of the security portfolios, which included both defense and law and order. Kissinger agreed earlier "that we would do our best to obtain agreement on that point,"[4] yet when Smith's *public* actions began to reflect this, Kissinger hurriedly deflated his expectations, instructing U.S. Ambassador Frank Wisner via cable to request an "urgent appointment" with Smith to inform him that the goal of installing whites in the positions he wanted had "become indeed difficult" (Document 41).

Particularly telling is Kissinger's anxiety—Wisner was to tell the prime minister, "the U.S. is appalled"— over Smith's public reference to Annex C of the Rhodesia proposal (Document 42), "which [had] not been given to the Africans," according to the cable. Annex C laid out "possible constitutional arrangements for the period of transition." Among other fundamental matters, it detailed a number of provisions, such as the need to change British law to allow the government to revamp Rhodesia's constitution while "the Queen...[remained] the sovereign of the territory" prior to independence, and the creation of new executive and legislative authorities for Rhodesia, including the possible breakdown of membership by race. The U.S. apparently had several reasons to be concerned about Annex C coming to light. For one thing, the African states believed strongly that the Zimbabwean conflict was essentially an African problem requiring an African solution, not one imposed from the outside as would be the case were Annex C implemented. For another thing, U.S. officials had good reason to expect a harsh reaction from black African governments to the provisions originally envisaged in Annex C for naming whites to the key cabinet positions of defense and of law and order. Finally, the annex touched on the issue of general amnesty, not only for political prisoners of conscience, but also for former Rhodesian officials—a sensitive issue indeed, because it could be perceived as another U.S. attempt to take sides with white racists in southern Africa.

Central to the Annex was a maneuver aimed at calming the fears of the white regime as it faced a dramatic change in the power structure: "It would also be necessary to provide for a political amnesty which would...protect members of the administration against prosecution or civil suit for past illegal acts."

In the end, the Kissinger initiatives did force Smith to shift his ground somewhat, but the Rhodesian leader ultimately caused the Geneva Conference on the country's new constitution to collapse by rejecting a set of British proposals just four days after Ford— and Kissinger—left office.

Despite this setback, in the final days of the Ford administration, Kissinger, with National Security Advisor Brent Scowcroft's concurrence, requested a one-time exception to the arms embargo against South Africa to ensure the latter's continued support on Rhodesia and Namibia. The request to export certain military navigational and control equipment to Pretoria would "provoke criticism in Congress and among Black African nations," Scowcroft admitted, but that would ultimately bring less "harm" than if South Africa refused to cooperate in the region in the event the White House denied the exception—a revealing acknowledgment of the hold Pretoria had over U.S. policy.[5]

JIMMY CARTER TURNS UP THE RHETORIC

After the failure of the U.S.- and U.K.-sponsored Geneva Conference, on April 1, 1977, the Carter administration welcomed a new British plan calling for a constitutional conference on Rhodesia. On May 20, Vice President Walter Mondale met Prime Minister Vorster in Vienna to pass along Washington's views: "Vice President Mondale set forth U.S. support for [British] Foreign Secretary Owens' initiative and efforts to draft a constitution...which will lead to free elections...and independence for Zimbabwe during 1978" (Document 43). However, Washington's efforts to maintain the momentum on Rhodesia fell short at first, largely because most governments in the region were unclear, and thus hesitant, about the new administration and its motives.

In contrast to Kissinger's country-by-country approach, which focused exclusively on Rhodesia, the Carter administration adopted a more regional view, which emphasized South Africa and Namibia as well. An initial step in this direction was the State Department's April 1981 "History of the Namibia Negotiations," which detailed Washington's attempts to bring the territory to independence (Document 44). As one means toward settling the destabilizing influence of Namibian strife (and, it was hoped, curbing Soviet expansionism in southern Africa), in May 1977 the Carter administration initiated an alliance of Western U.N. Security Council members—the United States, Canada, the United Kingdom, France, and West Germany, otherwise known as the "Contact Group" or "Western Five."

One of the first moves of the Contact Group was to launch an unprecedented campaign to stabilize Namibia, a former German colony that in the wake of World War I the League of Nations had mandated to South Africa to administer temporarily. At the heart of the problem was the fact that despite several warnings from the U.N., the South African government was determined to implement its apartheid policies in administering the territory. Based on the principles of Security Council Resolution 385 of January 1976, the five-nation group drafted a proposal calling for a cease-fire, U.N.-supervised elections for a constituent assembly, and a U.N. peacekeeping force. Both South Africa and the South West Africa People's Organization (SWAPO)—the internationally recognized national movement of Namibia, which had been fighting South African colonialism since 1966—accepted the proposal. However, the initial optimism generated by their agreement dissipated after major differences erupted over how to implement its stipulations.

In September 1978, the Security Council adopted Resolution 435, approving the U.N. secretary-general's plan for implementing the proposal. In May 1979, however, South Africa rejected the blueprint. According to a U.S. State Department briefing paper, the South African government "feared that Namibia under a SWAPO government could serve as a communist foothold in southern Africa,"[6] and, after the General Assembly had designated SWAPO as "the sole and authentic representative of the Namibia people,"[7] Pretoria publicly questioned the U.N.'s ability to supervise elections impartially. South Africa's rejection of the plan led most African members of the United Nations to conclude that Pretoria never intended to proceed with an internationally acceptable settlement in Namibia. The frontline states believed—and continue to believe—that since they brought SWAPO to accept the Contact Group's plan, it was up to the Western Five to obtain South Africa's agreement. Meanwhile, the South African government embarked on a two-pronged strategy of participating in the settlement effort while promoting an internal settlement within Namibia. Although the Western Five and the frontline states found Pretoria's reasons for rejecting the proposed Namibian solution unacceptable, the Reagan administration would establish an entirely different standard.

THE REAGAN APPROACH:
ACCOMMODATION, CONFRONTATION,
AND MEDIATION

Under the Reagan presidency, the perceived strategic importance of southern Africa increased dramatically. The new administration saw the growing number of pro-Soviet regimes in the region, the increasingly radicalized anticolonial organization in Namibia, and the antiapartheid organizations in South Africa as concrete evidence of Moscow's efforts to weaken Western influence. Beyond other blunt measures intended to check the Soviets, Reagan policymakers decided they would be well served by accelerating peaceful resolutions to local conflicts. Even though this strategy meant granting indigenous groups a larger role in developments in the region, it did not contradict the broader goal of keeping the upper hand there; rather, it reflected Washington's realization that it needed to generate some consensus among its allies—who at this stage believed that the United States was adopting an overly conciliatory attitude toward the white minority regimes. It was clear that crude intervention, rationalized only in terms of the Cold War, would not be enough: the United States needed a moral justification for its involvement in southern Africa as well.

The Reagan policy of "constructive engagement" sought to meet all of these requirements. Conceived by Assistant Secretary of State for African Affairs Chester Crocker, the program consisted of two basic ideas: change in Southern Africa must be controlled, and the region must be made "stable" before any such change could be instituted. The policy embraced both "accommodationist" and "confrontationist" elements in a strategy designed to accomplish several goals: contain the Soviet Union and its allies; cut short the potential for radical revolutionary change; create conditions for a dominant U.S. role in the area; generate a safe environment for American interests; and give the American people the impression that the administration was fulfilling its moral obligations in Africa as a "custodian" of peace, democracy, and human rights.

When the administration came to office in 1981, it ordered a review of U.S. policy in the region. According to a briefing memorandum prepared later for Secretary of State George Shultz, "strong pressure from key NATO allies to reinvigorate the Namibia settlement effort" led President Reagan and Shultz's predecessor, Alexander Haig, "to launch an ambitious and active diplomatic effort in southern Africa" (Document 45). In April 1981, Crocker set off on a mission to try to forge a consensus with allies and southern African countries on the recently concluded review.

A month later, South African officials Pik Botha and Magnus Malan followed up Crocker's trip with a meeting with Haig in Washington, D.C. The South Africans focused on regional issues, arguing that

South Africa faced a total onslaught directed by the Soviet Union and its allies. They found a sympathetic audience in both Haig and Crocker, whose strategy aimed at removing the Soviet "menace" by linking Namibian independence to the withdrawal of Cuban troops from Angola. However, the Reagan initiative's aim of "improving relations with Pretoria" did not lead South Africa to "move toward constructive change" as expected (Document 45); instead, Pretoria exploited the optimistic new administration's easing of pressure to turn the apparent rapprochement to its own advantage. Some U.S. government officials recognized this, as the conclusions of a report of the Secretary of State's Advisory Committee on South Africa make clear:

> South African government hardened its bargaining position in Namibian negotiations; embarked on a concerted military and economic campaign to establish regional dominance by intimidating and destabilizing neighboring states, particularly Angola, Mozambique, Zimbabwe, and Lesotho; and failed to make a clear and persuasive commitment to move toward extending meaningful individual political rights to black South Africans.[8]

By the mid 1980s, constructive engagement began to meet with intensified opposition. Responding to congressional criticism and South Africa's escalating spiral of cross-border raids, the White House expanded its self-appointed role as mediator between Pretoria and its neighbors. This effort yielded some results in 1984. In February of that year, Angola and South Africa agreed in Lusaka to a U.S.-brokered "framework for the completion of the SADF's withdrawal from southern Angola and for joint monitoring of the area both during and after that withdrawal" (Document 46).

Subsequently, Washington established a U.S. Liaison Office (USLO) in Windhoek, Namibia, to put itself "in a position to play the facilitative role envisaged for us in the Lusaka disengagement agreement" (Document 47). Within a year, however, the State Department suspended operations at the office, partly because South African forces were not pulling out as quickly as the Reagan administration had hoped. An information memorandum for Secretary Shultz explained the situation in this way:

> As long as there was a realistic chance for early completion of the disengagement, the office served as a link to the South African military and as a symbol of U.S. commitment…. There is little to be gained by continuing USLO's operations in present circumstances…. (Document 48)

The State Department's decision had a political element as well: the memorandum noted that the USLO had "begun to draw fire from some African and congressional critics of our policy, who claim it lends legitimacy to South African rule in Namibia." Ironically, as Document 47 shows, denunciations also came from the Right about the direction the U.S. was taking vis-à-vis the Lusaka Accord and, ultimately, U.N. Resolution 435: "The conservative press and several conservative political organizations have begun to target our policy, predicting a sell-out of UNITA, early recognition of Marxist Angola, and a general softening of our position, especially on Cuban withdrawal."

During this period, the White House was becoming increasingly concerned about the tarnished image of the United States as a supporter both of guerrilla groups committed to destabilizing the region and of the regime in South Africa. Partly to counter this impression, the administration embarked on a policy intended to compete with the Soviet Union by offering economic assistance and political support to the government of Mozambique. War with the South African–backed RENAMO insurgents and widespread famine had ravaged Mozambique's economy and infrastructure, and the scope of suffering among the Mozambican people was approaching staggering proportions. Responding to President Samora

Machel's appeals to the international community, the United States soon became one of the leading donors of aid that proved critical to the survival of Mozambique against RENAMO attacks.

The administration's policy toward the Marxist government of Mozambique differed somewhat from its treatment of other communist governments around the world. Reagan did not pursue the policy of assisting "freedom fighters" in their struggle against "Marxist" regimes with the same vigor in Mozambique as he did, for example, in Angola and Nicaragua. Rather, the administration actively sought to win the allegiance of the FRELIMO government away from the Soviets, using carrots instead of sticks. As described in a September 1985 secret memorandum for Secretary of Defense Weinberger, the administration's "objectives towards Mozambique [were] to replace Soviet influence with our own…and to induce Machel's FRELIMO Government to enter into substantive negotiations with the very active RENAMO insurgents" (Document 49). This strategy was justified as necessary to keep Cuban combat troops out of Mozambique and to win favor across much of the African continent, particularly among the frontline states.

Because this approach ran contrary to Reagan's declared intentions to reverse communist gains in the third world, the policy came under fire from conservatives in Congress and the White House, who urged the president to review personally the State Department–inspired strategy and shift his support to RENAMO.[9] Other administration officials resisted this pressure, however, and worked instead to change their opponents' minds. Document 49 notes that the State Department's first objective of an upcoming Machel visit to Washington, D.C., would be to "improve the FRELIMO government image in conservative congressional eyes." In arguing with conservatives, these administration officials defended their position by pointing to concerns regarding RENAMO's origins, the cohesiveness of its leadership, and its ability to lead effectively—assuming it ever gained military ascendancy. The pro-FRELIMO advocates also reasserted that they favored national reconciliation between FRELIMO and RENAMO as a way to reduce the Mozambican government's reliance on the Soviet Union. (As Document 49 indicates, the State Department also hoped to draw Mozambique closer to the United States and the West by increasing its level of cooperation with the International Monetary Fund and World Bank, and by pressing for "a renewed CIA liaison presence" in Mozambique.) Conservative members of Congress ultimately lost the battle for U.S. support for RENAMO, but they retaliated by repeatedly rejecting administration requests for nonlethal military assistance for Mozambique.

Nevertheless, the administration's strategy toward Mozambique had already borne fruit as Washington found itself in a position to extract a number of concessions from Machel along the lines later summarized in Document 49. Using its economic leverage, the United States had extracted a shift in Mozambique's hard-line stance on South Africa's apartheid policy. And in exchange for security assistance, the White House had persuaded the FRELIMO government to enter into a dialogue with Pretoria, which led to the Nkomati Accord, signed by Mozambique and South Africa on March 16, 1984. In addition to reducing tensions in the region, the practical effects of the accord were to end each country's support of an insurgent group hostile to the other and to open the door to increased economic cooperation between the two countries.

For U.S. officials, the Nkomati Accord was a regional turning point. "In a nutshell, we are witnessing a potential watershed in southern Africa's evolution," read a lengthy April 1984 cable from Shultz to diplomatic posts; the pact was "the prominent symbol of a broader process" of peaceful change, which included dealing "a severe blow" to "the notion of 'armed struggle' as the solution to South Africa's Apartheid system" (Document 50).

THE REAGAN DOCTRINE IN ANGOLA
Unfortunately, this détente was short-lived. In viola-

tion of the Nkomati Accord, South Africa resumed active support to the RENAMO rebels in Mozambique and its relations with Angola deteriorated in the wake of Pretoria's increased military aid to UNITA. South Africa's military activities in Angola led U.S. officials to conclude that

> While the South Africans publicly remain committed to UNSCR 435, their contention that there is a serious military threat fits conveniently into what may be Pretoria's preferred scenario for Namibia: to…limit SWAPO's power in an independent Namibia. Anti-SWAPO operations in Angola also provide cover for assisting UNITA…. (Document 51)

To prevent further deterioration, in March 1985 Assistant Secretary Crocker submitted a set of proposals to South Africa and Angola on procedures for implementing Resolution 435, and on the question of Cuban withdrawal from southern Angola. Neither party followed up on them.

In the meantime, even while the United States seemed to show concern about South Africa's continued military activities in Angola, and pursued a negotiated settlement, it nevertheless engaged in a certain degree of hypocrisy by covertly providing assistance to UNITA rebels in Angola. As part of the so-called Reagan Doctrine of supporting third-world "freedom fighters" in their struggle against "Marxist" governments, the administration embraced UNITA leader Jonas Savimbi and, in August 1985, managed to win repeal of the Clark Amendment, which had banned aid to any forces fighting in Angola. Needless to say, this side of U.S. policy had adverse consequences for the peace process. The Angolan government suspended all negotiations with Washington; the White House, in turn, sent a strong signal to Luanda in January 1986 by inviting Savimbi to the United States, where he met with President Reagan, Secretary of State Shultz, Defense Secretary Weinberger, CIA Director William Casey, and other senior officials. Savimbi was assured that we support him, are proceeding on the aid front and will not abandon him after an agreement on the withdrawal of foreign forces.... [W]e will continue efforts to turn [UNITA's] military pressure on the MPLA into a negotiated settlement on the withdrawal of all foreign troops from the region (Document 52).

By mid 1986, the United States had provided the Pretoria-backed rebel group with $15 million in aid, including Stinger antiaircraft missiles;[10] by the following year, the administration had promised another $15 million.

On February 10, 1986, the White House affirmed its objectives in Angola in National Security Decision Directive 212, entitled "United States Policy Toward Angola" (Document 53). Topping the list was the intention to "[r]educe and possibly eliminate Soviet and Soviet-proxy influence and opportunities in Angola and southern Africa." To achieve its goals, the administration adopted a two-track strategy of "continuing to negotiate with the MPLA and South Africa on Cuban withdrawal in the context of Namibian independence" while "applying pressure on the MPLA to negotiate seriously and to accept a negotiated settlement." The administration later reaffirmed this strategy in NSDD 274, dated May 7, 1987 (Document 54).

RETURNING TO THE TABLE

Following the Reagan-Gorbachev summits in 1987 and 1988 and the waning of U.S.-Soviet tensions worldwide, administration officials—particularly Crocker—became more actively engaged in brokering peace in the region. In an effort to revive negotiations, Crocker returned to Angola on July 14, 1987, for discussions with the Angolan foreign minister. Based on those talks, on August 4 the Angolan government presented new proposals to Washington setting out conditions for the withdrawal of Cuban and South African troops from southern Angola, and preparing the way for implementing Resolution 435.[11]

This new round of negotiations, combined with increased U.N. pressure on South Africa to withdraw its forces from southern Angola, eventually pushed Pretoria to announce a troop withdrawal on December 5, 1987. UNITA, on the other hand, was not at all deterred by the announcement, and it pressed on with its military campaign against the government of Angola—and South Africa, in turn, exploited the ongoing hostilities to launch attacks against SWAPO forces from southern Angola. Fighting escalated further in early 1988 when more Angolan and Cuban troops were deployed to counter these South African strikes.

As a result, according to a secret State Department memo to the acting secretary in April 1988, South Africa's civilian and military leadership found themselves "in the throes of a major policy debate... over...the US-brokered CTW [Cuban Troop Withdrawal] negotiations" (Document 55). In describing the internal conflict, the memo noted that the government "chose a diplomatic response" to the buildup, while elements in the military continued "to voice the belief that a preemptive military strike against the Cubans—which in their view would be successful—would enhance South Africa's negotiating position."

A Defense Intelligence Agency report later noted that among its far-reaching effects, the Cuban buildup ultimately "provided new impetus to peace negotiations and resulted in the December 1988 accords among South Africa, Angola and Cuba."[12]

THE BUSH ADMINISTRATION:
PRESSURING SAVIMBI

President George Bush continued the U.S. commitment to eliminate Soviet and Cuban military influence in Angola and the region. His efforts to promote a political reconciliation between the MPLA and UNITA were part of a broader attempt, very much in keeping with the aims of his predecessors, to reduce the prospects for revolutionary change throughout southern Africa.

As part of this approach, the Bush administration encouraged African leaders, including President Mobutu Sese Seko of Zaire, to try to bring Angolan President dos Santos and Jonas Savimbi together. According to a secret memorandum from Crocker to newly appointed Secretary of State James Baker in early February 1989,

> we have received reports of at least three active efforts by African countries to arrange a direct meeting between dos Santos and Savimbi.... Also, UNITA offered a ceasefire to the MPLA on January 31, [1989,] opening a new context for the two sides to deal with each other (Document 56).

Crocker went on to assure Baker that "[t]hese developments are grounds for optimism" about an impending "national reconciliation" in Angola, "although progress will continue to be incremental, and it will be difficult for us to force the pace."

On June 22, 1989, a National Reconciliation meeting did indeed take place in Zaire, where Savimbi met face to face with dos Santos to conclude a groundbreaking cease-fire accord. A State Department cable exulted that "the summit at Gbadolite, organized and chaired by President Mobutu, turned out to be a resounding success against considerable odds" (Document 57). The "symbol-laden" meeting, attended by at least eighteen African heads of state who "warmly received" Savimbi, granted the rebel leader "a level of political legitimacy unimaginable just one month ago." Department officials managed to stop short of total euphoria, though, noting that "[i]t is, of course, far too early to declare the Angolan civil war at an end."

> Nonetheless, more than a page has been turned: in what has long been a particularly bitter and politically charged conflict out of proportion to the importance of the country it was being fought in, the seeds for political compromise between former enemies have been laid. It will be difficult, if not impossible to turn the clock back.

It took almost two years for the government of Angola and UNITA to sign, in May 1991, an agreement to end the civil war and prepare for free elections in 1992. In a September 1992 nationwide ballot, the MPLA won a plurality of the votes but not the necessary 50 percent majority; this forced a second round of balloting. A U.N. special representative and a number of international observer teams verified the results and the State Department agreed with their findings: "The UN concluded that the elections held Sept. 29–30 were generally free and fair. We support that conclusion" (Document 58). However, UNITA rejected the outcome, claiming that the process had been rigged. Within a week, near civil war had broken out again.

The most concrete conclusion one can draw from the above outline of southern African political developments is that for at least the last fifteen years, the region has been a microcosm of the broader political and economic forces at work in the international system. In particular, southern Africa has definitely felt the impact of U.S. foreign policy, which has traditionally been oriented toward its Cold War rivalry with the former Soviet Union. As in other parts of the world—the Horn of Africa and Southeast Asia to name just two—U.S. policy has left a deep political and economic imprint, both to the benefit and the detriment of those regions. Because of South Africa's past influence and its ongoing importance as a military and economic power, the likelihood of positive change there will be integrally linked to whatever new perspectives may emerge from Washington in the post–Cold War era.

NOTES

1. Department of State cable, "RSA Media Reaction," July 14, 1986. This document is included in the National Security Archive's microfiche collection, *South Africa: The Making of U.S. Policy, 1962–1989*.

2. As a result of heavy MPLA-dominated fighting in key parts of Angola around August 1975, UNITA and the FNLA reduced their representation in the transitional government, leaving it in effect in the hands of the MPLA. The MPLA immediately took control of Luanda and the surrounding areas; later, it announced its intention to assume full authority for governing Angola after the territory achieved independence, which was set for November 11.

3. Colby is quoted in William Blum, *The CIA: A Forgotten History* (London: Zed Books, 1986), p. 285.

4. Henry Kissinger, cable for Ambassador Schaufele, "Talking Points for Your Meeting with the Rhodesians," October 2, 1976. This document is available at the National Security Archive.

5. Brent Scowcroft, Memorandum for the president, "Request for an Exception to the Arms Embargo against South Africa," January 15, 1977. This document is available at the National Security Archive.

6. Department of State briefing paper, "Namibia," November 19, 1980. This document is included in the National Security Archive's microfiche collection, *South Africa: The Making of U.S. Policy, 1962–1989*.

7. Department of State document, "Question of UN Impartiality," December 15, 1980. This document is available at the National Security Archive.

8. "A U.S. Policy Toward South Africa," the Report of the Secretary of State's Advisory Committee on South Africa, January 1987. This document is included in the National Security Archive's microfiche collection, *South Africa: The Making of U.S. Policy, 1962–1989*.

9. Interestingly, the authors of Document 49 also appear to question the administration's approach, calling for a review of Mozambique policy (see the handwritten notes at the end of the memo).

10. Department of State cable, "British Journalist Alleges U.S. Officials Confirm U.S. Arms for Savimbi Sent Through South Africa CIA Director Said to Have Set Conduit Up," July 18, 1986. This document is included in the National Security Archive's microfiche collection, *South Africa: The Making of U.S. Policy, 1962–1989*.

11. The State Department did not think it was worth presenting the proposals to Pretoria at the time, according to a September 26, 1987, cable: "It is our view that no useful purpose would be served by our taking this MPLA proposal to the [South African Government] which in any case knows of it and has commented negatively on it" ("Conversation with Gabréel Akunwafor, Nigerian Ambassador-Designate to Angola," September 26, 1987). Nevertheless, in a cable of October 10, 1987, the State Department agreed that the plan was "positive," and could, in conjunction with talks held in early September between Washington and Luanda, "set the stage for further progress" ("Angola: The South African Connection," October 10, 1987). Both of these cables are available at the National Security Archive.

12. Defense Intelligence Agency briefing text, "The 1987–88 Combat in Southern Angola: Lessons Learned," December 1988. This document is available at the National Security Archive.

DOCUMENT 34: Central Intelligence Agency, Special Report, "Subversive Movements in South Africa," May 10, 1963.

PAGE 1 OF 7

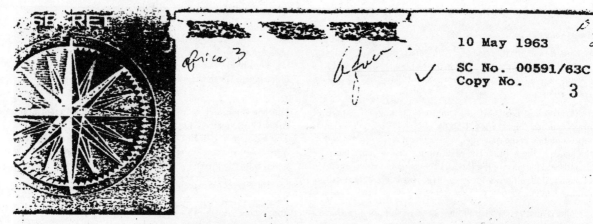

10 May 1963

SC No. 00591/63C
Copy No.

3

SPECIAL REPORT

OFFICE OF CURRENT INTELLIGENCE

SUBVERSIVE MOVEMENTS IN SOUTH AFRICA

CENTRAL INTELLIGENCE AGENCY

NO FOREIGN DISSEM

DOCUMENT 34: Central Intelligence Agency, Special Report, "Subversive Movements in South Africa," May 10, 1963.

PAGE 2 OF 7

~~SECRET~~

10 May 1963

SUBVERSIVE MOVEMENTS IN SOUTH AFRICA

Subversive groups in the Republic of South Africa have recently displayed a growing capability to use sabotage and terrorism to harass the white community. However, they are not likely to confront the whites with a serious challenge for several years. The recent history of these groups, although it does attest to improved conspiratorial techniques, tends to confirm their basic weaknesses when pitted against the power of the South African state.

Nonwhite Nationalism and Communism

Antigovernment activities in South Africa are distinguished from similar activities farther north by two important features: the large number of Westernized and politically active non-Europeans in South Africa, and the operations there of the oldest orthodox Communist party on the continent.

Fully a third of the 12 million nonwhites (including Asiatics and persons of mixed blood as well as Africans) are involved in the complex economic and social world of the country's urban centers. Many of the urban Africans have few ties with their tribal heritage, and as a group they are far better educated and far more sophisticated politically than Africans to the north. Until recently, nationalist ideas have come almost entirely from this relatively large group of educated nonwhites.

This situation has had two effects on nationalist activity. First, most of its leaders in the past have been genuine moderates who realize that South Africa's economic and social complexities make interracial cooperation a prerequisite for stability. Second, the large number of people involved and the hundreds of miles separating urban areas--all of them important centers of nationalist activity--have made it nearly impossible to work out nationwide plans of action. Periodic efforts to streamline existing mass organizations have usually produced large, racially moderate groups which are excellent propaganda platforms but too amorphous for positive action in the face of the government's security activities.

Circumstances have also forced the South African Communist Party into a moderate attitude on the crucial question of racial attitudes. Founded in 1921 and operating illegally since 1950, the party has always been mainly white and Indian in membership. Since World War II the number of African members has increased, and the party has become identified with nonwhite

DOCUMENT 34: Central Intelligence Agency, Special Report, "Subversive Movements in South Africa," May 10, 1963.

PAGE 3 OF 7

SECRET

nationalism, for which it has provided an organizational know-how which was unavailable from any other source. It is still mainly a non-African group, however, and thus cannot fully exploit the racial issue, potentially its most effective weapon. The Communists therefore have turned for allies to such racially moderate leaders as Albert Luthuli of the African National Congress (ANC).

Congress Alliance

Communists dominate the top echelons of the Congress Alliance, a coalition of "congresses" of the various racial groups, of which the ANC is the most important. However, the moderate racial attitude to which the Communists are tied --and perhaps their ability to understand the motivation of the African rank and file --has blinded them to most issues which might stimulate mass action. With rare exceptions the Congress Alliance's line has been devoted to high-sounding appeals to multiracialism, and the issues on which it has chosen to make specific calls for action have been poorly selected.

In May 1961, for instance, when South Africa became a republic, the alliance decreed a general strike to protest the event. By skillfully using the alliance's organization, the African strike leader operated covertly for weeks despite frenzied police efforts

LITHULI

to find him; by adept propaganda he threw the government into a virtual state of siege. But the strike itself was a failure, not just because of the government's countermeasures, but because the issue on which it was called had no relevance for most of the nonwhites.

The failure of the May 1961 strike apparently was a turning point for the alliance. The Communists and many moderate non-Communist Africans seem to have decided that there was no chance of ever setting up an effective mass movement, and Luthuli was persuaded by Communists and sympathizers to countenance a campaign of sabotage. The first bombs-- very amateurish devices--went off the following October, and two or three white Communists were caught aiding the Africans who did the actual planting. There was another outbreak of bombings in December, and

SECRET

2

DOCUMENT 34: Central Intelligence Agency, Special Report, "Subversive Movements in South Africa," May 10, 1963.

PAGE 4 OF 7

sabotage of one kind or another has been going on fairly steadily since June 1962.

This policy shift seems to have been accompanied by much soul-searching in the Communist hierarchy. The party apparently did not circulate a statement advocating violence to its members until August 1962, and it did not publish a program incorporating the new line until the last few weeks of the year. As revealed in both overt and unpublished documents, the new program still painstakingly tries to avoid alienating the moderate Africans or jeopardizing the present position of non-African Communists in the nationalist movement; at the same time, it aims at exploiting the conspiratorial techniques instilled in some elements of the ANC.

"Spear of the Nation"

The group which seems to have perpetrated most of the sabotage is called "Spear of the Nation." It allegedly is the action arm of the ANC, but direction reportedly is centered in a small and highly secret group, most of whose members are Communists or sympathizers. The organization is said to be highly compartmentalized so that disclosure of part of the structure would not compromise the rest.

In line with Luthuli's reported desires, "Spear of the Nation" has devoted itself almost entirely to sabotage of

power installations, buildings associated with the government, and the like; only one of its acts so far has endangered human life. One source reports that in the future it plans political assassinations. The movement has so far avoided any open suggestion of mass terrorism or racism, although a confidential party circular does call for greater emphasis on the ANC as the "racial organ of the African people."

The Pan-Africanists

As early as 1959 a so-called "Africanist" wing split off from the ANC and set up the Pan-Africanist Congress (PAC) under Robert Sobukwe. Deriving its stand from Ghanaian ideas of a unique African personality, the PAC condemned the ANC's multiracial approach; it also denounced the Communists and their ideology as un-African.

Sobukwe himself is a moderate, but his demand for recognition of Africans as a unique group brought racism closer to the surface. His appeal, translated as "Africa for the Africans," was far easier to understand than the ANC's multiracial abstractions, particularly among the mass of African workers. Even under moderate leadership the appeal of the idea was evident in March and April 1960, when PAC-inspired demonstrations led to the shootings at Sharpeville and--perhaps more spectacular--the orderly march of 30,000 Africans on the parliament buildings at Cape Town.

3

DOCUMENT 34: Central Intelligence Agency, Special Report, "Subversive Movements in South Africa," May 10, 1963.

PAGE 5 OF 7

~~SECRET~~

SOBUKWE

The PAC was weak, however, just where the ANC was relatively strong: in organization. Sobukwe and his associates were flabbergasted by the enthusiasm at the time of Sharpeville; when they were sent to jail and their organization was banned, the PAC virtually disappeared as an entity. The Congress Alliance and the ANC, although subject to the same restrictions, did keep a bare skeleton of organization in being.

Poqo

The idea of "Africa for the Africans" dies hard, however. Remnants of the PAC managed to keep together, particularly in the large African housing areas near Cape Town. Deprived of any direction or restraint from a central authority, these ele-

ments seem to have taken a violently antiwhite line. Their movement was named Poqo, an African word meaning "pure"-- an implied criticism of the ANC's multiracialism and perhaps of Sobukwe's moderation as well.

Little is known about Poqo's early history. It was heavily influenced by the criminal gangs which operate in the African areas. It probably exploited discontent with the announced government policy of gradually removing all Africans from the Cape Town region and sending them back to their "homeland" to the east. In the "homeland," Poqo apparently associated with other violence-minded groups which had grown up within the traditional society. From the first it seems to have used intimidation to enforce silence on anyone who knew about the movement, and for several months no information leaked out. As recently as February 1963, a police official confessed that his organization had not been able to find out very much about Poqo.

Even by that time, however, the situation was beginning to change. Outbreaks of rioting and assassination in late 1962 and early 1963 gave the police some insight into Poqo's organization and personnel. At about the same time, establishment of a headquarters in the nearby British-administered territory of Basutoland was proclaimed

~~SECRET~~

4

DOCUMENT 34: Central Intelligence Agency, Special Report, "Subversive Movements in South Africa," May 10, 1963.

PAGE 6 OF 7

SECRET

by Potlako Kitchener Leballo, formerly Sobukwe's second-in-command in the PAC and only recently released from jail. Leballo began issuing a stream of clandestine directives and making grandiloquent statements to the press, claiming that Poqo and PAC were identical.

Partly to keep ahead of his radical followers and partly because he apparently reveled in the activity, Leballo began to agitate for an outbreak of widespread racial violence between late March and May 1963. His directives aimed to foster the growth of PAC/Poqo cells in key urban areas such as Johannesburg, where the movement had been weak. In issuing them, however, he confused the branches and compromised their security. Late in March a wide police sweep of PAC/Poqo adherents began, and almost 3,000 have been arrested so far. Simultaneously, police in Basutoland raided Leballo's headquarters, confiscating membership lists and driving Leballo himself into hiding.

Present Situation

PAC/Poqo members reportedly are still holding meetings, and some of them may even be willing to try racial violence on their own initiative. Police are confident, however, that the organization as such has been shattered. It seems probable that Leballo has been discredited both among potential followers

LEBALLO

inside the country and among PAC leaders abroad. The government has rushed through a new battery of draconian security laws, one of whose aims is to keep Sobukwe locked up indefinitely.

Nevertheless, Leballo and Poqo demonstrated once again the effectiveness of appeals based on racism. As was the case at the time of Sharpeville, the PAC and movements associated with it lack the ability to maintain themselves for long; while their enthusiasm lasts, however, they produce far more spectacular results than does the more cautious, better disciplined "Spear of the Nation."

"Spear of the Nation," although some of its activists have been picked up recently, seems to have suffered less than PAC/Poqo from the police

SECRET

5

Document 34: Central Intelligence Agency, Special Report, "Subversive Movements in South Africa," May 10, 1963.

PAGE 7 OF 7

sweeps of the past few months. Its activities have been hampered more severely by the government's numerous house arrest orders, which have immobilized many known Communists and sympathizers and have driven others out of the country. Although part of its underground apparatus may have escaped police notice, the movement is likely to try to husband its resources until police vigilance has abated somewhat.

Outlook

Members of both ANC and PAC reportedly are undergoing training in subversion in various foreign countries, including Tanganyika, Algeria, Morocco, Ghana, and perhaps some countries of the Sino-Soviet bloc as well. There have been reports that militants from both groups have begun to return to South Africa. Their expertise will make the subversive movement somewhat more effective, but their zeal will be dampened by recent legislation which includes even attendance at a sabotage course abroad on the long list of capital crimes.

It seems likely that the character of nonwhite nationalist movements will undergo considerable change in the next few years. As ANC activists learn conspiratorial techniques of their own, they may try to reduce their dependence on non-African Communists. At the same time, the PAC presumably will be acquiring the operational know-how to go with its latent capability for stirring up the mass of its followers. With the ANC edging away from multi-racialism and the PAC working out its organizational problems, the ideological and practical differences between the two groups could become blurred, and eventually both could have a violent, essentially racial solution to South Africa's problems as their acknowledged goal.

This blurring of differences might lead them into a united front, but the odds appear to be against it. In 1960 and 1961 exiles from the PAC and the Congress Alliance were joined in such a front, but mutual distrust forced its break-up. Moreover, at least a few of their leaders—Leballo for one—seem to believe reports that both groups are already forming assassination squads directed against the rival organization. The South African police are aware of these fears and can be expected to encourage them. It seems likely, therefore, that the ANC and PAC will use up much of their meager potential in struggles with each other. (SECRET NO FOREIGN DISSEM)

6

DOCUMENT 35: Ambassador Joseph Satterthwaite, Airgram for Department of State, "U.S. Overseas Internal Defense Policy—South Africa," December 18, 1962 (partially transcribed by the editors).

AIRGRAM

SANITIZED
NLK-7L-285

A-278

~~TOP SECRET~~

(With SECRET enclosure)

AIR POUCH

HANDLING INDICATOR

FOR RM USE ONLY

TO : DEPARTMENT OF STATE, WASHINGTON

COPY NO. 22 SERIES B

This document consists of 9 pages.
Copy No. --- of 60 copies, Series B

FROM   AmEmbassy, PRETORIA   DATE: December 18, 1962.

SUBJECT : U.S. Overseas Internal Defense Policy - South Africa

REF   CA-2783 - September 13, 1962.

FILE

In compliance with the Department's instruction under reference, all key U.S. officials attached to the Country Team of this Mission have read a copy of the document "U.S. Overseas Internal Defense Policy", with the exception of the TOP SECRET Annex A which was seen only by the Ambassador, the Deputy Chief of Mission [   ]

As called for in the basic document, a Country Internal Defense Plan for South Africa has been prepared, following the format contained in Annex C of the basic document. In preparing the Plan the Embassy has "made a study on how the document applies to this country and what measures should be taken to implement the policy" as required by the Action paragraph of the Department's instruction under reference. The Embassy's conclusions are incorporated in the Plan, which is attached as an Enclosure to this airgram.

Bearing in mind the unique status of the Republic of South Africa, in contrast with Counter-Insurgency Requirements of "less developed countries" care must be taken in this instance to distinguish the types of "insurgency" which the U.S. would wish to discourage in South Africa. Basic to this Embassy's mission is a policy which would deny to the South African Government materiel, facilities or any form of support for programs which suppress legitimate claims of non-White groups. Particular care must be taken in this instance, therefore, to consider the South African Plan only in relation to (1) communist inspired, supported or directed subversion or insurgency or (2) those other types of subversion and insurgency which are inimical to

~~TOP SECRET~~
(With SECRET enclosure)

FOR DEPT. USE ONLY

FORM
4-61 OS-323

GFClark/ihh   JCSatterthwaite/ihh

SANITIZED
. . . 7L-285

[195]

DOCUMENT 35: Ambassador Joseph Satterthwaite, Airgram for Department of State, "U.S. Overseas Internal Defense Policy—South Africa," December 18, 1962 (partially transcribed by the editors).

PAGE 2 OF 3

A-218, Dec. 18, 1962, from AmEmbassy, Pretoria, to Department.

~~TOP SECRET~~

37

U.S. national security interests vis-a-vis South Africa. In this context, the Embassy agrees fully with Section V. A of the basic document: "The U.S. does not wish to assume a stance against revolution, *per se*, as an historical means of change."

In compliance with Section VI A. 4, page 24 of the basic document, I have designated G. Edward Clark, the Deputy Chief of Mission, as the officer responsible for assisting me in meeting the Embassy's responsibilities for internal defense.

Original contributions to the Internal Defense Plan for South Africa were made by the following members of the Country Team: Mr. Herman HORTON, Miss Ruth TORRANCE, Mr. Theodore NELSON, Lt. Col. Don DAVIS, and Dr. Argus TRESIDDER.

J. C. Satterthwaite

Enclosure:

GEClark/ihh

~~TOP SECRET~~

DOCUMENT 35: Ambassador Joseph Satterthwaite, Airgram for Department of State, "U.S. Overseas Internal Defense Policy—South Africa," December 18, 1962 (partially transcribed by the editors).

PAGE 3 OF 3

Enclosure to A–278, dated December 18, 1962, from AmEmbassy, Pretoria, to Department.

[Following is an excerpt from pages 3 and 4 of the above document]

A Congress Alliance committee was organized in late 1961 under the leadership of Nelson Mandela to perform sabotage. It performed two trial acts of sabotage in October 1961 and 13 acts of sabotage on 16 December 1961. Due to the number of saboteurs who were arrested by the South African Police, it was believed by the Committee that the sabotage movement was penetrated and needed complete reorganization. In late January 1962, Nelson Mandela was sent throughout Africa and to England to obtain aid for the sabotage effort. During his absence there was very little sabotage performed in South Africa. In mid-June, 1962 the Natal Provincial Committee of the ANC adopted violence as part of its program. In mid-July the Transvaal Provincial ANC Committee also adopted violence. About this time, the SACP (South African Communist Party) prepared a very sophisticated 43 page document calling for revolution in South Africa. At approximately the same time, the Central Committee of the SACP issued a directive which abolished the Congress Alliance and which directed that the ANC become more prominent in sabotage. On 23 July 1962 Nelson Mandela returned to Bechuanaland where he was met by Cecil Williams, a prominent South African Communist. He drove to Johannesburg in Williams' car. In late July Mandela, acting as chauffeur for Williams, drove to Durban and had at least one meeting with the sabotage committee there. He also met with ANC leaders and announced the ANC was no longer under the Congress Alliance. The rank anf [sic] file of the ANC did not know that this new tactic had been directed by the SACP and thought instead that Mandela was moving away from the white Communist domination of the Congress Alliance. While returning to Johannesburg from Durban, Mandela was arrested by the South African Police and was subsequently convicted of incitement and illegally leaving the country. He was sentenced to five years imprisonment. In 1959 the ANC was reorganized under a plan called the M Plan (Mandela Plan). Beginning in September, 1962 members were reorganized again into a highly secret organizational structure known as the Revised M Plan. This new structure is similar to the organization of the SACP and is in existance [sic] today.

DOCUMENT 36: National Security Advisor Henry Kissinger, National Security Study Memorandum 39, "Southern Africa," April 10, 1969, with Attached "Study in Response to National Security Study Memorandum 39: Southern Africa," December 9, 1969 [Parts I–III (transcribed by the editors)].

PAGE 1 OF 21

NATIONAL SECURITY COUNCIL
WASHINGTON, D.C. 20506

Dir., OEP
USecState
J. Clark, BO
LCol. Lemni
Halperi
Allen
Lynn
Eaglebu:
Haig
Moose
Osgood
R. Morri
E. Robe:

April 10, 1969

National Security Study Memorandum 39

TO: The Secretary of State
             The Secretary of Defense
             Director, Central Intelligence Agency

SUBJECT: Southern Africa

The President has directed a comprehensive review of U.S. policy toward Southern Africa (south of Congo (K) and Tanzania).

The study should consider (1) the background and future prospects of major problems in the area; (2) alternative views of the U.S. interest in Southern Africa; and (3) the full range of basic strategies and policy options open to the United States.

The review of interests and policy options should encompass the area as a whole -- including Southern Rhodesia, South Africa, the Portuguese territories, and adjacent African states.

The President has directed that the NSC Interdepartmental Group for Africa perform this study.

The study should be forwarded to the NSC Review Group by April 25th.

Henry A. Kissinger

cc: Secretary of the Treasury
    Secretary of Commerce
    Chairman, Joint Chiefs of Staff
    Administrator, AID
    Acting Director, NASA

DOCUMENT 36: National Security Advisor Henry Kissinger, National Security Study Memorandum 39, "Southern Africa," April 10, 1969, with Attached "Study in Response to National Security Study Memorandum 39: Southern Africa," December 9, 1969 [Parts I–III (transcribed by the editors)].

PAGE 2 OF 21

97pr   X-TRA

19274

AF/NSC-IG 69-8 Rev. A
December 9, 1969

S/S-7)09618

NATIONAL SECURITY COUNCIL

INTERDEPARTMENTAL GROUP FOR AFRICA

Study in Response to National Security Study Memorandum 39:

Southern Africa

DOCUMENT 36: National Security Advisor Henry Kissinger, National Security Study Memorandum 39, "Southern Africa," April 10, 1969, with Attached "Study in Response to National Security Study Memorandum 39: Southern Africa," December 9, 1969 [Parts I–III (transcribed by the editors)].

PAGE 3 OF 21

NATIONAL SECURITY COUNCIL INTERDEPARTMENTAL GROUP FOR AFRICA

Study in Response to National Security Study Memorandum 39:

Southern Africa

Table of Contents

DOCUMENT 36: National Security Advisor Henry Kissinger, National Security Study Memorandum 39, "Southern Africa," April 10, 1969, with Attached "Study in Response to National Security Study Memorandum 39: Southern Africa," December 9, 1969 [Parts I–III (transcribed by the editors)].

PAGE 4 OF 21

AF/NSC-IG 69-8 Rev. A
December 9, 1969

I. A. U.S. INTERESTS IN SOUTHERN AFRICA

Our policy positions on southern African issues affect a range of U.S. interests. None of the interests are vital to our security, but they have political and material importance. Some of these interests are concrete and evident in the region itself, while others relate to our position in black Africa and the world. The interests can be summarized as follows:

1. Political

Racial repression by white minority regimes in southern Africa has international political ramifications extending beyond the region itself. Politically conscious blacks elsewhere in Africa and the world deeply resent the continuation of discrimination, identify with the repressed majorities in southern Africa and tend in varying degrees to see relationships of outside powers with the white regimes as at least tacit acceptance of racism. Many others in the non-white world tend to share this view in some measure. The communist states have been quick to seize on this issue and to support black aspirations. Thus our policy toward the white regimes of southern Africa affects, though it may not necessarily govern, our standing with African and other states on issues in the United Nations and bilaterally. Depending on its intensity, adverse reaction to our policy in southern Africa could make more difficult our relationships elsewhere in Africa on a variety of matters including U.S. defense installations, over-flight rights and the use of port facilities. The same consideration applies to economic relations: direct investment in Africa outside the white regime states currently totals about $1.5 billion (of which the greater part is in black Africa south of the Sahara), or about two-thirds of the total U.S. investment in Africa. U.S. exports split about 60% to the black states of Africa and 40% to the white regime countries.

Because of the multi-racial character of our society and our own racial problems, other countries tend to see our relationships with southern Africa as reflections of domestic attitudes on race. This situation is exacerbated by the extension of South African racial discrimination to black Americans who may be refused visas or who are subjected to segregated facilities in South Africa.

If violence in the area escalates, U.S. interests will be increasingly threatened. In these circumstances the U.S. would find it increasingly difficult without sacrificing interests to find a middle ground in the UN on questions of insurgent violence and counter-violence in the region and to resist demands for more positive actions against the white regimes.

2. Economic

U.S. direct investment in southern Africa, mainly in South Africa, is about $1 billion and yields a highly profitable return. Trade, again mainly with South Africa, runs a favorable balance to the U.S. (Our exports to South Africa were about $450 million in 1968 against imports of $250 million.) In addition the U.S. has indirect economic interest in the key role which South Africa plays in the U.K. balance of payments. U.K. investment in South Africa is currently estimated at $3 billion, and the British have made it clear that they will take no action which would jeopardize their economic interests. South Africa produces over 75% of the free world supply of gold. The long-term importance of South African gold sales has been reduced by the creation of IMF Special Drawing Rights but they are nonetheless significant in the international monetary system and very important to South Africa.

3. Defense

Southern Africa is geographically important for the U.S. and its allies, particularly with the closing of the Suez Canal and the increased Soviet activity in the Indian Ocean.

The U.S. uses overflight and landing facilities for military aircraft in the Portuguese Territories and

DOCUMENT 36: National Security Advisor Henry Kissinger, National Security Study Memorandum 39, "Southern Africa," April 10, 1969, with Attached "Study in Response to National Security Study Memorandum 39: Southern Africa," December 9, 1969 [Parts I–III (transcribed by the editors)].

PAGE 5 OF 21

South Africa. Any of a number of contingencies could require U.S. military air transit to the Indian Ocean/Mid East areas. All but one feasible air route across Africa south of the Sahara would depend upon overflight and, in some cases, landing rights in South Africa or Zambia and Mozambique. The DOD [*Department of Defense*] has proposed periodic use of these routes in normal times. However, apart from tracking station support aircraft, the policy has been to request clearance for South Africa as infrequently as possible.

There are major ship repair and logistic facilities in South Africa with a level of technical competence which cannot be duplicated elsewhere on the African continent. We have not permitted U.S. naval vessels to use South African port facilities since early 1967, except for emergencies. We have made use of U.S. Navy or foreign oilers to refuel carriers transiting to and from S.E. Asia via the Cape of Good Hope. Navy force reductions now call for the deactivation of two Atlantic Fleet and one Pacific Fleet oiler, which will attenuate already meager oiler assets so that, the DOD considers, assignment of oiler support to a carrier transit would seriously degrade our fleet posture vis-a-vis commitments and requirements. Regular use is made of ports in Angola and Mozambique, however, but these ports cannot accommodate carriers.

The DOD has a missile tracking station in South Africa under a classified agreement, and some of the military aircraft traffic involves support of this station. The future need for the DOD station is under review. The tentative conclusions are that the station is no longer required for research and development of missiles. We also finance a U.K. atmosphere testing station for nuclear materials located in Swaziland which helps us monitor nuclear atmospheric explosions worldwide.

4. Scientific

NASA has a space tracking facility of major importance in South Africa, and overflight and landing rights for support aircraft are utilized in connection with various space shots. The NASA station is particularly oriented towards support of unmanned spacecraft and will be of key significance for planetary missions.

We have an atomic energy agreement with South Africa initiated under the Atoms for Peace Program; this relationship is important in influencing South Africa to continue its policy of doing nothing in the marketing of its large production of uranium oxide which would have the effect of increasing the number of nuclear weapons powers.

B. VIEWS OF THE U.S. INTEREST IN SOUTHERN AFRICA

In weighing the range of U.S. interests in southern Africa, there is basic consensus within the U.S. Government:

1. Although the U.S. has various interests in the region, it has none which could be classified as vital security interests.

2. Our political interests in the region are important because the racial policies of the white states have become a major international issue. Therefore, because other countries have made it so, our foreign policy must take into account the domestic policies of the white regimes. Most non-white nations in the world in varying degrees would tend to judge conspicuous U.S. cooperation with the white regimes as condoning their racial policies.

3. The racial problems of southern Africa probably will grow more acute over time, perhaps leading to violent internal upheavals and greater involvement of the communist powers. Though these developments may be years or even decades ahead, U.S. policy should take account now of the risks to our interests and possible involvement over this uncertain future.

There are specific differences of view within the government regarding future trends in southern Africa and the U.S. role in the area. These contrasting views are central to a judgement of U.S. policy options. The following reflect a basic intellectual disagreement within the government in approaching the southern African problem:

DOCUMENT 36: National Security Advisor Henry Kissinger, National Security Study Memorandum 39, "Southern Africa," April 10, 1969, with Attached "Study in Response to National Security Study Memorandum 39: Southern Africa," December 9, 1969 [Parts I–III (transcribed by the editors)].

PAGE 6 OF 21

(1) *U.S. Involvement to Promote Change*

U.S. efforts for constructive change: Some argue that racism and colonialism are central issues in African and world-politics. The race issue in southern Africa has already led to armed conflict and disharmony which will spread if left unchecked. The U.S. is obligated under the UN Charter to do what we can to promote the non-discriminatory observance of human rights.

Non-involvement: Others reply that our disagreement with the domestic policies of any state should not govern the pursuit of our foreign policy interests in that state. Our concern with internal human rights problems has caused us to ignore serious cross-border infiltration which is a more legitimate UN concern and could lead to larger conflicts in the area. The actions taken against the white states, particularly on South West Africa and Rhodesia, have no valid basis in international law.

(2) Violent vs. Evolutionary Change

Violent Change: Some argue that mounting violence is inevitable unless change occurs and that there is no prospect for peaceful change in the racial policies of the white regimes, embedded as they are in prejudice, religious doctrine and self-interest and bolstered by economic prosperity, particularly, in South Africa. The results will be: (a) black guerrilla and terrorist activity on a growing scale within these countries until change occurs, and (b) because of their support of the blacks, the Soviets and Chinese will become the major beneficiaries of the conflict.

Evolutionary Change: Others contend that there will be violence up to a point, since change can only come slowly. But there is some prospect for peaceful change in the white states in response to internal economic and social forces. In any event, peaceful evolution is the only avenue to change because (a) black violence only produces internal reaction, and (b) military realities rule out a black victory at any stage. Moreover, there are reasons to question the depth and permanence of black resolve. Recently there has been a decline in the level of insurgency. Neighboring black states—vital to successful guerrilla activity—will

choose to preserve their own security in the face of inevitable punishing white retaliation at an early stage of any significant guerrilla warfare.

(3) The Possibility of U.S. Influence Toward Evolutionary Change

No Influence: Some contend that we can neither reform the whites nor restrain the blacks. Racial repression is deeply ingrained in the whites—the product of tradition, economic privilege and fears for their survival. These attitudes are not amenable to the kinds of influence one nation exerts upon another through peaceful international relations. Only isolation and stronger forms of pressure (i.e. force or mandatory economic sanctions backed by blockade) could have any impact.

Yet, they argue, without some change in the whites we cannot hope to influence the blacks to accept "peaceful evolution" as a substitute for force. The blacks will see such advice as a fundamental U.S. betrayal of their cause.

A related school of thought believes that in this sensitive area any effort by the U.S. to exert influence on internal policies could retard rather than stimulate the natural dynamics of change in the white-dominated societies.

Some Influence: Others argue that our tactical encouragement of economic and social forces already at work within the white regimes can constitute marginal but important influence for change. That influence, however, can be exerted only subtly and over several years. We should not give up whatever chance we have—through contacts with whites as well as blacks—to defuse the dangerous tensions in the area and to demonstrate the alternatives to the disastrous racial policies of the white regimes. Exposure of these regimes to the outside world is necessary if there is to be peaceful change. Isolation of the white societies has only intensified repressive policies, [*sic*] Moreover, external efforts to force change by pressure or coercion have unified the whites and produced an obdurate counter-reaction.

DOCUMENT 36: National Security Advisor Henry Kissinger, National Security Study Memorandum 39, "Southern Africa," April 10, 1969, with Attached "Study in Response to National Security Study Memorandum 39: Southern Africa," December 9, 1969 [Parts I–III (transcribed by the editors)].

PAGE 7 OF 21

(4) Importance of Political vs. Other Tangible Interests

Political Interests: Some argue that racial hostility as a reaction to centuries of white predominance is a relatively new political force in the world, gaining power and effectiveness as the developing countries become independent and control access to their own territories. We cannot forseeexactly [*sic*] when race will become a major factor in the international power balance, but that time is coming. It is equally clear that the racial repression by the white regimes in southern Africa is now the most volatile racial problem on the international scene.

For the non-white states, they also argue, the reckoning of support on the racial issue in their time of weakness will determine their friendship or hostility for the U.S. a generation hence when their importance in world politics may be substantially greater. Thus failure to demonstrate an appreciation today of African aspirations may eventually (a) forfeit great influence to the communist powers, who have taken a clear position in support of black states and liberation movements and (b) jeopardize our strategic and economic interests in non-white Africa. Any anti-U.S. or pro-communist reactions, however, are likely to be either solid or early and many black states are very aware of the dangers of association with the communists.

Other Tangible Interests: Others reply that our interests in the white states of southern Africa—albeit having a relatively low priority among such interests worldwide—are clearly worth retaining at their present political cost. These interests include access to air and naval facilities for which alternatives are expensive or less satisfactory, a major space tracking station, and significant investment and balance of trade advantages. Our political concerns and other interests may be accommodated because (a) the great majority of non-white states in Africa and elsewhere will put their own immediate self-interest ahead of penalizing us for our interests in the white states, and (b) even the most directly involved black states (Zambia and Tanzania) will temper their reaction because our continued good will and support for their cause will be important, and they know it. In any event other countries will judge our standing on the racial issue worldwide by the outcome of the racial problems in the United States.

DOCUMENT 36: National Security Advisor Henry Kissinger, National Security Study Memorandum 39, "Southern Africa," April 10, 1969, with Attached "Study in Response to National Security Study Memorandum 39: Southern Africa," December 9, 1969 [Parts I–III (transcribed by the editors)].

PAGE 8 OF 21

II. PRESENT POLICY

The aim of present policy is to try to balance our economic, scientific and strategic interests in the white states with the political interest of dissociating the U.S. from the white minority regimes and their repressive racial policies. Decisions have been made *ad hoc*, on a judgment of benefits and political costs at a given moment. But the strength of this policy—its flexibility—is also its weakness. Policy is not precisely recorded. And because there have been significant differences of view within the government as to how much weight should be given to these conflicting factors in any given instance, certain decisions have been held in suspense "pending review of the over-all policy"—e.g., visits of naval vessels to South African ports enroute to and from the Indian Ocean or Viet-Nam [*sic*], export licensing of equipment for South Africa, Angola and Mozambique, which might be used either for military or civilian purposes, participation of South African military personnel in Department of Defense correspondence courses.

This policy seeks progress towards majority rule through political arrangements which guarantee increasing participation by the whole population. Tangible evidence of such progress has been considered a precondition for improved U.S. relations with the white states. In the case of South Africa, the following are illustrative of the types of actions which that government might take to improve relations with the U.S.:

A. *Bilateral*. Permit assignment of non-whites to U.S. Embassy and consulates. Non-discriminatory treatment of U.S. naval personnel and merchant marine crews ashore. Non-discriminatory visa policy. Permit more South African non-whites in U S. exchange programs. Facilitate U.S. official access to non-white areas of South Africa and South West Africa.

B. *Internal*. Eliminate job reservation and abolish pay differentials based an race. Recognize African labor unions as bargaining units. Abolish pass laws and repressive security legislation. Move towards qualified franchise for non-whites.

C. *Regional and International*. Recognize UN responsibility for South West Africa and permit UN presence in territory; cease applying repressive legislation there. Withdraw economic and paramilitary support from Rhodesia. Give generous customs treatment to Botswana, Lesotho and Swaziland. Expand exceptions to apartheid in cases of visiting non-whites such as sportsmen and businessmen.

(It is realized that most of the foregoing are unrealistic under present circumstances, but they illustrate the directions in which change might be sought.)

Following are the actions taken toward the different countries and areas which, in sum, constitute our present policy toward southern Africa:

Republic of South Africa

We maintain limited but formally correct diplomatic relations, making clear our opposition to apartheid. In the early 1960's the U.S. played a leading role in the UN in denouncing South Africa's racial policies. We led the effort in 1963 to establish and we continue to support the UN arms embargo on South Africa. We have avoided association with the South African Defense Force except for limited military attache contacts. We supported the UN declaration that South Africa's mandate over South West Africa had terminated, and calling for it to withdraw and to acknowledge direct UN responsibility for the territory. On the other hand, we have acted on the premise that the problems of South Africa and South West Africa do not justify either the use of force or the imposition of mandatory economic sanctions, in part because there is no evidence that these actions would be efficacious. Moreover, we have sought to avoid the involvement of any U.S. military forces which might be required for such measures. Negro personnel have not been assigned to the U.S. mission and consulates in South Africa.

We have supported efforts to protest the legal rights of victims of discriminatory and repressive legislation in South Africa and South West Africa. This has involved aide memoires, attendance at trials to assure international observation of certain legal and judicial practices, and cooperation with private groups in the American bar to reinforce in South Africa traditions of respect for the rule of law. We also have sought to deepen our identification with the non-white majorities through personal contacts, public appearances and our exchange program. We have sought to support through the UN and private agencies humanitarian relief for South African and South West African victims of repression.

There is limited overflight and landing activity by U.S. aircraft in South Africa. Except for three emergencies, there have been no U.S. naval ship calls in South African ports since early 1967, pending a review of policy towards South Africa. We rely heavily on the NASA tracking station near Johannesburg, particularly for planetary missions, but at the same time maintain less satisfactory alternate facilities outside South Africa in case it becomes necessary or desirable to close the station. The future need for the DOD tracking station at Pretoria is under review. The tentative conclusions are that the station is no longer required for research and development of missiles. We enjoy very profitable economic relations with South Africa despite the official approach of neither encouraging nor discouraging investment (apart from the Foreign Direct Investment Program) and keeping trade facilitative services in low key. EXIM loans are not authorized, but export guarantees up to five years are permitted, subject to review for political implications. In general, the restrictions imposed on our economic relations with South Africa, especially the constraints on EXIM financing, may have limited somewhat the growth of our exports and investment there. Profit prospects in South Africa, however, attract U.S. business regardless of official endorsement.

Southern Rhodesia

The U.S. voted for the Security Council resolutions of December 1966 and May 1968 which imposed mandatory sanctions against Southern Rhodesia on the basis of a finding of a threat to the peace under Chapter VII of the UN Charter. Executive Orders implementing the sanctions program were issued in Janaury [sic] 1967 and July 1968 under authority of the UN Participation Act of 1945. (Although Portugal and South Africa have assisted Southern Rhodesia, the U.S. has not supported the extension of mandatory sanctions to them.)

The mandatory sanctions program was devised by the British as a compromise between the use of force, which they were unwilling to contemplate largely because of domestic considerations, and doing nothing, which would have jeopardized their relations with the black African states and other Afro-Asian members of the Commonwealth. The United States cooperated with the U.K. largely for the same reasons. We also anticipated that failure to devise peaceful means to influence the Smith regime toward a satisfactory settlement would encourage extremists and dangerous instability in the area. Although it was recognized from the start that the sanctions program would be an imperfect instrument there was a tendency to overestimate the effectiveness of sanctions, which have been weakened by numerous and sometimes large (South Africa and Portugal) loopholes. Similarly, although there was awareness that the convenience of certain economic interests would be disrupted through sanctions, there was a tendency to underestimate the extent to which criticism, both political and economic, would multiply with the passage of time and evidence of the program's lack of success.

The U.S. has continued to recognize British sovereignty in the colony, and refused to support the use of force by either side to the dispute. We maintain a reduced staff at our Consulate General in Salisbury which continues to operate under exequaturs from the British Crown. With the Southern Rhodesian determination to declare itself a republic, increasingly negative reactions may be anticipated from African nations to our continuing presence in Salisbury. The Consulate General provides citizenship and welfare services to approximately 1,100 American residents, three-fourths of whom are missionary families.

Portuguese Territories

Our approach to Angola and Mozambique is influenced by countervailing factors. On the one hand Portugal is a NATO ally to which we currently supply about one million dollars in military assistance and

DOCUMENT 36: National Security Advisor Henry Kissinger, National Security Study Memorandum 39, "Southern Africa," April 10, 1969, with Attached "Study in Response to National Security Study Memorandum 39: Southern Africa," December 9, 1969 [Parts I–III (transcribed by the editors)].

PAGE 10 OF 21

whose islands, the Azores, we find important for use as a naval and air base. On the other hand we sympathize with the aspirations of the Angolans and Mozambicans for self-determination.

In implementation of these policies we maintain a unilateral embargo on military equipment of U.S. origin for use in the Portuguese Territories either directly from the U.S. or indirectly from our NATO supplies to Portugal. U.S. export controls restrain possible sales of dual-purpose items, such as jet transports and communications equipment to the government of Portugal for uses in Africa.

We cooperate with Portugal on NATO matters and continue to use the Azores facilities. U.S. naval vessels and aircraft also use facilities in the Portuguese African territories for refueling and space support missions. Trade relations with the territories are normal and there are no USG restraints on American investment there apart from the Foreign Direct Investment Program. EXIM Bank facilities are available, subject to review for political implications.

Black African States of Southern Africa

The U.S. maintains cordial relations with the five black-ruled states of the area, Malawi, Zambia, Botswana, Lesotho, and Swaziland. We have Ambassadors in Malawi and Zambia. Since their independence we have maintained Charges in Botswana, Lesotho and Swaziland and these countries are pressing us for the assignment of resident Ambassadors. These countries consider the level of our diplomatic representatives to be an important manifestation of U.S. sympathy and support.

As with all developing countries, an important factor in our relations is the level and kind of aid we can provide. Under current policies AID provides funds for regional and multi-donor projects and for the small Special Self-Help and Development Program. Investment guarantees are available, and the U.S. extends additional help through PL 480 food donations, and Peace Corps programs in four of the five black countries. However, there is a body of opinion which considers that programs of bilateral technical assistance are necessary in these states because of their generally isolated and en-

clave location. Bilateral assistance has been limited as a matter of policy to 10 concentration countries in Africa, none of which are in the southern region. World-wide AID policy is currently under review. (See Annex 7 for a discussion of considerations involved in bilateral aid to the black states of the region).

A further problem with these countries is the Conte amendment to foreign assistance legislation. Zambia, fearful of attacks by the white regimes in retaliation for passage of liberation groups through her territory, is purchasing air defense missiles and possibly jet aircraft from the U.K. and Italy. The Conte amendment requires the cancellation of U.S. aid of bilateral and some regional types in the amount of weapons expenditures. We have introduced legislation to change the amendment to provide greater flexibility. Despite our explanations of the intent of Congress, application of the Conte amendment may be seen by the black states as evidence that the U.S. is more sympathetic to the status quo of the white regimes than the aspirations of the blacks.

Liberation Groups

The U.S. maintains contact with exile nationalist movements from the white-controlled states. We also assist refugee students from these states through the Southern African Student Program and two secondary schools which are operated for refugee students. The U.S. takes the position that force is not an appropriate means to bring about constructive change in southern Africa.

United Nations

On southern African issues in the UN the relationship between the U.S. position and that of Afro-Asian UN members has altered considerably over the last five years. We played a leading role in the arms embargo against South Africa, the determination that South Africa's mandate over South West Africa had terminated, and on mandatory economic sanctions against Southern Rhodesia. However, these actions largely exhausted the store of measures we were prepared to take on these issues.

DOCUMENT 36: National Security Advisor Henry Kissinger, National Security Study Memorandum 39, "Southern Africa," April 10, 1969, with Attached "Study in Response to National Security Study Memorandum 39: Southern Africa," December 9, 1969 [Parts I–III (transcribed by the editors)].

PAGE 11 OF 21

The Afro-Asians have steadily increased pressures to exclude South Africa from the UN, for sanctions against South Africa and Portugal, and for use of force to give effect to UN actions. These demands have moved these states far out in front of the U.S. and some other Free World countries. We have consistently resisted efforts to exclude South Africa from international bodies and to extend mandatory sanctions or useforce [sic] on southern African issues. Thus the U.S. has made it clear that we have gone as far as we can in the direction of greater UN pressures on the white regimes. (The U.K. and France have adopted an even more restrained position on southern African issues, in their abstentions on the UN General Assembly resolution determining that South Africa's mandate over South West Africa had terminated on which we voted in favor, and the U.K.'s somewhat more permissive policy on the arms embargo against South Africa, which is virtually a dead letter in the case of France.)

III.   THE RANGE OF POLICY OPTIONS

U.S. Objectives

There are several broad objectives of U.S. policy toward southern Africa. Arranged without intent to imply priority, they are:

— To improve the U.S. standing in black Africa and internationally on the racial issue.

— To protect economic, scientific and strategic interests and opportunities in the region.

— To minimize the likelihood of escalation of violence in the area and the risk of U.S. involvement.

— To minimize the opportunities for the USSR and Communist China to exploit the racial issue in the region for propaganda advantage and to gain political influence with black governments and liberation movements.

— To encourage moderation of the current rigid racial and colonial policies of the white regimes. These objectives are to a degree contradictory—pursuit of may make difficult the successful pursuit of one or more of the others. Moreover, views as to the relative priority among these objectives vary widely, depending primarily upon the perception of the nature of the problems in the area and U.S. interests there (see I.B).

Range of Choice

The general policy question centers on U.S. posture toward the white regimes—a key element in our relations with the black states in the area and a factor of varying degrees of importance throughout the continent.

But the range of feasible policy options is limited. On one extreme our interests do not justify consideration of U.S. military intervention in the area. On the other extreme we cannot accept or endorse either the racial or colonial policies of the white regimes. Nor can we identify ourselves with violent or repressive solutions to the area's problems on either side of the confrontation. The essential choice is among:

(a) Movement towards normal relations with the white regimes to protect and enhance our economic, strategic and scientific interests (Option 1).

(b) Broader association with both black and white states in an effort to encourage moderation in the white states, to enlist cooperation of the black states in reducing tensions and the likelihood of increasing cross-border violence, and to encourage improved relations among states in area (Option 2).

(c) Increased identification with and support for the black states of the region, as a pre-condition to pursuit of our minimum necessary economic, strategic and scientific interests in the white states (option 3).

(d) Limited association with the white states and closer association with the blacks in an effort to retain some economic, scientific and strategic interests in the white states while maintaining a posture on the racial issue which the blacks will accept, though opposing violent solutions to the problems of the region (option 4).

(e) Dissociation from the white regimes with closer relations with the black states in an effort to enhance our standing on the racial issue in Africa and internationally (Option 5).

(f) Increased U.S. measures of coercion, short of armed force, bilaterally and on an international basis, to induce constructive change in white-regime race policies (Option 6).

Each option represents a range of actions, with some flexibility of choice among specific means without altering the premise or general strategy of the option. The purpose of this paper is to afford the NSC a choice on basic posture toward southern Africa. It is not intended to be a specific scenario for operational action, and the examples in each option are the types of action which would be consistent with the option's thrust but are neither comprehensive nor necessarily in each case the specific action which would be selected.

A satisfactory arrangement regarding South Africa's handling of gold can continue to be sought

DOCUMENT 36: National Security Advisor Henry Kissinger, National Security Study Memorandum 39, "Southern Africa," April 10, 1969, with Attached "Study in Response to National Security Study Memorandum 39: Southern Africa," December 9, 1969 [Parts I–III (transcribed by the editors)].

PAGE 13 OF 21

under any of the options, but it would probably be more difficult to achieve under option 5, and particularly under Option 6.

OPTION 1

Premise

Our disagreements with the internal policies of governments in power in the region should not govern our relations with either the black or white states. We should follow a policy of pursuing our tangible interests throughout the region. In seeking to induce change, we have erroneously supported UN actions on Rhodesia and South West Africa based on questionable premises. While we cannot reverse our participation in these actions overnight, we can begin to withdraw from implementation of them. The political costs of closer relations with the white states will not be excessive.

General Posture

We would move to normalize our relations with all governments of the area, recognizing that reversal of our support for international actions already taken on Rhodesia and South West Africa will require some time. While we would make limited declarations of moral disapproval of the racial and colonial policies of the white governments, we would take no concrete measures to induce change and place no restrictions on the pursuit of our tangible interests. We would assume the risks of reaction against us in the black areas of the region and the rest of Africa.

Operational Examples

— Gradually terminate arms embargo against South Africa, beginning with liberal treatment of equipment which could serve either military or civilian purposes or the common defense, e.g., anti-submarine warfare equipment.

— Authorize routine U.S. naval visits and use of airfields.

— Retain tracking station in South Africa as long as needed.

— Promote U.S. exports and facilitate investment (within the framework of U.S. Foreign Direct Investment Program) in South Africa, South West Africa, the Portuguese Territories and eventually Rhodesia; afford unrestricted EXIM bank facilities.

— Continue sugar quota for South Africa.

— Recognize South African authorities in South West Africa and place no limitations on dealing with them.

— Cease enforcement of sanctions against Rhodesia; retain Consulate; if Republic is declared consider recognition.

— Quietly terminate unilateral U.S. arms embargo on Portuguese Territories, beginning with authorization of export of dual-purpose equipment.

— Economic assistance to the black states on the same basis as elsewhere in Africa; no special assistance and no arms supply; possible minority participation in development consortium with South Africa and Rhodesia.

— Public discouragement of insurgent movements and no assistance to political refugees.

— Limited information and exchange programs in both black and white areas.

PROS

1. Would reduce danger that U.S international commitments on problems of the region may involve us in possible future conflict.

2. Would preserve and expand U.S. scientific strategic, and economic interests in white–controlled areas.

3. Would remove irritant in U.S. relations with Portugal.

CONS

1.   Would require repudiation of previous U.S. actions in UN and, in the case of Rhodesia, violation of mandatory provisions of the UN Charter.

2.   Would tend to encourage the white regimes in their intransigence.

3.   Would provoke strong black African reaction with possible adverse effects on U.S. interests in those countries.

4.   Would risk forfeiting to communist powers primary influence with black states of region, the insurgent movements and to degree elsewhere in Africa.

5.   Unrestricted pursuit of tangible interests would result in greater restrictions on future actions.

6.   Does nothing to deal with problems of potential violence in region.

OPTION 2

Premise

The whites are here to stay and the only way that constructive change can come about is through them. There is no hope for the blacks to gain the political rights they seek through violence, which will only lead to chaos and increased opportunities for the communists. We can, by selective relaxation of our stance toward the white regimes, encourage some modification of their current racial and colonial policies and through more substantial economic assistance to the black states (a total of about $5 million annually in technical assistance to the black states) help to draw the two groups together and exert some influence on both for peaceful change. Our tangible interests form a basis for our contacts in the region, and these can be maintained at an acceptable political cost.

General Posture

We would maintain public opposition to racial repression but relax political isolation and economic restrictions on the white states. We would begin by modest indications of this relaxation, broadening the scope of our relations and contacts gradually and to some degree in response to tangible—albeit small and gradual—moderation of white policies. Without openly taking a position undermining the U.K. and the UN on Rhodesia, we would be more flexible in our attitude toward the Smith regime. We would take present Portuguese policies as suggesting further changes in the Portuguese Territories. At the same time we would take diplomatic steps to convince the black states of the area that their current liberation and majority rule aspirations in the south are not attainable by violence and that their only hope for a peaceful and prosperous future lies in closer relations with white-dominated states. We would emphasize our belief that closer relations will help to bring change in the white states. We would give increased and more flexible economic aid to black states of the area to focus their attention on their internal development and to give them a motive to cooperate in reducing tensions. We would encourage economic assistance from South Africa to the developing black nations.

This option accepts, at least over a 3 to 5 year period, the prospect of unrequited U.S. initiatives toward the whites and some opposition from the blacks in order to develop an atmosphere conducive to change in white attitudes through persuasion and erosion. To encourage this change in white attitudes, we would indicate our willingness to accept political arrangements short of guaranteed progress toward majority rule, provided that they assure broadened political participation in some form by the whole population.

The various elements of the option would stand as a whole and approval of the option would not constitute approval of individual elements out of this context.

Operational Examples

— Maintain public stance against apartheid but relax political isolation and economic restrictions against the white states.

— Enforce arms embargo against South Africa but with liberal treatment of equipment which could serve either military or civilian purposes.

DOCUMENT 36: National Security Advisor Henry Kissinger, National Security Study Memorandum 39, "Southern Africa," April 10, 1969, with Attached "Study in Response to National Security Study Memorandum 39: Southern Africa," December 9, 1969 [Parts I–III (transcribed by the editors)].

PAGE 15 OF 21

— Fuel stops only, or naval visits in South Africa with arrangements for non-discrimination toward U.S. personnel in organized activity ashore;° authorize routine use of airfields.

— Retain tracking stations in South Africa as long as required.

— Remove constraints on EXIM Bank facilities for South Africa; actively encourage U.S. exports and facilitate U.S. investment consistent with the Foreign Direct Investment Program.

— Continue sugar quota in South Africa.

— Conduct selected exchange programs with South Africa in all categories, including military.

— Without changing the U.S. legal position that South African occupancy of South West Africa is illegal, we would play down the issue and encourage accommodation between South Africa and the UN.

— On Rhodesia, retain Consulate; gradually relax sanctions (e.g. hardship exceptions for chrome) and consider eventual recognition.

— Continue arms embargo on Portuguese Territories, but give more liberal treatment to exports of dual purpose equipment.

— Continue discussions with Portuguese on African policy. Be prepared to offer discreet good offices in restoring and improving Portuguese relations with Zambia and the Congo.

— Encourage trade and investment in Portuguese Territories; full EXIM Bank facilities.

— Establish Southern African Development Fund for aid projects in Botswana, Lesotho and Swaziland with U.S. Ambassador accredited to three states to be U.S. representative to Fund Council. Consider possibility of Malawi participation in Fund at later stage, if this appears politically advisable.

— Provide bilateral technical assistance to Tanzania and Zambia; continue at least one major regional development project involving them.

° This would not necessarily preclude individual shore leave.

— Respond to reasonable requests for purchase of non-sophisticated arms but seek no change in Conte amendment.

— Official visits for Tanzanian and Zambian heads of state.

— By diplomatic means seek to persuade black states (importantly Zambia and Tanzania) to adopt policy of peaceful coexistence with white regimes.

— Towards African insurgent movements take public position that U.S. opposes use of force in racial confrontation. Continue humanitarian assistance to refugees.

— Increase information and exchange activities in both white and black states.

PROS

1. Would encourage existing tendencies to broaden relations between black states and white and thus reduce tensions—South Africa's new outward policy, Zambia's trade and *sub-rosa* political contacts with South Africa and Portugal.

2. Would preserve U.S. economic, scientific and strategic interests in the white states and would expand opportunities for profitable trade and investment.

3. Relaxation of the U.S. attitude toward the whites could help lift their present siege mentality; and it would encourage elements among the whites seeking to extend South African relationships with black Africa.

4. U.S. diplomatic support and economic aid offer the black states an alternative to the recognized risks of mounting communist influence.

5. Increased aid would also give us greater influence to caution the black states against violent confrontation and give them a tangible stake in accepting the prospects of gradual change.

6. Would reduce a major irritant in our relations with Portugal, and afford the Caetano government opportunity for liberalization.

CONS

1. Relaxation of the U.S. stance toward white states could be taken by the whites as a vindication of their policies. Many black states, led by Zambia and Tanzania, probably would charge us with subordinating our professed ideals to material interests and tolerating white-regime policies. This reaction could adversely affect, in varying degrees, our political, economic and strategic interests in the black states.

2. There is a serious question whether pro-Western leaders of the black states could continue to justify their stance to their populations if the U.S. officially declared its opposition to current liberation efforts. Radical and communist states would be the beneficiaries.

3. Unilateral U.S. relaxation of sanctions against Rhodesia would be a highly visible violation of our international obligations and would be damaging both to the U.S. and to the UN.

4. The current thrust of South African domestic policy does not involve any basic change in the racial segregation system, which is anathema to the black states. There is virtually no evidence that change might be forthcoming in these South African policies as a result of any approach on our part.

5. Requires extensive diplomatic and economic involvement in a situation in which the solution is extremely long-range and the outcome doubtful at best.

6. It is doubtful that the additional aid contemplated would be sufficiently great to influence the black states in the direction indicated.

OPTION 3

Premise

An effective U.S. role in the region and in Africa requires credibility with the black states. A more active demonstration of interest in the black states of the region is necessary to meet this need and to provide a basis for carrying out with minimum political risk, essential official policies in the white states. We can by so doing meet our minimal requirements in the area and exert a greater influence on the course of events in the black states.

General Posture

We would begin as soon as possible to improve our position in the black states, including a high-level public statement stressing our commitment to the peaceful advancement of human freedoms and dignity in southern Africa. If progress achieved in the first six months should warrant it, we could consider possibility for steps in pursuit of our minimum necessary economic, strategic and scientific interests in the white states.

Operational Examples

— Maintain active stance, publicly, officially and in UN against apartheid.

— Continue arms embargo against South Africa.

— Retain NASA tracking station but with alternative facilities elsewhere.

— Neither encourage nor discourage investment; low-key commercial services.

— No EXIM loans; insurance and credit guarantees subject to political review.

— Encourage Congressional revocation of South African sugar quote [*sic*] and reallocation to less developed African producers.

— Encourage U.S. companies to apply liberal employee policies.

— Maintain persistent opposition and non-recognition of South African rule in South West Africa.

— Discourage U.S. investments in South West Africa; no EXIM Bank facilities.

— Take initiatives in UN on behalf of alternatives to Chapter VII sanctions on South West Africa—such as reference to ICJ. Avoid veto if possible.

— Support through exchanges and contacts groups in South Africa and South West Africa seeking wiser racial policies and the rule of law; encourage U.S. private organizations supportive of these groups.

— Terminate U.S. investment in Rhodesia by closing Consulate and permitting release of chrome stocks if they would clearly fall under Treasury hardship rule (even though this would violate our UN obligations). Make clear no further transactions with current regime will be permitted. Continue sanctions enforcement.

— Continue discussions with Portuguese on African policy. Be prepared to offer discreet good offices in restoring and improving Portuguese relations with Zambia and the Congo.

— Maintain embargo on the supply of arms to either side in the conflict in Portuguese Africa. Continue operational naval visits.

— Normal trade and neutral policy on investment in Portuguese Territories; continue routine EXIM financing and be prepared to grant major EXIM loans when economic and political circumstances warrant.

— Maintain discreet contact with but give no new assistance (other than educational and humanitarian) to political refugees from Portuguese Africa.

— Establish Southern African Development Fund for aid projects in Botswana, Lesotho and Swaziland with U.S. Ambassador accredited to three states to be U.S. representative to Fund Council. Consider possibility of Malawi participation in Fund at later stage, if this appears politically advisable.

— Provide bilateral technical assistance to Tanzania and Zambia; continue at least one major regional development project involving them.

— Official visits for Tanzanian and Zambian heads of states.

— Maintain discreet contact and selective non-military support to liberation groups (other than those from Portuguese Africa). Extend educational and humanitarian assistance to individual political refugees.

— Maintain present information and exchange programs in white areas and expand programs in black states.

○ ○ ○ ○ ○ ○

— After a period of six months from the inception of the program to strengthen relations and understanding with the black states, consider the following actions in pursuit of limited U.S. economic and strategic interests in South Africa:

— Reconsider EXIM policy.

— Flexibility in arms embargo on sale of dual purpose items.

— Unclassified military correspondence courses where there is clearly direct benefit to U.S. in resulting contact.

— Operational naval visits on the basis of fuel stops only or with shore leave restricted to racially integrated activities.

PROS

1. Would preserve most of our minimum necessary economic, strategic and scientific interests in the white states.

2. Would afford access to black states of region and improve our standing elsewhere in Africa and with Afro-Asian states at UN.

3. Expanded aid to the black states would enable us to offset criticisms of our necessary activities in white states.

4. Would retain flexibility for future movements towards either white or black states.

CONS

1. Preparatory moves in black states might not give clear enough results nor be sufficient to offset African criticism for possible later activities in white states.

2. Association with the white regimes at any time is vulnerable to exploitation by the communists and African extremists.

3. Substantial EXIM loan in Portuguese Territories could cause adverse repercussions in Zambia and Tanzania.

4. Chrome "exception" by U.S. would be in violation of a mandatory provision of the UN Charter and might tend toward further weakening of sanctions against Southern Rhodesia.

OPTION 4

Premise

The situation in the region is not likely to change appreciably in the foreseeable future, and in any event we cannot influence it. Consequently we can retain some economic, scientific and strategic interests in the white states at the same time as we protect our world-wide standing on the racial issue by limiting the nature and scope of our associations with these states and by maintaining present levels and types of aid to the black states of the region. To do so provides us with a posture of flexibility to enable us best to adapt our policy to future trends.

General Posture

This is a codification and extension of present policy.

In the UN and bilaterally we would continue basic opposition to the racial and colonial policies of the white states but seek to maintain correct relations with them. We would retain some military access, scientific installations etc., under conditions which do not imply our condoning of racial repression. In concert with the British, we would stand firmly against the Smith regime, closing our Consulate and continuing sanctions. We would lower the level of public criticism of Portuguese policy in Africa to encourage liberalizing tendencies of the Caetano government. We would give economic aid to black states of the region. We would continue to oppose violent solutions to the problems of the region, and to oppose the outward thrust of South African influence where this strengthens South African domination of neighboring states.

Operational Examples

— Strict application of arms embargo against South Africa.

— Permit U.S. naval calls in South Africa with arrangements for non-discrimination toward U.S. personnel ashore.

— Retain NASA station in South Africa but with alternative facilities elsewhere.

— Neither encourage nor discourage investment in South Africa, give low-key commercial-services, no direct EXIM Bank loans but permit insurance and guarantees of commercial credits.

— Support Congressional revocation of sugar quota for South Africa and its reallocation to less developed African producers.

— Continue to view South African administration of South West Africa as illegal; urge South Africa to accept UN supervisory authority; discourage U.S. investments, no EXIM facilities.

— Support through exchanges and contacts groups in South Africa and South West Africa seeking wiser racial policies and rule of law; encourage U.S. private organizations supportive of such groups.

— Follow British lead on representation and recognition of Southern Rhodesia and on UN sanctions program; withdraw consulate.

— Maintain embargo on supply of arms to either side in the conflict involving the Portuguese Territories, take neutral attitude on investment and permit EXIM facilities for U.S. exports short of major infra-

DOCUMENT 36: National Security Advisor Henry Kissinger, National Security Study Memorandum 39, "Southern Africa," April 10, 1969, with Attached "Study in Response to National Security Study Memorandum 39: Southern Africa," December 9, 1969 [Parts I–III (transcribed by the editors)].

PAGE 19 OF 21

structural projects. Soften criticisms of Portuguese African policy in UN and bilaterally.

— Establish flexible economic assistance programs in the black states of the region permitting the retention of present aid levels.

— Maintain discreet contact with African insurgent movements and extend educational and humanitarian assistance to individuals.

— Maintain modest information and exchange programs in white-rules [*sic*] areas (except Rhodesia); expand activities in the black states.

PROS

1. Preserves most of our major economic, scientific and strategic interests in the region at least in the short run.

2. Affords access to black states in the region and preserves some standing elsewhere in Africa and with Afro-Asian states at the UN.

3. Retains some flexibility for movement closer to either white or black states, depending upon future developments.

CONS

1. Position would be seen as expedient and hypocritical by both sides. Our condemnation of whites hurts us with them, yet fails to satisfy the blacks, exposing us to pressures for more decisive measures.

2. Policy does nothing to deal actively with problem of violence in the area or increasing communist influence.

3. Restrictions on association with white regimes involve some loss of potential U.S. economic and defense assets.

OPTION 5

Premise

We cannot influence the white states for constructive change, and therefore increasing violence is likely.

Only by cutting our ties with the white regimes can we protect our standing on the race issue in black Africa and internationally. Since our tangible interests are not vital, this is a reasonable price to pay.

General Posture

We would maintain only minimal relations with the white regimes, emphasizing that improved relations are impossible until they moderate present policies and avoiding actions vis-a-vis these states likely to provoke an adverse reaction in the black African states. This disassociation would be at the *official* level only: private trade, travel, and other forms of communication would continue, but without USG assistance or encouragement. We would at the same time stress to the black African states the extent to which we were sacrificing certain of our material interests and would make it clear that (1) we had gone as far as we were prepared to go in this direction, and (2) we would not support any violent solution to their problems nor sanctions against the white states (except Rhodesia). We would take positive official stands against racial and colonial oppression. We would afford economic aid to the black states and sell them reasonable quantities of non-sophisticated military equipment.

Operational Examples

— Strictest application of arms embargo against South Africa.

— Remove NASA tracking station.

— Prohibit official use of South African ports and airfields except in emergency.

— Neither encourage nor discourage trade or investment but provide no commercial services or EXIM facilities in South Africa.

DOCUMENT 36: National Security Advisor Henry Kissinger, National Security Study Memorandum 39, "Southern Africa," April 10, 1969, with Attached "Study in Response to National Security Study Memorandum 39: Southern Africa," December 9, 1969 [Parts I–III (transcribed by the editors)].

PAGE 20 OF 21

— Encourage Congressional revocation of the sugar quota for South Africa, and its reallocation to less developed African producers.

— Match diplomatic mission and consulates in South Africa to reduced official relationships.

— Make clear that we regard South Africa's continued occupation of South West Africa as illegal. Discourage U.S. investment; deny commercial services and EXIM facilities; hold to minimum U.S. contacts with South African authorities in South West Africa.

— Support through exchanges and contacts groups in South Africa and South West Africa seeking wiser racial policies and rule of law; encourage U.S. private organizations supportive of such groups.

— Support strict international enforcement of sanctions and maintain non–recognition of Southern Rhodesia; withdraw Consulate.

— Limit EXIM Bank activities and official trade promotion in Portuguese Territories. Maintain arms embargo and continue to support self-determination for the Portuguese Territories.

— Establish Southern African Development Fund for aid projects in Botswana, Lesotho and Swaziland with U.S. Ambassador accredited to three states to be U.S. representative to Fund Council. Consider possibility of Malawi participation in Fund at later stage, if this appears politically advisable.

— Provide bilateral technical assistance to Tanzania and Zambia; continue at least one major regional development project involving them.

— Official visits for Tanzanian and Zambian heads of states.

— Open contact and sympathy for aspirations of African insurgent groups short of material support.

— Reduce information and exchange programs in white areas to a minimum; expand programs in the black states.

PROS

1. Would significantly increase our credibility in black Africa and the UN by demonstrating U.S. is prepared to back its pronouncements on the race issue at some material sacrifices.

2. Would provide maximum leverage to limit Soviet and Chinese influence among liberation groups and in their host countries.

3. Would put white regimes on notice that U.S. is not prepared to bail them out for material or strategic reasons.

4. Would provide a more defensible basis to counter Afro-Asian demands for more far-reaching proposals.

CONS

1. It would tend to identify us with the cause of the insurgent movements and would stimulate demands for more far-reaching action.

2. Would sacrifice economic, strategic and scientific interests.

3. We would forfeit economic opportunities to France, the U.K. and other major trading nations who would be unlikely to take similar steps.

4. Might reinforce the siege mentality of the white regimes and their resistance to constructive change.

5. Would make our relations with the Portuguese more difficult.

OPTION 6

Premise

The repressive policies of the white regimes are leading to eventual conflict in the region, which in the long run cannot end other than in victory for the

DOCUMENT 36: National Security Advisor Henry Kissinger, National Security Study Memorandum 39, "Southern Africa," April 10, 1969, with Attached "Study in Response to National Security Study Memorandum 39: Southern Africa," December 9, 1969 [Parts I–III (transcribed by the editors)].

PAGE 21 OF 21

African majority. Such conflict would be a tragedy, but for the U.S. to permit communist monopoly of the insurgent struggle would be worse for our long-range interests. Both to obviate a major armed conflict if possible, and to identify with the eventual winners if it is inevitable, the U.S. should now move to active measures to force change in white-regime race policies.

General Posture

After appropriate diplomatic warnings of our impending action, the U.S. would move to active measures of coercion, short of armed force, against the white regimes. We would try to get maximum UN support for these measures. Our actions would include efforts to extend UN mandatory economic sanctions to include South Africa and Portugal, but would be carried out unilaterally if necessary. We would sharply increase assistance to the black states, and give non-military aid to the liberation movements.

Operational Examples

— Advocate in UN the extension of mandatory economic sanctions to Portuguese Territories and South Africa because of their evasion of sanctions against Rhodesia.

— Toughen present sanctions against Rhodesia to include bans on tourism, postal facilities, telecommunications, and transportation, and include such provisions in eventual sanctions against Portuguese Territories and South Africa.

— Reduce representation in South Africa to charge and small staff, close consulates in white regime countries.

— Withdraw NASA tracking station from South Africa.

— Afford substantial economic assistance to black states of the region, particularly Botswana, Lesotho and Swaziland.

— Furnish non-sophisticated defense materiel and training in the United States for selected military personnel from Zambia and Tanzania.

— Declare public support for the objectives of the liberation organizations and furnish them non-military assistance.

— Withdraw USIS and terminate U.S. exchange programs in white-regime areas; expand these programs in the black states.

PROS

1. Clear U.S. position on side of majority rule brings our actions into alignment with our declared political position and therefore would increase our influence throughout black Africa.

2. Decisive action by U.S. might induce white regimes to make needed reforms before violence erupts.

3. Policy puts U.S. on eventual winning side, thus undercutting communist influence on liberation effort and insuring long-term dominant U.S. influence in most developed part of Africa.

CONS

1. U.S. initiative in UN would be unlikely to gain support of U.K., France and perhaps others, leaving us to go it alone.

2. Experience with Rhodesia suggests that even stringent sanctions tend to increase siege mentality and unify white minorities.

3. Heavy repercussions from sanctions would fall on new, economically weak African states, particularly Botswana, Lesotho and Swaziland. These would have to be given economic compensation.

4. The U. S. would have sacrificed a range of valuable material interests in the southern region without reasonable assurances that disruptive conflict would be thereby averted.

DOCUMENT 37: State Department, Memorandum for the Senate Foreign Relations Committee, "U.S. Policy Toward Angola," December 16, 1975.

PAGE 1 OF 7

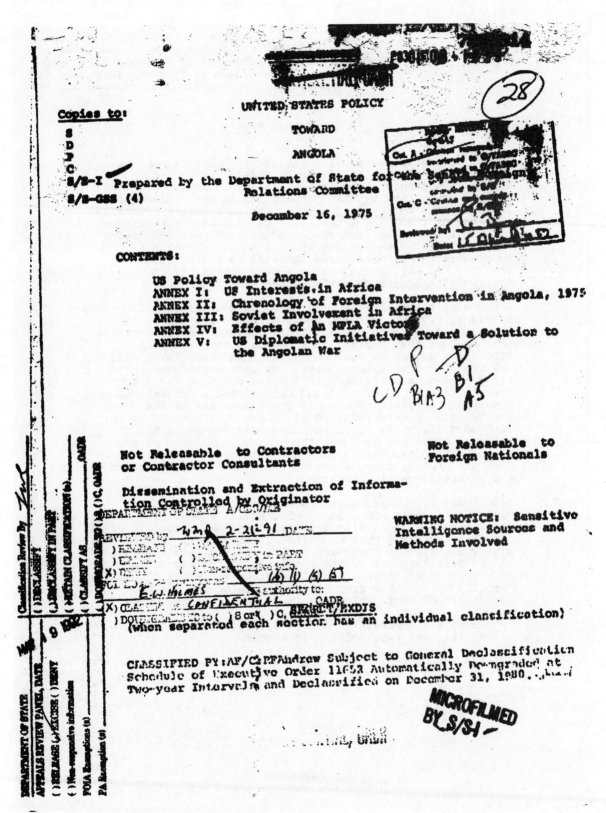

Copies to:

S

D

P

C

S/S-I   Prepared by the Department of State for the Senate Foreign
S/S-GSS (4)   Relations Committee

December 16, 1975

UNITED STATES POLICY

TOWARD

ANGOLA

CONTENTS:

US Policy Toward Angola
ANNEX I: US Interests in Africa
ANNEX II: Chronology of Foreign Intervention in Angola, 1975
ANNEX III: Soviet Involvement in Africa
ANNEX IV: Effects of An MPLA Victory
ANNEX V: US Diplomatic Initiatives Toward a Solution to
            the Angolan War

Not Releasable to Contractors
or Contractor Consultants

Not Releasable to
Foreign Nationals

Dissemination and Extraction of Information Controlled by Originator

WARNING NOTICE: Sensitive
Intelligence Sources and
Methods Involved

(when separated each section has an individual classification)

CLASSIFIED BY: AF/C: PFAndrew Subject to General Declassification
Schedule of Executive Order 11652 Automatically Downgraded at
Two-year Intervals and Declassified on December 31, 1980.

Subject to General Declassification Schedule of Executive Order 11652 Automatically Downgraded at Two-year Intervals and Declassified on December 31, 1978.

U.S. Policy Toward Angola

United States interests with respect to Angola extend beyond that country alone. We of course wish to protect our modest investments there, primarily in oil production ($225 million investment by Gulf Corporation in the enclave of Cabinda), and to assure future access to Angola's extensive reserves of other raw materials. We also have some slight strategic interests from the standpoint of port facilities and overflight rights. But none of these interests in themselves can be considered as vital to United States security and well-being. (For a description of U.S. interests in Africa as a whole, see Annex I.)

Because of these limited interests, United States policy toward Angola throughout 1974 and until mid-1975 was one of non-involvement. Despite the political upheavals in Portugal it was our hope that Portugal and Angola's three competing liberation movements could work out some means for a peaceful transition to independence. We were encouraged by the Alvor Agreement of January 1975 which provided the framework for such a transition and established a provisional government providing for equal representation of the three movements. We were under no illusions with respect to the serious differences which divided these movements and the chances they could work together effectively; but we remained determined not to take any actions that might undermine the chances for a peaceful resolution of the problem by the parties directly concerned.

Unfortunately, other outside powers did not share this view. Portuguese Communists, with Soviet support,1/ were working hard with Marxist-oriented Agostinho Neto, leader of the MPLA, to build up the political strength of that movement vis-a-vis the other two. (We estimate Neto's support at not more than 30% of the population.) More worrisome were reports of large-scale clandestine shipments of military supplies to the MPLA from the Soviet Union and its bloc allies.2/ As these shipments increased in frequency and

---

1/ Annex III presents an analysis of Soviet interests in Africa, and particularly in Angola.

2/ Annex II gives a chronology of the involvement of foreign powers in support of Angolan movements after January 1975.

BEST COPY AVAILABLE

DOCUMENT 37: State Department, Memorandum for the Senate Foreign Relations Committee, "U.S. Policy Toward Angola," December 16, 1975.

PAGE 3 OF 7

2.

quantity during the first six months of this year, it became increasingly evident that the Soviet Union was committed to a power play designed to pre-empt a compromise solution by enabling the MPLA to forcefully take control of the country before independence in November. In fact, by August the MPLA, with Soviet arms and Portuguese Communist connivance, had driven the Western-oriented FNLA and UNITA -- representing 55-60% of the population -- out of Luanda and then physically prevented them from reoccupying their rightful positions in the transitional government. The MPLA proceeded to press its offensive in other parts of the country and occupied areas that were ethnically tied to the other two movements.

The result of the big Soviet arms shipments that began arriving in March was a gradual but radical change in the balance of power among the three movements -- a balance which had previously offered hope for a compromise. By September the MPLA was openly refusing any accommodation with FNLA and UNITA, even though together these two movements still controlled a majority of Angola's people and land.

The MPLA-Soviet alliance to seize power in Angola needed to be stopped. Portugal being neither willing nor able to resist MPLA encroachments, FNLA and UNITA appealed to us for help. Moreover, Angola's neighbors were increasingly alarmed and also looked to us to counter the Soviet intrusion. Our failure to heed President Mobutu's repeated requests for help in Angola created strains in our traditionally close relations with this important power in Africa.

It was clear that the establishment of a radical and potentially hostile regime in Angola could have grave consequences for the security and stability of both Zaire and Zambia; it was equally clear that our failure to react could seriously harm our own relations with these and other countries in the area.

Another factor we had to weigh was the effect of a Marxist-oriented Angola on future developments in southern Africa. Our conclusion was that it would increase the prospects for violent rather than peaceful change and perhaps fatally undermine the incipient trend toward detente between South Africa and Black African states.

BEST COPY AVAILABLE

DOCUMENT 37: State Department, Memorandum for the Senate Foreign Relations Committee, "U.S. Policy Toward Angola," December 16, 1975.

PAGE 4 OF 7

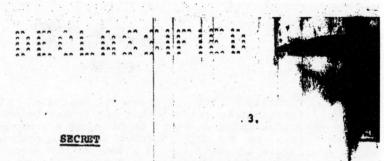

3.

SECRET

Finally, and most importantly, we believed it was essential to the credibility of our policies throughout the world not to permit such a power play by the USSR to go totally unchallenged. In Africa and elsewhere, this means showing that the United States, despite recent reverses in southeast Asia and our preoccupations at home, is still able to react when a power — the Soviet Union in this instance — moves to upset the international political environment. We do not regard Africa as a political vacuum in danger of being filled by Soviet power. Africa is not threatened with recolonization. At the same time, Africans and other militarily vulnerable peoples of the world could not fail to be impressed, in their assessment of the global context in which they operate and in which they must make foreign policy decisions, by a demonstration of Soviet will and ability to intervene militarily to determine the political complexion of a government far from its shores and far from areas of traditional Russian interest.

We also feared the demonstration effect on the Soviet government itself of a successful, unopposed intervention in Africa, enhancing the temptation to it to exploit other similar targets of opportunity.

It was only after exhaustive review and assessment of all of these factors that the Executive Branch approved, in June of this year, undertaking a program of covert activities which Mr. Colby and Mr. Sisco discussed with the Senate Foreign Relations Committee in executive session on November 6. The program is not intended to crush the MPLA. Rather, our limited commitments have been geared to our limited objectives: (1) preventing the MPLA and its Soviet and Cuban backers from achieving a quick military take-over of Angola; and (2) sufficiently redressing the balance among Angola's political movements to facilitate a political solution in which the MPLA does not dominate UNITA AND FNLA.

We believe we have thus far been successful in achieving our first objective: the non-Marxist FNLA and UNITA have been able to withstand the MPLA's heavy military pressure (reinforced by 3500-4000 Cuban troops) and thereby survive as viable political movements. At the same time only 14 African states, out of 46, have recognized MPLA's claim to be the sole government of Angola. It is doubtful whether FNLA and UNITA would have been able to survive without our help. South African military help, has been entirely independent of our own assistance, was also an important factor, but it is becoming a growing political liability to FNLA and UNITA.

SECRET

DOCUMENT 37: State Department, Memorandum for the Senate Foreign Relations Committee, "U.S. Policy Toward Angola," December 16, 1975.

PAGE 5 OF 7

4.

Achieving the second part of our objective -- a political settlement -- depends primarily upon turning the Soviet Union from commitment to an MPLA victory to acceptance of a political compromise. This means bringing home to the Soviets the diplomatic costs of persisting in their present course.

The call of the OAU's conciliation commission for a unity government and an end of outside interference in Angola has laid part of the groundwork for this. The OAU will hold a summit meeting soon to discuss ways to bring about a peaceful settlement, and we have been working through diplomatic channels with friendly African countries to build support for a settlement involving a ceasefire and the establishment of a coalition government.

More critical to diverting the Soviets from their present course, however, will be our own success in convincing them that the risks of their policy reach beyond their African interests. We have given warning in general terms, publicly and privately, that continued Soviet/Cuban intervention in Angola is a threat to detente. We have offered to cooperate in seeking a general disengagement of foreign interference in Angola.

Our hope has been that the Soviets would reconsider their policy of unrestrained involvement and permit the OAU or the UN to take the lead in obtaining a ceasefire, withdrawal of foreign forces, and a political compromise among the Angolan factions.

Our first warnings were answered, in private and in public, with hard-line propaganda. Subsequently, in diplomatic exchanges, both with us and Zaire, the Soviets have shown some respect for our warnings and indicated a possible willingness to consider compromise. This may prove to be a false hope. If it does, we will have to consider whether to raise the stakes and make them more specific: grain, technology exchange, etc.

We see little chance of success for any of these diplomatic initiatives unless they are supported by continued military pressure on the ground. The MPLA and the Soviets must see no prospect of a quick military victory. Only if the military and

1/ Annex V describes US diplomatic initiatives in connection with Angola.

DOCUMENT 37: State Department, Memorandum for the Senate Foreign Relations Committee, "U.S. Policy Toward Angola," December 16, 1975.

PAGE 6 OF 7

5.

SECRET

psychological stalemate can be maintained can we expect diplomacy to have a chance to work and the basis for a political settlement to be laid.

If we were publicly to terminate our support to FNLA and UNITA at this time, placing our relations entirely on diplomacy, the psychological impact would, we believe, be destructive to our interests. UNITA and FNLA, and their African supporters, would feel abandoned and dispirited. The MPLA would be encouraged in its resistance to compromise and its quest from military victory. We believe our withdrawal would also precipitate a South African withdrawal. Although they made their decision to intervene without consultation or encouragement for the US, we think that their own assessment of the likely military outcome, as well as growing internal political problems and external diplomatic pressures, would make them unwilling to stay on after our disengagement. We would expect the consequences of these reactions to such a decision on the part of the US would be a rapid MPLA military victory. Room, time and reason for diplomacy would quickly disappear.

The South African involvement on the side of FNLA/UNITA creates a dilemma for us. It is essential for maintenance of the present military balance but diverts African concern from the Soviet/Cuban intervention, creates pressure among Africans to recognize the MPLA in reaction, and risks bringing discredit by association upon the US. At the same time, there is African sentiment, admitted only in private but probably more extensive than we know, which accepts the necessity of South Africa's balancing intervention if a Soviet victory is to be prevented and the military balance necessary to achieve political compromise is to be maintained. We are dealing with the risks created by the South African involvement by clearly stating our opposition to all external involvement in Angola. We are also stating our willingness to cooperate with others and use our influence to end all foreign intervention, including that by South Africa, in the context of a balanced disengagement which leaves neither Angolan party militarily at the mercy of the other.

We have no intention of continuing our support program endlessly. Nor, however, can the Soviet Union contemplate an intervention escalating and ramifying without limit. Our ability to test the Soviet limits and work what leverage we have with them will depend, however, on not manifesting the specific limits of our own commitment. We believe that the interaction of multilateral diplomacy, focused in the OAU and perhaps the UN, bilateral diplomatic efforts with the Soviet Union, and a military stalemate over the coming weeks and months offers some promise of the solution we seek.

SECRET

DOCUMENT 37: State Department, Memorandum for the Senate Foreign Relations Committee, "U.S. Policy Toward Angola," December 16, 1975.

PAGE 7 OF 7

6.

SECRET

This prospect must be constantly reassessed and we would plan to do this in consultation with the Congress.

It is our belief that we should not prematurely terminate our activities. It is our hope that we will be able to look back at Angola's tumultuous beginnings with the satisfaction of knowing that we were not unresponsive to the appeals for help from the leaders of the Angolan majority and their friends and that our efforts helped them to avert a situation prejudicial to their interest and our own.

SECRET

DOCUMENT 38: House Select Committee on Intelligence, Selection from the Pike Report Relating to Angola, February 1976 (transcribed by the editors).

PAGE 1 OF 2

For reasons not altogether clear, and despite the opposition of senior government officials, the U.S. has been heavily involved in the current civil war in Angola.

The CIA has informed the Committee that since January 1975, it had expended over $31 million in military hardware, transportation costs, and cash payments by the end of 1975. The Committee has reason to believe that the actual U.S. investment is much higher. Information supplied to the Committee also suggests that the military intervention of the Soviet Union and Cuba is in large part a reaction to U.S. efforts to break a political stalemate, in favor of its clients.

The beneficiaries of U.S. aid are two of the three contesting factions: the National Front for the Independence [sic: Liberation] of Angola (FNLA) and the National Union for the Total Independence of Angola (UNITA). The third faction contesting for control of the government, following independence on November 11, 1975, is the Soviet-backed Popular Movement for the Liberation of Angola (MPLA). CIA estimates that the fighting had claimed several thousand casualties by the end of 1975.

The main U.S. client is the National Front, headed by Holden Roberto, a long time associate and relative of President Mobutu Sese Seko of neighboring Zaire. Subsequent to President Mobutu's request last winter to Dr. Kissinger, as independence for Angola became a certainty and liberation groups began to jockey for position, the Forty Committee approved furnishing Roberto $300,000 for various political action activities, restricted to non-military objectives.

Later events have suggested that this infusion of U.S. aid, unprecedented and massive in the underdeveloped colony, may have panicked the Soviets into arming their MPLA clients, whom they had backed for over a decade and who were now in danger of being eclipsed by the National Front. Events in Angola took a bellicose turn as the U.S. was requested by President Mobutu to make a serious military investment.

In early June, 1975, CIA prepared a proposal paper for military aid to pro-U.S. elements in Angola, the cost of which was set at $6 million. A revised program costing $14 million was approved by the Forty Committee and by President Ford in July. This was increased to $25 million in August and to about $32 million in November. By midsummer it was decided that U.S. aid

should not be given solely to Roberto, but instead, divided between him and UNITA's Jonas Savimbi.

The Committee has learned that a task force composed of high U.S. experts on Africa strongly opposed military intervention; instead, last April they called for diplomatic efforts to encourage a political settlement among the three factions to avert bloodshed. Apparently at the direction of National Security Council aides, the task force recommendation was removed from the report and presented to NSC members as merely one policy option. The other two alternatives were a hands-off policy or substantial military intervention.

Of CIA's $31 million figure, said to represent expenditures to the end of 1975, about half is attributed to supply of light arms, mortars, ammunition, vehicles, boats, and communication equipment. The balance includes shipping expenses and cash payments. The Committee has reason to question the accuracy of CIA's valuation of military equipment sent to Angola.

A staff accountant on loan from the General Accounting Office has determined the CIA "costing" procedures and the use of surplus equipment have resulted in a substantial understatement of the value of U.S. aid. Examples include .45 caliber automatic weapons "valued" by CIA at $5.00 each and .30 caliber semi-automatic carbines at $7.55. Based on a sampling of ordnance cost figures and a comparison with Department of Defense procedures, staff advises that the CIA's ordnance figure should at least be doubled.

Dr. Kissinger has indicated that U.S. military intervention in Angola is based on three factors: Soviet support of the MPLA and the USSR's increased presence in Africa, U.S. policy to encourage moderate independence groups in southern Africa, and the U.S. interest in promoting the stability of Mobutu and other leadership figures in the area. Past support to Mobutu, along with his responsiveness to some of the United States [sic] recent diplomatic needs for Third World support, make it equally likely that the paramount factor in the U.S. involvement is Dr. Kissinger's desire to reward and protect African leaders in the area. The U.S.'s expressed opposition to the MPLA is puzzling in view of Director's Colby's statement to the Committee that there are scant ideological differences among the three factions, all of whom are nationalists above all else.

DOCUMENT 38: House Select Committee on Intelligence, Selection from the Pike Report
Relating to Angola, February 1976 (transcribed by the editors).

PAGE 2 OF 2

Control of resources may be a factor. Angola has significant oil deposits and two American multinationals, Gulf and Texaco, operate in the off-shore area. Gulf had deposited some $100 million in concession fees in a national bank now under MPLA control. At the suggestion of the U.S. government, the company suspended further payments.

Until recently, the U.S.-backed National Front was supported by the People's Republic of China, which had provided about 100 military advisors. Moboutu [sic] has provided a staging area for U.S. arms shipments and has periodically sent Zairois troops, trained by the Republic of North Korea, into Angola to support Roberto's operations. Small numbers of South African forces have been in the country and are known to have been in contact with Savimbi's UNITA troops.

Pursuant to Section 662 of the Foreign Assistance Act of 1974, the President has found that the Angola action program is "important to the national security." As directed by the Act, CIA had briefed the Congressional oversight committees as to the Forty Committee approvals of increased amounts of military aid.

CIA officials have testified to the Committee that there appears to be little hope of an outright MPLA military defeat. Instead, U.S. efforts are now aimed at promoting a stalemate, and in turn the cease-fire and the coalition government urged by the long-forgotten NSC task force.

DOCUMENT 39: Assistant Secretary of State William Schaufele, Action Memorandum for Secretary Henry Kissinger, "Rhodesia—A Proposed Course of Action," April 1, 1976.

PAGE 1 OF 8

P760057-0559

7606874

C/FADRC

R

DEPARTMENT OF STATE

ACTION MEMORANDUM

O/FADRC (ORIG)
COPIES TO:
S/P
AF
INR
RF/hjb

CONFIDENTIAL

April 1, 1976

TO: The Secretary

FROM: AF - William E. Schaufele, Jr.

Rhodesia - A Proposed Course of Action

The Problem

Any moves we make with respect to Rhodesia must be in concert with an over-all Southern African strategy which will consider our relationships with the Soviet Union, Cuba, our European allies, black African countries, China and South Africa. S/P will shortly present you with a paper on this broader conceptualization of a rationale of action regarding the Southern African problem. However, in terms of immediacy, we should focus on Rhodesia - on what we can do in the near future to preempt the Soviets and Cubans, improve our position in Africa, and possibly help avert widespread, intensified conflict in Rhodesia itself.

The Strategic Imperatives

The Soviet/Cuban intervention in Angola has drastically affected the determinants of our policies toward Rhodesia. Our essentially passive stance no longer is the most appropriate approach. Preclusion of further expansion of Soviet/Cuban presence and influence in Southern Africa will require us to become more directly involved there than we might prefer.

As you have pointed out, failure to try to counter Soviet/Cuban designs in Southern Africa would contribute to the belief that the U. S. is unwilling

CONFIDENTIAL
GDS

9/13/96

DOCUMENT 39: Assistant Secretary of State William Schaufele, Action Memorandum for Secretary Henry Kissinger, "Rhodesia—A Proposed Course of Action," April 1, 1976.

PAGE 2 OF 8

CONFIDENTIAL

- 2 -

or unable to formulate and carry out appropriate policies. We must continue to make clear our opposition to Soviet/Cuban expansionism. However, because the Communists are backing what the world regards as the right side in Southern Africa, any steps we take against the Soviet/Cuban objectives there must be such that they are not viewed as supportive of white minority regimes. Regarding Rhodesia our efforts should be aimed at, and perceived as, supporting an early transition to self-determination and majority rule, with consideration given to minority rights.

What is required, then, is a preemptive strategy - moves to take the play away from the Soviets and Cubans in a manner that will be viewed favorably by the Africans and supported by majority opinion in the United States.

More assertive steps toward Rhodesia need not put us distinctly at odds with South Africa. The South Africans are anxious for a peaceful settlement in Rhodesia and have concluded that there must be majority rule there before long. Thus, the Rhodesian question is to some extent separable from the South African problem, and from the South Africans' concern about their own survival.

With the breakdown of talks between Smith and Nkomo, intensified guerrilla warfare is inevitable. The Africans have said they want an African solution for Rhodesia, and the Soviets may be wary about deep military involvement - including Cuban combat forces - there. But the Africans are likely to ask for Soviet/Cuban participation in the war if their guerrilla effort is checked, if the Rhodesians make preemptive strikes into Mozambique, or employ a considerable number of foreign mercenaries, or if the South Africans intervene on the side of Smith.

The preferred outcome in Rhodesia, a negotiated settlement leading to majority rule, is still possible, but only if military losses and other circumstances

CONFIDENTIAL

DOCUMENT 39: Assistant Secretary of State William Schaufele, Action Memorandum for Secretary Henry Kissinger, "Rhodesia—A Proposed Course of Action," April 1, 1976.

PAGE 3 OF 8

<u>CONFIDENTIAL</u>

- 3 -

drive home to the Rhodesians that they are going to lose, and to suffer greatly in the process. We should continue to try to convince Rhodesian whites that the world is arrayed against them and they cannot possibly win a military victory. The steps we will be taking with Chissano regarding the Mozambique offset are one way open to us to support African aspirations more directly than before, and yet in a way that could encourage the Africans to keep Soviet/Cuban involvement restricted to logistical and training support at the most. Other approaches we take - with the Soviets, Cuba, Mozambique, the Europeans, the Smith regime, and the Africans - must encompass this two-pronged approach: thwarting the Soviets and Cubans and yet adding to pressures on Smith to capitulate.

<u>Current Situation and Prospects</u>

<u>Rhodesia</u>

Following the collapse of the Smith-Nkomo talks on March 19, British Foreign Secretary Callaghan on March 22 proposed a two-stage program for proceeding to majority rule. Essentially Callaghan called on Smith to agree to majority rule with protection of minority rights as a precondition for British participation in negotiations and assistance for economic development.

Rhodesian Prime Minister Smith's almost instantaneous rejection of Callaghan's proposals has reinforced those Africans who see increasing insurgency within Rhodesia mounted by black nationalist guerrillas from Mozambique and very probably Zambia, as the only route to majority rule.

For the time being there is no single person or group with whom Smith can negotiate. Nkomo lost his already uncertain mandate to negotiate when his talks with Smith collapsed. Until such time as Smith, or his regime, is prepared to accept the concept of majority rule and seriously to negotiate on its

<u>CONFIDENTIAL</u>

DOCUMENT 39: Assistant Secretary of State William Schaufele, Action Memorandum for Secretary Henry Kissinger, "Rhodesia—A Proposed Course of Action," April 1, 1976.

PAGE 4 OF 8

CONFIDENTIAL

- 4 -

attainment, neither Nkomo nor anyone else is likely to risk his position by resuming the talks.

Even before the breakdown of the talks, Rhodesian guerrillas in Mozambique, along the 800-mile common border with Rhodesia, had stepped up their cross-border incursions into Rhodesia. These infrequent attacks have been so far more of a harrassment than a serious threat to the regime. Now, however, that the focus is shifting to armed struggle as the only method of obtaining a solution, these actions can be expected to increase in both frequency and intensity. There are 4,000 to 6,000 nationalist guerrillas in various stages of training and readiness in Mozambique. Already it is estimated that up to 1,000 armed guerrillas are inside Rhodesia at any given time. While we stand by our assessment that it will take another 6 to 8 months before the nationalist forces are sufficiently organized to mount a sustained guerrilla action inside Rhodesia, they do have a demonstrated present capacity for short-term, hit-and-run incursions - which, if spread out along the length of the Mozambican and possibly Zambian borders, can stretch the capacity of the Rhodesian security forces and provide increasing pressure and stress on the white population.

Between now and roughly next October, the prospects would seem to be for an uneasy stand-off, accompanied by escalating guerrilla activity over increasingly wider areas along Rhodesia's borders with Mozambique and Zambia and occasional forays deeper into Rhodesia. As the nationalists become better trained, more numerous (their forces could double to 8,000-12,000 by the rainy season in October) and more seasoned, they could well be in a position to mount and sustain a major guerrilla effort and, in the process, so stretch the Rhodesian security forces that their effectiveness would be greatly impaired.

South Africa

Further pressure by South Africa on Smith could have a major impact on the Rhodesian situation.

CONFIDENTIAL

DOCUMENT 39: Assistant Secretary of State William Schaufele, Action Memorandum for Secretary Henry Kissinger, "Rhodesia—A Proposed Course of Action," April 1, 1976.

PAGE 5 OF 8

CONFIDENTIAL

- 5 -

However, Vorster has said that because of domestic political considerations, he cannot twist Smith's arm any more than he already has. In view of South Africa's own vulnerability to economic sanctions, the South African Government continues to be opposed to their imposition. Nevertheless, because Vorster remains convinced that peaceful transition to majority rule in Rhodesia is in South Africa's interest, he could yet begin quietly to increase economic pressures on Rhodesia. We do not, though, have any concrete indications that Vorster will move in this direction.

The Cuban Spectre

Speculation about possible direct Cuban involvement in Rhodesia is yet another pressure factor on Smith. The regime's reaction to date has been to seize upon our and British warnings against such outside involvement as evidence of ultimate support for the Rhodesian regime.

There is no hard evidence that the Soviets and Cubans are preparing for direct involvement and it seems clear that neither the nationalists nor concerned African leaders want it at the present time. They may change their minds, however, as frustrations mount at the insurgents' inability to break the stalemate with the Rhodesian forces. If Cuban intervention occurs, it is most likely under the following circumstances:

-- inability of Rhodesian liberation forces to make significant progress toward their goal soon enough;

-- repeated Rhodesian incursions into Mozambique;

-- significant or repeated guerrilla defeats;

-- South African intervention supporting the Rhodesian regime.

CONFIDENTIAL

DOCUMENT 39: Assistant Secretary of State William Schaufele, Action Memorandum for Secretary Henry Kissinger, "Rhodesia—A Proposed Course of Action," April 1, 1976.

PAGE 6 OF 8

CONFIDENTIAL

- 6 -

The UN

The forthcoming Security Council meeting on Rhodesia, during which an extension of economic sanctions against Rhodesia is expected to be approved, will probably serve to isolate Rhodesia even further, thereby placing an additional increment of psychological pressure on Smith.

Immediate Steps We Can Take to Influence the Situation

Although we have at best only very limited means to influence developments in Rhodesia, there are steps we could take to preempt a Soviet-Cuban intervention, to demonstrate our full support for majority rule with protection for minority rights and to attempt to stem the tide of violent confrontation. S/P will be recommending what we can do in the broader context, with our allies, the Soviets, the Chinese, etc. The following steps can be taken immediately in the more restricted context of Rhodesia itself:

1. Support the latest effort to repeal the Byrd Amendment - which white Rhodesians, Rhodesian nationalists, and other African countries all look upon as a symbol of basic American support for the white Rhodesian regime.

2. Respond to Mr. Callaghan's call for developmental and educational assistance to an independent majority-ruled Rhodesia where the rights of the minority would be respected. This could be done first in a private message to Mr. Callaghan which would later be noted by you in a public forum.

CONFIDENTIAL

DOCUMENT 39: Assistant Secretary of State William Schaufele, Action Memorandum for Secretary Henry Kissinger, "Rhodesia—A Proposed Course of Action," April 1, 1976.

PAGE 7 OF 8

CONFIDENTIAL

- 7 -

3. Send an emissary to Smith bearing a message that will make it clear that he can count on no help from the U. S. in his fight to maintain white rule. Smith should also be warned that we believe his forces will face overwhelming odds and be defeated and that our opposition to Soviet/Cuban intervention will not be carried to an extent that would put us on the side of the white minority in Rhodesia.

4. Have the Department's spokesman issue a "travel alert", noting the potentially dangerous situation that could erupt in Rhodesia and the fact that since we have no representation there and have no way of providing any assistance or protection, we strongly advise American citizens against traveling to Rhodesia as tourists and encourage those now resident there to make contingency plans for an orderly departure. Such a statement, aside from discouraging travel, would also serve as another signal to Smith and the white population of their growing isolation and potential danger.

5. Inform Vorster of the steps we are taking, remind him of the urgency of the matter as it applies to South Africa, and encourage him to increase his political and economic pressure to persuade Smith that further resistance to a negotiated settlement is futile. In no way should our demarche to Vorster imply a quid pro quo.

6. Inform Kaunda, Nyerere, Khama and Machel of our intended actions.

7. You could convey to the EC-9 Foreign Minister's Meeting (April 5-6) our position on Rhodesia, spelling out as appropriate the concepts behind any new initiatives we have taken or contemplate taking. At the same time you could say that we look forward to cooperating with the 9 in determining and carrying out our strategy in Rhodesia.

CONFIDENTIAL

DOCUMENT 39: Assistant Secretary of State William Schaufele, Action Memorandum for Secretary Henry Kissinger, "Rhodesia—A Proposed Course of Action," April 1, 1976.

PAGE 8 OF 8

CONFIDENTIAL

– 8 –

Recommendation:

That you meet as soon as possible with the appropriate Department officers to consider the steps we have raised.

Approve: _K_ APR 1 1976 Disapprove _____

ALTERNATIVELY, that you wait until you have seen S/P's over-all Southern African strategy paper before convoking such a meeting.

Approve_____ Disapprove_____

Drafted:AF/S:TGCole:S/P:DPetterson:jk
x-28252:3/31/76
Concurrence: INR/RAF:TThorne
S/P:WLord

CONFIDENTIAL

DOCUMENT 40: Secretary Henry Kissinger, Cable for U.S. Embassy Pretoria, "Message to Prime Minister Vorster," September 20, 1976.

PAGE 1 OF 2

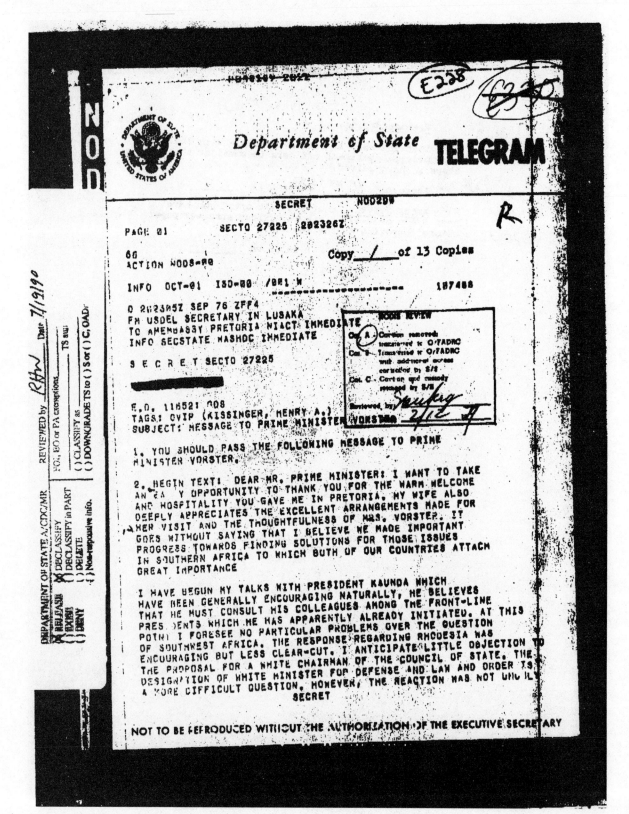

Department of State TELEGRAM

SECRET N0028W

PAGE 01 SECTO 27225 2023262

60
ACTION NODS-00

Copy / of 13 Copies

INFO OCT-01 ISO-00 /001 W   107408

O 2023052 SEP 76 ZFF4
FM USDEL SECRETARY IN LUSAKA
TO AMEMBASSY PRETORIA NIACT IMMEDIATE
INFO SECSTATE WASHDC IMMEDIATE

S E C R E T SECTO 27225

E.O. 11652: GDS
TAGS: OVIP (KISSINGER, HENRY A.)
SUBJECT: MESSAGE TO PRIME MINISTER VORSTER

1. YOU SHOULD PASS THE FOLLOWING MESSAGE TO PRIME
MINISTER VORSTER.

2. BEGIN TEXT: DEAR MR. PRIME MINISTER: I WANT TO TAKE
AN EARLY OPPORTUNITY TO THANK YOU FOR THE WARM WELCOME
AND HOSPITALITY YOU GAVE ME IN PRETORIA. MY WIFE ALSO
DEEPLY APPRECIATES THE EXCELLENT ARRANGEMENTS MADE FOR
HER VISIT AND THE THOUGHTFULNESS OF MRS. VORSTER. IT
GOES WITHOUT SAYING THAT I BELIEVE WE MADE IMPORTANT
PROGRESS TOWARDS FINDING SOLUTIONS FOR THOSE ISSUES
IN SOUTHERN AFRICA TO WHICH BOTH OF OUR COUNTRIES ATTACH
GREAT IMPORTANCE

I HAVE BEGUN MY TALKS WITH PRESIDENT KAUNDA WHICH
HAVE BEEN GENERALLY ENCOURAGING NATURALLY, HE BELIEVES
THAT HE MUST CONSULT HIS COLLEAGUES AMONG THE FRONT-LINE
PRESIDENTS WHICH HE HAS APPARENTLY ALREADY INITIATED. AT THIS
POINT I FORESEE NO PARTICULAR PROBLEMS OVER THE QUESTION
OF SOUTHWEST AFRICA. THE RESPONSE REGARDING RHODESIA WAS
ENCOURAGING BUT LESS CLEAR-CUT. I ANTICIPATE LITTLE OBJECTION TO
THE PROPOSAL FOR A WHITE CHAIRMAN OF THE COUNCIL OF STATE. THE
DESIGNATION OF WHITE MINISTER FOR DEFENSE AND LAW AND ORDER IS
A MORE DIFFICULT QUESTION. HOWEVER, THE REACTION WAS NOT UNDULY

SECRET

DOCUMENT 40: Secretary Henry Kissinger, Cable for U.S. Embassy Pretoria, "Message to Prime Minister Vorster," September 20, 1976.

PAGE 2 OF 2

PB40109-2323

Department of State **TELEGRAM**

SECRET

PAGE 02   SECTO 27225   2023262

HOSTILE, I WILL PROBABLY BE ASKED TO RETURN TO LUSAKA OR DAR
ON WEDNESDAY TO GET AN OFFICIAL REPLY.

3. PROBABLY BECAUSE OF THE AFRICAN FEELINGS ABOUT THE
RHODESIAN AUTHORITIES, OUR CONVERSATIONS MAKE IT CLEAR TO ME
THAT WHEN IAN SMITH SPEAKS ON FRIDAY, IT IS IMPERATIVE THAT HE
PUT FORWARD STRICTLY THE LANGUAGE OF THE UNDERSTANDING WE
REACHED. HE SHOULD OFFER NO EXPLANATIONS OR GRATUITOUS COM-
MENTARY WHICH COULD BE MISINTERPRETED AND GIVE THE BLACK AFRICAN
PRESIDENTS REASON TO REJECT A SETTLEMENT. IF THE RHODESIAN
PRIME MINISTER GOES BEYOND THE LANGUAGE WE DISCUSSED, I PREDICT
SERIOUS CONSEQUENCES FOR OUR UNDERTAKING. YOU AND I HAVE
INVESTED TOO MUCH IN POSITIVE OUTCOME TO LET SUCCESS SLIP
BY NOW. I WOULD APPRECIATE YOUR USING YOUR CONTINUING AND
CONSTANT INFLUENCE BETWEEN NOW AND FRIDAY TO MAKE SURE THAT
MR. SMITH LIVES UP TO THIS PART OF HIS COMMITMENT.

4. IN MY JUDGMENT OUR MEETINGS OVER THE PAST MONTHS
HAVE LAID MORE SOLID FOUNDATIONS FOR RELATIONS BETWEEN
THE UNITED STATES AND SOUTH AFRICA. I LOOK FORWARD TO STAYING
IN CLOSE TOUCH WITH YOU DURING THE DECISIVE WEEKS THAT LIE
AHEAD. WARM REGARDS, HENRY A. KISSINGER. END TEXT.
KISSINGER

SECRET

NOT TO BE REPRODUCED WITHOUT THE AUTHORIZATION OF THE EXECUTIVE SECRETARY

DOCUMENT 41: Secretary Henry Kissinger, Cable for Ambassador Frank Wisner, "Smith's Comments about Annex C," October 26, 1976.

PAGE 1 OF 2

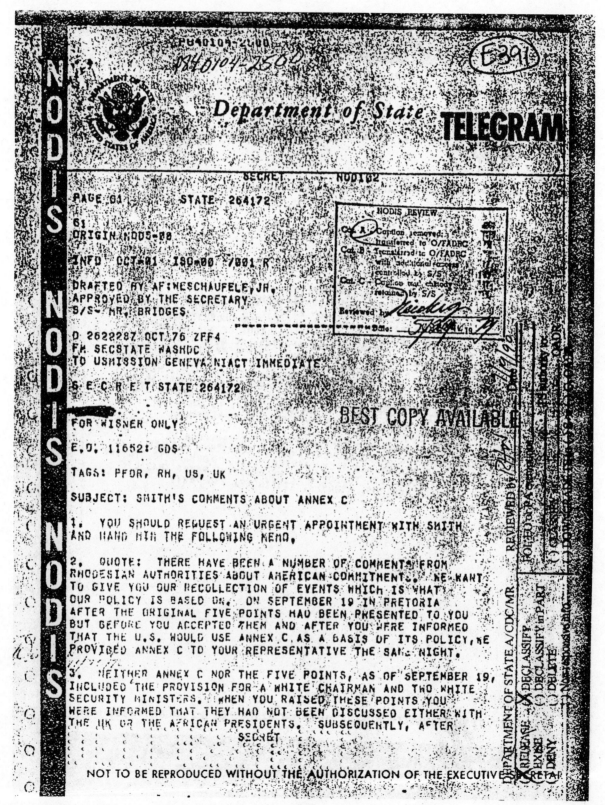

Department of State TELEGRAM

SECRET NODIS

PAGE 01 STATE 264172

61
ORIGIN NODS-00

INFO OCT-01 ISO-00 /001 R

DRAFTED BY AF:WESCHAUFELE, JR.
APPROVED BY THE SECRETARY
S/S - MR. BRIDGES

O 262228Z OCT 76 ZFF4
FM SECSTATE WASHDC
TO USMISSION GENEVA NIACT IMMEDIATE

S E C R E T STATE 264172

FOR WISNER ONLY

E.O. 11652: GDS

TAGS: PFOR, RH, US, UK

SUBJECT: SMITH'S COMMENTS ABOUT ANNEX C

1.   YOU SHOULD REQUEST AN URGENT APPOINTMENT WITH SMITH
AND HAND HIM THE FOLLOWING MEMO.

2.   QUOTE: THERE HAVE BEEN A NUMBER OF COMMENTS FROM
RHODESIAN AUTHORITIES ABOUT AMERICAN COMMITMENT. WE WANT
TO GIVE YOU OUR RECOLLECTION OF EVENTS WHICH IS WHAT
OUR POLICY IS BASED ON. ON SEPTEMBER 19 IN PRETORIA
AFTER THE ORIGINAL FIVE POINTS HAD BEEN PRESENTED TO YOU
BUT BEFORE YOU ACCEPTED THEM AND AFTER YOU WERE INFORMED
THAT THE U.S. WOULD USE ANNEX C AS A BASIS OF ITS POLICY, WE
PROVIDED ANNEX C TO YOUR REPRESENTATIVE THE SAME NIGHT.

3.   NEITHER ANNEX C NOR THE FIVE POINTS, AS OF SEPTEMBER 19,
INCLUDED THE PROVISION FOR A WHITE CHAIRMAN AND TWO WHITE
SECURITY MINISTERS. WHEN YOU RAISED THESE POINTS YOU
WERE INFORMED THAT THEY HAD NOT BEEN DISCUSSED EITHER WITH
THE UK OR THE AFRICAN PRESIDENTS. SUBSEQUENTLY, AFTER

SECRET

NODIS

BEST COPY AVAILABLE

NOT TO BE REPRODUCED WITHOUT THE AUTHORIZATION OF THE EXECUTIVE SECRETAR

[238]

DOCUMENT 41: Secretary Henry Kissinger, Cable for Ambassador Frank Wisner, "Smith's Comments about Annex C," October 26, 1976.

PAGE 2 OF 2

Department of State TELEGRAM

SECRET

PAGE 02   STATE 264178

CONSULTATIONS WITH THE UK AND THE AFRICAN PRESIDENTS, YOU
WERE INFORMED THAT THESE TWO ISSUES WOULD BE DIFFICULT BUT
PERHAPS MANAGEABLE AND COULD BE INCLUDED AS MODIFICATIONS
OF THE ORIGINAL FIVE POINTS.

6. THIS SEQUENCE OF EVENTS CLEARLY DEMONSTRATES THAT
THESE TWO POINTS, WHICH HAVE BECOME INDEED DIFFICULT, WERE
ADDED LATER AND WERE NOT INCLUDED IN THE ORIGINAL FIVE
POINTS AS THEY WERE PRESENTED TO YOU IN PRETORIA. UNQUOTE.

8. ORALLY YOU SHOULD MAKE THE FOLLOWING POINTS TO SMITH:

--IT SEEMS TO US THAT HE SHOULD NOT BE EXPOSING HIMSELF
TO THE PRESS OR ALLOW HIMSELF TO BE LED INTO DISCUSSION
OF DETAILS.

--THE U.S. IS APPALLED THAT HE HAS MADE PUBLIC REFERENCE
TO ANNEX C (WHICH HAS NOT BEEN GIVEN TO THE AFRICANS)
DESPITE REQUESTS FROM US DIRECTLY AND THROUGH SOUTH
AFRICA AND GREAT BRITAIN THAT HE NOT DO SO.

--THE END RESULT CAN ONLY MAKE IT MORE DIFFICULT FOR HIS
OWN POSITION IN THE CONFERENCE.

--THE U.S. CANNOT BE PUT UNDER PRESSURE BY PUBLIC STATE-
MENTS.

--IF IT CONTINUES WE WILL HAVE TO WASH OUR HANDS OF OUR
EFFORTS AND SMITH WILL HAVE TO DO WHAT HE CAN ON HIS
OWN.

--HOWEVER, YOU MAY TELL HIM THAT WE CONTINUE TO STAND
BEHIND ANNEX C AND WILL NOT PUSH HIM BEYOND IT AS STATED
IN YOUR ORIGINAL INSTRUCTIONS.

--YOU MAY ALSO INFORM HIM OF THE SECRETARY'S HIGH PERSONAL
REGARD FOR SMITH, HIS DESIRE TO WORK WITH HIM, AND THE
GREAT SYMPATHY HE HAS FOR HIM AND HIS POPULATION IN THESE
CIRCUMSTANCES.   KISSINGER

SECRET

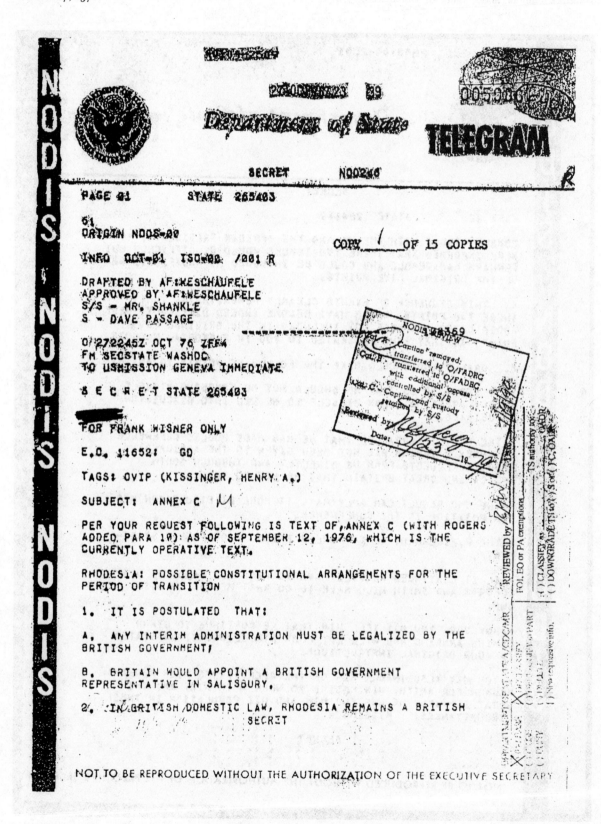

Department of State

TELEGRAM

SECRET   N00246

PAGE 01   STATE 265403

61
ORIGIN NODS-00   COPY 1 OF 15 COPIES

INFO OCT-01 ISO-00 /001 R

DRAFTED BY AF:WESCHAUFELE
APPROVED BY AF:WESCHAUFELE
S/S - MR. SHANKLE
S - DAVE PASSAGE

O 272245Z OCT 76 ZFF4
FM SECSTATE WASHDC
TO USMISSION GENEVA IMMEDIATE

S E C R E T STATE 265403

FOR FRANK WISNER ONLY

E.O. 11652:   GD

TAGS: OVIP (KISSINGER, HENRY A.)

SUBJECT: ANNEX C

PER YOUR REQUEST FOLLOWING IS TEXT OF ANNEX C (WITH ROGERS
ADDED PARA 10) AS OF SEPTEMBER 12, 1976, WHICH IS THE
CURRENTLY OPERATIVE TEXT.

RHODESIA: POSSIBLE CONSTITUTIONAL ARRANGEMENTS FOR THE
PERIOD OF TRANSITION

1. IT IS POSTULATED THAT:

A. ANY INTERIM ADMINISTRATION MUST BE LEGALIZED BY THE
BRITISH GOVERNMENT;

B. BRITAIN WOULD APPOINT A BRITISH GOVERNMENT
REPRESENTATIVE IN SALISBURY.

2. IN BRITISH DOMESTIC LAW, RHODESIA REMAINS A BRITISH
                              SECRET

NOT TO BE REPRODUCED WITHOUT THE AUTHORIZATION OF THE EXECUTIVE SECRETARY

DOCUMENT 42: Secretary Henry Kissinger, Cable for Ambassador Frank Wisner, "Annex C," October 27, 1976.

PAGE 2 OF 7

Department of State TELEGRAM

SECRET

PAGE 02 STATE 265423

COLONY AND THE QUEEN (AS QUEEN OF THE UNITED KINGDOM) IS THE SOVEREIGN OF THE TERRITORY. THIS WOULD REMAIN THE LEGAL POSITION UNTIL THE TIME CAME TO GRANT INDEPENDENCE.

3. IN ORDER TO LEGALIZE THE SITUATION IN RHODESIA, FOLLOWING AGREEMENT ON A CONSTITUTIONAL SETTLEMENT, IT WOULD BE NECESSARY FOR THE BRITISH PARLIAMENT TO PASS A NEW ACT. THE 1965 SOUTHERN RHODESIA ACT DOES NOT CONFER POWERS TO SUSPEND OR REVOKE THE RHODESIAN CONSTITUTION OF 1961 OR TO AMEND THAT CONSTITUTION OUT OF ALL RECOGNITION. BUT THE 1961 CONSTITUTION WOULD NOT PROVIDE AN APPROPRIATE FRAMEWORK FOR THE PERIOD OF TRANSITION.

4. THE NEW ACT WOULD BE AN ENABLING INSTRUMENT, I.E, IT WOULD EMPOWER THE BRITISH GOVERNMENT TO IMPOSE CONSTITUTIONAL CHANGE IN RHODESIA BY ORDERS IN COUNCIL (WHICH WOULD PROBABLY HAVE TO BE SUBJECT TO AN AFFIRMATIVE RESOLUTION BY BOTH HOUSES OF THE BRITISH PARLIAMENT). A BILL TO ENACT AN AMENDMENT TO THE 1965 LEGISLATION COULD NOT BE INTRODUCED IN THE BRITISH PARLIAMENT UNTIL IT REASSEMBLES IN MID-OCTOBER (UNLESS IT WERE TO BE RECALLED EARLIER FOR THAT SPECIAL PURPOSE).

5. IT WOULD IN ANY CASE TAKE TIME TO PREPARE THE NECESSARY CONSEQUENTIAL LEGISLATION. ONE MAJOR TECHNICAL PROBLEM IS POSED BY THE NEED TO DETERMINE WHICH OF THE POST-UDI ENACTMENTS OF THE RHODESIAN PARLIAMENT SHOULD BE RETROSPECTIVELY VALIDATED AND WHICH SHOULD BE ANNULLED OR AMENDED. IT WOULD ALSO BE NECESSARY TO PROVIDE FOR A POLITICAL AMNESTY WHICH WOULD, ON THE ONE HAND, FREE POLITICAL DETAINEES AND PRISONERS FROM RHODESIAN RESTRAINTS AND, ON THE OTHER, PROTECT MEMBERS OF THE ADMINISTRATION AGAINST PROSECUTION OR CIVIL SUIT FOR PAST ILLEGAL ACTS.

LEGISLATIVE AND EXECUTIVE AUTHORITY IN RHODESIA

6. THE NEW ACT WOULD HAVE TO VEST LEGISLATIVE AND

SECRET

DOCUMENT 42: Secretary Henry Kissinger, Cable for Ambassador Frank Wisner, "Annex C," October 27, 1976.

PAGE 3 OF 7

 **TELEGRAM**

SECRET

PAGE 03   STATE 265483

EXECUTIVE AUTHORITY WITHIN RHODESIA IN LOCAL ORGANS
OF GOVERNMENT. WE ENVISAGE THE FORMATION OF A TWO TIER
SYSTEM, COMPRISING A "COUNCIL OF STATE" AND A "COUNCIL
OF MINISTERS" AND PROVIDING FOR INTERNAL CHECKS AND
BALANCES, DESIGNED AS FAR AS POSSIBLE TO BE SELF-
REGULATING AND TO OBVIATE THE NEED FOR THE BRITISH
PARLIAMENT TO INTERVENE IN THE GOVERNMENT OF RHODESIA
DURING THE TRANSITIONAL PERIOD.

7. WHILE FOR FORM OF ANY INTERIM ADMINISTRATION WOULD
BE PARTLY A MATTER FOR THE BRITISH PARLIAMENT, ITS

COMPOSITION WOULD BE A MATTER FOR DECISION BY THE
RHODESIANS THEMSELVES. THE RESPONSIBILITY FOR CHOOSING
THE MEMBERS OF THE COUNCIL OF STATE AND OF THE COUNCIL
OF MINISTERS MUST LIE IN RHODESIA, EVEN THOUGH THE FORMAL
APPOINTMENT OF MEMBERS OF THE FORMER WILL HAVE TO BE
MADE BY THE QUEEN OF THE UNITED KINGDOM. AT THE SAME
TIME, THE ALLOCATION OF RESPONSIBILITIES SET OUT BELOW
MUST BE BASED ON THE ASSUMPTION THAT THE MEMBERS OF THE
ORGANS OF GOVERNMENT DURING THE INTERIM PERIOD WOULD,
BY AND LARGE, HAVE BEEN CHOSEN FROM AMONG THOSE WHO
GENUINELYSUBSCRIBEDTO, OR ACQUIESCED IN, THE AIM OF A
RAPID AND ORDERLY TRANSITION OF MAJORITY RULE.

THE COUNCIL OF STATE

8. FOR THE COUNCIL OF STATE, WE COULD ENVISAGE THE
FOLLOWING:

1. COMPOSITION: THE COUNCIL WOULD BE COMPOSED OF
BETWEEN 5 TO 7 MEMBERS, WITH A PRE-DETERMINED RATIO,
WHICH WOULD HAVE TO BE MAINTAINED THROUGHOUT, BETWEEN
THE EUROPEAN AND THE AFRICAN MEMBERS. THE MEMBERS OF
THE COUNCIL WOULD ELECT THEIR OWN CHAIRMAN. HE WOULD
BE PRIMUS INTER PARES AND WOULD HAVE NO SPECIAL
STATUS. THE RATIO OF MEMBERSHIP COULD BE 3 TO 2 OR 4 TO 3
IN FAVOR OF THE AFRICANS: OR THERE COULD BE PARITY BUT
IN THAT EVENT IT WOULD BE LAID DOWN THAT THE CHAIRMAN
OF THE COUNCIL WOULD BE AFRICAN.

SECRET

DOCUMENT 42: Secretary Henry Kissinger, Cable for Ambassador Frank Wisner, "Annex C," October 27, 1976.

PAGE 4 OF 7

Department of State TELEGRAM

SECRET

PAGE 04   STATE 265403

II. APPOINTMENT OF MEMBERS: BY THE QUEEN OF THE
UNITED KINGDOM, FORMALLY ACTING ON THE ADVICE OF HER
SECRETARY OF STATE FOR FOREIGN AFFAIRS, BUT THE LATTER
WOULD HAVE NO POWER OF CHOICE: HE WOULD ENDORSE
LOCAL RHODESIAN CHOICES

(A) THE COMPOSITION OF THE FIRST COUNCIL OF STATE WOULD
BE DECIDED IN THE COURSE OF NEGOTIATIONS BETWEEN THE
EUROPEAN CARETAKER GOVERNMENT AND THE AFRICAN NATIONALISTS.
IN THE EVENT THAT THEY WERE UNABLE TO REACH CONSENSUS,
THE EUROPEAN AND AFRICAN SIDES WOULD BOTH HAVE THE RIGHT
TO NOMINATE THE NUMBER OF REPRESENTATIVES TO WHICH THEY
WERE RESPECTIVELY ENTITLED. NEITHER SIDE COULD VETO THE
CHOICE OF THE OTHER: ALL THOSE NOMINATED WOULD HAVE TO
TAKE AN OATH BINDING THEMSELVES TO WORK FOR A RAPID AND
ORDERLY TRANSITION TO MAJORITY RULE. AN ADDITIONAL
SAFEGUARD (AND THIS WOULD POINT TO A 7-RATHER THAN
A 5 OR 6 MAN COUNCIL) WOULD BE TO PROVIDE THAT THE
EUROPEANS AND AFRICANS WOULD HAVE THE RIGHT TO NOMINATE

ONE MEMBER OF THE OTHER RACE.

(B) SUBSEQUENT APPOINTMENTS WOULD BE BY CO-OPTION,
REQUIRING AT LEAST A TWO-THIRDS MAJORITY. THE ONLY PROVISO
WOULD BE THAT A DEPARTING MEMBER MUST BE REPLACED BY SOME-
ONE OF THE SAME RACE OR THAT, WHERE A DEPARTING MEMBER
HAD BEEN INITIALLY NOMINATED BY THE OTHER SIDE, THE CHOICE
OF THE REPLACEMENT WOULD LIE SOLELY WITH THE MEMBERS OF
THAT OTHER SIDE.

III. VOTING: THE DECISIONS OF THE COUNCIL WOULD NORMALLY
BE TAKEN BY CONSENSUS, WHERE A VOTE WAS NECESSARY, AT
LEAST A TWO-THIRDS MAJORITY SHOULD BE REQUIRED, EXCEPT
THAT A DECISION TO DISMISS THE CHIEF MINISTER OR THE CHIEF
OF STAFF OF THE ARMED FORCES WOULD HAVE TO BE UNANIMOUS.

IV. LEGISLATIVE AUTHORITY: FULL LEGISLATIVE AUTHORITY
WOULD BE VESTED IN THE COUNCIL: IT ALONE WOULD HAVE
POWER TO ENACT PRIMARY LEGISLATION, THOUGH IT COULD
DELEGATE ITS POWERS IN RESPECT OF SUBORDINATE LEGISLATION
TO THE COUNCIL OF MINISTERS OR TO INDIVIDUAL MINISTERS.
                              SECRET

SECRET

PAGE 05　　　STATE 265403

RESPONSIBILITY FOR INITIATING PROPOSALS FOR LEGISLATION
WOULD REST WITH THE COUNCIL OF MINISTERS THOUGH, IN THE
SPHERES MENTIONED IN (V) (A) BELOW, THE COUNCIL OF STATE
WOULD HAVE POWER TO AMEND THE FORMER'S PROPOSALS AND
ELSEWHERE TO SUGGEST AMENDMENTS. THESE LATTER WOULD
STAND UNLESS OVERRIDEN BY A VOTE OF A PRE-DETERMINED SIZE
IN THE COUNCIL OF MINISTERS.

V. EXECUTIVE POWERS:

A. THE COUNCIL OF STATE WOULD HAVE ULTIMATE AUTHORITY
IN MATTERS RELATED TO THE IMPLEMENTATION OF THE PROGRAMME
FOR PROGRESS TO MAJORITY RULE AND (SEE ALSO VI BELOW)
TO DEFENSE AND INTERNAL SECURITY. IN BOTH SPHERES, IT
COULD ISSUE DIRECTIVES TO THE COUNCIL OF MINISTERS TO
INDIVIDUAL MINISTERS OR TO OFFICIALS.

B. IT WOULD HAVE THE RIGHT TO BE KEPT INFORMED OF THE
PROCEEDINGS OF THE COUNCIL OF MINISTERS (ONE
POSSIBILITY WOULD BE TO ARRANGE FOR A JOINT SECRETARIAT
TO SERVICE BOTH COUNCILS).

C. THE COUNCIL WOULD BE RESPONSIBLE FOR THE APPOINTMENTS
AND DISMISSAL OF ALL MEMBERS OF THE COUNCIL OF MINISTERS,
AT ITS DISCRETION ALONE; OTHER APPOINTMENTS AND DISMISSALS,
AND THE ALLOCATION OF PORTFOLIOS, WOULD, HOWEVER, BE
MADE ONLY AFTER CONSULTATION WITH THE CHIEF MINISTER,
WHOSE ADVICE WOULD BE BINDING.

D. THE COUNCIL WOULD ALSO BE RESPONSIBLE FOR THE
APPOINTMENT AND DISMISSAL OF: MEMBERS OF THE JUDICIARY
(WHOSE DISMISSAL WOULD, HOWEVER, BE SUBJECT TO THE USUAL
SAFEGUARDS); THE CHIEFS OF THE ARMED FORCES AND OF THE
POLICE; AND THE SENIOR MEMBERS (DOWN TO A GRADE TO BE
DETERMINED) OF THE PUBLIC SERVICE.

E. THE COUNCIL WOULD ALSO EXERCISE THE PREROGATIVE OF
MERCY.

THE COUNCIL OF MINISTERS

SECRET

DOCUMENT 42: Secretary Henry Kissinger, Cable for Ambassador Frank Wisner, "Annex C," October 27, 1976.

PAGE 6 OF 7

SECRET

PAGE 06   STATE 265403

9. FOR THE COUNCIL OF MINISTERS, WE COULD ENVISAGE
THE FOLLOWING:

I. APPOINTMENT OF MEMBERS: SEE PARAGRAPH 8 (IV) (C)
ABOVE.

II. COMPOSITION: THE COUNCIL WOULD BE COMPOSED OF A
CHIEF MINISTER, WHO WOULD BE AN AFRICAN, AND WOULD
CONTAIN A MAJORITY OF AFRICAN MEMBERS.

III. VOTING: NORMALLY, UNDER THE DOCTRINE OF COLLECTIVE
RESPONSIBILITY, NO VOTE OUGHT TO BE NECESSARY BUT, WHERE
THERE WAS A CLEAR DIVISION OF OPINION, IT MIGHT BE
NECESSARY TO PROVIDE FOR A VOTE TO BE TAKEN IN SUCH AN
EVENT, IT WOULD BE IMPORTANT TO ENSURE THAT A MERE
MAJORITY DID NOT SUFFICE; FOR THAT COULD, THEORETICALLY
LEAD TO A SITUATION IN WHICH THE EUROPEAN MEMBERS WERE
PERMANENTLY OUTVOTED. ONE POSSIBILITY WOULD BE TO PRO-
VIDE FOR A TWO THIRDS MAJORITY TO BE REQUIRED AS THE
NORM AND, WHERE THIS COULD NOT BE ACHIEVED, FOR THE
DECISION TO LIE WITH THE COUNCIL OF STATE.

IV. THE QUORUM: IT WOULD BE NECESSARY TO MAKE PROVISION
FOR A QUORUM, PERHAPS OF A LEAST HALF OF THE AFRICAN
AND HALF OF THE EUROPEAN MEMBERS.

V. THE COUNCIL'S BUSINESS: THE INITIATIVE FOR PROPOSING
THE AGENDA WOULD LIE WITH THE CHIEF MINISTER, BUT
EVERY MEMBER OF THE COUNCIL WOULD BE ENTITLED TO PROPOSE
ITEMS FOR AGENDA AND SHOULD HAVE THE RIGHT TO INSIST
ON THEIR BEING DISCUSSED.

THE BRITISH ROLE

10. THE ORGANS OF GOVERNMENT WOULD HAVE AUTHORITY FOR
A PREDETERMINED PERIOD PERHAPS NOT EXCEEDING TWO YEARS.

11. BRITAIN WOULD REMAIN RESPONSIBLE FOR EXTERNAL
AFFAIRS DURING THE INTERIM PERIOD AND THERE WOULD BE
A BRITISH GOVERNMENT REPRESENTATIVE IN SALISBURY.
HE WOULD NOT BE A REPRESENTATIVE OF THE QUEEN. HIS
SECRET

DOCUMENT 42: Secretary Henry Kissinger, Cable for Ambassador Frank Wisner, "Annex C," October 27, 1976.

PAGE 7 OF 7

Department of State TELEGRAM

SECRET

PAGE 07   STATE 265403

FUNCTION WOULD BE QUASI-DIPLOMATIC: TO MONITOR THE
PROGRAMME OF PROGRESS TO MAJORITY RULE AND, WHERE
NECESSARY, TO MAKE AVAILABLE HIS GOOD OFFICES TO
MEDIATE IN ANY MATTER AFFECTING THE CARRYING THROUGH
OF THE PROGRAMME.   ROBINSON

SECRET

DOCUMENT 43: U.S. Embassy Vienna, Cable for National Security Advisor Zbigniew Brzezinski and Secretary Cyrus Vance, "First Meeting Between Vice President Mondale and Prime Minister Vorster, Morning, May 19," May 20, 1977.

PAGE 1 OF 8

PAGE 01   VIENNA 04122   01 OF 02   208324Z
ACTION NODS-03

INFO OCT-01 ISO-00 /001 W
              ——————————— 208339Z 095865 /58

O 200113Z MAY 77
FM AMEMBASSY VIENNA
TO SECSTATE WASHDC IMMEDIATE 1800

S E C R E T SECTION 1 OF 2 VIENNA 4122

DEPARTMENT PLEASE PASS WHITE HOUSE, ATTN: DR. BRZEZINSKI

DEPT PASS GENEVA EYES ONLY FOR SECRETARY VANCE

EO 11652: GDS
TAGS: PFOR, OVIP, (MONDALE, WALTER F.) US, BF, RH
SUBJECT: FIRST MEETING BETWEEN VICE PRESIDENT MONDALE AND
PRIME MINISTER VORSTER, MORNING, MAY 19

SUMMARY: DURING INITIAL SESSION, ON RHODESIA, VICE PRESIDENT
MONDALE SET FORTH U.S. SUPPORT FOR OWEN INITIATIVE AND
EFFORTS TO DRAFT A CONSTITUTION WITH CLEAR GUARANTEES FOR
ALL, WHICH WILL LEAD TO FREE ELECTIONS WITH FULL PARTICIPATION
AND INDEPENDENCE FOR ZIMBABWE DURING 1978. VORSTER

END SUMMARY.

1. FOLLOWING INITIAL PHOTO SESSION AT HOFBURG CONFERENCE
ROOM, VICE PRESIDENT MONDALE, JOINED BY AARON, AND
PRIME MINISTER VORSTER, JOINED BY BOTHA, MET PRIVATELY
AS PER EARLIER AGREEMENT. DURING THAT SESSION,
WHICH LASTED APPROXIMATELY 35 MINUTES, VORSTER OPENED BY
                    SECRET

DOCUMENT 43: U.S. Embassy Vienna, Cable for National Security Advisor Zbigniew Brzezinski and Secretary Cyrus Vance, "First Meeting Between Vice President Mondale and Prime Minister Vorster, Morning, May 19," May 20, 1977.

PAGE 2 OF 8

PHFAD/D 7496

Department of State

INCOMING TELEGRAM

NODIS

SECRET

PAGE 02   VIENNA 04122 01 OF 02   200324Z

2. PRINCIPLES THEN RETURNED TO OPEN SESSION, ON SOUTH
AFRICAN SIDE WERE, IN ADDITION TO VORSTER AND BOTHA,
VAN DEN BERGH, FOURIE, SOLE, FRANKLIN, AND EKSTEEN,
WITH THE VICE PRESIDENT AND AARON WERE AMBASSADORS BOWDLER
AND MCHENRY, LAKE, CLIFT, JOHNSON, AND KATZEN, AS AGREED,
OPENING SESSION WAS DEVOTED TO DISCUSSION OF RHODESIA,
AND LASTED 2 HOURS.

3. SOUTHERN RHODESIA: VICE PRESIDENT MONDALE SET FORTH
USG SUPPORT FOR FOREIGN SECRETARY OWENS' INITIATIVE AND
EFFORTS TO DRAFT A CONSTITUTION WHICH WILL LEAD TO FREE
ELECTIONS AND INDEPENDENCE FOR ZIMBABWE DURING 1978.
WHILE THE ORIGINAL SUGGESTION WAS TO HAVE A CONSTITUTIONAL
CONFERENCE AS PART OF THE PROCESS, HE SAID WE NOW ARE
BEGINNING BILATERAL CONSULTATIONS WITH THE HOPE THAT A
CONSENSUS WILL RESULT CONCERNING A CONSTITUTION. WE HAVE
APPOINTED A SENIOR AMERICAN DIPLOMAT, AMBASSADOR LOW, TO
PARTICIPATE IN THE PROCESS. WE HOPE THAT SOUTH AFRICA WILL
ENCOURAGE SMITH TO WORK WITH THE PROCESS, SUPPORTING
FREE ELECTIONS WITH ALL PARTICIPATING, AND AN
INDEPENDENT GOVERNMENT IN ZIMBABWE IN 1978.
WE HAVE NOT DEVELOPED DETAILS CONCERNING THE
CONSTITUTION; THESE ARE FOR THE CONSULATIVE PROCESS
TO DETERMINE. THE CONSULTATIVE GROUP WILL BE IN
SALISBURY, MAY 2223.

4. VORSTER REVIEWED EATIER SMITH EFFORTS TO REACH A
SOLUTION, BEGINNING IN 1973. HE OUTLINED SOUTH AFRICAN
STEPS TO BRING THE PARTIES TOGETHER, INCLUDING THE
LIBERATION OF NKOMO AND SITHOLE. SOUTH AFRICA AT ALL
TIMES HAS BEEN PREPARED TO HELP, AND IS PREPARED NOW.

SECRET

DOCUMENT 43: U.S. Embassy Vienna, Cable for National Security Advisor Zbigniew Brzezinski and Secretary Cyrus Vance, "First Meeting Between Vice President Mondale and Prime Minister Vorster, Morning, May 19," May 20, 1977.

PAGE 3 OF 8

DECLASSIFIED

Department of State

INCOMING TELEGRAM

SECRET

PAGE 03   VIENNA 04122   01 OF 02   200384Z

SMITH IS WILLING TO FIND A SOLUTION; HE WILL ACCEPT
MAJORITY RULE, WHICH MEANS BLACK RULE, BUT WITH WHOM
IS HE TO NEGOTIATE? GENEVA SHOWED HOW SPLIT THE
NATIONALISTS ARE.

5. VICE PRESIDENT MONDALE COMMENTED THAT PRECISELY BECAUSE
OF THE MANY DIFFERENT GROUPS HAVING DIFFERENT OBJECTIVES,
IT WAS DESIRABLE TO PROCEED NOW WITH A PROCESS WHICH
WOULD LEAD TO A CONSTITUTION AND GOVERNMENT.
BUT, WE DO NOT WISH TO CHOOSE THE LEADERS. VORSTER
INTERJECTED THAT IF AN ELECTION WERE HELD TOMORROW
IN RHODESIA, MUSOREWA WOULD BE ELECTED OVERWHELMINGLY.
VICE PRESIDENT MONDALE REPLIED THAT THE CRUCIAL ELEMENT
IS NOT WHO IS ELECTED BUT THAT THE ELECTIONS ARE HELD,
IN A SPIRIT OF FAIRNESS, EQUALITY, AND INTEGRITY.
THIS IS OUR OBJECTIVE, AND WE BELIEVE IT WILL LEAD TO
THE CREATION OF A MODERATE GOVERNMENT. HE AGAIN
APPEALED TO SOUTH AFRICA TO INFLUENCE SMITH TO ACCEPT
THE PROCESS AND THE RESULTS OF FAIR ELECTIONS. WE
WILL ENCOURAGE THOSE WITH WHOM WE HAVE INFLUENCE.

6. VORSTER STATED THAT SMITH ALREADY HAD ACCEPTED
THE PROCESS, WHICH HAD CAUSED A REBELLION WITHIN HIS OWN
POLITICAL PARTY. THE QUESTON REMAINS1 TO WHOM SHOULD
HE TURN OVER POWER? THE IDEAL WOULD BE A REFERENDUM
AMONG BLACKS TO CHOOSE A LEADER WHO, IN TURN, WOULD
NEGOTIATE THE TURNOVER WITH SMITH. VICE PRESIDENT MONDALE SAID
THE BLACKS HAVE ALREADY REJECTED THIS "INTERNAL OPTION",
AND THE OWEN MISSION SEEKS TO CIRCUMVENT THAT VERY
PROCESS. WE REJECT THE INTERNAL OPTION. WE ARE NOT AS
SURE AS VORSTER THAT SMITH HAS FULLY ACCEPTED THE PROCESS.

SECRET

DOCUMENT 43: U.S. Embassy Vienna, Cable for National Security Advisor Zbigniew Brzezinski and Secretary Cyrus Vance, "First Meeting Between Vice President Mondale and Prime Minister Vorster, Morning, May 19," May 20, 1977.

PAGE 4 OF 8

ᴵᴺᵁᴼᴰ0Y0 7ᴬᵀᴴ

DECLASSIFIED

Department of State

INCOMING TELEGRAM

SECRET

PAGE 04   VIENNA 04122   01 OF 02   2003242

VORSTER REPLIED THAT IN SMITH'S AND KISSINGER'S PRESENCE,
HE, VORSTER, HAD SPECIFICALLY SAID THAT IF SMIGH DID NOT
ADHERE TO THE FIVE POINTS SMITH HAD ACCEPTED, VORSTER
WOULD DROP HIM. VORSTER ADDED THAT HE ALSO HAD
SAID HE WOULD GUARANTEE SMITH HONORED HIS COMMITMENTS.
"I CAN'T DO ANY MORE", HE ADDED. "IF SMITH AGREES
TOTHE ELECTION PROCESS, I WILL SUPPORT THE RESULTS".

7. THE VICE PRESIDENT CONCLUDED THAT AGREEMENT SEEMED
TO EXIST NOW ON THAT POINT. HE ADDED THAT WHILE WE
SEEK MAJORITY RULE, WE DO NOT SAY THAT THIS NECESSARILY MEANS
BLACK MAJORITY RULE. BLACKS OFTEN ARE ELECTED IN
PRIMARILY WHITE ELECTORATES AND VICE VERSA, IN THE
UNITED STATES. VORSTER WAS QUICK TO RESPOND THAT ONE
COULD NOT EQUATE THE UNITED STATES SITUATION TO THAT
EXISTING IN EITHER RHODESIA OR SOUTH AFRICA.

8. VORSTER ADDED THAT A GUARANTEE STILL WAS NEED FOR
WHITES AND ASKED FOR IT FROM THE VICE PRESIDENT OR OWEN.
THE VICE PRESIDENT REPLIED THAT THE MORE PROMPT THE
PROGRESS TO HONEST MAJORITY GOVERNMENT, WITH
CONSTITUTIONAL PROTECTON OF PERSONAL LIBERTIES, PROPERTY,
RELIGION, AND INDIVIDUAL CHOICE, WITH AN INDEPENENT
JUDICIARY, THE MORE ATTRACTIVE IT WOULD BE FOR ALL TO
REMAIN IN RHODESIA. THESE RIGHTSWOULD GUARANTEE WHAT THE
WHITES SEEK. VORSTER RESPONDED THAT SUCH CONSTITUTIONAL
GUARANTEES WOULD NOT MEAN ANYTHING, BUT THAT IF THE
AMERICANS STATED THAT THEIR OBJECTIVES INCLUDED SUCH
CONSTITUTIONAL GUARANTEES, THE WHITE RHODESIANS AND THE
MAJORTIY OF BLACK RHODESIANS WOULD ACCEPT, SO WOULD

SECRET

DOCUMENT 43: U.S. Embassy Vienna, Cable for National Security Advisor Zbigniew Brzezinski and Secretary Cyrus Vance, "First Meeting Between Vice President Mondale and Prime Minister Vorster, Morning, May 19," May 20, 1977.

PAGE 5 OF 8

Department of State

INCOMING TELEGRAM

SECRET   NODIS

PAGE 01   VIENNA 04122 02 OF 02 2003012
ACTION NODS-00

INFO OCT-01 ISO-00 /001

-------------------- 2003072 096073 /12

O 2001102 MAY 77
FM AMEMBASSY VIENNA
TO SECSTATE WASHDC IMMEDIATE 1001

S E C R E T SECTION 2 OF 2 VIENNA 4122

NODIS

DEPARTMENT PLEASE PASS WHITE HOUSE, ATTN: DR. BRZEZINSKI

DEPARTMENT PASS GENEVA EYES ONLY FOR SECRETARY VANCE

THE SAG, SUCH ASSURANCES, COUPLED WITH
IMPLEMENTATION OF THE ZIMBABWE FUND (AND ITS
INCLUSION IN THE CONSTITUTION) WOULD LEAD TO A
SETTLEMENT. "IF YOU CAN GUARANTEE NKOMO AND MUGABE
FALL INTO LINE", HE SAID, "I WILL GUARANTEE SMITH
DOES".

9. THE VICE PRESIDENT REPLIED THAT WHILE HE CAN'T
GUARANTEE RESULTS, OUR OBJECTIVE IS TO PURSUE THE OWEN

MISSION AND, AS PART OF THE PROCESS TRY TO GAIN FRONT
LINE SUPPORT, AND DO WHAT HE CAN TO SUPPORT AN INDEPDENENT
GOVERNMENT ONCE IT IS ESTABLISHED. SPECIFICALLY WE ASK
VORSTER:

A) FOR SAG SUPPORT, HOPEFULLY PUBLICLY, FOR THE
OWEN MISSION;

B) TO PRESS SMITH TO NEGOTIATE FOR MAJORITY RULE,
ATTAINED THROUGH FAIR ELECTIONS, IN 1978;

SECRET

DOCUMENT 43: U.S. Embassy Vienna, Cable for National Security Advisor Zbigniew Brzezinski and Secretary Cyrus Vance, "First Meeting Between Vice President Mondale and Prime Minister Vorster, Morning, May 19," May 20, 1977.

PAGE 6 OF 8

የቀ፡በበ፯ለ ፯ለ፡በ

Department of State

INCOMING TELEGRAM

SECRET

PAGE 02   VIENNA 04122   02 OF 02 2003012

C) TO OBTAIN SMITH'S AGREEMENT TO INDEPENDENCE
AT THAT DATE!

D) FOR SOUTH AFRICA TO WORK AS WE WILL WITH A
ZIMBABWE GOVERNMENT THUS CHOSEN!

E) TO HELP IN REDUCING TENSIONS WHICH TEAR AT
THAT PROCESS.

10. VORSTER CAME UP SHARPLY, SAYING THAT HE DID NOT
LIKE THE WORD "PRESSURE", THAT HE HAD NEVER PRESSED
SMITH; INSTEAD, "I TALK SENSE TO HIM". VORSTER
REITERATED THAT THE PROBLEM IN RHODESIA
IS NOT SMITH, BUT THE NATIONALISTS. HE RETURNED
TO HIS ARGUMENT FAVORING AN INTERNAL SETTLEMENT
IN RHODESIA THEN, FEIGNING COMPROMISE, SAID HE WOULD
ACCEPT HIS SECOND CHOICE, WHICH WOULD BE ALONG THE
LINES OF OWEN'S PROPOSAL. BUT, THE CONSTITUTION,
HE REPEATED, WOULD HAVE TO INCLUDE ALL ELEMENTS THE VICE
PRSIDENT HAD DESCRIBED AND US/UK GUARANTEES THAT THE
ELECTED GOVERNMENTS WOULD BE UPHELD AND NOT BE OVERTHROWN
FROM THE OUTSIDE, AND THAT SANCTIONS WOULD BE LIFTED.

11. RETURNING TO THE QUESTION OF THE ZIMBABWE FUND,
THE VICE PRESIDENT SAID THAT HE ENVISAGED IT AS HELPING
IN ECONOMIC DEVELOPMENT, GROWTH, INFRASTURCUTE, AND
TRAINING; THAT WAS THE PATH TO ECONOMIC STABILITY. WE
ARE PREPARED TO CONSIDER OTHER KINDS OF HELP TO STRENGTHEN
AGAINST THE FEARS AND THREATS VORSTER HAS MENTIONED.
WE CANNOT GUARANTEE THAT THE PEOPLE OF ZIMBABWE WILL
CHOOSE A GOVERNMENT THA WILL RENOUNCE ALL PUBLIC
OWNERSHIP. BUT, THE CONSTITUTION WOULD INCORPORATE
GUARANTEES ON CONFISCATION. THE FUND ITSELF CANNOT BE
USED SIMPLY TO BUY OUT WHITES.

SECRET

DOCUMENT 43: U.S. Embassy Vienna, Cable for National Security Advisor Zbigniew Brzezinski and Secretary Cyrus Vance, "First Meeting Between Vice President Mondale and Prime Minister Vorster, Morning, May 19," May 20, 1977.

Department of State

INCOMING TELEGRAM

SECRET

PAGE 03   VIENNA 04122   02 OF 02   2003517

BIA5

12. BOTHA [DESCRIBED AGREEMENTS AS HAVING BEEN REACHED IN THE DEPARTMENT WHEREBY THE FUND HAS TO HAVE A COMPENSATORY FUNCTION. HE SAID THAT SOUTH AFRICA HAD BEEN TOLD THERE WERE TO BE FORMAL GUARANTEES THAT A "SLIDING SCALE" OF COMPENSATIONS WOULD BE PAID IF THINGS WENT BADLY AND WHITE RHODESIANS WANTED TO LEAVE. THE VICE PRESIDENT CONFIRMED THAT THE U.S. GOVERNMENT HAD CHANGED ITS THINKING ON THIS.

BIA3 + 5

13. THE VICE PRESIDENT AGREED TO LOOK INTO THE QUESTION AT LUNCH TIME, AND TURNED TO THE MATTER OF INCURSIONS BY SMITH FORCES. VORSTER ACKNOWLEDGED THAT BOTH SIDES WERE ESCALATING THE VIOLENCE AND STRESSED THAT ON MANY OCCASIONS SOUTH AFRICA HAD SERVED AS CHANNEL TO COMMUNICATE APPEALS TO SMITH. BUT, VORSTER ADDED, RHODESIA HAS RESPONSIBILITY TO PROTECT ITS OWN POPULATION, AND FRONT LINE STATES MUST DO THEIR PART TO RESTRAIN NATIONALISTS. VICE PRESIDENT SAID THAT AS PRACTICAL MATTER, THE SITUATION WILL NOT IMPROVE UNLESS THERE IS PROGRESS TOWARD ELECTIONS AND INDEPENDENCE. VICE PRESIDENT AND VORSTER AGREED THAT U.S. AND SAG WOULD USE

SECRET

DOCUMENT 43: U.S. Embassy Vienna, Cable for National Security Advisor Zbigniew Brzezinski and Secretary Cyrus Vance, "First Meeting Between Vice President Mondale and Prime Minister Vorster, Morning, May 19," May 20, 1977.

PAGE 8 OF 8

Department of State

INCOMING TELEGRAM

SECRET

PAGE 01   VIENNA 04122   02 OF 02   2003561Z

WHAT INFLUENCE THEY HAVE ON BOTH SIDES. BEFORE
BREAKING FOR LUNCH, VICE PRESIDENT AND VORSTER AGREED
NOT TO SPEAK TO PRESS AT THIS TIME. MEEHAN

SECRET

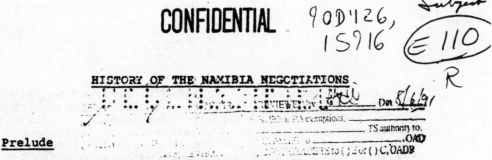

CONFIDENTIAL 90D426,
15916 E 110
R

HISTORY OF THE NAMIBIA NEGOTIATIONS

Prelude

Following years of condemnatory UN General Assembly resolutions calling for South African withdrawal from Namibia, and the 1971 International Court of Justice opinion reiterating the SAG's obligation to remove its administration, the Secretary General in 1972 under Security Council mandate contacted all parties concerned with a view to establishing the necessary conditions to enable Namibians to exercise their right to self-determination and independence.

The Secretary General visited South Africa and Namibia in March, 1972, and held discussions with South African government officials and representatives of various groups and parties in Namibia. Seven months later the SYG's special representative had extended discussions with the SAG and the Namibian parties, at which time the SAG Foreign Minister stated that his government:

-- would fully respect the wishes of the entire population of Namibia regarding future constitutional organization and would impose no constitutional system;

-- would permit all political parties to participate in the process leading to self-determination and independence;

-- would not delay the act of self-determination, would cooperate with the Secretary General, and consult with the people of Namibia to determine measures to insure the achievement of self-determination;

-- did not envisage individual population groups becoming independent as separate entities;

-- anticipated that it might not take longer than 10 years for the population to be ready to exercise its right to self-determination.

However, the Secretary General concluded that these statements did not provide the clarification of South Africa's policy required by the Security Council. On the basis of his opinion, and a period of South African repression of political activities in Namibia, the Security Council in 1973 formally terminated the SYG's mandate.

CONFIDENTIAL
GDS - 4/3/87

- 2 -

In September 1974, the National Party of Namibia announced that various population groups (white, colored, and black) should select leaders to come together to discuss Namibia's future pattern of constitutional development. The "Turnhalle Conference" eventually called for independence for the territory and produced proposals for a constitution for an interim government which would bring the country to independence by December, 1978. The Conference proposed a complex three tier government of central, regional, and municipal governing bodies along ethnic lines. SWAPO participation was effectively ruled out by a provision in the "bill of rights" prohibiting participation in the political process by groups with a Marxist-Leninist ideology. Moreover, a five year residency requirement for participation in the central government Council of Ministers and National Assembly eliminated possible participation by political exiles.

In January 1976, the Security Council adopted Resolution 385, which called for an end to SAG occupation of Namibia, and declared that Namibians should determine their future through UN supervised and controlled elections. Additionally, 385 called for release of all political prisoners, return to the territory of all Namibians currently in exile for political reasons, and demanded the abolition of all racially discriminatory and politically repressive laws and practices.

The Western Five Initiative

Proposed in 1978 by the Contact Group, the Western Plan calls for a ceasefire between South Africa and SWAPO, and an election to a constituent assembly to decide on a constitution for an independent Namibian state. A UN force would supervise the ceasefire, and oversee an election to be held seven months after the ceasefire. The election date would be contingent upon fulfillment of truce arrangements and other preparations for a fair election. Under the Western Plan, South Africa would organize the elections, maintain law and order with its local police forces, and would assure that all discriminatory legislation was repealed prior to election.

In April 1978, Prime Minister Vorster accepted the Western proposal "in principle." Under considerable pressure from the Front Line states and Nigeria, SWAPO accepted the Plan. Secretary General Waldheim then submitted to the Security Council his recommendations for implementation, including:

CONFIDENTIAL

- 3 -

-- SAG troops in Namibia be reduced to a force of 1,500, which would remain until shortly after an election;

-- provision of a UN force of 5,000 troops and an additional 2,500 support personnel;

-- selection of national contingents for the UN force in consultation with the Security Council and the parties concerned, according to the principle of equitable geographic distribution.

Sam Nujoma accepted the Plan soon thereafter. However, South Africa claimed on September 30, 1978 that the Plan was unacceptable, primarily because the UN military contingent would be too large, and the interval between the ceasefire and elections too long. Vorster announced that the South African administration in Namibia would conduct an election for a constituent assembly by the end of 1978. The Security Council on September 29 passed Resolution 435, which approved Waldheim's plan, called on South Africa to cooperate with the Secretary General in implementing the Plan, and declared null and void any election conducted solely by South Africa.

The Foreign Ministers of the five Western sponsors of the UN Plan for Namibia visited Pretoria in October 1978, to attempt resolution of the impasse. Botha turned down their requests that an election be cancelled, but vowed that after election of the assembly, he would try to persuade its members "to consider achieving international recognition through the good offices of the UN Special Representative for Namibia and the South African Administrator General. Botha said Western assurances had cleared up South African reservations about the size and composition of the UN force, and the Western Foreign Ministers recommended to Waldheim that he send UN Special Representative Martti Ahtisaari on a tour of Namibia, Pretoria, and the Front Line capitals to seek agreement on implementation.

The African Group in New York maintained that the "internal" election would undercut the UN program, opposed the Western Plan to go ahead with Ahtisaari's mission, and pressed for sanctions against South Africa unless the election were cancelled. In November 1978, the Security Council, with Western members abstaining, passed Resolution 439, which called on South Africa to cancel the election, and warned that sanctions might be proposed if they failed to cooperate in implementation of the Plan.

CONFIDENTIAL

CONFIDENTIAL
- 4 -

In December, the newly elected Constituent Assembly after a session with Prime Minister Botha agreed "in principle" to a new election under UN auspices if adequate truce arrangements were enforced. Botha announced that South Africa would cooperate in fulfilling Security Council Resolution 435, that UNTAG should begin its deployment by February 26 and that elections should be held by September 30. The response, however, indicated that Pretoria might accept a ceasefire plan if two points in the ceasefire plan were changed. First, the plan must include effective UN monitoring of SWAPO bases in Angola and Zambia, and second, must not allow guerrillas inside Namibia at the time of cease-fire to set up bases, even under UN monitoring. The Front Line refused to allow the UN to monitor SWAPO bases, and SWAPO insisted on having bases inside Namibia after a cease-fire. In May 1979, the SAG rejected the Western proposal for resolving the impasse and at the same time elevated the Constituent Assembly to a Namibian National Assembly and gave it some legislative functions.

In July 1979, President Neto of Angola suggested to Don McHenry and Waldheim a compromise on the bases issue. Angola had previously discussed secretly with South Africa the establishment of a demilitarized zone along the northern Namibia border. In August the Front Line approved Neto's proposal and agreed to accept UN "liaison" offices in Angola, Botswana, and Zambia which would coordinate monitoring opera-tions by UN troops within the DMZ. SWAPO was persuaded not to insist on bases inside Namibia, but predicated their agreement on SAG agreement to implementation.

In September 1979, the Contact Group completed a plan for establishing a DMZ which would supplement the original cease-fire plan. The DMZ would encompass a 50 kilometer strip on both sides of Namibia's northern border, but some population centers and military bases would be excluded. The SAG bases excluded would be closed three months after ceasefire, in keeping with the earlier proposals, which provided for a phased withdrawal of SAG troops to bases at Grootfontein and Oshivelo. Only UN troops and aircraft would operate within the DMZ, but UN ground patrols would be accompanied by South African, Angolan, or Zambian civil personnel in their portions of the DMZ.

In November 1979, delegates from South Africa, the Front Line, and SWAPO met in Geneva under UN auspices to consider the plan for establishing the DMZ. The Front Line states and SWAPO accepted the concept of a DMZ and agreed to participate in detailed technical discussions, provided Pretoria accepted it.

In December, Waldheim was notified that South Africa accepted the concept of the zone provided agreement was reached in further discussions on a number of technical arrangements. Among the SAG's specified preconditions were agreement on the number of forward bases to be excluded from the DMZ, confirmation that SWAPO's claim to bases would not be revived, and that the Western settlement proposal accepted by the SAG in April 1978, would not be changed. Waldheim then met with the Front Line in New York, who tentatively agreed to go ahead with technical discussions, despite their dissatisfaction with Pretoria's conditional acceptance of the DMZ concept.

Technical discussions on the DMZ between UN and South African officials were held in February 1980. Considerable progress was made, but South Africa seemed to be reconsidering its position in light of Robert Mugabe's overwhelming victory in Zimbabwe's first elections. The SAG promised a formal reply on its position by March 24. In their May 12 reply, South Africa raised further questions on the DMZ, stated the necessity of UNITA cooperation in making the DMZ effective, called for an end to UN impartiality toward SWAPO, and equal treatment of the internal parties during the electoral process.

On June 20, Waldheim responded to Botha and noted that:

-- the Front Line agreed that South Africa could retain 20 selected locations in the DMZ during the first 12 weeks after the ceasefire, that the Front Line would disarm SWAPO at bases in their territory and prohibit SWAPO infiltration into Namibia;

-- the question of SWAPO bases would no longer arise once the SAG accepted 435;

-- the UN would not deal with UNITA, since it was not a party to the negotiations;

-- UNTAG, as a force established by the Security Council, would act with complete impartiality, and that all parties, as soon as implementation began, would be treated with complete impartiality.

In late August 1980, South Africa responded to the Secretary General and essentially laid to rest its questions on

CONFIDENTIAL
- 6 -

the operation of the DMZ. However, Foreign Minister Botha reiterated that the UN should immediately cease its preferential treatment of SWAPO and henceforth include the internal parties in all future consultations.

The South African letter indicated that all major substantive problems of the Plan having been resolved, the major South African objections now centered on the more subjective question of UN impartiality and treatment of the internal parties. In UN/SAG consultations in October 1980, the South Africans concentrated on "mutual distrust and lack of confidence" between the internal parties and SWAPO as a result of UN partiality toward SWAPO and exclusion of the internals from the negotiations. The South African position reflected in part its desire to send the internal parties to a "multi-party" conference, a proposal which originated in Front Line and particularly Angolan initiatives over previous months to set up direct talks between SWAPO and South Africa.

In his report of November 24, 1980, the Secretary General stated that South Africa had informed the October UN delegation that "mistrust and lack of confidence" affected the setting of a date for implementation, but independence for Namibia could be achieved by the end of 1981 if this obstacle could be overcome. It was agreed, at South African urging, that the "internal parties" would be included in the SAG delegation and that any party could raise "any other practical proposals" bearing on implementation.

The "pre-implementation" conference was convened under UN auspicies in Geneva from January 7-14, 1981. SWAPO at the outset stated its willingness to begin implementation of the Plan. South Africa used the PIM to push the internal parties to the fore, and through the sometimes inflammatory statements by internal representatives, attempted to goad Sam Nujoma into reacting negatively. However, Nujoma was well coached by the Front Line, and demonstrated a measured reasonableness and a forthcoming attitude. The PIM never actually got down to what were perceived as the remaining points of contention. Please refer to papers entitled "UN Impartiality toward SWAPO" and "Constitutional Issues" for a fuller examination of points raised during the PIM.

IO/UNP:DLMcElhaney:ek   Clearances:IO/UNP:MLevitsky
4/2/81   x22597   AF/S:PHare

DOCUMENT 45: Assistant Secretary Chester Crocker, Briefing Memorandum for Secretary
George Shultz, "Your Meeting with the President on the Southern Africa Negotiations, Thursday,
September 23 at 11:00 a.m.," September 22, 1982, with Attached Chart of Issues.

PAGE 1 OF 8

DEPARTMENT OF STATE

BRIEFING MEMORANDUM

S/S

REVIEW

Caption removed;
transferred to O/FADRC

Cat. B - Transferred to O/FADRC
with additional access
controlled by S/S

Cat. C - Caption and custody
retained by S/S

Reviewed by: Elijah Kelly Jr.

Date: 2/11/91 19____

SECRET/NODIS

TO: The Secretary

FROM: AF - Chester A. Crocker

SUBJECT: Your Meeting with the President on the Southern Africa
          Negotiations, Thursday, September 23 at 11:00 a.m.

When you met with the President September 15 to discuss
funding for the UN Transition Assistance Group (UNTAG), you
offered to brief him at greater length on our southern Africa
negotiations. This memorandum provides background on the
Namibia independence negotiations and on our discussions with
Angola on Cuban troop withdrawal, along with talking points
for briefing the President. We have also prepared a chart of
unresolved issues on the Namibia and Angola tracks, indicating
positions taken by the parties to the negotiations.

EXCIS.

Reagan Administration Initiative

The Administration's initiative on southern Africa grew
out of the collapse of the Geneva conference on Namibia in
January 1981 and the negotiating deadlock which followed.
Faced with strong pressure from key NATO allies to reinvigorate
the Namibia settlement effort, along with South African probing
for evidence that the new Administration would abandon the UN
negotiating framework which developed from Security Council
Resolution 435, the President and Secretary Haig decided to
launch an ambitious and active diplomatic effort in southern
Africa, with two principal objectives. Our approach was aimed
at improving relations with Pretoria, on the understanding that
the SAG would move toward constructive change -- in Namibia and
at home -- and at capitalizing on African interest in Namibian
independence to lever the Cubans out of Angola.

BIAS

We soon reached an

SECRET/NODIS
OADR

[261]

DOCUMENT 45: Assistant Secretary Chester Crocker, Briefing Memorandum for Secretary George Shultz, "Your Meeting with the President on the Southern Africa Negotiations, Thursday, September 23 at 11:00 a.m.," September 22, 1982, with Attached Chart of Issues.

PAGE 2 OF 8

SECRET/NODIS

2

understanding with the SAG on a three-phase framework and a timetable for negotiating the remaining Namibia issues, and, in September 1981, we obtained the support of our Contact Group (CG) partners for our approach on Namibia and their reluctant acceptance that there would be no deal if the Angola track failed. The African Front Line States (FLS) and SWAPO also agreed to our three-phase Namibia approach, despite substantial misgivings about our Angola track, because they recognized, as did the CG, that our unique relationship with the SAG was essential to resolution of the Namibia question.

In the year which has followed, we have established a necessary minimum of credibility as honest broker by responding fully to African, UN Secretariat, and SAG concerns on Namibia. At the same time, by defining the Angolan issue as "separate", "not formally linked", and "not part of SCR 435", we have obtained growing acceptance of the legitimacy of bilateral US-Angolan negotiations on Cuban withdrawal.

The Namibia Track

Since October 1981, we have reached agreement among all parties on virtually all the Namibia issues. Phase I, involving a set of "constitutional principles" to guide the parties elected to the Constituent Assembly, is fully agreed, apart from the question of which electoral system will be used (proportional representation or single-member constituency). The FLS/SWAPO have said they can accept either system, provided the SAG indicates prior to Security Council action -- as it has promised to do -- which system will be used.

Intensive discussions between the CG, the FLS, and SWAPO in New York this summer, along with our talks with the SAG, have produced agreement on measures to ensure impartial conduct of UN-supervised elections and on most issues regarding the size, composition, and deployment of UNTAG.

Aside from these UNTAG questions, responsibility for which lies with the UN Secretariat, there are a relatively few hurdles to be cleared before Phase II could be concluded and a Namibia package could go to the Security Council for adoption of a resolution to implement SCR 435 -- which would begin Phase III, to end with Namibian independence within approximately one year.

SECRET/NODIS

DOCUMENT 45: Assistant Secretary Chester Crocker, Briefing Memorandum for Secretary George Shultz, "Your Meeting with the President on the Southern Africa Negotiations, Thursday, September 23 at 11:00 a.m.," September 22, 1982, with Attached Chart of Issues.

SECRET/NODIS

3

This rapid progress has produced strong FLS/SWAPO rumblings over Cuban "linkage", but the President's recent letters to the FLS leaders made clear that we will go no further on Namibia without satisfactory progress on Angola.

The Angola Track

Our bilateral discussions on the Angola track are beginning to show possible grounds for agreement. Frank Wisner will soon be returning to Luanda with what we hope will be South African agreement in principle to the procedural framework concept we presented to the MPLA in August. We also hope to be able to tell them the South Africans are prepared to engage in military-to-military proximity talks on a ceasefire before implementation of SCR 435 (CBI), which would set the stage for the arrival of UNTAG.

The procedural framework, if finally agreed, would pro- vide for parallel commitments from Angola with respect to Cuban withdrawal and from South Africa with respect to non- use of force against Angola, which would be provided to us as separate written documents. We are seeking an Angolan docu- ment which would spell out in detail the timetable and sequence for withdrawal of Cuban combat forces, both of which would have to be acceptable to the SAG. Upon receipt of documents agreed to by both sides, we would, in cooperation with our CG allies, request final Security Council action to implement SCR 435.

While not an essential precondition to such an arrangement, the CBI would establish an important basis for confidence on both sides. We have proposed to the South Africans -- and will do so with the Angolans -- that proximity talks, with our facili- tative assistance, should work out final agreement on the CBI.

8145

SECRET/NODIS

[263]

DOCUMENT 45: Assistant Secretary Chester Crocker, Briefing Memorandum for Secretary George Shultz, "Your Meeting with the President on the Southern Africa Negotiations, Thursday, September 23 at 11:00 a.m.," September 22, 1982, with Attached Chart of Issues.

PAGE 4 OF 8

SECRET/NODIS

4

BIAS

Our objective remains the withdrawal of all Cuban combat forces from Angola during Phase III. The MPLA has already backed off its maximum position that the Cubans can only be withdrawn after Namibian independence -- their position through our September 1981 to May 1982 discussions with them -- and have agreed to develop specific proposals for withdrawal during Phase III. As the negotiation progresses, we will be carefully evaluating the Angolan proposals to determine what our bottom line realistic expectations should be in terms of both numbers and timing of Cuban withdrawal in the context of Phase III.

BIAS
]

UNITA

UNITA remains a key factor in the negotiations. Our public and private position with all the parties to the negotiation has been that UNITA is a viable force which must be taken into account in Angola. UNITA probably has the capacity to sabotage any settlement it does not agree to through stepped-up military activity.

BIAS

] My Director of Southern African Affairs, Dan Simpson, met with senior UNITA representatives in Kinshasa earlier this month to bring them up to date on our efforts, reassuring them that we continue to envisage a role for UNITA in Angola. The UNITA representatives reaffirmed support for our southern Africa initiative.

SECRET/NODIS

DOCUMENT 45: Assistant Secretary Chester Crocker, Briefing Memorandum for Secretary George Shultz, "Your Meeting with the President on the Southern Africa Negotiations, Thursday, September 23 at 11:00 a.m.," September 22, 1982, with Attached Chart of Issues.

SECRET/NODIS

5

We have reassured UNITA that national reconciliation in Angola remains one of our objectives, but both we and UNITA agree that Cuban withdrawal is a prerequisite for reconciliation. While the MPLA has remained adamant in its refusal to deal with UNITA, there are signs that Dos Santos realizes that some sort of internal accommodation may be necessary if the Cubans are to leave. Savimbi appreciates that this is a tremendously sensitive question for the MPLA. When I meet with him, I will try to draw him out on possible confidence-building gestures by both the MPLA and UNITA to lay the groundwork for reconciliation if agreement is reached on Cuban withdrawal.

South Africa

While the South Africans have been cooperative in resolving the remaining Namibia Phase II issues, they are increasingly nervous about the Angola track. Recent public statements by senior South African officials on the necessity for Cuban withdrawal are signals to us about the sensitivity of the Namibia question in South African domestic politics and the need to be able to show a Cuban withdrawal quo for the quid of Namibia.

B1A5

We have repeatedly reassured the SAG of our commitment to achieving Cuban withdrawal. However, Prime Minister Botha's government faces increasing opposition on the right and may, if it sees its domestic base of support eroding, decide to back out of the Namibia process. Part of the problem is persistent South African doubt about the value of an exercise which appears likely to place a SWAPO government in office. Additionally, South African demands on the sequence of Cuban withdrawal -- all Cubans out within twelve weeks -- are completely unsaleable in the context of the phased, confidence-building concept we have presented to the Angolans.

B1A5

t

'rk

SECRET/NODIS

DOCUMENT 45: Assistant Secretary Chester Crocker, Briefing Memorandum for Secretary George Shultz, "Your Meeting with the President on the Southern Africa Negotiations, Thursday, September 23 at 11:00 a.m.," September 22, 1982, with Attached Chart of Issues.

PAGE 6 OF 8

SECRET/NODIS

6

Soviet Involvement

The Soviets are increasingly nervous that our southern Africa strategy may succeed, but they do not want to be seen overtly blocking the peace process. Last week the Soviets sent a letter to the Secretary General condemning our insistence on Cuban withdrawal as a requirement for a Namibia settlement, and we have seen their hand behind various critical statements out of African capitals and disinformation press reports seeking to exacerbate Angolan security fears.

Our strategy in the southern Africa negotiations has been to deal directly with the African parties involved, while at the same time talking quietly with the Soviets in an effort to check any temptation they may have to try and block our efforts.

BIAS

Attachments:

Tab 1.   Talking Points
Tab 2.   Chart of Issues

Drafted:AF/S:PReams/MRanneberger:lr
9/22/82 x-28252
Cleared:AF/S:DHSimpson
        IO/UNP:DMcElhaney
        L/AF:NHEly

SECRET/NODIS

[266]

DOCUMENT 45: Assistant Secretary Chester Crocker, Briefing Memorandum for Secretary George Shultz, "Your Meeting with the President on the Southern Africa Negotiations, Thursday, September 23 at 11:00 a.m.," September 22, 1982, with Attached Chart of Issues.

SECRET

THE KEY ISSUES AND PLAYERS IN THE SOUTHERN AFRICA NEGOTIATION

PLAYERS / ISSUES	Soviets and Cubans	U.S.	UNITA	Angola (MPLA)	Front Line States (FLS)
Angolan-SAG Proximity Talks	No Position	This is US proposal to work out details of CBI.	Does not oppose.	Agrees in principle.	No position.
Ceasefire Before Implementation (CBI)	No Position	This is US proposal.	Agrees to cooperate in not disrupting CBI.	Agrees to CBI concept with differences over details.	Favors concept.
Angolan National Reconciliation	Soviets insist UNITA is puppet of South Africa	US feels national reconciliation is necessary for peace in Angola.	Key objective is peaceful reconciliation after Cubans depart.	Refuses to discuss; views UNITA as puppet of SAG.	Appreciate practical necessity but remain skeptical and refuse active involvement.
Cuban Withdrawal	Soviets insist should not be "linked" to Namibia settlement and Cubans withdraw only after SAG threat removed.	Withdrawal of Cuban combat forces must occur during Phase III	Supports US objective	Has agreed to consider scenarios for withdrawal during Phase III, but has given no specifics or numbers or timing.	Oppose formal "linkage" but favor compromise leading to withdrawal and have given carte blanche support to MPLA.
Namibia Negotiations (Phases I, II, and III)	Soviets and Cubans have no formal role in Namibia process but actively oppose "linkage".	US supports UN plan; ready to seek UNSC resolution to implement UN Plan if Angola first gives commitment and plan for withdrawal of Cuban combat forces during Phase III	Agrees it has no formal role in Namibia negotiations but supports US efforts.	Opposes formal "linkage" between Cuban withdrawal and Namibia settlement; has cooperated in moving Phase I and Phase II discussions along and putting pressure on SWAPO to cooperate	Same as MPLA position.

SECRET

DEPARTMENT OF STATE
( )RELEASE
( )EXCISE ( )DELETE
( )DENY ( )NON-RESPONSIVE INFO.
( )DECLASSIFY ( )CLASSIFY ( )TS AUTH. TO.
( )TS AUTH. TO. ( )OAD
( )IN PART ( )IN FULL ( )OADR
( )DECLASSIFY IN PART TS10( )S10( )Sat( )C,OADR

[267]

DOCUMENT 45: Assistant Secretary Chester Crocker, Briefing Memorandum for Secretary George Shultz, "Your Meeting with the President on the Southern Africa Negotiations, Thursday, September 23 at 11:00 a.m.," September 22, 1982, with Attached Chart of Issues.

PAGE 8 OF 8

SECRET

KEY ISSUES AND PLAYERS
Page 2

Contact Group (CG)	South Africa (SAG)	SWAPO
No position.	Has agreed to consider.	No position.
Favors concept.	Agrees to CBI concept with differences over details.	Has not been discussed with SWAPO; MPLA expected to get SWAPO agreement.
Same as FLS position.	Wants role for UNITA and vague on bottom line, but objective may not be same as US.	No position.
Supports US efforts to obtain Cuban withdrawal, but opposes formal "linkage" with Namibia settlement	Requires agreement to Cuban withdrawal to occur in Phase III as requirement to proceed with UN plan for Namibia.	SWAPO opposes "linkage" and nervous about US-MPLA discussions.
Formally oppose linkage but supports US position that Cuban issue must be resolved.	SAG has cooperated in resolving Phase I and Phase II issues but will not move beyond Phase II without agreement on Cuban withdrawal.	As result of FLS pressure, SWAPO has cooperated in resolving Phase I and Phase II issues.

SECRET

DOCUMENT 46: Secretary George Shultz, Cable for Secretary Caspar Weinberger, "South Africans and Angolans Reach Agreement on Military Disengagement," February 15, 1984.

PAGE 1 OF 4

(E-105)

 Department of State **TELEGRAM**

SECRET

AN: 0840101-0072

R

SECRET

PAGE 01   STATE 048799
ORIGIN SS-10

INFO   OCT-00   COPY-01 ADS-00   SSO-00   /011 R

66011
DRAFTED BY:AF/I:JSDAVIDOW
APPROVED BY:AF:FGWISNER
S/S-O:HO'HARA
------------334537   150633Z /11
O 150443Z FEB 84
FM SECSTATE WASHDC
INFO SECDEF WASHDC IMMEDIATE 0000
OJCS WASHDC IMMEDIATE
USCINCEUR VAIHINGEN GE IMMEDIATE 0000
USMISSION USUN NEW YORK IMMEDIATE
NSC WASHDC IMMEDIATE 0000

S E C R E T STATE 048799

EXDIS

MILITARY ADDRESSEES HANDLE AS SPECAT EXCLUSIVE

SECDEF FOR USD/P; OJCS FOR J-5; USCINCEUR FOR POLAD; NSC
FOR WETTERING

FOLLOWING LUSAKA 00717, DTD FEB 14, SENT ACTION SECSTATE, CAPE TOWN,
JOHANNESBURG AND PRETORIA; BEING REPEATED TO YOU FOR YOU IFORMATION:

QUOTE:

S E C R E T LUSAKA 00717

EXDIS

AF FOR DAS WISNER

SECRET
SECRET

PAGE 02   STATE 048799

CAPE TOWN FOR EMBASSY

DEPARTMENT OF STATE		IS/FPC/CDR Date:
(✓) RELEASE (✓) DECLASSIFY	MR Cases Only: EO Citations	
( ) EXCISE ( ) DECLASSIFY		
( ) DENY IN PART		TS authority to
( ) DELETE Non-Responsive Info	( ) CLASSIFY as ( ) S or ( ) C OADR	
FOIA Exemptions___	( ) DOWNGRADE TS to ( ) S or ( ) C OADR	
PA Exemptions___		

Reviewed by: Elijah Kelly Jr
Date: 6/18/92

EXDIS REVIEW

Cat. A - Caption removed; transferred to O/FADRC
Cat. B - Transferred to O/FADRC with additional access controlled by S/S
Cat. C - Caption and custody retained by S/

SECRET

DOCUMENT 46: Secretary George Shultz, Cable for Secretary Caspar Weinberger, "South Africans and Angolans Reach Agreement on Military Disengagement," February 15, 1984.

PAGE 2 OF 4

DECLASSIFIED

SECRET

E.O. 12356: DECL: OADR
TAGS: PREL, MOPS, SF, AO, US
SUBJECT: SOUTH AFRICANS AND ANGOLANS REACH AGREEMENT
ON MILITARY DISENGAGEMENT

1. SECRET - ENTIRE TEXT.

2. JOHANNESBURG PASS TO CHET CROCKER AT JAN SMUTS
DURING TRANSIT.

3. IN INTENSIVE TALKS OVER A TWENTY-FOUR HOUR PERIOD,
THE SOUTH AFRICANS AND ANGOLANS REACHED FULL AGREEMENT
IN LUSAKA ON FEBRUARY 14 ON A FRAMEWORK FOR THE
COMPLETION OF THE SADF'S WITHDRAWAL FROM SOUTHERN
ANGOLA AND FOR JOINT MONITORING OF THE AREA BOTH
DURING AND AFTER THAT WITHDRAWAL. (FULL TEXT OF THE
AGREED MINUTE IS IN PARA SEVEN.) THE NEGOTIATIONS
WERE HELD UNDER U.S. CHAIRMANSHIP AND LARGELY CONDUCTED
IN A PROXIMITY FORMAT WITH THE U.S. BROKERING POSITIONS.

4. BOTH SIDES CAME TO DEAL AND DEMONSTRATED SIGNIFICANT
FLEXIBILITY IN THE COURSE OF THE TALKS. BOTH SIDES WERE
WILLING TO GIVE UP TROUBLESOME POSITIONS WHEN IT BECAME
APPARENT THAT AGREEMENT WOULD BE HINDERED. IN PARTICULAR,
THE ANGOLANS IN EFFECT CONCEDED THAT ALL SADF UNITS WILL
NOT BE OUT OF ANGOLA UNTIL PERHAPS LATE MARCH; A FIRMLY
STRUCTURED JOINT MONITORING COMMISSION IS ESSENTIAL NOW
AND AFTER THE FINAL DEPARTURE OF SA TROOPS; AND
RIGOROUS RESTRAINT OF SWAPO BY LUANDA IS REQUIRED IF
THIS IS TO WORK. FOR THEIR PART, THE SOUTH AFRICANS
GAVE UP THEIR DEMAND FOR UNILATERAL MONITORING, I.E.
SECRET
SECRET

PAGE 03   STATE   045799

SADF RECCE UNITS OPERATING INDEPENDENTLY, AND THEIR
ASSERTION THAT A SIXTY DAY WITHDRAWAL SCHEDULE TO BEGIN
IN LATE FEBRUARY WOULD BE REQUIRED TO ASSURE THAT THE
ANGOLANS RESTRAIN SWAPO. THE SOUTH AFRICANS RAISED
THEIR CONCERN ABOUT SWAPO VIOLATIONS BUT DID NOT
HIGHLIGHT THE POINT EXCESSIVELY.

5. BOTH THE SOUTH AFRICANS AND THE ANGOLANS FAVOR A
SYMBOLIC, TOKEN U.S. PRESENCE -- THREE TO SIX PEOPLE --
TO BE ATTACHED TO THE JOINT COMMISSION. THEY DO NOT

SECRET

DECLASSIFIED

DOCUMENT 46: Secretary George Shultz, Cable for Secretary Caspar Weinberger, "South Africans and Angolans Reach Agreement on Military Disengagement," February 15, 1984.

DECLASSIFIED

SECRET

SEE THE NEED FOR AN ACTIVE U.S. ROLE: RATHER, THESE PEOPLE WOULD BE ESSENTIALLY OBSERVERS. BOTH SIDES APPEARED TO ACCEPT THAT A SECTOR BY SECTOR SA DISENGAGEMENT AND ANGOLAN REASSERTION OF AUTHORITY DURING A THIRTY DAY PERIOD MIGHT BE THE BEST PROCEDURE AS IT WOULD PREVENT THE CREATION OF VACUUMS IN THE AREA WHICH COULD BE EXPLOITED BY SWAPO.

6. THE SOUTH AFRICAN DELEGATION INCLUDED GENERAL GELDENHUYS, DAVID STEWART FROM DFA (WHO FUNCTIONED AS HEAD OF DELEGATION), BRIGADIER JOUBERT FROM SWA SECTOR TEN (OSHIKATI) AND NILS VON TONDER. THE ANGOLAN SIDE INCLUDED LT. COL. MONTEIRO (NGONGO), LT. COL. SEGUEIRA OF THE FIFTH MILITARY DISTRICT (LUBANGO) AND MAJOR ANTONIO JOSE MARIA FROM PRESIDENT DOS SANTOS' OFFICE. JOUBERT AND SEGUEIRA HAVE BEEN NAMED BY THEIR RESPECTIVE SIDES TO HEAD DELEGATIONS FOR JOINT MILITARY TALKS ON FEBRUARY 16 TO INNAUGURATE THE JOINT COMMISSION AND TO MAKE PRACTICAL ARRANGEMENTS FOR ITS ACTIVITIES.

7. FULL TEXT OF THE AGREED "MULUNGUSHI MINUTE."

BEGIN TEXT:
MULUNGUSHI MINUTE

SECRET
SECRET

PAGE 04   STATE 045799

-- BOTH SIDES AGREED THAT A JOINT SOUTH AFRICAN/ANGOLAN COMMISSION WILL BE CONSTITUTED AS SOON AS POSSIBLE TO MONITOR THE DISENGAGEMENT.

-- THE FIRST MEETING OF THAT COMMISSION WILL OCCUR IN LUSAKA ON FEBRUARY 16, 1984.

-- THE COMMISSION, WITH A PARITY OF FORCES FROM BOTH SIDES, WILL BE LOCATED AT NGIVA, A MUTUALLY AGREEABLE LOCATION WITHIN THE AREA IN QUESTION.

-- THE COMMISSION WILL BE EMPOWERED TO TRAVEL IN THE AREA IN QUESTION AS NECESSARY AT THE BEHEST OF EITHER OR BOTH OF THE PARTIES.

-- THE PURPOSE OF THE COMMISSION WILL BE TO MONITOR THE

SECRET

DECLASSIFIED

DOCUMENT 46: Secretary George Shultz, Cable for Secretary Caspar Weinberger, "South Africans and Angolans Reach Agreement on Military Disengagement," February 15, 1984.

PAGE 4 OF 4

DECLASSIFIED

SECRET

DISENGAGEMENT PROCESS AND TO DETECT, INVESTIGATE AND REPORT ON ANY ALLEGED VIOLATIONS.

-- ON THE DAY ON WHICH BOTH SIDES AGREE THAT THE COMMISSION IS IN OPERATION ON SITE, A THIRTY DAY PERIOD WILL COMMENCE WHICH WILL CONCLUDE WITH THE FINAL WITHDRAWAL OF ALL SOUTH AFRICAN FORCES FROM THE AREA IN QUESTION, ASIDE FROM THOSE ATTACHED TO THE COMMISSION AND ITS JOINT MONITORING TEAMS.

-- BOTH SIDES BELIEVE THAT A SYMBOLIC AMERICAN OBSERVER PRESENCE IN THE ACTIVITIES OF THE COMMISSION WOULD BE USEFUL.

-- THE ANGOLAN SIDE REITERATED ITS FIRM COMMITMENT TO RESTRAIN SWAPO AS THE PROCESS PROCEEDS, INCLUDING NO SWAPO OR CUBAN PRESENCE IN THE RECOVERED TERRITORY.
SECRET
SECRET

PAGE 05   STATE   048799

-- BOTH SIDES AGREED THAT THE DISENGAGEMENT PROCESS, INCLUDING THE SUCCESSFUL OPERATION OF THE JOINT COMMISSION, WOULD BE AN IMPORTANT STEP IN ESTABLISHING CONDITIONS LEADING TO THE PEACEFUL RESOLUTION OF THE PROBLEMS OF THE REGION INCLUDING THE QUESTION OF THE IMPLEMENTATION OF UNSC RESOLUTION 435.

FEBRUARY 14, 1984
LUSAKA, ZAMBIA
END TEXT.PLATT UNQUOTE SHULTZ

SECRET

DECLASSIFIED

DOCUMENT 47: Assistant Secretary Chester Crocker, Information Memorandum for Deputy
Secretary Kenneth Dam, "Update on the Southern Africa Negotiations," March 3, 1984.

PAGE 1 OF 2

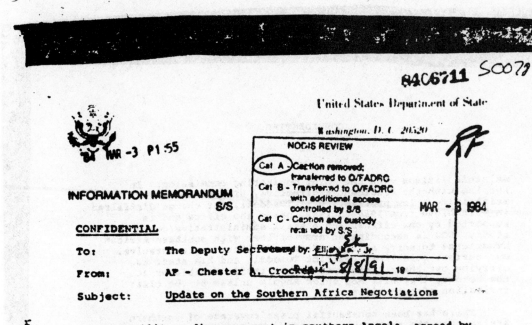

8406711 S0079

United States Department of State

Washington, D.C. 20520

NODIS REVIEW

Cat A - Caption removed:
transferred to O/FADRC
Cat B - Transferred to O/FADRC
with additional access
controlled by S/S
Cat C - Caption and custody
retained by S/S

MAR - 3 1984

INFORMATION MEMORANDUM
S/S

CONFIDENTIAL

To: The Deputy Secretary by: Elliot ___ Jr.

From: AF - Chester A. Crocker 8/8/91 19___

Subject: **Update on the Southern Africa Negotiations**

The military disengagement in southern Angola, agreed by
South Africa and Angola on February 16 in Lusaka, appears
to be taking hold. The first on-site meeting of the
Angolan/South African joint monitoring commission was held
February 25, with both sides contributing to serious business-
like talks. They agreed on the composition of the commission
and on the terms for its establishment in Cuvelai, in southern
Angola. The formal work of the commission was to have begun
March 1, but was delayed one day due to transportation
difficulties for the Angolans in reaching Cuvelai. Subsequent
meetings are to be held at progressively southerly locations,
in parallel with South African withdrawal until, with
completion of disengagement, hopefully by March 31, the
commission is finally sited on the Namibia/Angola border.

We have firmly established with both sides that the
disengagement is not an end in itself, but only a step along
the way to implementation of UNSCR 435. We have made clear
our own hope that the disengagment, if successful, will
create conditions (absence of South African forces on Angolan
territory and a credible mechanism to satisfy Angola of a
diminished threat to its territorial integrity) that will allow
Angola to take the step necessary -- agreement on Cuban
troop withdrawal -- to allow implementation of UNSCR 435
to proceed. If, in our bilateral talks with them, the Angolans
are prepared to take that necessary step, we would hope to
be able to move directly from the disengagement into the
UN-supervised ceasefire that would launch the UNSCR 435
period of transition to Namibian independence.

In order that we can be in a position to play the
facilitative role envisaged for us in the Lusaka disengagement
agreement, we have established in Windhoek a small office to

CONFIDENTIAL
OADR

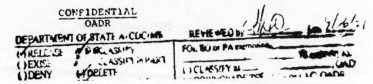

DEPARTMENT OF STATE A/CDC/MR

( ) RELEASE   ( ) DECLASSIFY
( ) EXCISE   ( ) CLASSIFY in PART
( ) DENY   ( ) DELETE

REVIEWED by ___

FOI, EO or PA exemptions ___

( ) CLASSIFY as ___

DOCUMENT 47: Assistant Secretary Chester Crocker, Information Memorandum for Deputy Secretary Kenneth Dam, "Update on the Southern Africa Negotiations," March 3, 1984.

PAGE 2 OF 2

CONFIDENTIAL

-2-

maintain liaison with the joint monitoring commission. In keeping with the President's directive, USLO Windhoek is maintaining a low profile. Bill Twaddell, our charge d'affaires in Mozambique from 1980 to 1983, heads the office and is supported by one officer and a small administrative/communications staff. DOD is seconding an army officer with southern African experience to serve as the office's military representative. Our current guidelines restrict Twaddell and his staff to carrying out their liaison functions inside Namibia or at the border; they will not enter Angola unless at the clear invitation of both sides.

There has been substantial press coverage of southern Africa over the past several weeks. We are holding to the general line that while progress has been made, the road ahead is long and tough, with key issues remaining to be resolved. The conservative press and several conservative political organizations have begun to target our policy, predicting a sell-out of UNITA, early recognition of Marxist Angola, and a general softening of our position, especially on Cuban withdrawal. We are repeating our basic line: our goal is peace in the region, acceptable to all parties, which undercuts Soviet influence. No agreement has been reached on the Cuban issue; recognition will only take place in the context of a package deal.

AF/S:PReams
3/3/84, x8252

Clearances:AF:FGWisner
AF/S:DPassage

CONFIDENTIAL

DOCUMENT 48: Ambassador Frank Wisner, Information Memorandum for Secretary George Shultz, "Suspension of the U.S. Liaison Office in Namibia," February 7, 1986.

PAGE 1 OF 3

P85 20SD- 279 ⋯ ⋯ United States Department of State

Washington, D.C. ⋯⋯⋯

EXGIS

INFORMATION MEMORANDUM S/S⋯

SECRET

FB - 7 1986

TO: The Secretary

THROUGH: P - Michael Armacost MAS

FROM: AF - Frank G. Wisner, Acting

SUBJECT: Suspension of the U.S. Liaison Office in Namibia

       With Undersecretary Armacost's authorization, we decided that we should suspend operations at the U.S. Liaison Office (USLO) in Windhoek, Namibia, effective February 15. This follows a detailed assessment, including extensive consultations with the posts concerned. We intend to notify the South Africans and the Angolans immediately and will make a public statement concerning the suspension immediately thereafter.

       The Liaison Office was established in February 1984 to support the symbolic U.S. observer role provided for under the U.S.-brokered Lusaka Agreement of last January between Angola and South Africa. The Lusaka Agreement has been an important success in two major respects: it produced an end to the violence between South Africa and Angola, and it built confidence for the breakthrough in the negotiations last fall, when we began discussing concrete proposals, including Cuban troop withdrawal. However, the full disengagement of South African forces has not been completed and they, with the JMC, remain 25 miles north of the Namibian border inside Angola. JMC meetings at the border, which would have allowed direct US participation, have not taken place.

       As long as there was a realistic chance for early completion of the disengagement, the office served as a link to the South African military and as a symbol of U.S. commitment. In recent months, however, it has become increasingly apparent that early completion is unlikely. ⌐

                                                                    ⌐

                                                                    ⌐

SECRET
DECL: OADR

BIAS

DOCUMENT 48: Ambassador Frank Wisner, Information Memorandum for Secretary George Shultz, "Suspension of the U.S. Liaison Office in Namibia," February 7, 1986.

PAGE 2 OF 3

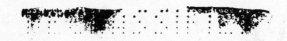

SECRET

-2-

BIAS

Moreover, the existence of USLO has begun to draw fire from some African and congressional critics of our policy, who claim it lends legitimacy to South African rule in Namibia. Despite our strong defense of USLO in the U.N., USLO was condemned in a recent resolution, which Angola supported.

BIAS

There is little to be gained by continuing USLO's operations in present circumstances, but the U.S. can leave without apology. The disengagement has already achieved two major goals -- ending the violence between the SAG and the MPLA and creating conditions for progress in the negotiations. We are thus in a strong position to defend our contribution and the results of our effort so far, without resort to finger-pointing. Moreover, there is every prospect that advances in the overall peace process will make possible completion of the disengagement. For that reason, the operation in Windhoek would be suspended, not terminated, and office facilities retained, so that we could quickly resume operations once the disengagement moves to the border. Meanwhile, we will continue to monitor developments in the disengagement through embassy Pretoria.

In our public posture, we need make no apology. Our announcement will stress our pride in the major contributions of the disengagement to bringing peace to southern Africa. We will recall that this incurred tragic costs: the killings of the USLO Director, FSO Dennis Keogh, and military representative Lt. Col. Kenneth Crabtree in May 1984. We will explain that, while the present need for monitoring doesn't justify keeping USLO operational, we are retaining facilities in Windhoek, so as to keep open the possibility of reactivating the office when the disengagement is completed -- and we fully expect that it will be completed as the peace process unfolds.

SECRET

DOCUMENT 48: Ambassador Frank Wisner, Information Memorandum for Secretary George Shultz, "Suspension of the U.S. Liaison Office in Namibia," February 7, 1986.

UNCLASSIFIED

Drafted: AF/SirPerany...
2/6/85 x9641 WANG 1545A

Clearances:
AF/Bishmith...
AV/FWisner
P/MHannoto...

~~SECRET~~   17

**INTERNATIONAL
SECURITY AFFAIRS**

THE ASSISTANT SECRETARY OF DEFENSE

WASHINGTON, D C 20301-2400

19 SEP 1985

In reply refer to:
I-20669/85

MEMORANDUM FOR THE SECRETARY OF DEFENSE

   THROUGH THE UNDER SECRETARY OF DEFENSE FOR POLICY $\mathcal{FI}$ ·19 SEP 1985

SUBJECT: Your Call on President and Field Marshal Samora
          Machel of Mozambique (U) - INFORMATION MEMORANDUM

(∅) DATE, TIME, AND PLACE: Friday, September 20; 1530-1600;
Presidential Suite (rooms 1213-1214), Vista International Hotel,
1400 M Street NW (429-1700, direct line 466-4374 or 466-5298).

(U) PARTICIPANTS: Secretary Weinberger, MGen Powell, Mr.
Armitage, LTC McConnell (notetaker).

(U) PURPOSE: This courtesy call on President Machel will add
importance to Machel's 18-20 September State visit, and provide
you an opportunity to personally assess this controversial head
of state and to emphasize to him the Administration's goals in
southern Africa.

(∅) ISSUE: Administration policy toward Mozambique is under
challenge from conservative elements, both elected and private.
Under the regional policy of "Constructive Engagement," the
Administration's specific objectives toward Mozambique are to
replace Soviet influence with our own, to reduce regional
violence vis a vis South Africa, and to induce Machel's FRELIMO
Government to enter into substantive negotiations with the very
active RENAMO insurgents. Machel is a self-avowed Marxist who
has relied almost exclusively on the Soviets for arms; RENAMO
states it is an anticommunist movement although it has made no
clear statement of its proposed political structure. These
characterizations - Marxist vs anticommunist movement - form the
basis of the Administration's policy difficulties, with
conservatives vigorously objecting to assistance to FRELIMO, and
some proposing instead assistance to RENAMO.

Most recently the Congress has denied the Administration's
request for modest ($1.15M in FY85, $3.15M in FY86) nonlethal
military assistance. The FY86 ESF ($15M for agriculture) was
also under serious congressional fire but has thus far survived.

              State's
~~Administration~~)objectives for the Machel visit are:

   -Improve the FRELIMO government image in conservative
    congressional eyes

LTC McConnell, ISA/Africa, x79755 ~~SECRET~~

DECLASSIFIED BY AUTHORITY OF
ASD(ISA) AFR
20Dec91   *91-FOI-1204*
  DATE   **CASE #**

DOCUMENT 49: Information Memorandum for Secretary Caspar Weinberger, "Your Call on President and Field Marshal Samora Machel of Mozambique," September 19, 1985.

PAGE 2 OF 3

~~SECRET~~

-Encourage continued adherence to the U.S.-brokered Nkomati Accord with South Africa, which specifies non-interference in the other's internal affairs (Mozambican support of the ANC; South African support of RENAMO);

-Encourage FRELIMO to negotiate power sharing with RENAMO;

-Seek FRELIMO cooperation in achieving an Angola/Namibia settlement;

-Achieve a renewed CIA liaison presence;

-Press FRELIMO toward serious economic reform and greater cooperation with the IMF and World Bank; and

-Moderate Mozambique's anti-U.S. votes in the United Nations

Internally, Mozambique's situation is bleak. Although firmly in charge of the government, Machel faces an economy that is in shambles and an insurgent group that essentially operates at will outside the cities. State sees - and we agree - his objectives for the visit as:

-"Establish Mozambique on the U.S. political map and reduce conservative criticism.

-"Increased economic and military assistance.

-"Increased private investment.

-"Frank review of internal developments in South Africa."

(§) <u>OBJECTIVES:</u> Your objectives for the meeting should be to:

-Emphasize your personal support of the regional policy of Constructive Engagement;

-Express satisfaction with Mozambique's continued adherance to the Nkomati Accord;

-Stress that meaningful negotiation with RENAMO is, in our view, the only possible and lasting solution to Mozambique's internal problems;

-Reiterate the Administration's intent to provide some security assistance. Caution him that Congressional acceptance of this initiative will only come if there is concrete movement away from the Soviets and Marxist principles, real economic reform, and genuine efforts to allow political expression for all factions in Mozambique;

~~SECRET~~

DOCUMENT 49: Information Memorandum for Secretary Caspar Weinberger, "Your Call on President and Field Marshal Samora Machel of Mozambique," September 19, 1985.

PAGE 3 OF 3

~~SECRET~~

-Thank him for his recent agreement to the accreditation of a resident Defense Attache, which we regard as an important channel of information and communication on defense matters.

(U) President Machel's biography is at the Bio Tab. A talking paper and supporting background is at the Talker Tab.

Phil

My advice is just listen to him – The Administration needs to review this whole issue. I'm not sure that the President isn't getting sold a bill of goods with this guy.

I agree, we need to review our Mozambique policy. Fred.

DOCUMENT 50: Secretary George Shultz, Cable for All African Diplomatic Posts, "Southern Africa: What About Change in South Africa and What Happens to the ANC?" April 14, 1984.

PAGE 1 OF 11

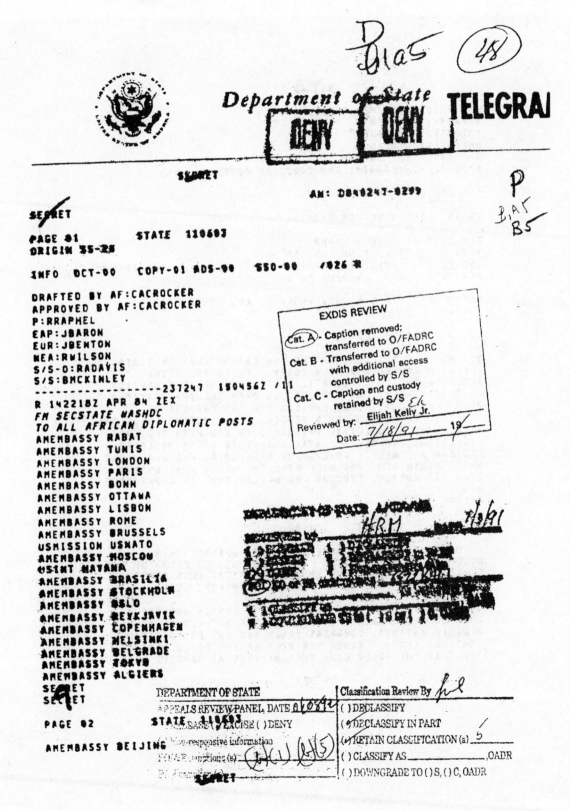

SECRET

AN: D840247-0299

SECRET

PAGE 01   STATE 110693
ORIGIN SS-25

INFO OCT-00   COPY-01 ADS-00   SSO-00   /026 R

DRAFTED BY AF:CACROCKER
APPROVED BY AF:CACROCKER
P:RRAPHEL
EAP:JBARON
EUR:JBENTON
NEA:RWILSON
S/S-O:RADAVIS
S/S:BMCKINLEY
----------------237247 150456Z /11

R 142218Z APR 84 ZEX
FM SECSTATE WASHDC
TO ALL AFRICAN DIPLOMATIC POSTS
AMEMBASSY RABAT
AMEMBASSY TUNIS
AMEMBASSY LONDON
AMEMBASSY PARIS
AMEMBASSY BONN
AMEMBASSY OTTAWA
AMEMBASSY LISBON
AMEMBASSY ROME
AMEMBASSY BRUSSELS
USMISSION USNATO
AMEMBASSY MOSCOW
USINT HAVANA
AMEMBASSY BRASILIA
AMEMBASSY STOCKHOLM
AMEMBASSY OSLO
AMEMBASSY REYKJAVIK
AMEMBASSY COPENHAGEN
AMEMBASSY HELSINKI
AMEMBASSY BELGRADE
AMEMBASSY TOKYO
AMEMBASSY ALGIERS
SECRET
SECRET

PAGE 02   STATE 110693

AMEMBASSY BEIJING

EXDIS REVIEW

Cat. A - Caption removed; transferred to O/FADRC
Cat. B - Transferred to O/FADRC with additional access controlled by S/S
Cat. C - Caption and custody retained by S/S

Reviewed by: Elijah Kelly Jr.
Date: 7/18/91   19

DEPARTMENT OF STATE
APPEALS REVIEW PANEL DATE
Non-responsive information

Classification Review By
( ) DECLASSIFY
( ) DECLASSIFY IN PART
( ) RETAIN CLASSIFICATION (a)
( ) CLASSIFY AS _____, OADR
( ) DOWNGRADE TO ( ) S, ( ) C, OADR

DOCUMENT 50: Secretary George Shultz, Cable for All African Diplomatic Posts, "Southern Africa: What About Change in South Africa and What Happens to the ANC?" April 14, 1984.

PAGE 2 OF 11

SECRET

USMISSION USUN NEW YORK
AMEMBASSY CANBERRA
AMEMBASSY BUCHAREST
AMEMBASSY BERLIN
AMEMBASSY THE HAGUE
INFO ALL DIPLOMATIC AND CONSULAR POSTS

S E C R E T STATE 110603

EXDIS USEC ALSO FOR EMBASSY

E.O. 12356 DECL: OADR
TAGS: PREL, PINS, US, SF
SUBJECT: SOUTHERN AFRICA: WHAT ABOUT CHANGE IN SOUTH
AFRICA AND WHAT HAPPENS TO THE ANC?

REFS: (A) STATE 077356 (NOTAL), (B) STATE 105303
(NOTAL)

1. S - ENTIRE TEXT.

2. REFTELS SET SOME OF THE CONTEXT OF WHAT IS TAKING
PLACE IN SOUTHERN AFRICA TODAY. (REFS ARE BEING
REPEATED TO ALL DIPLOMATIC POSTS.) A MAJOR DIMENSION
OF THAT CONTEXT, HOWEVER, IS TO DRAW THE IMPLICATIONS
OF THE REGIONAL PEACE PROCESS FOR THE PROCESS OF
DOMESTIC CHANGE IN SOUTH AFRICA. IN A NUTSHELL, WE ARE
WITNESSING A POTENTIAL WATERSHED IN SOUTHERN AFRICA'S
EVOLUTION. THERE IS A REAL RISK THAT MEDIA OBSERVERS,
AFRICAN AND ALLIED GOVERNMENT OFFICIALS, AND BLACK AND
WHITE SOUTH AFRICANS WILL DRAW THE WRONG CONCLUSIONS
FROM THE CURRENT PROCESS AND DECIDE THAT IT REPRESENTS
SECRET
SECRET

PAGE 03   STATE 110603

A POSTPONEMENT OF CHANGE AWAY FROM APARTHEID; A
SELL-OUT BY THE AFRICAN FRONT LINE STATES (FLS) OF THE
BLACK AFRICAN MAJORITY IN SOUTH AFRICA; LESS PRESSURE
ON THE SOUTH AFRICAN SYSTEM AND THEREFORE LESS

OPPORTUNITY FOR THOSE INSIDE SOUTH AFRICA WHO ARE
WORKING FOR CHANGE; AND FINALLY THE EXTINCTION OF THE
AFRICAN NATIONAL CONGRESS (ANC) AND THE PAN-AFRICAN
CONGRESS (PAC). GIVEN OUR ROLE IN THE PEACE PROCESS,
THERE IS THE ADDED RISK THAT WE WILL BE SADDLED WITH

SECRET

DOCUMENT 50: Secretary George Shultz, Cable for All African Diplomatic Posts, "Southern Africa: What About Change in South Africa and What Happens to the ANC?" April 14, 1984.

PAGE 3 OF 11

SECRET

ALLEGATIONS OF COLLUSION WITH SOUTH AFRICA TOWARD THESE ENDS. CERTAINLY THESE DISTORTIONS ARE THE MESSAGE OF SOVIET/PROXY AGITPROP IN RECENT WEEKS. THEY ARE FINDING AN ECHO IN AFRICAN DIPLOMATIC CIRCLES AND MAINSTREAM WESTERN MEDIA. IN LIGHT OF UPCOMING FLS, LUSOPHONE AND OAU MEETINGS, AS WELL AS GENERALLY HEIGHTENED INTERNATIONAL SCRUTINY OF THE REGION, IT IS CENTRAL THAT ADDRESSEES BE ARMED WITH WASHINGTON'S PERSPECTIVE AND EQUIPPED TO GET OUR MESSAGE ACROSS IN THE RIGHT CHANNELS. AFRICAN ADDRESSEES SHOULD GIVE THOUGHT TO THOSE CHANNELS AND TO MEANS FOR COMBATTING, REACTIVELY OR PRE-EMPTIVELY, ADVERSE MEDIA THEMES AND GOVERNMENT ATTITUDES WITH THE ANALYSIS IN THE PARAGRAPHS BELOW.

3. FIRST, IT IS A FACT THAT THE NOTION OF "ARMED STRUGGLE" AS THE SOLUTION TO SOUTH AFRICA'S APARTHEID SYSTEM HAS BEEN DEALT A SEVERE BLOW BY EVENTS OF THE PAST MONTHS. THE MARCH 16 NKOMATI PACT OF NON-AGGRESSION BETWEEN MOZAMBIQUE AND SOUTH AFRICA IS THE PROMINENT SYMBOL OF A BROADER PROCESS. ON MARCH 31, SOUTH AFRICA AND SWAZILAND ANNOUNCED PUBLICLY THAT THEY HAD PREVIOUSLY CONCLUDED A SIMILAR PACT. LATE LAST YEAR, SOUTH AFRICA SUCCESSFULLY PRESSED LESOTHO TO EXPEL CERTAIN ANC FIGURES. LESOTHO AND SOUTH AFRICA MAY BE HEADED TOWARD A FORMAL AGREEMENT ON MUTUAL PREVENTION OF GUERRILLA ACTIVITY FROM EACH OTHER'S
SECRET
SECRET

PAGE 04   STATE 110982

TERRITORY OR THE EQUIVALENT IN INFORMAL ARRANGEMENTS.

BIA

[   ] WE ARE WITNESSING THE ATTEMPTED ELABORATION OF CERTAIN GROUND-RULES OF CO-EXISTENCE IN SOUTHERN AFRICA AMONG THE GOVERNMENTS THERE. GUERRILLA GROUPS HAVE NOT BEEN DIRECT PARTICIPANTS IN THIS PROCESS AND COULD, IN ONE SENSE, BE ITS VICTIMS.

4. SECOND, HOWEVER, THERE IS NOTHING TERRIBLY NEW

SECRET

DOCUMENT 50: Secretary George Shultz, Cable for All African Diplomatic Posts, "Southern Africa: What About Change in South Africa and What Happens to the ANC?" April 14, 1984.

PAGE 4 OF 11

SECRET

ABOUT SECURITY DIALOGUES BETWEEN SOUTH AFRICA AND ITS
NEIGHBORS. MALAWI HAS LONG ESPOUSED A DOCTRINE OF
DIALOGUE RATHER THAN CONFRONTATION WITH SOUTH AFRICA
AND HAS MAINTAINED OVERT DIPLOMATIC RELATIONS.
TRADITIONALLY, BOTSWANA, LESOTHO AND SWAZILAND HAVE
EVOLVED TACIT GROUND-RULES FOR LIVING WITH THEIR
DOMINANT NEIGHBOR. SINCE ITS INDEPENDENCE, ZIMBABWE
HAS ESPOUSED A POLICY WHICH IN PRACTICE IS NOT AT ALL
UNLIKE THE NKOMATI PACT - POLITICAL/DIPLOMATIC SUPPORT
FOR THE ANC AND FOR THE PRINCIPLE OF BASIC CHANGE
TOWARD MAJORITY RULE COMBINED WITH A COMMITMENT TO
PREVENT VIOLENT ACTIONS AGAINST SOUTH AFRICA FROM ITS
TERRITORY. WITH STARTS AND STOPS, ZAMBIA HAS EVOLVED
TOWARDS A DELICATELY BALANCED BLEND OF LINKS WITH THE
ANC AND THE SAG THAT TODAY CAN ONLY BE TERMED A FORMULA
FOR CO-EXISTENCE. LIKE MOZAMBIQUE, EACH OF THESE
GOVERNMENTS HAS ALTERNATIVES TO CO-EXISTENCE AND
SECRET
SECRET

PAGE 05   STATE 110603

DIALOGUE WITH SOUTH AFRICA. THEY COULD HAVE CHOSEN THE
COURSE OF CONFRONTATION (SEVERAL DABBLED WITH THIS
COURSE AND THE EXTERNAL ALLIANCES INVOLVED) BUT HAVE
OPTED DIFFERENTLY AFTER CAREFULLY CALCULATING THE ODDS
AND ASSESSING NATIONAL INTERESTS.

5. WHAT IS NEW IS THE INCLUSION OF MOZAMBIQUE, A
CLEARLY MARXIST-ORIENTED AND SOVIET-ALIGNED STATE UNTIL
NOW, IN THIS PROCESS AND THE EMERGENCE OF FORMAL,
WRITTEN AGREEMENTS AS THE VEHICLE FOR RECORDING
PRACTICAL SECURITY ARRANGMENTS BETWEEN NEIGHBORS.
MOZAMBIQUE, ACCORDING TO SOME REPORTS, ACCOUNTED FOR AS
MUCH AS 90 PERCENT OF CROSS-BORDER OPERATIONS AGAINST
SOUTH AFRICA. IF IMPLEMENTED, THE NKOMATI PACT WILL
DEPRIVE GUERRILLA STRATEGISTS OF THEIR BEST
INFILTRATION ZONES AND PLACE THEM IN THE POSITION OF
SEEKING ALTERNATIVE ROUTES, MOUNTING PRESSURE ON HOST
GOVERNMENTS TO REVERSE RECENT DECISIONS, OR CONSIDERING
A WHOLLY NEW STRATEGY FOR PURSUIT OF THEIR GOALS. AS
FOR THE FORMALIZING OF DETENTE, THIS TREND TENDS TO
REDUCE SOUTH AFRICA'S PARIAH STATUS. BUT IT HAS OTHER
CONSEQUENCES OF NOTE. IT UNDERSCORES THE LEGITIMACY
AND SANCTITY OF BORDERS IN THE REGION - AN OAU DOCTRINE
OF CARDINAL IMPORTANCE AND ONE THAT OBVIOUSLY CUTS BOTH
WAYS. THE PRINCIPLE OF RECIPROCITY IS ENTRENCHED IN

SECRET

Document 50: Secretary George Shultz, Cable for All African Diplomatic Posts, "Southern Africa: What About Change in South Africa and What Happens to the ANC?" April 14, 1984.

PAGE 5 OF 11

SECRET

THE MOZAMBICAN-SOUTH AFRICAN UNDERSTANDINGS AND THIS IN
ITSELF REPRESENTS A VICTORY - NOT A DEFEAT FOR AFRICAN
DIPLOMACY. THESE FACTS, IN OTHER WORDS, CAN SERVE NOT
ONLY AS INSTRUMENTS FOR RESTRAINT OF ANC/PAC VIOLENCE
BUT ALSO AS INSTRUMENTS FOR COUNTERING SOUTH
AFRICAN-SUPPORTED GUERRILLA MOVEMENTS DIRECTED AT
NEIGHBORING COUNTRIES. NKOMATI, IN SUM, MAY BE A
WATERSHED FOR THE ANC BUT MAY ALSO BE A WATERSHED IN
THE UNHAPPY RECORD OF SOUTH AFRICAN DESTABILIZATION
EFFORTS IN THE REGION. THAT, AT LEAST, IS THE US
APPROACH TO THE WHOLE PROCESS.
SECRET
SECRET

PAGE 06   STATE   110603

6.   THIRD, ARMED STRUGGLE AGAINST SOUTH AFRICA FROM
OUTSIDE ITS BORDERS WAS NEVER A VIABLE STRATEGY. THE
ARMED STRUGGLE MYSTIQUE EMBODIED IN LIBERATIONIST
THEOLOGY IS PERHAPS NOWHERE LESS RELEVANT TO THE FACTS
OF GEOGRAPHY AND POWER THAN IN SOUTHERN AFRICA. WE
RECOGNIZE THAT THE CONCEPTS OF ARMED NATIONAL
LIBERATION STRUGGLE SWEEPING DOWN THE CONTINENT UNTIL
ALL COLONIES ARE FREE AND SOUTH AFRICA BECOMES AZANIA
HAS BEEN A MAINSTAY OF THE AFRICAN RHETORICAL LEXICON.
THE DECOLONIZING EXPERIENCE OF RHODESIA AND PORTUGUESE
AFRICA ADDED SOME TEMPORARY CREDIBILITY TO THIS IDEA,
AND THE MORE CANDID AMONG OUR SOUTHERN AFRICAN
INTERLOCUTORS TODAY QUIETLY ADMIT THAT THEY WERE TAKEN
WITH THE JUGGERNAUT THEORY OF AFRICAN LIBERATION. BUT
THESE CONCEPTS OR CLICHES OF LIBERATION NEVER MADE
SENSE IN SOUTH AFRICA'S CASE. THE STRENGTH AND
DETERMINATION OF THE WHITE SOUTH AFRICAN ESTABLISHMENT,
INCLUDING ITS ECONMIC RESOURCES AND SECURITY APPARATUS,
REMAIN LITERALLY AWESOME IN REGIONAL TERMS. IF
ANYTHING, SOUTH AFRICA'S HEIGHTENED ISOLATION, ITS
CONFRONTATION WITH NEIGHBORS AND ITS SUSTAINED PROGRAM
OF ARMAMENT AND MOBILIZATION SINCE 1975 HAVE ONLY
INCREASED THE POWER DISPARITY. THE FLS PERFORMANCE
WITH OR WITHOUT SOVIET/PROXY ASSISTANCE - HAS NOT IN
ANY MEANINGFUL SENSE PRODUCED AN INDIGENEOUS REGIONAL
BALANCE OF POWER. IN SUM, THE DOCTRINE OF
EXTERNALLY-BASED ARMED STRUGGLE APPLIED TO SOUTH AFRICA
IS A FORMULA FOR THE DESTRUCTION OF SOUTH AFRICA'S
NEIGHBORS. IT ALSO IMPLIES THE POLARIZATION OF THE
REGION INTO HOSTILE CAMPS WITH DANGEROUS GLOBAL

SECRET

DOCUMENT 50: Secretary George Shultz, Cable for All African Diplomatic Posts, "Southern Africa: What About Change in South Africa and What Happens to the ANC?" April 14, 1984.

PAGE 6 OF 11

SECRET

IMPLICATIONS AND THE DIVERSION OF SOUTH AFRICAN ENERGIES INTO THE COUNTER-MYSTIQUE OF DEFENDING AGAINST

SECRET

SECRET

PAGE 07   STATE 110603

THE "TOTAL MARXIST ONSLAUGHT". IT PROMISED THE OPPOSITE OF ECONOMIC PROGRESS TO THE PEOPLES AND GOVERNMENT ALONG SOUTH AFRICA'S BORDERS, SEVERAL OF WHOM HAD FOUGHT HARD FOR A BETTER FUTURE.

7. FOURTH, IT IS CLEAR THAT THESE CONCLUSIONS ARE NOT OURS ALONE. AFTER SEVERAL YEARS OF PURSUING POLICIES OF POLARIZATION, CONFRONTATION AND DESTABILIZATION, SOUTH AFRICA AND ITS NEIGHBORS ARE EXPLORING THE DIPLOMACY OF REALISM. THAT ROAD IS NOT A ONE-WAY STREET, BUT A POTENTIAL HIGHWAY OF MUTUAL BENEFIT. AT NKOMATI, PRETORIA AND MAPUTO DID MORE THAN AGREE TO CONTROL THE GUERRILLAS EACH HAD MAINTAINED AND

TARGETTED OR ALLOWED TO MOVE ACROSS THEIR COMMON BORDER. THEY SET THE STAGE FOR A WIDE RANGE OF ADDITIONAL TIES THAT COULD EXPAND INTO A COOPERATIVE WEB WITH BENEFITS ON ALL SIDES. THE FLS AND OTHER NEIGHBORS OF SOUTH AFRICA HAVE SEVERAL KINDS OF LEVERAGE IN THESE RELATIONSHIPS: (A) THEY CAN REDUCE SOUTH AFRICA'S ISOLATION AND EXPAND ITS LEGITIMACY REGIONALLY AND INTERNATIONALLY; (B) THEY OFFER MARKETS, INFRASTRUCTURE LINKS, LABOR, TOURIST OUTLETS, ENERGY SOURCES, INTELLIGENCE TIES AND A HOST OF POSSIBILITIES FOR THE PEACEFUL PROJECTION OF SOUTH AFRICAN INFLUENCE - THINGS A PARIAH SOCIETY AND A DYNAMIC ECONOMY CRAVE; (C) THEY CAN POTENTIALLY IMPORT AND ABSORB LARGE AMOUNTS OF SOUTH AFRICAN CAPITAL, KNOW-HOW AND EXPERTISE, THUS ENABLING SOUTH AFRICA'S REGIONAL DOMINANCE TO ACQUIRE A LEGITIMATE FORM. CLEARLY, THAT WHICH CAN BE OFFERED TO SOUTH AFRICA CAN ALSO BE DENIED; THIS IS THE ESSENCE OF INFLUENCE. SIMILARLY, SUCH RELATIONSHIPS STRIPPED OF SOME OF THEIR PAST TABOOS CAN HAVE PROFOUND POLITICAL AND PSYCHOLOGICAL CONSEQUENCES. THE CURRENT PEACE PROCESS IS A JOLT TO EVERYONE'S SYSTEM IN THE REGION AND BEYOND. IT IS NOT

SECRET

SECRET

PAGE 08   STATE 110603

SECRET

DOCUMENT 50: Secretary George Shultz, Cable for All African Diplomatic Posts, "Southern Africa: What About Change in South Africa and What Happens to the ANC?" April 14, 1984.

SECRET

NOW AND NEED NOT BECOME A ONE-SIDED HUMILIATION. IF AFRICAN SENTIMENT IN THE FLS AND MORE BROADLY IS OBLIGED TO SHED THE MYSTIQUE OF ARMED STRUGGLE, SO TOO WILL WHITE SOUTH AFRICAN LEADERS AND OPINION-SHAPERS FIND IT FAR MORE DIFFICULT TO SUSTAIN THE SELF-GENERATED ILLUSIONS AND STEROTYPES OF THE "TOTAL ONSLAUGHT" WITH AN ENEMY DUBBED "MARXIST" BUT IN PRACTICE SUBSTANTIALLY AFRICAN AND NATIONALIST. "ARMED STRUGGLE" AND "TOTAL ONSLAUGHT" ARE MIRROR IMAGES OF EACH OTHER, SELF-DEFEATING CLICHES THAT SERVE ONLY TO DIVERT ENERGY AND ATTENTION FROM THE PRACTICAL AGENDAS OF CHANGE AND CO-EXISTENCE. HENCE, THE CURRENT PEACE PROCESS IN FACT CONTAINS THE SEEDS NOT ONLY OF STRENGTHENED REGIONAL SECURITY BUT ALSO EXPANDED ECONOMIC PROGRESS AND REDUCED POLITICAL POLARIZATION IN THE REGION AND IN SOUTH AFRICA ITSELF.

8. FIFTH, THERE IS NO REASON WHATEVER TO SUPPOSE THAT THIS PROCESS WILL POSTPONE CHANGE INSIDE SOUTH AFRICA OR IS AT THE EXPENSE OF BLACK SOUTH AFRICANS. IN FACT, ONE CAN ARGUE THAT THE "ARMED STRUGGLE"/"TOTAL ONSLAUGHT" PHASE HAS ENABLED WHITES TO DUCK MANY OF THE IMPERATIVES OF CHANGE. AS LONG AS WHITE SOUTH AFRICA DEFINES ITSELF AS AT WAR WITH THE ENTIRE NEIGHBORHOOD, THE STRESS IS PLACED ON MILITITARIZATION OF SOCIETY, GIRDING OF THE SOUTH AFRICAN DEFENSE FORCE'S (SADF) NOW HEFTY LOINS AND THE SUPERVISION BY SOUTH AFRICA'S

SUBSTANTIAL SECURITY APPARATUS OF ALL ELEMENTS OF POLICY - "TOTAL STRATEGY". A PHRASE BORROWED FROM THE LEXICON OF FRANCE'S GENERALS DURING THE FOURTH REPUBLIC.

9. BY CONTRAST, THE NKOMATI PACT SIGNALS AND
SECRET
SECRET

PAGE 09   STATE 110503

LEGITIMIZES THE POTENTIAL FOR BLACK AND WHITE TO DO BUSINESS, TO CUT DEALS, TO NEGOTIATE. IF PRETORIA CAN DO THIS WITH NEIGHBORING STATES AND SELL IT AT HOME, IT BECOMES INCONSISTENT AND ARTIFICIAL TO MAINTAIN THAT THERE CAN BE NO NEGOTIATION BETWEEN BLACK AND WHITE SOUTH AFRICANS AT HOME. IN FACT, OF COURSE, THE NEW CONSTITUTION IN SOUTH AFRICA ALREADY REPRESENTS A BEGINNING HERE: THE WHITE AND BROWN NEGOTIATION THAT

SECRET

DOCUMENT 50: Secretary George Shultz, Cable for All African Diplomatic Posts, "Southern Africa: What About Change in South Africa and What Happens to the ANC?" April 14, 1984.

PAGE 8 OF 11

SECRET

HAS ALREADY OCCURRED OVER THAT CONSTITUTION IS BUT AN OPENING OF THE WEDGE. MOREOVER, IN A REGIONAL ATMOSPHERE OF SECURITY PACTS AND CROSS-BORDER COOPERATION, THERE IS A NEW POTENTIAL ROLE FOR NEIGHBORING STATES. IF THEY CHOOSE TO RISE TO THE CHALLENGE, THE FLS COULD LAUNCH THEIR OWN EFFORTS TO FOSTER DIALOGUE AND NEGOTIATION WITHIN SOUTH AFRICA. AS LINKS AND CONTACTS GROW, THERE WILL BE MANY OPENINGS FOR DISCREET TRIAL BALLOONS, PROBES AND SIGNALS THAT COULD MOVE THINGS FORWARD IN SOUTH AFRICA. SUCH OPENINGS MULTIPLY IN A REGIONAL CLIMATE OF DETENTE.

10.   SIXTH, AND PERHAPS MOST TELLING, SOUTH AFRICA IS TODAY A CHANGING SOCIETY, AND THE PRINCIPAL DYNAMICS OF THAT CHANGE ARE INDEED INTERNAL. THE GOVERNMENTAL SYSTEM REMAINS WEDDED OFFICIALLY AND PRACTICALLY TO A MODEL THAT EXCLUDES THE BLACK AFRICAN MAJORITY FROM THE NATIONAL POLITICAL ARENA. THAT IS WHAT GRAND APARTHEID MEANS - DENIAL OF THE VOTE AND OF CITIZENSHIP IN A UNITARY SOUTH AFRICA, DENIAL OF FREEDOM OF MOVEMENT, RIGID INFLUX CONTROL, RESIDENTIAL SEGREGATION BY RACE, "PROVISION" FOR BLACK POLITICAL RIGHTS SOLELY IN THE CONTEXT OF TRIBAL HOMELANDS, AND SO FORTH. HOWEVER, THE SYSTEM DOES NOT OPERATE IN A VACUUM. SOCIAL, ECONOMIC AND POLITICAL DYNAMICS HAVE PRODUCED DRAMATIC CHANGES IN THE FIELD OF LABOR LAW IN RECENT YEARS; TODAY, THE TRADE UNION MOVEMENT IS PERHAPS THE MOST ACTIVE ARENA FOR BLACK ORGANIZATION AND COMPETITIVE SECRET

SECRET

PAGE 10   STATE 110583

POLITICS IN SOUTH AFRICA. SIGNIFICANT DEVELOPMENTS, SOME OF THEM POSITIVE, ARE OCCURRING IN THE FIELDS OF SECURITY POLICY AND PRACTICES, BLACK EDUCATION AND BLACK URBAN HOUSING. THERE IS FERMENT OVER THE FUTURE THROUGHOUT THE CULTURAL, POLITICAL AND RELIGIOUS ORGANS OF AFRIKANERDOM. THE SOUTH AFRICAN GOVERNMENT HAS INITIATED SOME MOVES ITSELF, AS IN THE NEW CONSTITUTION WHICH OFFERS LIMITED POLITICAL RIGHTS TO COLOREDS AND

ASIANS. FOR AFRIKANERDOM, EXTENDING AN OVERDUE BRANCH TO THE COLOREDS - A SISTER PEOPLE - IS AN ACT OF MAJOR IMPORTANCE. EQUALLY IMPORTANT, REALISTS IN THE GOVERNING ESTABLISHMENT ARE INCREASINGLY AWARE THAT GRAND APARTHEID IS A DEAD-END MODEL THAT CANNOT STOP

SECRET

DOCUMENT 50: Secretary George Shultz, Cable for All African Diplomatic Posts, "Southern Africa: What About Change in South Africa and What Happens to the ANC?" April 14, 1984.

PAGE 9 OF 11

SECRET

THE EVOLUTIONARY CLOCK. BLACKS ARE ACQUIRING A STEADILY EXPANDING BASE OF DE FACTO LEVERAGE AS CONSUMERS, WORKERS, PROFESSIONALS AND FELLOW SOUTH AFRICANS, EVEN AS THE GOVERNMENT FORMALLY AND FIRMLY CLINGS ONTO THE APARTHEID BLUEPRINT WHILE HINTING VAGUELY AT AN ULTIMATE "CONFEDERATION".

11. WE HAVE NO ILLUSIONS ABOUT THE GULF OF RACIAL DISTRUST IN SOUTH AFRICA OR THE LENGTH OF THE ROAD AHEAD BEFORE WE AND OTHERS CAN SAY THAT BASIC CHANGE HAS HAPPENED. NOR DO WE CONCLUDE THERE WILL BE NO VIOLENCE IN THE PROCESS WITHIN SOUTH AFRICA IN THE MONTHS AND YEARS AHEAD. BUT WE EQUALLY BELIEVE THERE ARE TODAY IMPORTANT OPPORTUNITIES TO LEVERAG. CONTRUCTIVE CHANGE, AS OUR PROGRAMS OF TANGIBLE SUPPORT TO BLACK ADVANCEMENT SEEK TO DO. WE ARE CONVINCED THAT SOUTH AFRICA MUST BE INTERPRETED AT MANY LEVELS. FORMAL POSITIONS OF THE SOUTH AFRICAN GOVERNMENT AND BLACK OPPOSITION GROUPS (BOTH INTERNAL AND EXTERNAL)

SECRET

SECRET

PAGE 11   STATE   110603

ARE IRRECONCILABLE. IN PRACTICE, BARGAINING OCCURS IN VARIOUS ARENAS AND THIS WILL INCREASE. PARTICIPANTS STRIVE FOR OPENINGS WHILE FIGHTING WITH EQUAL FEROCITY TO SAVE FACE AND RETAIN THEIR NATURAL CONSTITUTENCIES. TO DATE, MUCH OF WHAT IS HAPPENING CAN BE TERMED "DENIABLE CHANGE", A SITUATION WHICH DISMAYS MODERATES OF ALL RACES AND ENABLES WHITE AND BLACK HARDLINERS TO MAINTAIN THEIR POSTURES. THE TIME FOR BROADENED AND OVERT POLITICAL BARGAINING INVOLVING BLACK AFRICANS (EXCEPT IN THE SOUTH AFRICA-HOMELAND CONTEXT) HAS NOT YET ARRIVED.

12. AS AFRICAN STATES AND THE ANC FACE UP TO THIS PICTURE, THEY FACE REAL CHOICES. THE FLS AND THE ANC MAY BE TEMPORARILY GOING IN OPPOSITE DIRECTIONS. BUT WE SHOULD REMEMBER THAT THE ANC IS A VENERABLE INSTITUTION THAT COMPROMISES AND SYMBOLIZES MANY THINGS. IT IS A HARDENED, SOVIET-BACKED TERRORIST CADRE AND TEENAGERS WITH AK-47S. BUT IT IS ALSO A RANGE OF VIEWPOINTS INTERNALLY INCLUDING URBAN ACTIVITS WHO USE OTHER LABELS, CAREFUL SYMPATHIZERS OF ALL SORTS, GRANNIES IN ROCKERS WHO WOULD LIKE TO SEE BLACKS GET A BETTER DEAL, A FULLER ROLE AS PARTICIPANTS IN THE LIFE

SECRET

DOCUMENT 50: Secretary George Shultz, Cable for All African Diplomatic Posts, "Southern Africa: What About Change in South Africa and What Happens to the ANC?" April 14, 1984.

PAGE 10 OF 11

SECRET

OF THE COUNTRY, ONE SHOULD NOT FORGET THAT FOR MOST OF ITS 22-YEAR HISTORY, THE ANC WAS NEITHER ILLEGAL NOR

DEDICATED TO VIOLENCE AS THE ONLY OR PRINCIPAL TECHNIQUE FOR PRIMARY CHANGE AND GAINING POLITICAL POWER FOR BLACKS. THE NEW REGIONAL CONTEXT IN SOUTHERN AFRICA, IF IT HOLDS, WILL REKINDLE DEBATE WITHIN AFRICAN NATIONALIST CIRCLES INCLUDING, PERHAPS, THE ANC. IT IS NOT INEVITABLE THAT THE ANC REMAIN HEAVILY ORIENTED TOWARD ARMED TERRORISM OR STRONGLY INFLUENCED BY MOSCOW VIA THE SOUTH AFRICAN COMMUNIST PARTY (SACP).

13. FREQUENTLY, THE USG IS ASKED TO DEFINE ITS
SECRET
SECRET

PAGE 12   STATE   110603

RELATIONSHIP WITH AND VIEW TOWARD THE ANC AS IF THIS WERE THE "MISSING PIECE" OF OUR POLICY TOWARD SOUTH AFRICA. THE QUESTION MISSES THE POINT. WE SEEK CONSTRUCTIVE RELATIONS WITH ALL ELEMENTS OF SOUTH AFRICAN SOCIETY THAT SEEK PEACEFUL, NEGOTIATED CHANGE AWAY FROM APARTHEID.

BIAS
B5

WE VIEW IT AS A RATHER MORE ABLE RELATIONS OF A FUNCTION OF THE CHANGING SOUTH AFRICAN CONTEXT AND ITS OWN DECISIONS. OUR RELATIONSHIP WITH IT WILL OF A FUNCTION OF THOSE DECISIONS.

BIAS
B5

                                    AS AND IF THE
ANC ENTERS THE BARGAINING ARENA - INDIRECTLY AND TACITLY IF NECESSARY, OVERTLY IF THE SAG PERMITS IT - ITS RELATIONS WITH US COULD ALSO DEVELOP IN A MORE POSITIVE DIRECTION.

14. THE ANC AND ITS SYMPATHIZERS MAY ASK HOW THE
SECRET

DOCUMENT 50: Secretary George Shultz, Cable for All African Diplomatic Posts, "Southern Africa: What About Change in South Africa and What Happens to the ANC?" April 14, 1984.

PAGE 11 OF 11

MOVEMENT CAN ENTER SOUTH AFRICA'S COMPETITIVE FRAY
GIVEN THE FACT IT IS A BANNED INSTITUTION. THE ANSWER
IS NOT SIMPLE: THE BANNING OF THE ANC IS NO MORE

SECRET
SECRET

PAGE 13   STATE 110603

ENGRAVED IN STONE TABLETS THAN WAS LIFE IMPRISONMENT
FOR TOIVO JA TOIVO. THE ANC HAS NEVER BEEN AT LOSS FOR
ALTERNATIVE FORMS OF EXPRESSION. ITS SYMPATHIZERS ARE
PRINCIPALLY TO BE FOUND INSIDE SOUTH AFRICA WHERE THE
REAL JOB REMAINS TO BE DONE. IT IS TIME FOR THE
LEADERSHIP OF THE ANC TO PUT THEIR RHETORIC AND WEIGHT

BEHIND THOSE INSIDE SOUTH AFRICA WHO COMPETE FOR CHANGE
AND NOT BEHIND THE MIRAGE OF A LIBERATION ARMY - STILL
UNFORMED AND WHOSE VERY CREATION PROMISES ONLY
DESTRUCTION AND VIOLENCE FOR ALL OF SOUTHERN AFRICA'S
PEOPLES - INCLUDING THEIR OWN SIBLINGS INSIDE SOUTH
AFRICA. IN SHORT AND FOR THE FIRST TIME IN MANY YEARS,
THE ANC HAS A CHOICE BETWEEN ARMAGEDDON AND SERIOUS
RELEVANCE TO CHANGE IN SOUTH AFRICA.
SHULTZ

DOCUMENT 51: Assistant Secretary Morton Abramowitz, Information Memorandum for Secretary George Shultz, "South African Anti-SWAPO Military Operations in Angola," January 24, 1986.

PAGE 1 OF 1

S0095A

ES SENSITIVE   8602324   *fil*

United States Department of State

Washington, D. C. 20520

January 24, 1986

EXCISI

DIST:
1/24

SECRET/SENSITIVE/NOFORN/NOCONTRACT/ORCON

S
D
P
S/S
S/S-I

INFORMATION MEMORANDUM
S/S

TO: The Secretary

FROM: INR - Morton I. Abramowitz

SUBJECT: South African Anti-SWAPO Military Operations in Angola

Caption removed; transferred to O/FADRC
Cat B - Transferred to O/FADRC with additional access controlled by S/S
Cat C - Caption and custody retained by S/S

Reviewed by Elizabeth M.
Date: 8/8/91   19___

B1A5+9

We believe the SADF is conducting substantial operations in southern Angola. But we doubt that SWAPO could send 800 insurgents (the figure the SADF has used for the last several years) into Namibia, given the SADF's control of the border. We do give some credence to reports of increased Angolan assistance to SWAPO infiltration operations.

While the South Africans publicly remain committed to UNSCR 435, their contention that there is a serious military threat fits conveniently into what may be Pretoria's preferred scenario for Namibia: to force changes in 435 or a regional settlement outside 435 which would limit SWAPO's power in an independent Namibia. Anti-SWAPO operations in Angola also provide cover for assisting UNITA, by occupying Angolan forces which otherwise could be used against Savimbi's troops and as cover for SADF or joint SADF/UNITA sabotage operations against preparations for the next government offensive. While the size of the SADF force in Angola may fluctuate, we believe it likely there will be a significant SADF presence in southern Angola at least for the remainder of the rainy season.

Drafted:INR/AA:L.Silverman
    1/24/86   x77174
Cleared:INR/AA:A.Dalsimer
        INR/PMA:G.Price
Approved:INR:R.A.Clarke

SECRET/SENSITIVE/NOFORN/NOCONTRACT/ORCON

DECL: OADR

DEPARTMENT OF STATE A/CDC/MR   REVIEWED by ___ Lim 9/24/91   TS authority to. ___ OAD
( ) RELEASE   ( ) DECLASSIFY   ( ) FOI ( ) EO or PA exemptions. B/   ( ) CLASSIFY as ___ OADR
( ) EXCISE   ( ) DECLASSIFY in PART   ( ) DOWNGRADE TS to ( ) S or ( ) C OADR
( ) DENY   ( ) DELETE
              ( ) Non-responsive info.

DOCUMENT 52: Assistant Secretary Chester Crocker, Briefing Memorandum for Secretary George Shultz, "Meeting with UNITA Leader, Jonas Savimbi, February 6, 1986, 6:30 pm–7:00 pm," February 5, 1986.

E23

United States Department of State

Washington, D. C. 20520

EXCISE

DECLASSIFIED

BRIEFING MEMORANDUM

SECRET/SENSITIVE S/S

DEPARTMENT OF STATE	IS/FPC/CDR F. / O Date. JUL 15 1992
( ) RELEASE ( ) DECLASSIFY	MR Cases Only:
✓ EXCISE (✓) DECLASSIFY	EO Citations _____
( ) DENY IN PART	
( ) DELETE Non-Responsive Info	_____,TS authority to.
FOIA Exemptions (b)(1)	( ) CLASSIFY as ( ) S or ( ) C OADR
PA Exemptions _____	( ) DOWNGRADE TS to ( ) S or ( ) C OADR

TO: The Secretary

FROM: AF - Chester A. Crocker

SUBJECT: Meeting with UNITA Leader, Jonas Savimbi,
         February 6, 1986, 6:30 pm - 7:00 pm.

<u>SETTING</u>

This meeting offers an opportunity to have a last exchange with Savimbi before he returns to the bush.

B|25

|Finally, we need to set the stage for continued liaison with Savimbi.

Savimbi will depart for New York after the evening's Heritage Foundation reception. He will have a one-day program there before returning to Angola. Savimbi has accepted your invitation to drive to the Heritage reception in your car, and you will leave together immediately after your meeting.

I.   <u>WHAT DOES UNITA WANT?</u>

o   In addition to briefing you on visit/

B|a5

SECRET/SENSITIVE
DECL: OADR

DOCUMENT 52: Assistant Secretary Chester Crocker, Briefing Memorandum for Secretary George Shultz, "Meeting with UNITA Leader, Jonas Savimbi, February 6, 1986, 6:30 pm–7:00 pm," February 5, 1986.

PAGE 2 OF 4

SECRET/SENSITIVE
- 2 -

DECLASSIFIED

B1 ᵘ ⁵

III. WHAT DO WE WANT?

o   To assure Savimbi that we support him, are proceeding on the aid front and will not abandon him after an agreement on the withdrawal of foreign forces.

o   To seek his views on the role of American business in Angola and to reaffirm US policy against threats to American lives and property.

o   To tell him that we do not believe it useful to alter the nature of the present formal negotiating process by making national reconciliation part of it but that we are prepared to sound out the MPLA and the Soviets on this issue.

o   To brief him on diplomatic developments and reaffirm our expectation of his continued support for our negotiating effort.

o   To brief him on the approach to aid we intend to pursue and to assure him that we will continue to monitor the situation on the ground, and his needs, carefully.

IV. POINTS TO MAKE

--   What are your impressions of your visit?

--   We are proceeding with aid while working with Congress on a supportive legislative strategy.

--   We will continue efforts to turn your military pressure on the MPLA into a negotiated settlement on the withdrawal of all foreign troops from the region.

--   Some press reports of your remarks suggest you would target American companies for their political activities here. Some suggest you do not favor the withdrawal of the oil companies. What are your views?

SECRET/SENSITIVE

DOCUMENT 52: Assistant Secretary Chester Crocker, Briefing Memorandum for Secretary George Shultz, "Meeting with UNITA Leader, Jonas Savimbi, February 6, 1986, 6:30 pm–7:00 pm," February 5, 1986.

SECRET/SENSITIVE
- 3 -

B| 25

-- ... we cannot accept any
   threats to American lives and property.

-- We believe national reconciliation is essential
   for peace and stability in Angola. You must be
   part of Angola's future for there to be one.

-- But we do not believe it would advance the
   negotiating process to make national
   reconciliation a formal part of it, but we are
   prepared to help you explore the issue.

-- Chet has spoken to you about this; he speaks for
   the President as well as myself.

-- We will continue on the negotiating path.

B| 25

-- It is important that we maintain contact over
   the coming months. The President looks to me to
   do this on our side, and I look to Chet.

SECRET/SENSITIVE

DOCUMENT 52: Assistant Secretary Chester Crocker, Briefing Memorandum for Secretary George Shultz, "Meeting with UNITA Leader, Jonas Savimbi, February 6, 1986, 6:30 pm–7:00 pm," February 5, 1986.

PAGE 4 OF 4

SECRFT/SENSITIVE
- 4 -

PARTICIPANTS

US	UNITA
The Secretary	Dr. Jonas Savimbi
Under Secretary Armacost	
Assistant Secretary Crocker	Miguel N'Zau Puna, Secretary General
Jeffrey Davidow, Office Director for Southern Africa	Jeremias Chitunda, Foreign Secretary
Gerard Gallucci, Angola Desk Officer (Notetaker)	Gen. Tito Chingunji, Assistant Secretary for Foreign Affairs

Drafted: AF/S:GGallucc
2/5/86   n246c
Cleared: AF/S:JDavidow
         AF:FGWisner
         P:MHArmacost

SECRET/SENSITIVE

DOCUMENT 53: National Security Decision Directive 212, "United States Policy Toward Angola," February 10, 1986.

PAGE 1 OF 3

THE WHITE HOUSE
WASHINGTON
February 10, 1986

SYSTEM II 91177

*National Security Decision
Directive Number 212*

UNITED STATES POLICY TOWARD ANGOLA

The United States and its allies have important political, commercial, and strategic interests in southern Africa, which are being threatened by the Angolan MPLA regime's hard-line policies and increased Soviet Bloc military assistance to that government. At this juncture, direct Soviet/Cuban challenges to our important interests in the region and the increased military confrontation inside Angola, coupled with the recent repeal of the Clark Amendment and continued uncertainty of U.S. negotiating efforts, make it necessary to reconsider and affirm U.S. southern Africa policy objectives in the Angolan context. These objectives are:

   -- Reduce and possibly eliminate Soviet and Soviet-proxy influence and opportunities in Angola and southern Africa;

   -- Encourage change away from apartheid and reform in southern Africa so as to enhance prospects for peace and improved relations between South Africa and its neighbors;

   -- Promote regional stability and improved relations between South Africa and its neighbors, particularly by participating in efforts to achieve negotiated settlements to regional problems and broker rules of engagement for the peaceful resolution of disputes;

   -- Seek an internationally acceptable solution to the Namibian problem based on UNSCR 435, and Cuban troop withdrawal from Angola.

In order to achieve these broad objectives, the U.S. will remain actively involved in southern Africa, and with respect to Angola, will pursue a two-track strategy of a) continuing to negotiate with the MPLA and South Africa on Cuban troop withdrawal in the context of Namibian independence while b) applying pressure on the MPLA to negotiate seriously and to accept a negotiated settlement.

Declassified/Released on 5-17-91
under provisions of E.O. 12356
by S. Tilley, National Security Council

(F87-1035)

SECRET
DECLASSIFY ON: OADR

SECRET

2

This strategy will consist of the following elements:

-- Develop overt means of increasing pressure on and pursue openings offered by the MPLA, including in the negotiating track, to achieve an agreement on Cuban troop withdrawal;

-- Work actively with our allies, the Front Line States, and other parties to encourage them to press the MPLA regime for a peaceful settlement;

-- Expand contacts with UNITA, and assist UNITA politically in its efforts to increase its international stature and acceptance in order to make it clear that:

o We have UNITA's interests in mind in the current negotiating process, which could set the stage for national reconciliation in Angola;

o Peace cannot be imposed on Angola by suppressing UNITA or ignoring its interests; what is required is a national reconciliation based on a political settlement acceptable to all Angolan parties;

-- Continue U.S. development, security assistance, and humanitarian food relief programs consistent with our national values and objectives in the southern African region;

-- Intensify U.S. efforts to improve relations between South Africa and its neighbors, maintain an effective dialogue in support of U.S. objectives with all relevant parties, condemn and help minimize violence and terrorism by any party;

-- Pursue discussions with the Soviet Union in an attempt to diminish and eventually eliminate Soviet Bloc military assistance to Angola, and to promote national reconciliation between UNITA and the MPLA;

-- USIA should enhance international media attention to increase the international stature of UNITA's political goals and military accomplishments, and to explain to the Cuban people the real costs of the Angola war to Cuba;

-- The Department of State should develop a political strategy to bolster UNITA within the U.N. and the Organization of African Unity, working both unilaterally and through friendly governments;

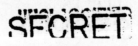

DOCUMENT 53: National Security Decision Directive 212, "United States Policy Toward Angola," February 10, 1986.

PAGE 3 OF 3

3

-- Inform senior management of all major American companies with operations in Angola to be aware of all the risks involved in their positions there, including the risk that commercial dealings with Angola may someday be banned or restricted, depending on future developments in that country as they affect major U.S. interests and objectives;

-- Inform EXIM Bank that it should neither seek nor accept any new business in Angola which would, broadly construed, enhance the ability of the MPLA to wage war or acquire the military or economic resources necessary to sustain its war effort. (X)

Accordingly, to further U.S. objectives, the following policies will apply. The U.S. will:

Apply pressure on the Angolan regime to cooperate in the current negotiations for a peaceful settlement in Angola/Namibia and restrict its ability to prosecute the war against UNITA through:

o Consideration of the use of economic measures available to the U.S. on a case by case basis.

o Use of all available means, including denial of export licenses, and use of other legal authorities, to prevent export of U.S. equipment, technology, projects or services which have end-user military application. (X)

DOCUMENT 54: National Security Decision Directive 274, "United States Policy Toward Angola," May 7, 1987.

PAGE 1 OF 3

UNCLASSIFIED

SYSTEM II
90470

THE WHITE HOUSE

WASHINGTON
May 7, 1987

NATIONAL SECURITY DECISION
DIRECTIVE NUMBER 274

UNITED STATES POLICY TOWARD ANGOLA

National Security Decision Directive 212 of February 10, 1986 determined that the policies of the Angolan MPLA regime and increased Soviet bloc military assistance to that government posed a threat to important political, strategic, and economic interests of the U.S. and its allies in southern Africa. NSDD 212 enumerated U.S. policy objectives in the Angolan context and established a U.S. strategy of a) continuing to negotiate with the MPLA and South Africa on Cuban troop withdrawal in the context of Namibian independence while b) applying pressure on the MPLA to negotiate seriously and to accept a negotiated settlement.

Since the approval of NSDD 212, the Angolan military conflict has stabilized. Neither the MPLA nor UNITA is in a position to achieve a military victory, despite Moscow's interjection of almost $1 billion in new Soviet military assistance in support of a continuing attempt by the Soviet Union and its MPLA client to achieve a military solution to the civil war. U. S. efforts to negotiate Cuban troop withdrawal in the context of Namibian independence have been stalled by the unwillingness of the MPLA regime to negotiate seriously.

UNITA has made some progress in its efforts to develop broader international ties, but the MPLA remains unwilling to afford UNITA a fair share of power in the context of national reconciliation. Although Soviet/Cuban costs have risen, Moscow and Havana remain committed to the Luanda regime and to the maintenance of their presence and influence in Angola.

In light of these developments, U.S. policy has been reviewed, and it has been determined that our objectives and strategy as established by NSDD 212 remain valid:

--To seek an internationally acceptable solution to the Namibian problem based on UNSCR 435, linked to Cuban troop withdrawal from Angola.

--To achieve an equitable internal settlement of the Angolan conflict that affords UNITA a fair share of power;

--To reduce and, if possible, eliminate Soviet and Soviet-proxy influence, military presence, and opportunities in Angola and southern Africa.

SECRET
Declassify on: OADR

SECRET

Declassified/Released on 12/20/91
under provisions of E.O. 12356
by S. Tilley, National Security Council
(F87-1035)

DOCUMENT 54: National Security Decision Directive 274, "United States Policy Toward Angola," May 7, 1987.

PAGE 2 OF 3

SECRET
UNCLASSIFIED

-2-

The two-track strategy for achieving the objectives established by NSDD 212 has also been reviewed and remains fundamentally valid. However, additional actions are warranted on both tracks to achieve U.S. policy objectives. (X)

With regard to negotiations with the MPLA and South Africa:

--The U.S. will continue to use all available diplomatic opportunities--including direct contacts with the parties to the Angola/Namibia negotiations--to bring negotiations on Cuban troop withdrawal and Namibian independence to a successful conclusion.

--The U.S. will continue to insist on withdrawal of Cuban forces in the context of a settlement. The U.S. will also continue to insist that any initiative for Namibian independence outside the framework of UNSCR 435 meet the test of international acceptability.

--With UNITA's interests in mind, the U.S. will actively promote diplomatic initiatives, to include talks on the reopening of the Benguela Railroad, which advance the objective of national reconciliation in Angola. (X)

With regard to pressures on the MPLA:

--The U.S. will actively seek and implement effective means of increasing pressure on the MPLA to agree to a negotiated settlement.

--A review will be conducted in order to ensure that U.S. support for UNITA is: consistent with our overall strategy; responsive to UNITA's needs; effective in raising the costs incurred by the MPLA regime and its Soviet and Cuban backers; acceptable to key African partners whose support is essential; and sustainable in Congress and with the American public.

--As a follow-up to the present interagency review, the Department of State shall convene an interagency group to consider feasible and effective means of increasing economic pressures on the MPLA regime and recommend appropriate options to me within one month. Pending completion of that review, the specific economic pressures against the MPLA government set forth in NSDD 212 will remain in force.

--The Department of State, together with other appropriate agencies, will explore means of increasing UNITA's stature within

UNCLASSIFIED SECRET

DOCUMENT 54: National Security Decision Directive 274, "United States Policy Toward Angola,"
May 7, 1987.

PAGE 3 OF 3

UNCLASSIFIED

UNCLASSIFIED

-3-

Angola and internationally through more effective information
programs. The U.S. information efforts will also seek to
undermine Cuba's ability to deploy troops to Angola through
specially focused radio programming broadcast to Cuba by Radio
Marti and through Spanish language programs aimed at the Cuban
troops deployed in Angola. To the greatest possible extent, the
U.S. should seek to exacerbate differences between the MPLA and
their Soviet bloc supporters and undermine Soviet/Cuban efforts
to portray themselves as assisting a legitimate and embattled
African government.

--Diplomatic efforts to obtain the support of our allies and
other international parties in pressing the MPLA regime for a
peaceful settlement and to assist UNITA in expanding its
international ties will be continued and, if possible, expanded.

The Department of State will continue efforts to engage the
Soviet Union in serious discussions to diminish and eventually
eliminate Soviet military assistance to Angola, to advance
negotiations on Cuban troop withdrawal and Namibian
independence, and to promote national reconciliation between
UNITA and the MPLA.

--The U.S. will continue development, security assistance,
and humanitarian relief programs to assist governments friendly
to the U.S. which are threatened by the Angolan conflict or
strained by refugee flows from that country.

SECRET

UNCLASSIFIED

DOCUMENT 55: Assistant Secretary Morton Abramowitz, Information Memorandum for the Acting Secretary, "South Africa's Angola-Namibia Dilemma," ca. April 1988.

United States Department of State

Washington, D. C. 20520

SECRET/NOFORN/SENSITIVE
INFORMATION MEMORANDUM
S/S

TO: The Acting Secretary

FROM: INR - Morton I. Abramowitz

SUBJECT: South Africa's Angola-Namibia Dilemma

--South Africa is in the throes of a major policy debate between the civilian and military elements of the Botha government over its position on the US-brokered CTW negotiations. This division is complicated by the recent deployment of crack Cuban units and sophisticated air defense systems only a few miles from the Namibian border. At this juncture, Pretoria's negotiating posture in the next round of talks in June is likely to reflect the lowest common denominator.

--Pretoria still does not see an acceptable solution for Namibian independence under procedures outlined in UNSCR 435. Optimally, it would like to "delink" CTW from 435. Realistically it knows it cannot, if it is to keep the US and other parties involved in CTW talks. Therefore, Pretoria is searching for solutions that will keep CTW alive but sidestep the more undesirable aspects of 435 including early implementation.

--Pretoria is serious about negotiating a share of power for UNITA as a precondition to a final settlement. It is convinced that a metamorphosis in Luanda is essential for its long-term security interests. But it knows its ambitions for UNITA run counter to US efforts to keep CTW and national reconciliation on separate, if parallel, tracks.

--South Africa's best-case scenario is a settlement which, while guaranteed by Moscow and Washington and approved by the international community, also ensures it continued regional dominance. But it is also intent on drawing other African countries into the negotiation process should international terms be unacceptable and as a long-term diplomatic hedge against a waning of Western interest in southern Africa.

*   *   *

SECRET/NOFORN/SENSITIVE
DECL: OADR

DOCUMENT 55: Assistant Secretary Morton Abramowitz, Information Memorandum for the Acting Secretary, "South Africa's Angola-Namibia Dilemma," ca. April 1988.

PAGE 2 OF 3

SECRET/NOFORN/SENSITIVE

<u>Confrontation on Angola</u>. With US mediation efforts entering a new phase and the threat of conflict with the Cubans in southwestern Angola growing stronger, President P. W. Botha sees merit in taking another look at prospects for Cuban Troop Withdrawal and Namibian independence. But Botha has yet to forge a consensus among his key advisers. He has come to realize that South Africa's protracted involvement in southern Angola has been costly in white lives and defense expenditures, and that a military victory for UNITA, even with continuing South African support, is not in the cards. To the discomfort of the military, Pik Botha's Department of Foreign Affairs has played up those costs in its efforts to use Angola to foster diplomatic, rather than military solutions, to South Africa's regional problems.

For reasons still not entirely clear, the South African military was slow to react to the recent build-up of Cuban forces in southwestern Angola, and still appears reluctant to force a showdown. In any event, the government chose a diplomatic response, warning the Angolans in Brazzaville and through other channels that a continued Cuban build-up could jeopardize CTW negotiations. Now, some of Botha's senior military commanders are expressing concern over what they see as a sharp deterioration in South Africa's position in Angola and Namibia while others continue to voice the belief that a preemptive military strike against the Cubans--which in their view would be successful--would enhance South Africa's negotiating position.

<u>Even More on Namibia</u>. Apart from CTW is the question of Namibian independence and the prospect that UNSCR 435 could come into play before Pretoria has a viable political structure in place there and before it has neutralized SWAPO. But here again, Botha is receiving conflicting advice. The SADF argues that it needs at least five years to neutralize SWAPO, militarily and politically. Others argue that a pacified Angola, in which UNITA shares power, will be adequate to ensure that a SWAPO-led government in Windhoek will not be threatening. In this connection, South African officials are encouraged by reports that the Soviets are prepared to accept a "neutral" Namibia--perhaps on the Botswana model.

The South African Defense Force (SADF) reportedly believes that 435 is too much of a political risk to accept at this time. Military Intelligence, which has a strong voice in such matters, and perhaps the foreign ministry as well, reportedly believe Namibia will have to be part of an Angolan settlement. Hence, Pretoria may follow the path of least resistence, at least over the near term, by accepting 435 in principle while at the same time expressing enough misgivings to extract concessions on the timing and procedures of implementation.

SECRET/NOFORN/SENSITIVE

DOCUMENT 55: Assistant Secretary Morton Abramowitz, Information Memorandum for the Acting Secretary, "South Africa's Angola-Namibia Dilemma," ca. April 1988.

PAGE 3 OF 3

SECRET/NOFORN/SENSITIVE

-3-

Support for UNITA. Pretoria also is serious about negotiating a share of power for UNITA. Malan and the military have been demanding that UNITA be a participant in the next round of talks. Because it recognizes that UNITA cannot win a military victory, Pretoria believes it must hit hard on the national reconciliation issue now--perhaps fearing that the momentum will be lost if the administration in Washington changes hands. The South Africans may also hope that the Soviets will counsel Luanda to be less intransigent on an accommodation with UNITA. Pretoria may be reading too much into recent Soviet statements that acknowledge UNITA's importance to a solution. It does, however, realize that national reconciliation cannot be imposed on Luanda and will need to be mediated.

Africa for the Africans. Botha, and probably most others in his government, is convinced that longer term western interests in southern Africa, focused as they are on CTW and Namibia, have a shorter time-span than his own, and derive from a different strategic view of the region. Thus, Foreign Minister "Pik" Botha's call at Brazzaville for African solutions to African problems, along with recent overtures toward Mozambique, suggests that Pretoria may also see the possibility of drawing African states into a regional security arrangement. And once western interest wanes, South Africa will be the dominant power and its decade-old vision of a regional Pax Pretoriana will become reality.

Keeping the Door Open. Given the many uncertainties it faces in the Angolan and Namibian situations, South Africa seems to be in a quandry about how best to proceed. The US negotiating effort probably is seen as useful in that it enables Pretoria to probe the intentions and take the measure of the various actors. At the same time, it deflects, for the time being, international opprobrium, buys time for UNITA to try to maneuver through the national reconciliation morass, and keep channels open to the US while Pretoria carefully calculates the advantages and disadvantages of closer cooperation with us.

Implications for the US. Even as it continues on the US-mediated track, Pretoria will try to keep open its other options, including the "Africans-only" track. Such a process would oblige South Africa to tread warily and respect the African countries' basic sovereign rights--foregoing aggressive acts when irritated, for instance--if it hopes to keep the process in its hands and not send the Africans scurrying for rescue to the US or USSR. Since regional peace and accommodation are at the heart of US policy objectives in southern Africa, any solutions the protaganists reach that point in that direction would have the advantage of being theirs, not ours. We would be free to encourage those aspects we like and keep away from costly commitments.

SECRET/NOFORN/SENSITIVE

DOCUMENT 56: Assistant Secretary Chester Crocker, Memorandum for Secretary James Baker, "Angola/Namibia Developments," February 3, 1989 (partially transcribed by the editors).

PAGE 1 OF 2

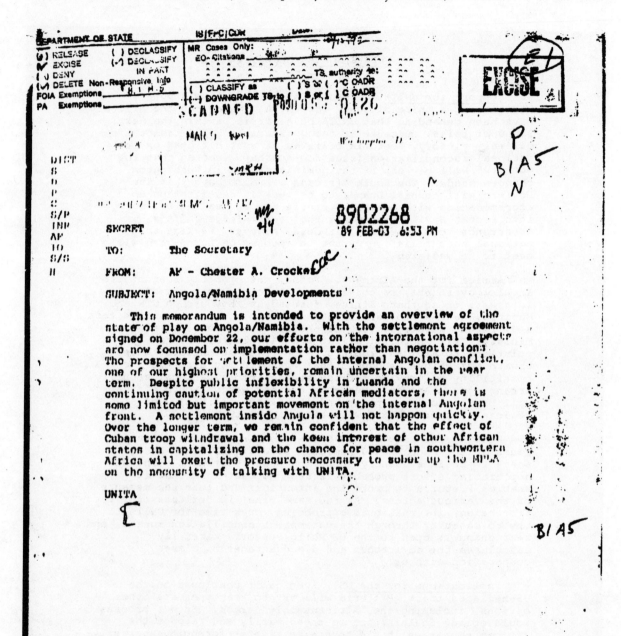

SECRET

8902268
'89 FEB-03 6:53 PM

TO: The Secretary

FROM: AF - Chester A. Crocker

SUBJECT: Angola/Namibia Developments

This memorandum is intended to provide an overview of the state of play on Angola/Namibia. With the settlement agreement signed on December 22, our efforts on the international aspects are now focussed on implementation rather than negotiations. The prospects for settlement of the internal Angolan conflict, one of our highest priorities, remain uncertain in the near term. Despite public inflexibility in Luanda and the continuing caution of potential African mediators, there is some limited but important movement on the internal Angolan front. A settlement inside Angola will not happen quickly. Over the longer term, we remain confident that the effect of Cuban troop withdrawal and the keen interest of other African states in capitalizing on the chance for peace in southwestern Africa will exert the pressure necessary to sober up the MPLA on the necessity of talking with UNITA.

UNITA

SECRET
DECL: OADR

[Eight lines deleted by State Department declassifiers under FOIA exemption B1(A5)]

MPLA

As authorized by Secretary Shultz and President Reagan, on January 18 we proposed to the GPRA that the U.S. establish a small official presence in Luanda for the purpose of communication on implementation of the settlement and for other purposes. We made clear to the MPLA that this stop would not represent a change of our policy of non-recognition and no diplomatic relations. On January 19, the GPRA informed us they could not accept our proposal without reciprocal treatment in Washington, which we were not prepared to offer. In New York at the first Joint Commission meeting I went over our January 18 proposal with Gen. Ndalu, the military chief of staff and their chief negotiator. The foreign minister had been dismissed in the interim, and it was apparent that our proposal had not been properly presented by the ambassador to his government. Ndalu said that he would report back to President Dos Santos, and let me know whether they had any further reaction. We have heard nothing since.

The Angolans' ultimate goal is recognition and diplomatic relations. Neither recognition nor relations is in the cards absent national reconciliation and full implementation of the Cuban troop withdrawal agreement. The ball is in the Angolan court on the Reagan Administration's offer of a modest improvement, if and when the Angolans get back to *[word illegible]* there will have to be a decision by the new Administration whether to stick to the previous offer, or modify it in some fashion.

National Reconciliation

National reconciliation (NR) is the primary objective of our past resettlement approach to Angola. There continues to be movement on this score. We understand for example that the MPLA is examining terms of reference for talking with UNITA about the recent cabinet changes, moreover, the man appointed as the new foreign minister, van Dunem *[illegible]*oi, also seems to be the point man in the government's halting efforts to talk to us about national reconciliation. Early in January *[three words illegible]* some preliminary thoughts through a third party on just how talks could get started between UNITA and the MPLA.

More immediately, we have received reports of at least three active efforts by African countries to arrange a direct meeting between dos Santos and Savimbi. While we cannot predict that these will bear fruit, the countries involved in the past have refused to play a role in this effort. Also, UNITA offered a ceasefire to the MPLA on January 31, opening a new context for the two sides to deal with each other. Earlier President dos Santos had indicated to New York Times columnist Anthony Lewis that the MPLA was also considering a ceasefire.

These developments are grounds for optimism about NR, although progress will continue to be incremental, and it will be difficult for us to force the pace. The conflict between the two sides has been going on for the better part of fifteen years, and Savimbi's larger than life persona is difficult for the rather faceless MPLA to come to terms with. The inevitability of a negotiated solution, however, is sinking into the MPLA's mindset with a combination of pressure from other African states, UNITA's continued military pressure on the ground, and our own efforts at persuasion. As Cuban troop withdrawal picks up pace in the coming months, there will an added inducement for the MPLA to face their own national reality.

[Approximately fifty-five lines deleted by State Department declassifiers as "non-relevant"]

Drafted:AF/S:JMOrdway/PMMCKinley
2/3/89 01020g   x78252
Cleared:AF/S:LCNapper
   AF/S:EClanpher
   AF/S:CWFreeman
   IO/UNP:HKirby

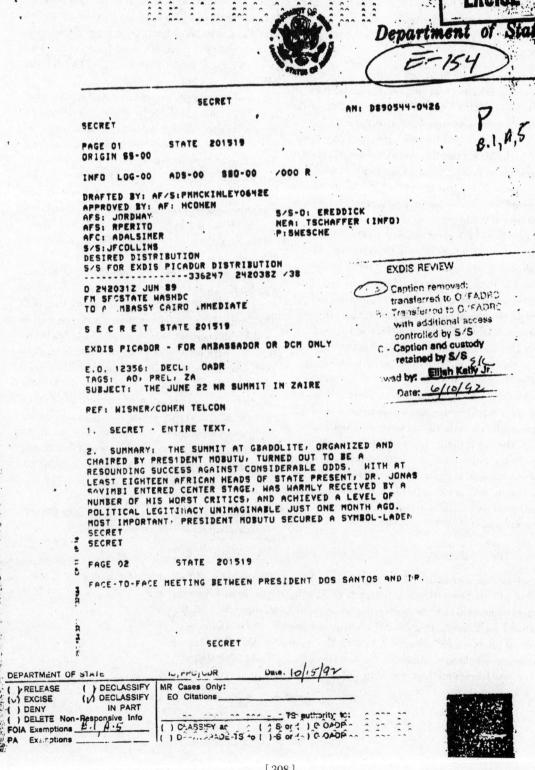

DECLASSIFIED

EXCISE

Department of State

Ē-154

SECRET

AN: D890544-0426

P
B.1, A.5

SECRET

PAGE 01   STATE 201519
ORIGIN SS-00

INFO LOG-00   ADS-00   SSO-00   /000 R

DRAFTED BY: AF/S:PMMCKINLEY0642E
APPROVED BY: AF: HCOHEN
AFS: JORDWAY   S/S-O: EREDDICK
AFS: RPERITO   NEA: TSCHAFFER (INFO)
AFC: ADALSIMER   P: SWESCHE
S/S: JFCOLLINS
DESIRED DISTRIBUTION
S/S FOR EXDIS PICADOR DISTRIBUTION
------------------336247   2420382 /38
O 242031Z JUN 89
FM SECSTATE WASHDC
TO AMBASSY CAIRO IMMEDIATE

S E C R E T STATE 201519

EXDIS PICADOR - FOR AMBASSADOR OR DCM ONLY

E.O. 12356: DECL: OADR
TAGS: AO, PREL, ZA
SUBJECT: THE JUNE 22 NR SUMMIT IN ZAIRE

REF: WISNER/COHEN TELCON

1. SECRET - ENTIRE TEXT.

2. SUMMARY: THE SUMMIT AT GBADOLITE, ORGANIZED AND
CHAIRED BY PRESIDENT MOBUTU, TURNED OUT TO BE A
RESOUNDING SUCCESS AGAINST CONSIDERABLE ODDS. WITH AT
LEAST EIGHTEEN AFRICAN HEADS OF STATE PRESENT, DR. JONAS
SAVIMBI ENTERED CENTER STAGE, WAS WARMLY RECEIVED BY A
NUMBER OF HIS WORST CRITICS, AND ACHIEVED A LEVEL OF
POLITICAL LEGITIMACY UNIMAGINABLE JUST ONE MONTH AGO.
MOST IMPORTANT, PRESIDENT MOBUTU SECURED A SYMBOL-LADEN
SECRET

SECRET

PAGE 02   STATE 201519

FACE-TO-FACE MEETING BETWEEN PRESIDENT DOS SANTOS AND DR.

SECRET

EXDIS REVIEW

A. Caption removed:
   transferred to O/FADRC
B. Transferred to O/FADRC
   with additional access
   controlled by S/S
C. Caption and custody
   retained by S/S S/C
wed by: Elijah Kelly Jr.

Date: 6/10/92

DEPARTMENT OF STATE   IO, FPC, CDR   Date. 10/15/92

( ) RELEASE   ( ) DECLASSIFY   MR Cases Only:
(✓) EXCISE   (✓) DECLASSIFY   EO Citations ____
( ) DENY   IN PART
( ) DELETE Non-Responsive Info   TS authority to:
FOIA Exemptions E.1, A.5   ( ) CLASSIFY as ( ) S or ( ) C OADR
PA Exemptions ____   ( ) DOWNGRADE TS to ( ) S or ( ) C OADR

DOCUMENT 57: Secretary James Baker, Cable for U.S. Embassy Cairo, "The June 22 NR Summit in Zaire," June 24, 1989.

PAGE 2 OF 5

SECRET
SAVIMBI, AND AGREEMENT ON A CEASEFIRE.

3. IT IS, OF COURSE, FAR TOO EARLY TO DECLARE THE
ANGOLAN CIVIL WAR AT AN END. THE MPLA AND UNITA ARE ONLY
BEGINNING A PROCESS OF DIALOGUE AND NEGOTIATION WHICH
COULD TAKE MANY MONTHS. THERE IS CONSIDERABLE ROOM FOR
DISAGREEMENT AND ARGUMENT ON THE VAGUE PRINCIPLES OF
NATIONAL RECONCILIATION SUPPOSEDLY AGREED TO IN
GBADOLITE.

                           AFRICAN LEADERS ARE
ALREADY INTERPRETING THE RESULTS OF THE SUMMIT IN LIGHT
OF THEIR OWN POLITICAL BIASES AND PERSPECTIVES ON THE
ANGOLAN CONFLICT.

4. NONETHELESS, MORE THAN A PAGE HAS BEEN TURNED. IN
WHAT HAS LONG BEEN A PARTICULARLY BITTER AND POLITICALLY
CHARGED CONFLICT OUT OF PROPORTION TO THE IMPORTANCE OF
THE COUNTRY IT WAS BEING FOUGHT IN, THE SEEDS FOR
POLITICAL COMPROMISE BETWEEN FORMER ENEMIES HAVE BEEN
LAID. IT WILL BE DIFFICULT, IF NOT IMPOSSIBLE TO TURN
THE CLOCK BACK. END SUMMARY.

5. GETTING TO THE SUMMIT: THE MAY 16 PRESIDENTIAL
SUMMIT IN LUANDA AT WHICH EIGHT AFRICAN HEAD OF STATE
WERE PRESENT (FROM GABON, ZAIRE, ZAMBIA, ZIMBABWE, CONGO,
MOZAMBIQUE, SAO TOME, AND THE HOST ANGOLA) WAS THE FIRST
SIGN THAT DRAMATIC DEVELOPMENTS WERE UNDERWAY. THE
GROUNDWORK HAD BEEN LAID BY WEEKS OF QUIET DIPLOMACY
INVOLVING A NUMBER OF ANGOLA'S NEIGHBORS, BUT WITH THE
LEAD CLEARLY BEING TAKEN BY PRESIDENT MOBUTU OF ZAIRE AND
PRESIDENT SASSOU OF THE CONGO.
SECRET
SECRET

PAGE 03   STATE 201519

6. THE LUANDA SUMMIT GAVE DOS SANTOS THE AFRICAN CONTEXT
-- AND POLITICAL COVER -- TO ANNOUNCE HIS CONVERSION TO
THE PRINCIPLE OF DIALOGUE WITH UNITA IN THE GUISE OF A
SEVEN POINT MPLA PEACE PLAN WHICH ADDRESSED PRACTICAL
CONCERNS AS WELL AS POLITICAL PRINCIPLES. WHILE STILL
STICKING TO HIS GOVERNMENT'S AMNESTY POLICY, HE PROMISED
MORE OPENLY THAN EVER POSITIONS IN THE GOVERNMENT FOR
UNITA CADRE, ENDORSED THE IDEA OF A CEASEFIRE, AND
INFORMED THE ASSEMBLED PRESIDENTS NO NEW MILITARY

SECRET

DOCUMENT 57: Secretary James Baker, Cable for U.S. Embassy Cairo, "The June 22 NR Summit in Zaire," June 24, 1989.

PAGE 3 OF 5

SECRET

OFFENSIVE AGAINST UNITA WOULD BE CARRIED OUT DURING THE
DRY SEASON. ONE AFRICAN LEADER LATER DEFINED THIS
PROPOSAL AS AN EFFORT TO RESPOND TO SAVIMBI'S PEACE
INITIATIVE OF MARCH 13, WHICH HAD CONSIDERABLY WIDENED
THE SCOPE FOR DIALOGUE BETWEEN THE TWO SIDES.

7. PRESIDENT DOS SANTOS WAS LEFT WITH THE UNENVIABLE
TASK OF ALIGNING THE PARTY BEHIND HIS SHIFT ON NATIONAL
RECONCILIATION (NR).

8. IN THE AFTERMATH OF THE SUMMIT, IT ALSO BECAME

APPARENT THAT PRESIDENT MOBUTU HAD BEEN GIVEN A SPECIAL
POLE IN BUILDING ON THE BREAKTHROUGH MADE ON MAY 16TH.
ON JUNE 5, A NEWLY CONFIDENT DOS SANTOS TRAVELLED TO
ZAIRE TO MEET WITH MOBUTU TO DISCUSS CONCRETE PRINCIPALS
AS WELL AS PRACTICAL STEPS FOR MOVING TOWARDS DIRECT
NEGOTIATIONS. THE TWO LEADERS AGREED THAT THE MPLA AND
UNITA SHOULD SEND NEGOTIATING TEAMS TO ZAIRE TO DECIDE A
SET OF PRINCIPLES THEY COULD AGREE ON. ONCE THIS WAS
DONE, MOBUTU WOULD CALL ANOTHER SUMMIT OF THE LUANDA
SECRET
SECRET

PAGE 04   STATE 201519

EIGHT TO FORMALLY LAUNCH THE PROCESS OF NATIONAL
RECONCILIATION IN ANGOLA.

9. EVENTS DID NOT PROCEED QUITE AS NEATLY AS THE
SCENARIO OUTLINED ON JUNE 5. THE MPLA BEGAN TO HEDGE
ABOUT THE NEED FOR DIRECT MEETINGS WITH UNITA BEFORE THE
SUMMIT, AND ADOPTED AN INCREASINGLY HARDLINE POSTURE ON
THE NEED FOR PRIOR UNITA ACCEPTANCE OF MPLA POSITIONS,
INCLUDING THE OFFER OF GENERAL AMNESTY. UNITA, NOT
UNNATURALLY, BEGAN TO QUESTION HOW FAR THE MPLA'S
ATTITUDES HAD ACTUALLY EVOLVED.

10. PRESIDENT MOBUTU, HOWEVER, WORKED WITH BOTH SIDES TO
SECURE AGREEMENT TO A BARE MINIMUM OF OBJECTIVES TO BE
ACHIEVED AT A SUMMIT. AS THE DEADLINE OF JUNE 22
APPROACHED THE OBJECTIVES NARROWED DOWN TO THREE:

SECRET

DOCUMENT 57: Secretary James Baker, Cable for U.S. Embassy Cairo, "The June 22 NR Summit in Zaire," June 24, 1989.

PAGE 4 OF 5

DECLASSIFIED

SECRET
FORMAL ANNOUNCEMENT BEFORE AFRICAN HEADS OF STATE
DECLARING NR TO BE UNDERWAY; DECLARATION OF A
CEASEFIRE; AND COMMENCING THE PROCESS OF DIALOGUE.
MOBUTU ALSO DESIGNED A CEREMONY FOR JUNE 22 WHICH WOULD
HAVE SAVIMBI RECEIVED BY THE ASSEMBLED GATHERING, AND
PROVIDE FOR A FACE TO FACE MEETING BETWEEN SAVIMBI AND
DOS SANTOS.

11. THE SUMMIT: IN THE MEANTIME, MOBUTU HAD SENT OUT
INVITATIONS TO A VERITABLE GALAXY OF AFRICAN PRESIDENTS.
SEVENTEEN TURNED UP AT THE PRESIDENTIAL PALACE IN
GBADOLITE: FROM MALI, ZAMBIA, ZIMBABWE, BOTSWANA,
BURUNDI, CAMEROUN, CAPE VERDE, CENTRAL AFRICAN REPUBLIC,
THE CONGO, GABON, GUNEA BISSAU, MOZAMBIQUE, NIGER'A,
RWANDA. CHAD, SAO TOME, ANGOLA. SENIOR REPRESENTATIVES
FROM MOROCCO AND TANZANIA ALSO ATTENDED.

SECRET
SF RET

PAGE 05   STATE 201519

12. THE HEADS OF STATE (INCLUDING DOS SANTOS) REPORTEDLY
DELIBERATED FOR THREE HOURS BEFORE SAVIMBI WAS BROUGHT
INTO THE CHAMBERS. NOT ONL' DID A HANDSHAKE BETWEEN
SAVIMBI AND DOS SANTOS TAKE PLACE, BUT EACH WAS GIVEN A
CHANCE TO ADDRESS THE PRESIDENTS. SAVIMBI REPORTEDLY WAS
APPLAUDED ON FOUR OCCASIONS AND RECEIVED A STANDING
OVATION. PRESIDENTS MOBUTU, MUGABE, CHISSANO, BABANGIDA,

TRAORE, AND PERREIRA WENT OUT OF THEIR WAY TO GREET HIM
WARMLY AND SHOW HIM AROUND. THE CEREMONY, IN SHORT, WAS A
TREMENDOUS POLITICAL SUCCESS WHICH LEGTIMIZED SAVIMBI AT
THE SAME TIME AS IT TRANSFORMED THE TERMS OF REFERENCE
FOP THE ANGOLAN CONFLICT.

13. IN PRACTICAL TERMS, A CEASEFIRE WAS AGREED TO, WITH
DELEGATIONS LEFT BEHIND TO WORK ON THE DETAILS OF
IMPLEMENTATION. NO ONE IS UNDER ANY ILLUSIONS THAT IT
WILL TAKE MORE THAN A FEW DAYS TO REACH ALL THE UNITS IN
THE FIELD, AND TO REACH AGREEMENT ON WHAT KIND OF
DEFENSIVE POSTURES EACH SIDE WILL TAKE IN DIFFEPENT
PEGIONS OF THE COUNTRY.

14. THE MPLA AND UNITA ALSO AGREED TO COMMENCE QUIET
NEGOTIATIONS UNDER ZAIPEAN MEDIATION AS EAPLY AS NEXT
WEEK ON POLITICAL ASPECTS OF A SETTLEMENT. GENEPAL

SECPET

DECLASSIFIED

DOCUMENT 57: Secretary James Baker, Cable for U.S. Embassy Cairo, "The June 22 NR Summit in Zaire," June 24, 1989.

PAGE 5 OF 5

SECRET
NDALU, WHO HEADED THE ANGOLAN DELEGATION TO THE
ANGOLA/NAMIBIA TALKS, WAS TAPPED TO DEAL WITH UNITA.
UNITA, HOWEVER, HAS YET TO NAME A DELEGATION HEAD.

15. THE NEXT PRESIDENTIAL SUMMIT, ANNOUNCED FOR THE NEAR
FUTURE, IS NOT LIKELY TO TAKE PLACE FOR A WHILE UNTIL
THERE IS CONCRETE PROGRESS IN THE NEGOTIATIONS.

16. MOST PROBLEMATIC OF ALL, WILL BE THE FLESHING OUT OF
THE SO-CALLED PRINCIPALS OF NATIONAL RECONCILIATION (THE
WORD FINALLY HAS CURRENCY IN OFFICIAL MPLA LITERATURE AS
SECRET
SECRET

PAGE 06   STATE 201519

OF THE GBADOLITE SUMMIT). AS POST NO DOUBT IS AWARE FROM
THE VARIOUS PRESS REPORTS, THERE IS SOME CONFUSION OVER
WHAT THEY CONTAIN. WE HAVE YET TO SEE A COPY, BUT HAVE
BEEN INFORMED THEY ARE WORDED GENERALLY ENOUGH TO ALLOW
FOR AMBIGUOUS INTERPRETATION, AND THEREFORE OPEN TO
NEGOTIATION WITHOUT UNDULY COMPROMISING THE INTERESTS OF
EITHER SIDE IN THE CONFLICT. THEY ADDRESS SUCH WORTHY
OBJECTIVES LIKE THE CEASEFIRE, NON-INTERFERENCE IN
ANGOLA'S INTERNAL AFFAIRS, AND CREATION OF COMMISSIONS TO
"EXAMINE" THE MODALITIES OF NR.

13. COMMENT: NO DOUBT THERE WILL BE LENGTHY NEGOTIATING
PROCESS. BOTH DOS SANTOS AND SAVIMBI ARE PLAYING THE
SUMMIT LOW-KEY, AND CHARACTERIZING IT AS A BEGINNING.
THIS IS PERHAPS JUST AS WELL, AND SUGGESTS THEY MAY
APPROACH THEIR UPCOMING DIALOGUE WITH A HEALTHY DOSE OF
REALISM.   BAKER

DOCUMENT 58: State Department Spokesman Richard Boucher, Statement, "Angola Elections," October 19, 1992.

PAGE 1 OF 1

U.S. DEPARTMENT OF STATE

Office of the Assistant Secretary/Spokesman

For Immediate Release   October 19, 1992

STATEMENT BY RICHARD BOUCHER, SPOKESMAN

ANGOLA ELECTIONS

The UN Secretary General's Special Representative for Angola, Margaret Anstee, made a statement Saturday, Oct. 17 on the Angolan elections. We concur in the UN's judgment that "while there were certainly some irregularities in the electoral process, these appear to have been mainly due to human error and inexperience." We further accept that there is "no evidence of major, systematic or widespread fraud, or that the irregularities were of a magnitude to have a significant effect on the results."

The UN concluded that the elections held Sept. 29-30 were generally free and fair. We support that conclusion. Because no presidential candidate obtained the requisite 50 percent majority, a second round of elections for president will be necessary. The UN has declared that it will be involved with the certification of this round as well, and we strongly support this effort. We urge the parties to make the necessary arrangements for this election as quickly as feasible.

ABOUT THE EDITOR

Kenneth Mokoena has been an analyst at the National Security Archive since 1986, specializing in southern African affairs. He served as project director for the Archive's 12,000-page microfiche collection, *South Africa: The Making of U.S. Policy, 1962–1989*. He has been active in South African political affairs since the early 1970s, and has worked as a development specialist for the United Nations Development Programme and the government of Botswana. He received his BA and MA degrees from Ball State University.

ABOUT THE NATIONAL SECURITY ARCHIVE

The National Security Archive is a nonprofit, nonpartisan organization that combines the functions of a foreign policy research institute, a library of declassified U.S. government documents, an indexer and publisher, and a legal advocate of the Freedom of Information Act and the public's right to know. The mission of the Archive is to serve scholars, students, journalists, Congress, public interest organizations, and concerned citizens by obtaining and disseminating internal U.S. government records that are indispensable for informed public inquiry and debate on important issues of foreign and national security policy. The Archive is supported by royalties from its publications and donations from foundations and individuals. The organization is located at 1755 Massachusetts Avenue, N.W., Washington, D.C., 20036. The Archive's published collections of indices and microfiched documents are available through Chadwyck-Healey, Inc., 1101 King St., Alexandria, VA, 22314.

THE TYPE

THIS BOOK IS SET IN NEW CALEDONIA — AN ADAPTATION OF
THE TYPEFACE DESIGNED BY W. A. DWIGGINS FOR LINOTYPE
IN 1939. CALEDONIA IS A "MODERN" TYPE PATTERNED LOOSELY
AFTER THE WORK OF SCOTCH TYPEFOUNDERS AROUND 1800.

TYPOGRAPHY, BINDING DESIGN, AND BOOK PREPARATION
BY CHARLES NIX